THE LADY IN T

Alison Weir was born in London and now resides in Surrey. Before becoming a published author in 1989, she was a civil servant, then a house-wife and mother. From 1991 to 1997, whilst researching and writing books, she ran a school for children with learning difficulties before taking up writing full-time. Her non-fiction books include *The Six Wives of Henry VIII, Lancaster and York, Children of England, Elizabeth the Queen, Eleanor of Aquitaine, Mary Queen of Scots, Henry VIII: King and Court, Isabella* and, most recently, *Katherine Swynford*. She is also the author of two best-selling novels, *Innocent Traitor* and *The Lady Elizabeth*.

ALISON WEIR

The Lady in The Tower

The Fall of Anne Boleyn

VINTAGE BOOKS
London

Published by Vintage 2010

2 4 6 8 10 9 7 5 3

First published in Great Britain in 2009 by
Jonathan Cape

Vintage
Random House, 20 Vauxhall Bridge Road,
London SW1V 2SA

www.vintage-books.co.uk

Addresses for companies within The Random House Group Limited can be found at:
www.randomhouse.co.uk/offices.htm

The Random House Group Limited Reg. No. 954009

A CIP catalogue record for this book is available from the British Library

ISBN 9780712640176

The Random House Group Limited supports The Forest Stewardship
Council (FSC), the leading international forest certification organisation.
All our titles that are printed on Greenpeace approved FSC certified paper
carry the FSC logo. Our paper procurement policy can be found at
www.rbooks.co.uk/environment

Mixed Sources
Product group from well-managed
forests and other controlled sources
www.fsc.org Cert no. TT-COC-2139
© 1996 Forest Stewardship Council
FSC

Typeset in Bembo by Palimpsest Book Production Limited,
Grangemouth, Stirlingshire

Printed and bound in Great Britain by
CPI Cox & Wyman, Reading RG1 8EX

This book is dedicated to a dear friend,
Father Luke
(Rev. Canon Anthony Verhees),
to mark his eightieth birthday,
and
to the memory of
Ronald Blackwood Weir,
1944–2009,
who touched so many lives.

Contents

Illustrations   ix

Preface   I
Prologue: 'The Solemn Joust'   5
1   'Occurrences that Presaged Evil'   9
2   'The Scandal of Christendom'   27
3   'The Frailty of Human Affairs'   55
4   'Plotting the Affair'   85
5   'Unlawful Lechery'   123
6   'Turning Trust to Treason'   147
7   'To The Tower'   166
8   'Stained in Her Reputation'   185
9   'The Most Mischievous and Abominable Treasons'   211
10   'More Accused than Convicted'   246
11   'Fighting Without a Weapon'   269
12   'Just, True and Lawful Impediments'   292
13   'For Now I Die'   318
14   'When Death Hath Played His Part'   351
15   'The Concubine's Little Bastard'   378
16   'A Work of God's Justice'   396
Appendix: Legends   419
Notes on Some of the Sources   429
Select Bibliography   439
Notes and References   455
Genealogical Tables   503
Index   507

Illustrations

FIRST SECTION

Anne Boleyn, as she probably looked at the time of her fall
(Artist unknown, sixteenth century, Nidd Hall, Yorkshire, © The Trustees of the 16th Viscount Mountgarret Will Trust)

Henry VIII
(Hans Holbein the Younger, c.1536–7, Thyssen-Bornemisza Collection, Madrid, Spain/The Bridgeman Art Library)

Jane Seymour
(Artist unknown, 1540s, The Society of Antiquaries of London/The Bridgeman Art Library)

Sir Nicholas Carew
(Workshop of Hans Holbein, 1530s?, by kind permission of The Trustees of the 9th Duke of Buccleuch's Chattels Fund)

The Lady Mary
(Hans Holbein the Younger, c.1536, The Royal Collection © 2009 Her Majesty Queen Elizabeth II)

Henry FitzRoy, Duke of Richmond
(Miniature by Lucas Horenbout, c.1534–5, The Royal Collection © 2009 Her Majesty Queen Elizabeth II)

Thomas Howard, Duke of Norfolk
(Hans Holbein the Younger, c.1539, The Royal Collection © 2009 Her Majesty Queen Elizabeth II)

Thomas Boleyn, Earl of Wiltshire
(Tomb brass, c.1539, St Peter's Church, Hever, Kent, photograph reproduced by kind permission of H. Martin Stuchfield)

Henry Parker, Lord Morley
(Albrecht Dürer, 1523, © The Trustees of the British Museum)

Signature of George Boleyn, Lord Rochford
(© British Library Board, Royal MS. 20 B XXI, f.2v)

Signature of Mark Smeaton
(© British Library Board, Royal MS. 20 B XXI, f.98)

Thomas Cromwell, 'Master Secretary'
(School of Hans Holbein the Younger, c.1533, Indianapolis Museum of Art, The Clowes Fund Collection)

Sir William FitzWilliam
(Hans Holbein the Younger, c.1536–40, The Royal Collection © 2009 Her Majesty Queen Elizabeth II)

Elizabeth Browne, Countess of Worcerster
(Tomb effigy, St Mary's Church, Chepstow, photograph © Archie Miles/Collections Picture Library)

Anne Boleyn
(English School, c. 1580–1600, by kind permission of Ripon Cathedral Chapter)

The Indictment against Anne Boleyn and Lord Rochford
(The National Archives, Kew KB 8/9)

Greenwich Palace, where Anne Boleyn was arrested
(Detail from 'The Panorama of London' by Anthonis van den Wyngaerde, 1558, © Ashmolean Museum, University of Oxford/The Bridgeman Art Library)

Anne Boleyn says a final farewell to her daughter, the Princess Elizabeth
(Gustaf Wappers, 1838, Collection SCHUNCK*, Heerlen, The Netherlands. Photograph Klaus Tummers, Heerlen)

The Tower of London
(Michael van Meer, 'Album Amicorum', 1615, Edinburgh University Library, Special Collections, ms. La. III. 283, fol. 346v)

Anne Boleyn at the Queen's Stairs
(Edward Matthew Ward, 1871, Sunderland Museum and Winter Garden, Tyne and Wear Archives and Museums)

SECOND SECTION

Anne Boleyn in the Tower
(Detail, Edward Cibot, 1835, Musée Rolin, Autun, France/Bridgeman Art Library)

Anne Boleyn, Lady Shelton
(Stained glass, St Mary's Church, Shelton, Norfolk, photograph by kind permission of Simon Knott www.suffolkchurches.co.uk)

Sir Thomas Wyatt
(Hans Holbein the Younger, c.1535, The Royal Collection © 2009 Her Majesty Queen Elizabeth II)

'To the King from the Lady in the Tower': a disputed letter
(© British Library Board, Cotton Otho MS. C.X. f.232r)

Westminster Hall, where four of Anne Boleyn's co-accused were tried on 12 May 1536
(Parliamentary copyright image reproduced with the permission of Parliament, photograph Deryc Sands)

Henry Percy, Earl of Northumberland
(Francis Lindo, eighteenth century, Collection of the Duke of Northumberland, photograph Geremy Butler)

Thomas Cranmer, Archbishop of Canterbury
(Gerlach Flicke, 1546, National Portrait Gallery, London / The Bridgeman Art Library)

Sir Francis Weston and his wife, Anne Pickering
(Carved heads from marriage chest, c.1530, by kind permission of Saffron Walden Museum, Essex, photographs © Saffron Walden Museum)

'Weston Esq. of Sutton Surrey'
(Artist unknown, sixteenth century, The Collection at Parham House, West Sussex)

Anne Boleyn driven mad: a later, melodramatic image
(Alessandro Guardassoni, 1843, Instituzione Galleria d'Arte Moderna, Collezioni Storiche, Bologna, photograph Mario Berardi)

Carving from the Martin Tower
(Photograph Mary Evans Picture Library)

Anne Boleyn's falcon badge, without its crown and sceptre, in the Beauchamp Tower
(Photograph © Historic Royal Palaces)

The site of the Queen's Lodgings in the Tower of London
(Photograph by Tracy Borman)

Gold and enamel pendant, made c.1520
(Victoria & Albert Museum, photograph, anonymous loan / V&A Images)

The site of the scaffold on which Anne Boleyn was executed
(Photograph by Tracy Borman)

The execution of Anne Boleyn
(Illustration from John Foxe's Acts and Monuments, seventeenth century)

The Royal Chapel of St Peter ad Vincula
(Photograph by Tracy Borman)

Inside St Peter ad Vincula
(Photograph © Historic Royal Palaces)

Memorial plaque said to mark the last resting place of Anne Boleyn
(Photograph © Historic Royal Palaces)

Carved initials of Henry VIII and Anne Boleyn, Hampton Court Palace
(Photograph © Angelo Hornak/Alamy)

Queen Elizabeth I's ring of c.1575
(By kind permission of The Trustees of the Chequers Estate/Mark Fiennes/The Bridgeman Art Library)

ENDPAPERS

The Tower of London in c.1597
(The Society of Antiquaries of London)

If any person will meddle with my cause, I require them to judge the best.

Queen Anne Boleyn, 1536

Preface

This is where my interest in history began, many years ago, with Anne Boleyn and the dramatic story of her fall. That interest has never abated – I have written at length on Anne in two earlier books, *The Six Wives of Henry VIII* and *Henry VIII: King and Court*, and in a number of unpublished works – and I know that it is shared by many: the crowds who visit the Tower of London to see the supposed site of Anne's scaffold, or flock to Hampton Court, where she stayed in happier days, or to Hever Castle, her family home, or Blickling, the place of her birth. The fascination is evident in numerous sites on the internet, the almost regular appearance of biographies, films and television dramas about her, and the numerous letters and emails I have received from readers over the years.

Yet never before – surprisingly – has there been a book devoted entirely to the fall of Anne Boleyn, and it has been a deeply satisfying experience having the scope to research in depth this most discussed and debated aspect of Anne's life. This has allowed me to achieve new insights and to debunk many myths and misapprehensions. It has been an exciting project, and I have constantly been amazed at what I have discovered.

Coming to this subject afresh, I have — as always — questioned all my preconceptions and assumptions, and sometimes had to revise them, which of course exposes errors in my own previous books, and indeed in nearly every other book on Anne, however diligently researched. In writing a full biography, the historian does not have the opportunity to go into such detail, in research, narrative and analysis, as I have had the good fortune to be able to do in a book that essentially covers a period of four months.

I wish to stress that this book is based largely on original sources, and that the conclusions in it are my own, sometimes reached objectively after reading the various theories. This might sound like a statement of the obvious, but in some aspects my conclusions coincide with others'. That has often been pure coincidence. I purposely left reading all the modern biographies of Anne until my research from contemporary sources was completed and the book was in its penultimate draft. I have gratefully given due credit to historians whose theories and interpretations have informed my work, but otherwise all conjectures, inferences and conclusions are my own, independently reached without reference to the biographies. I wish in particular to pay tribute to those by Professor Eric Ives, whose theories about the reasons for Anne Boleyn's fall have been particularly illuminating.

Since contemporary sources are key factors in studying Anne Boleyn's fall, readers may wish to look at the section Notes on Some of the Sources, which appear after the main text, before reading the book. Historians must always decide what weight to give each source, and this guide is there to evaluate the reliability and veracity of the chief ones for the period.

The approximate modern worth of monetary amounts has been given in brackets after each sum mentioned in the text.

Above all, this book has been a labour of love, as well as an exciting quest for the truth — or as near as anyone can get to the truth.

I am deeply grateful for the help and support of many kind

and generous people: first and foremost, two dear friends and fellow historians, Tracy Borman, for so generously lending me the first chapter of her forthcoming book on Elizabeth I, for hours spent in convivial discussion about aspects of Anne and Elizabeth that are common to both our subjects, and for joining me for sell-out events mischievously entitled 'The Whore and the Virgin'; and Sarah Gristwood, for so thoughtfully obtaining for me the one rare biography of Anne that I had no time to track down, and for showing me a better way to write a book!

I should also like to thank Glen Lucas and Karen Marston for so generously giving of their time, without charge, to translate documents from Latin and French, and Patricia Macleod of Sutton Library for putting me in touch with Glen Lucas and for organising such wonderful events; Sue Wingrove of *BBC History* magazine for very kindly sending me photocopies of out-of-print articles; Canon Anthony Verhees (Father Luke) for advice and information on funeral masses in the sixteenth century and other issues raised by Anne Boleyn's fate; the historian Christopher Warwick, another dear friend, for advice, and for photographing a model of the Tower of London based on the 1597 map; Monica Tandy and Alan Mudie for information on ghost stories about Anne Boleyn; and last, but certainly not least, Samantha Brown and Ann Morrice of Historic Royal Palaces for their wonderful enthusiasm for Tudor history and for making it possible for me to speak about Anne and Henry VIII at Hampton Court, which has been an enormous privilege.

The list of people who have supported me in various ways whilst I was writing this book is a long one, but I wish especially to mention my agent, Julian Alexander, my commissioning editors, Will Sulkin at Jonathan Cape in London and Susanna Porter at Ballantine Books in New York, my editorial director, Anthony Whittome, his assistant, James Nightingale, the production director, Neil Bradford, the picture researcher, Sophie Hartley, who has worked particularly hard to track down the pictures

I chose, and the dedicated and helpful publishing teams at Random House in the UK and the USA. I am tremendously grateful to you all.

More special thanks must go to my family and friends, who have all had to put up with me during the writing of this book, in particular my wonderfully supportive husband, Rankin, my son, John, my daughter, Kate, my mother, Doreen Cullen, and my cousin, Christine Armour. I wish also to express my gratitude to (in no particular order) Ian Robinson, Kate Williams, Siobhan Clarke, Anthony Cunningham, Leza Mitchell, Richard Foreman, Alison Montgomerie, Roger England, Joan and John Borman, David Crothers, Richard Stubbings, Kathleen Carroll, Ian Franklin, Jean and Nick Hubbard, Nicholas and Carol Bennett, Anthony and Jackie Goodman, Pauline Hall, Karin Scherer, Gary and Barbara Leeds, Rose Lukas, John and Joanna Marston, Anita Myatt, Josephine Ross, Burnell and Shelley Tucker, Monica and John Tyler, Peter Taylor, Frank and Janet Taylor, Nicola Tallis, Alex von Tunzelmann, Jane Robins, Alice Hogge, Justin Pollard, Nellie Verhees, Kenneth and Elizabeth Weir, Ronald and Alison Weir, Martha Whittome, Jessie Childs, Helen Rappaport, Lynn and Anne Saunders, Jane Furnival, Mavis Cheek, Molly Bradshaw, Dr Linda Saether, Dave Musgrove and many more! You have all been wonderful in so many ways – thank you.

Alison Weir,
Carshalton, Surrey
Christmas 2008

Prologue: 'The Solemn Joust'

May Day was one of the traditional highlights of the English royal court's spring calendar, and was customarily celebrated as a high festival. The May Day of 1536 was no exception, being marked by a great tournament, or 'solemn joust', which was held in the tiltyard at Greenwich, the beautiful riverside palace much favoured by King Henry VIII, who had been born there in 1491. It was a warm day, and pennants fluttered in the breeze as the courtiers crowded into their seats to watch the contest.[1] At the appointed time, the King took his place at the front of the royal stand, which stood between the twin towers of the tiltyard, in front of the recently built banqueting hall. He was not yet the bloated and diseased colossus of his later years, but a muscular and vigorous man of forty-five, over six feet tall,[2] red-bearded and magnificently dressed: 'a perfect model of manly beauty', 'his head imperial and bald'.[3]

His queen of three years, Anne Boleyn, seated herself beside him. One of the most notorious women in Christendom, she was ten years younger than her husband, very graceful, very French – she had spent some years at the French court – and stylishly attired, but 'not the handsomest woman in the world': her skin was swarthy, her bosom 'not much raised' and she had a double nail on one of her fingers; her long brown hair was her crowning glory, and her other claim to beauty was her eyes, which were 'black and beautiful' and 'invited to conversation'.[4]

It was outwardly a happy occasion – May Day was traditionally the time for courtly revelry – and there was little sign of any gathering storm. Henry 'made no show' of being angry or in turmoil, 'and gave himself up to enjoyment'.[5] He watched as the contestants ran their chivalrous courses, lances couched, armour gleaming. At this 'great jousting', the Queen's brother, George Boleyn, Viscount Rochford, was the leading challenger and 'showed his skill in breaking lances and vaulting on horseback', while Sir Henry Norris, one of the King's most trusted friends and household officers, led the defenders, 'presenting himself well-armed'. When Norris's mount became uncontrollable, 'refused the lists, and turned away as if conscious of the impending calamity to his master', the King presented him with his own horse.[6] In the jousting, the poet-courtier Thomas Wyatt 'did better than the others', although Norris, Sir Francis Weston and Sir William Brereton all 'did great feats of arms, and the King showed them great kindness. The Queen looked on from a high place, and often conveyed sweet looks to encourage the combatants, who knew nothing of their danger.'[7]

Fifty years later, Nicholas Sander, a hostile Catholic historian, would claim that, 'the Queen dropping her handkerchief, one of her gallants [traditionally assumed to have been Henry Norris] took it up and wiped his face with it', and that Henry VIII, observing this and seething with jealousy, construed the gesture as evidence of intimacy between them, and rising 'in a hurry', left the stand; but there is no mention of this incident in contemporary sources such as the reliable chronicle of Charles Wriothesley, Windsor Herald. In the late seventeenth century, Gilbert Burnet, Bishop of Salisbury, who painstakingly researched Anne Boleyn's fall in order to refute the claims of Sander, would conclude that the handkerchief incident never happened, since 'this circumstance is not spoken of by [Sir John] Spelman, a judge of that time who wrote an account of the whole transaction with his own hand in his commonplace book'.

Halfway through the jousts, a message was passed to Henry VIII, and suddenly, to everyone's astonishment, especially the Queen's, 'the King departed to Westminster, having not above six persons with him',[8] leaving Anne to preside alone over what remained of the tournament. 'Of which sudden departing, many men mused, but most chiefly the Queen.'[9] She must have felt bewildered and fearful at the very least, because for some days now, the King had been distant or simmering with rage, and she had very good reasons to suspect that something ominous had happened – and that it concerned herself.

She was the Queen of England, and she should have been in an invincible position, yet she was painfully aware that she had failed Henry in the most important thing that mattered. She could not but have realised that his long-cherished passion for her had died and that his amorous interest now had another focus, but she clearly also knew that there was more to this present situation than mere infidelity. For months now, the court had been abuzz with speculation that the King might take another wife. But that was not all.

A week before the tournament, Anne's brother, one of the most powerful men at court, had been publicly slighted. That could have been explained in a number of ways, but many saw it as a slur upon herself. Since then, her father, a member of the King's Council and privy to state secrets, who could have told her much that would frighten her, may have said something that gave her cause for alarm. She had perhaps guessed that members of her household were being covertly and systematically questioned. How she found out is a matter for speculation, but there can be no doubt that she knew something was going on. Just four days earlier, she had sought out her chaplain and begged him to look to the care of her daughter should anything happen to her, the Queen. Plainly, she was aware of some undefined, impending danger.

She knew too that, only yesterday, her tongue, never very guarded, had run away with her and that she had spoken rashly, even treasonously, overstepping the conventional bounds of courtly banter between queen and servant, man and woman, and also that her words had been overheard. She was fretting about that, and had gone so far as to take steps to protect her good name. But it was too late. Others were putting their own construction on what she had said, and it was damning.

Anne perhaps feared that the King had been told of her compromising words. On the day – or the morning – before the tournament, she had made a dramatic, emotional appeal to him, only to be angrily rebuffed. Then had come the startling announcement, late the previous evening, that a planned – and important – royal journey had been postponed.

The signs had not been good, but the exact nature of the forces that menaced Anne was almost certainly a mystery to her. So she surely could not have predicted, when the King got up and walked out of the royal stand on that portentous May Day, that that was the last time she would ever set eyes on him, and that she herself and those gallant contestants in the jousts were about to be annihilated in one of the most astonishing and brutal *coups* in English history.

1

'Occurrences that Presaged Evil'

Three months earlier, on the morning of 29 January 1536,[1] in the Queen's apartments at Greenwich Palace, Anne Boleyn, who was Henry VIII's second wife, had aborted – 'with much peril of her life'[2] – a stillborn foetus 'that had the appearance of a male child of fifteen weeks' growth'.[3] The Imperial ambassador, Eustache Chapuys, called it 'an abortion which seemed to be a male child, which she had not borne three-and-a-half months',[4] while Sander refers to it as 'a shapeless mass of flesh'. The infant must have been conceived around 17 October.

This was Anne's fourth pregnancy, and the only living child she had so far produced was a girl, Elizabeth, born on 7 September 1533; the arrival of a daughter had been a cataclysmic disappointment, for at that time, it was unthinkable that a woman might rule successfully, as Elizabeth later did, and the King had long been desperate for a son to succeed him on the throne. Such a blessing would also have been a sign from God that he had been right to put away his first wife and marry Anne. Now, to the King's 'great distress',[5] that son had been born dead. It seemed like an omen. Anne had, famously, 'miscarried of her saviour'.[6]

Henry had donned black that day, out of respect for his first wife, Katherine of Aragon, whose body was being buried in Peterborough Abbey with all the honours due to the Dowager Princess of Wales, for she was the widow of his brother Arthur Tudor, Prince of Wales. Having had his own marriage to her declared null and void in 1533, on the grounds that he could never lawfully have been wed to his brother's wife, Henry would not now acknowledge her to have been queen of England. Nevertheless, he observed the day of her burial with 'solemn obsequies, with all his servants and himself attending them dressed in mourning'.[7] He did not anticipate that, before the day was out, he would be mourning the loss of his son with 'great disappointment and sorrow'.[8]

Henry VIII's need for a male heir had become increasingly urgent in the twenty-seven years that had passed since 1509, when he married Katherine.[9] Of her six pregnancies, there was only one surviving child, Mary. By 1526, the King had fallen headily in love with Katherine's maid-of-honour, Anne Boleyn, and after six years of waiting in vain for the Pope to grant the annulment of his marriage that he so passionately desired, so that he could make Anne his wife, he defied the Catholic Church, severed the English Church from Rome, and had the sympathetic Thomas Cranmer, his newly appointed Archbishop of Canterbury, declare his union with the virtuous Katherine invalid. All this he did in order to marry Anne and beget a son on her.

It had not been the happiest marriage. Anne's apologist George Wyatt's roseate view of it reads touchingly: 'They lived and loved, tokens of increasing love perpetually increasing between them. Her mind brought him forth the rich treasures of love of piety, love of truth, love of learning; her body yielded him the fruits of marriage, inestimable pledges of her faith and loyal love.'

Yet while some of this is true, in the three years since their secret wedding in a turret room in Whitehall Palace, Henry VIII had not shown himself to be the kindest of husbands.

In marrying Anne for love, he had defied the convention that kings wed for political and dynastic reasons. The only precedent was the example of his grandfather, Edward IV, who in 1464 had taken to wife Elizabeth Wydeville, the object of his amorous interest, after she refused to sleep with him. But this left Anne vulnerable, because the foundation of her influence rested only on the King's mercurial affections.[10]

His 'blind and wretched passion'[11] had rapidly subsided, and from the time of Anne's first pregnancy, following true to previous form, he had taken mistresses, telling her to 'shut her eyes and endure as more worthy persons had done' – a cruel and humiliating comparison with the forbearing and dignified Katherine of Aragon – and that 'she ought to know that he could at any time lower her as much as he had raised her'.[12] And this to the woman whom he had frenziedly pursued for at least seven years, and for whom he had risked excommunication and war; the woman who had been the great love of his life and was the mother of his heir.

'The King cannot leave her for an hour,' Chapuys had written of Anne in 1532. 'He accompanies her everywhere,' a Venetian envoy had recorded at that time,[13] and was so amorous of her that he gladly fulfilled all her desires and 'preferred all that were of [her] blood'.[14] Similarly, a French ambassador, Jean du Bellay, had reported that the King's passion was such that only God could abate his madness. That was hardly surprising, since the evidence suggests he did not sleep with Anne for six or seven frustrating years. It has been dubiously suggested that it was Henry who, having enjoyed a sexual relationship with Anne during the early stages of their affair, resolved to abstain as soon as he had decided upon making her his wife, since the scandal of an unplanned pregnancy would have ruined all hope of the Pope granting an annulment.[15]

The theory that the couple were lovers before 1528 rests on the wording of the Papal bull for which the King applied that year. Because Anne's sister Mary had once been his mistress, he needed – in the event of his marriage to Katherine being dissolved – a dispensation to marry within the prohibited degrees of affinity, which was duly granted; and he also asked for permission to marry a woman with whom he had already had intercourse.[16] He must have been referring throughout to Anne, whom he had long since determined to make his wife. But the wording of this bull does not necessarily imply that he had already slept with her: he was looking to the future and hopefully to making Anne his mistress in anticipation of their marriage. He was covering every contingency. Moreover, his seventeen surviving love letters to Anne strongly suggest that the more traditional assumption is likely to be correct, and that it was she who kept *him* at arm's length for all that time, only to yield when marriage was within her sights.

Despite all the years of waiting and longing, there had been 'much coldness and grumbling' between the couple since their marriage,[17] for Anne, once won, had perhaps been a disappointment. She had not been born to be a queen, nor educated to that end. She had found it difficult, if not impossible, to make the transition from a mistress with the upper hand to a compliant and deferential wife, which was what the King, once married, now expected of her. Years of frustration, of holding Henry off while waiting for a favourable Papal decision that never came, of pregnancies, miscarriages and the inevitable hormonal disturbances they brought, had taken their toll on her as well as the King, and made her haughty, overbearing, shrewish and volatile, qualities that were then frowned upon in wives, who were expected to be meek and submissive, not defiant and outspoken. And Henry VIII was nothing if not a conventional husband.[18] George Wyatt observed that, rather than upbraiding him for his infidelities, Anne would have done better to follow 'the general liberty and custom' of the age by suffering in dignified silence.

These days, Anne was no longer the captivating twenty-something who had first caught the King's eye, but (according to Chapuys) a 'thin old woman' of thirty-five, a description borne out by a portrait of her done by an unknown artist around this time, which once hung at Nidd Hall in Yorkshire; one courtier even thought her 'extremely ugly'.[19] She was unpopular, and she had made many enemies in the court and the royal household through her overbearing behaviour and offensive remarks.

Nor had her much-vaunted virtue, employed as a tactical weapon in holding off the King's advances, been genuine. We may set aside Sander's malicious assertion that Anne's father had sent her to France at the age of thirteen after finding her in bed with his butler and his chaplain, but she did go to the notoriously licentious French court at an impressionable age. 'Rarely, or ever, did any maid or wife leave that court chaste,' observed the sixteenth-century French historian, the Seigneur de Brantôme, and in 1533, the year of Anne's marriage to Henry VIII, King Francis I of France confided to Thomas Howard, Duke of Norfolk, her uncle, 'how little virtuously [she] had always lived'.[20] Given the promiscuity of Anne's brother George and her sister Mary, and the suspect reputation of their mother, Elizabeth Howard, as well as the fact that their father was ready to profit by his daughter's liaison with the King, it would be surprising if Anne herself had remained chaste until her marriage at the age of about thirty-two. In 1536, a disillusioned Henry told Chapuys in confidence that his wife had been 'corrupted' in France, and that he had only realised this after their marriage.[21]

Anne, however, would stand up one day in court and protest that she had maintained her honour and her chastity all her life long, 'as much as ever queen did'.[22] But that chastity may have been merely technical, for there are many ways of giving and receiving sexual pleasure without actual penetration. Henry VIII, perhaps not the most imaginative of men when it came to sex, and evidently a bit of a prude, was clearly shocked to discover that Anne had already had some experience before he slept with her, and his disenchantment had probably been festering ever since.[23] It would explain the rapid erosion of his great passion for her, his straying from her bed within months of their marriage, and his keeping her under constant scrutiny. He believed she had lied to him, now knew her to be capable of sustained duplicity, and he may also have been suspicious of her naturally coquettish behaviour with the men in her circle.

On the surface, however, he had maintained solidarity with Anne. He could not have afforded to lose face after his long and controversial struggle to make her his wife, nor would he admit he had been wrong in marrying her. He took the unprecedented step of having her crowned with St Edward's crown as if she were a queen regnant, crushed opposition to her elevation, slept with her often enough to conceive four children in three years, gave her rich gifts and looked after the interests of her family, and in 1534 named her regent and 'absolute governess of her children and kingdom' in the event of his death. That year he pushed through an act of Parliament that settled the royal succession on his children by 'his most dear and entirely beloved wife, Queen Anne', and made it high treason to slander or deny 'the lawful matrimony' between them.[24]

The conventional expressions of devotion in the Act of Succession concealed the fact that Henry was already 'tired to satiety' of his wife.[25] The French ambassador, Antoine de Castelnau, Bishop of Tarbes, reported in October 1535 that 'his regard for the Queen is less than it was and diminishes every day'.[26] According to a French poem written by the diplomat Lancelot de Carles in June 1536, 'the King daily cooled in his affection'. He was seen to be unfaithful, suspicious and increasingly distant towards Anne, and her influence had been correspondingly eroded.[27] Nevertheless, every quarrel or estrangement between them had so far ended in reconciliation, leading many, even Chapuys, to conclude that the King still remained to a degree in thrall to his wife. 'When the Lady wants something, there is no one who dares contradict her, not even the King himself, because when he does not want to do what she wishes, she behaves like someone in a frenzy.'[28]

The Queen's subsequent pregnancies had failed to produce the longed-for son. After the birth of the Princess Elizabeth in September 1533, Chapuys had written of the King: 'God has forgotten him entirely.' Anne had quickly conceived again, but, in the summer of 1534, had borne probably a stillborn son near full term. So humiliating was this loss that no announcement of the birth was made, and the veil of secrecy surrounding the tragedy ensured that not even the sex of the infant was recorded, although we may infer from Chapuys' reference in 1536 to Anne's 'utter inability to bear male children' that it was a boy.[29] In the autumn of 1534, Anne thought she was pregnant again, but her hopes were premature. 'The Lady is not to have a child after all,' observed Chapuys gleefully. He would never refer to Anne as queen; for him, Katherine, the aunt of his master, the Holy Roman Emperor Charles V, was Henry's rightful consort, and he could only regard Anne Boleyn as 'the Lady' or 'the Concubine', or even 'the English Messalina or Agrippina'.[30]

Anne's third pregnancy ended in another stillbirth around June 1535.[31] To Henry, who was perhaps already despairing of her bearing him a son,[32] it might have seemed as if she were merely repeating the disastrous pattern of Katherine of Aragon's obstetric history: before reaching the menopause at thirty-eight, Katherine had borne six children — three of them sons — in eight years, yet the only one to survive early infancy was Mary, born in 1516. Now, after four pregnancies, Anne too had just the one surviving daughter.

Daughters were of no use to the King. It was seen as against the laws of God and Nature for a woman to hold dominion over men, and so far England's only example of a female ruler had been the Empress Matilda, who had briefly emerged triumphant from her civil war with King Stephen in 1141, and seized London. Yet so haughty and autocratic was she that the citizens speedily sent her packing, never to regain control of the kingdom. The whole disastrous episode merely served to underline the prevailing male view that women were not fit to rule. England had yet to experience an Elizabeth or a Victoria, so there was no evidence that could overturn that thinking. Thus, even though he was the father of a daughter, Henry VIII had felt justified in claiming that his marriage to Katherine was invalid because the divine penalty for marrying his brother's widow was childlessness. Without a son, he was effectively childless.

This was not just a chauvinistic conceit, but a very pressing issue. A king such as Henry, who ruled as well as reigned, and led armies into battle, needed an heir. The Wars of the Roses, that prolonged dynastic conflict between the royal Houses of Lancaster and York, were still within living memory, and sixteenth-century perceptions of them were alarming, if overstated. There were those who regarded the Tudors – who had ruled since 1485, when Henry's father, Henry VII, had defeated Richard III, the last Plantagenet king – as an usurping dynasty, and there was no shortage of potential Yorkist (or 'White Rose') claimants to challenge the succession of the Princess Elizabeth, should Henry die without a son. 'The King was apprehensive that, after his own decease, civil wars would break out, and that the crown would again be transferred to the family of the White Rose if he left no heir behind him.'[33] The spectre of a bloody conflict loomed large in the King's mind, and he had done his best ruthlessly to eradicate or neutralise anyone with pretensions to the throne. But there could be little doubt that, were he to die and leave no son to succeed him, the kingdom would soon descend into dynastic turmoil and even war.

Henry – and his contemporaries – must sincerely have wondered if, in withholding the blessing of a son, God was manifesting the same divine displeasure that had blighted the King's first marriage, when it had become clear to Henry that he had offended the Deity by marrying his brother's widow. Now it seemed that he had offended again in some way, by marrying Anne.

The writing was on the wall, and Anne had known it for some time. It fuelled her insecurity. When she had attempted in September 1534 unsuccessfully to banish from court 'a handsome young lady' on whom Henry's eye had lighted, he had crushingly told her that 'she had good reason to be content with what he had done for her, for were he to begin again, he would certainly not do as much, and that she ought to consider where she came from'.[34] In February 1535, she had become distracted and near-hysterical when, conversing with the Admiral of France at a banquet, she had watched Henry flirting with a lady of the court; and that same month, she had even gone so far as to manoeuvre her husband into seducing one of her cousins, 'Madge' (Mary) Shelton, in the hope that Madge would at least be sympathetic to herself and unlikely to ally with Chapuys and his friends against her.[35]

Yet still the Queen was racked with jealousy. Her mood ricocheted between anger, despair, hope and grief, and these were often ill-concealed beneath a façade of gaiety. She argued with the King in public, was said to have ridiculed his clothes and his poetry in private, and sometimes appeared bored in his company.[36] But she was treading a dangerous course: before the former Lord Chancellor, Sir Thomas More, was executed for treason in 1535, he is said to have spoken of Anne – who was believed by many to have been the cause of his death – to his daughter, Margaret Roper, come to visit him in the Tower of London with bitter tales of the Queen's 'dancing and sporting'. 'Alas,' More sighed, 'it pitieth me to think into what misery she will shortly come. Those dances of hers might spurn off our heads like footballs, but it will not be long ere her head will dance the like dance.'[37]

His grim prophecy may have been made up by his biographer

– William Roper, his son-in-law – with the benefit of hindsight, but it was soon to be fulfilled.

It was perhaps during a royal progress to the West Country in the autumn of 1535 that Henry's amorous eye lighted upon Jane Seymour, one of Anne's maids-of-honour, possibly when, without the Queen, he visited the Seymours' family home, Wulfhall in Somerset, in early September. He had known Jane for some years, for she had been at court in the service of both his wives[38] and received New Year's gifts; it may be that he had fancied her for some time already, or their affair had begun prior to the progress, although there is no evidence for that. In early October, the Bishop of Tarbes, having heard gossip or observed Henry and Jane together, noticed that the King's love for Anne 'diminishes every day because he has new amours'.[39]

Jane Seymour was then about twenty-eight, and still unwed because her father had not the means to provide her with a rich dower. According to Chapuys' later description, 'she is of middle stature and no great beauty, so fair that one would call her rather pale than otherwise'.[40] She was Anne's opposite in nearly every way.[41] Where Anne was slender and dark, Jane was plump and insipidly fair;[42] where Anne was witty and feisty, Jane was studiedly humble and demure; and where Anne was flirtatious by nature, Jane made a great show of her meekness and virtue.

Jane's kinsman, Sir Francis Bryan, no friend to Anne, had some time since secured her a placement at court as maid-of-honour to the Queen,[43] and it has been suggested that this was arranged in the autumn of 1535 in order to capitalise on the King's interest,[44] but that cannot be correct, because Jane must have been in post by January 1534, when, alongside other ladies of Anne's household, she received a New Year's gift from the King.[45]

Jane Seymour was to make no secret of the fact that she was sympathetic to the cause of the former Queen Katherine and bore 'great good will and respect' to the Lady Mary.[46] As a maid-of-honour to Katherine, she would have been a witness to the trials that courageous lady had suffered; she had probably been dismayed when the King exiled Katherine and Mary from court in 1531, and could only have deplored his refusal to allow them to see each other thereafter.

If George Wyatt is to be believed, Anne's enemies seized every opportunity to thrust Jane in Henry's path: 'She waxing great again and not so fit for dalliance, the time was taken to steal the King's affection from her, when most of all she was to have been cherished. And he once showing to bend from her, many that least ought shrank from her also, and some leant on the other side.' By the time Anne realised that she was pregnant with her fourth child, probably in December 1535, the King, while outwardly solicitous, 'shrank from her in private'.

By January, his affair with Jane was well established, and Anne had become so violently jealous that the royal couple were barely communicating – in late February 1536, Chapuys was to state – perhaps with some exaggeration – that Henry had not spoken to her ten times in the past three months.[47] 'Unkindness grew,' observed George Wyatt, who believed that this led to Anne being 'brought abed before her time'. He was certainly correct in asserting that, from the first signs of Henry's amorous intentions, Anne's enemies saw Jane as a means of discountenancing or dislodging her.

The King of France, Francis I, had always been a friend to Anne, but by 1535, Henry's relations with the French had grown cool, especially after Francis had refused to consider the Princess Elizabeth as a bride for his son. In December 1535, Henry learned that Katherine of Aragon was dying; aware that her death would remove a significant barrier to a rapprochement with Spain and the Holy Roman Empire, both of which were ruled by the Emperor Charles V, Katherine's nephew and advocate and Francis's great rival, he had made a point of receiving Chapuys at Greenwich with calculated courtesy, clapping an arm about the ambassador's neck and walking up and down with him thus for some time 'in the presence of all the courtiers'. In January, Chapuys reported that the King was 'praising him to the skies'.[48] It seemed obvious which way the political wind might be blowing.

But Henry was keeping his options open. In one sphere above all others, Anne Boleyn still had the power to influence him, and that was in the cause of church reform. Anne was a passionate and sincere evangelical, the owner of a library of controversial reformist literature, and she was sympathetic to radical and even Lutheran ideas; Chapuys believed her to be 'the cause and principal nurse' of all heresy in England.[49] Perhaps seeing herself as a Renaissance Queen Esther, she had encouraged Henry to read controversial anti-clerical books like Simon Fish's *Supplication for the Beggars* (1531), and reportedly introduced him to William Tyndale's heretical *The Obedience of a Christian Man*.[50] She herself possessed a copy of Tyndale's illegal translation of the New Testament. During her years of ascendancy, not a single heretic had been burned in England, and no fewer than ten evangelical bishops had been appointed to vacant sees. Her radical stance had earned her many enemies, but while Chapuys accused her of being more Lutheran than Luther himself, Anne was a reformist, not a convert to the Protestant faith – that would have been a step too far for Henry – and she was to die a devout Catholic.

Henry VIII's assumption of the royal supremacy over the Church had left him politically isolated in a Europe dominated by those two mighty rival Catholic powers, France and the Empire. He was therefore toying with the idea of an alliance with the Lutheran princes of Germany. According to Alexander Aless, a Scots Protestant theologian and doctor of medicine who, in August 1535, had taken up residence in London and won the friendship of Archbishop Cranmer and the King's Principal Secretary, Thomas Cromwell, it was Anne who persuaded Henry, late in 1535, to send a delegation to Wittenberg in Saxony, where, in 1517, Martin Luther had set in motion the Reformation by pinning his ninety-five theses against indulgences and other doctrines to the door of the Schlosskirche; the envoys' purpose was to seek the friendship and support of the German princes, although the reformer Philip Melanchthon, summoned to Wittenberg by no less a person than Luther himself, was to report on 22 January: 'The English have not begun to deliberate with our party about anything. They are too fond of quibbling.' However, they were willing, in their official capacity, to show courtesy to Luther, who 'received them affectionately'.[51]

Thus it was by no means certain at this time that the King was ready to forge a more conservative alliance with the Emperor. In France, it was being said that Henry even 'wished to join the Lutherans, binding himself to live in his kingdom according to their usages, and to defend them against everyone, if they would have bound themselves equally to defend him'. But the King had no intention of going that far. In fact, the discussions at Wittenberg seem to have centred on the rights and wrongs of the divorce.[52]

Katherine of Aragon died, professing her love for Henry and styling herself queen to the last, on 7 January 1536, in her lonely exile at Kimbolton Castle in Huntingdonshire. 'Now I am indeed a queen!' Anne had crowed in triumph, on hearing of her rival's passing, and she had 'worn yellow for the mourning'.[53] It is a misconception that yellow was the colour of Spanish royal mourning: Anne's choice of garb was no less than a calculated insult to the memory of the woman she had supplanted.

Although Katherine's last letter made him weep,[54] the King was 'like one transported with joy' and expressed relief at her death, praising God for freeing his realm from the threat of war with the Emperor; also provocatively resplendent in yellow, he was to be seen jubilantly parading the two-year-old Elizabeth about the court and into chapel 'with trumpets and other great triumphs'.[55]

Anne joined in the celebrations, but her rejoicing perhaps masked anxiety. However, Chapuys did not give much credence to whoever told him, some days prior to 29 January, 'that notwithstanding the joy shown by the Concubine at the news of the good Queen's death, she had frequently wept, fearing that they might do with her as with the good Queen'.[56] The ambassador was right to be sceptical, as Henry would hardly have contemplated ridding himself of Anne when he was hoping that she would soon deliver a son. But Anne must have realised that, with Katherine dead, the legions of people who had never recognised her own marriage to Henry now regarded him as a widower who was free to take another wife. And Henry was highly suggestible, as she well knew; his passion had cooled, and she had failed so far to bear that vital male heir, despite all he had done, and the great upheavals he had initiated, to marry her. She must have been aware that much depended on the embryonic life in her womb. She could not fail Henry another time.

While Katherine lived, he would not have contemplated putting Anne away, for that would have been seen as tantamount to admitting that he had been wrong to marry her and that Katherine was his true wife, to whom the greater part of Christendom would press him to return. As far back as early 1535, he had privately enquired if, were his second marriage to be annulled, his first would thereby be held valid, and had asked Master Secretary Cromwell whether it would be possible to set Anne aside without returning to Katherine.[57] His rejoicing at Katherine's death may have been for more than one reason,[58] although that is unlikely, given that Anne was then pregnant. But now, with Katherine dead, all that stood between the Queen and disaster was her unborn child.

Days later, Anne 'met with divers ominous occurrences that presaged evil'. First, there was 'a fire in her chamber'.[59] This may have called to mind the uncannily prescient prophecy of the Abbot of Garadon, made in 1533, that by 1539,

When the Tower is white, and another place green,
Then shall be burned two or three bishops and a queen,
And after all this be passed we shall have a merry world.[60]

This prediction had been publicly recited by her detractors, while Anne herself had voiced the hope that Katherine was the Queen in question, not herself[61] – and it had now so nearly come true. She was unharmed, but probably badly shaken. It had been Katherine who had been meant to suffer martyrdom, not herself. Anne may also have been remembering a book containing another prophecy, which had been left in her apartments for her to find in 1532, open at a page bearing an illustration of her with her head cut off. She can have been in no doubt that there were those who sought her downfall, and that only the King's protection stood between her and her enemies, who would not hesitate to move in on her and destroy her, given the chance.

Then, as if Anne's ever-present fears were not enough to contend with, she received a nasty shock. She was not present when, on 24 January, 'the King, being mounted on a great horse to run at the lists' at Greenwich, 'fell so heavily that everyone thought it a miracle he was not killed'. Chapuys, who was at court at the time, adds only that he 'sustained no injury',[62] and therefore the report written on 12 February by the Bishop of Faenza, the Papal Nuncio in France and a notoriously unreliable source, that Henry 'was thought to be dead for two hours',[63] and that of Dr Pedro Ortiz, the Emperor's ambassador in Rome (6 March), that 'the French King said that the King of England had fallen from his horse and had been two hours without speaking'[64] are both probably unfounded and perhaps reflect European gossip, otherwise Chapuys, who was close to events, would surely have mentioned these details. Nevertheless, according to Lancelot de Carles, it was thought at the time that the King's fall 'would prove fatal'.

Anne was informed of what had happened by her maternal uncle, Thomas Howard, Duke of Norfolk. Chapuys says he broke the news gently so as not to alarm her, and that she received it with composure,[65] yet maybe her dawning realisation that the King could have been killed forcibly brought home to her the fearful prospect of a future without him there to protect her from her many enemies in a hostile world, in which the spectre of dynastic war loomed large. It was said that she 'took such a fright withal that it caused her to fall in travail, and so was delivered afore her full time' five days later.[66]

This latest calamity – 'a great discomfort to all this realm' – left Henry understandably devastated and unable to hide his 'great distress',[67] and Anne in 'greater and most extreme grief'. George Wyatt, who says that it made her 'a woman full of sorrow', wrote that when 'the King came bewailing and complaining to her the loss of his boy, some words were heard [to] break out of the inward feeling of her heart's dolours, laying the fault upon unkindness, which the King more than was cause (her case at this time considered) took more hardly than otherwise he would if he had not been somewhat too much overcome with grief, or not so much alienate'.

Plainly, Anne's accusation of unkindness had stung. Wyatt says that 'wise men' judged at the time that if she had kept quiet and borne with Henry's 'defect of love, she might have fallen into less danger' and tied him closer to her 'when he had seen his error'; instead, she had railed at him, and in consequence 'the harm still more increased'. Yet she perhaps had good cause to complain. That very morning – according to the account of Jane Dormer, Duchess of Feria, who got her information years later from her mistress, the King's daughter Mary – Anne had encountered Henry with Jane Seymour on his knee, and had become hysterical.[68] Abashed at being caught *in flagrante*, and aware of the need to appease his gravid wife, Henry had hastened to calm Anne. 'Peace be sweetheart, and all shall go well with thee,' he soothed.[69] But it was too late: the damage had been done, and it was said that

Anne, 'for anger and disdain, miscarried'.[70]

Now, having lost her baby, Anne reportedly was 'attributing her misfortune to two causes'.[71] She 'wished to lay the blame on the Duke of Norfolk, whom she hates, saying he frightened her by bringing the news of the fall the King had five days before'; that, she asserted, had triggered her premature labour and miscarriage.[72] 'But it is well-known that this is not the cause,' Chapuys wrote, 'for it was told her in a way that she should not be too alarmed nor attach much importance to it.'[73] Nevertheless, the tale gained currency, and on 12 February, in France, the Bishop of Faenza would report that the Queen 'miscarried in consequence' of being told of the King's fall, while the same would be claimed in Rome by Dr Ortiz, who asserted on 6 March that Anne 'was so upset that she miscarried of a son'.[74]

Anne also told Henry 'that he had no one to blame but himself for this latest disappointment, which had been caused by her distress of mind about that wench Seymour'.[75] Chapuys says she averred that 'because the love she bore him was greater than the late Queen's, her heart broke when she saw that he loved others. At this remark the King was much grieved.'[76] According to Jane Dormer, though, he softened and 'willed her to pardon him, and [said] he would not displease her in that kind thereafter'; but that is at variance with what George Wyatt heard, which was that Henry angrily told Anne 'he would have no more boys by her'. This is more in keeping with Chapuys' account of the conversation, in which he states that the King 'scarcely said anything to her, except that he saw clearly that God did not wish to give him male children, and in leaving her, he told her, as if for spite, that he would speak to her after she was up'. Then, 'with much ill grace', he left her.[77]

These parting shots sounded ominous, and we can only imagine how Anne felt, but Chapuys was 'credibly informed that, after her abortion', she put on a brave face and told her weeping attendants that it was all for the best 'because she would be the sooner with child again, and that the son she bore would not be doubtful like this one, which had been conceived during the life of the [late] Queen, thereby acknowledging a doubt about the bastardy of her daughter',[78] and also her awareness that some people still regarded Katherine as Henry's only lawful wife, and did not recognise her own marriage.

One of those people was undoubtedly Jane Seymour, who may not only have felt genuine grief at Katherine of Aragon's death, but must also have realised that, in the eyes of many people like herself – and indeed of most of Europe – Henry VIII was now a free man. And suddenly, in the light of the Queen's miscarriage, Anne's enemies saw in this pallid young woman, who up till now probably had been of no more significance than any other of the King's passing fancies, an opportunity to bring her down.[79]

2

'The Scandal of Christendom'

Henry's fall had no doubt brought forcibly home to him the
fact that he was without an heir; had he died in the
Greenwich tiltyard, the realm would have been plunged into
dynastic chaos. During those five days between his fall and Anne's
miscarriage, he must have brooded often on his urgent need for
a living son. Hence the understandably bitter remarks that he
flung at her in the pain of his unbearable disappointment, and
his need to apportion blame. He had been through all this before
with Katherine's fruitless pregnancies, and it seemed that he was
fated to lose his sons by Anne as well – his reaction is further
proof that the infant Anne had lost in 1534 had been a boy. But
now time was no longer on his side: he was forty-four, too old
to wait much longer for an heir, and he was evidently beginning
to believe that God would never grant him a son while he remained
married to Anne.

Anne was now older than Katherine had been when her last
child was conceived, and Henry may well have been aware of
this.[1] Yet there was perhaps another, deeply atavistic reason for the
King's growing conviction that he had incurred the wrath of
the Deity through marrying Anne. In a superstitious age, in which

it was widely believed – even by educated, rational people – that supernatural powers governed or subverted the natural order of things, a string of miscarriages or stillbirths did not happen without good reason. Either they were the result of divine displeasure – as Henry believed had been his punishment for marrying Katherine of Aragon, his brother's widow – or they were brought about by witchcraft. It may have been in this context that Anne's latest miscarriage 'made an ill impression on the King's mind' and reinforced his growing conviction that this second marriage too 'was displeasing to God'.[2]

On the day of Anne's miscarriage, Chapuys – not yet having heard of it, for he does not mention it in this dispatch, and was not to report it until 10 February – was told by the King's cousin, Henry Courtenay, Marquess of Exeter, and the Marchioness, Gertrude Blount, how they had been 'informed by one of the principal persons at court' that the King 'had said to someone in great confidence and, as it were, in confession, that he had made this marriage seduced and constrained by sortileges [i.e. divination or sorcery], and for this reason he considered it null, and that this was evident because God did not permit them to have any male issue, and that he believed he might take another wife, which he gave to understand that he had some wish to do'.[3]

It is easy to conjure up an image of a bitterly disappointed Henry railing at cruel Fate and saying such things. Possibly he uttered these chilling words in the heat of the moment, needing someone to blame for the loss of his son. Probably he perceived the avenging hand of God in the tragedy. But he might also have felt the need to explain his having been so long in thrall to this woman he had ill-advisedly married, and who had so grievously failed him, and one way to do this was by claiming that he had been bewitched.

It has been argued that, in speaking of sortileges, Henry – if he uttered these words at all – was merely referring to his having been seduced into marriage by predictions that it would bring him heirs,[4] yet the rest of the reported speech makes it clear he believed there was an element of sorcery involved, for predictions or divinations regarding its fruitfulness would not have rendered the marriage invalid.

Chapuys was rightly sceptical. 'The thing is very difficult to believe, although it comes from a good source,' he wrote to his master. 'I will watch to see if there are any indications of its probability.'[5] Anne, the ambassador added, had already repented of her hasty words of reproach, and was 'in great fear'.[6]

Certainly she had good reason to be so, for Henry might now consider her as barren of sons as Katherine, and find a pretext to have their marriage annulled and their daughter declared a bastard, just as he had done with Katherine and Mary. But Anne did not have Katherine's powerful friends – in fact she had not very many friends at all – so there would be few to champion her cause, and the outcome would be alarmingly predictable. Without Henry, she would be an object of derision, calumny and hatred; her very life might well be at risk.

We might wonder if Anne's great fear sprang from finding out that Henry believed her guilty of witchcraft. At that time, witchcraft was not an indictable offence; it was not until 1542 that an act was passed under Henry VIII making it a secular crime, and it did not become a capital offence until 1563, under Elizabeth I. Prior to that, the penalty for witchcraft had been determined according to evidence of actual criminality, with proof of evil deeds being necessary to obtain a conviction; in the cases of persons of high rank, there was often a suspicion of treason against the Crown.

In the previous century, three royal ladies had famously been accused of witchcraft. In 1419, Joan of Navarre, the widow of Henry IV, had been imprisoned for three years on trumped-up charges of sorcery on the orders of her stepson, Henry V, who wanted her dowry to pay for his wars, and she had not been freed until after his death in 1422. In 1441, Eleanor Cobham, the wife of Humphrey, Duke of Gloucester, uncle of Henry V, was convicted of practising witchcraft upon Henry VI, and was incarcerated on the Isle of Man for the rest of her life. Unlike Queen Joan, she was probably guilty as charged. Lastly, in 1469, Richard Neville, Earl of Warwick, then in rebellion against Edward IV, had paid two informers to accuse Jacquetta of Luxembourg, Duchess of Bedford and mother of Edward's consort, Elizabeth Wydeville, of having made obscene leaden image of the King and Queen and practising her black arts upon them to bring about her daughter's marriage to Edward – a marriage that Warwick had opposed. The Duchess was also accused of casting another image to bring about Warwick's death. When the witnesses whom Warwick had bribed refused to testify upon oath, the case against her collapsed, and she was freed and declared innocent.

Sir Thomas More also asserted that, in 1483, the future Richard III accused Elizabeth Wydeville of using sorcery to wither his arm, although this tale is probably apocryphal. Nevertheless, to the medieval mind, witchcraft was a very real threat; there was a history of it being used as a political weapon for nefarious ends, and Henry VIII's suspicion of sorcery would have been fully in keeping with the spirit of the times. He would surely have known about these precedents.

Had Henry said much the same thing to Anne as he had to the unnamed person referred to by Chapuys? And had he given voice to suspicions that had perhaps been festering in his imagination for some while? If so, then Anne had every reason to be fearful. For if Henry was talking about witchcraft, then he might well be casting about in his mind for ways of getting rid of her, weighing the idea of having their marriage dissolved, since canon law provided for an annulment on the grounds of sorcery.

Was that what Henry really intended? Given Anne's unpopularity, the fact that she had no powerful connections to defend her, and her having a rudimentary sixth fingernail on one hand, as well as 'certain small moles'[7] – which might have been regarded as devil's marks in a superstitious age, or as signs of inner corruption and even divine disfavour – a charge of witchcraft might appear very credible, and would almost certainly lead to her condemnation.

What of the slender possibility that Anne had indeed dabbled in witchcraft? She had a hound called Urian, which was one of the more obscure names of Satan; in fact, he was given to her by, and named after, the courtier Urian Brereton. Then there would be her prediction, made probably out of sheer desperation and bravado, in the Tower of London, that if she were to die, there would be no rain for seven years, seven being a magical number used by witches, who were believed to be able to control the weather. Was Henry's long-standing infatuation with Anne that of a man under a spell? Again, there is more likely to have been a less-than-occult reason for it.[8] It is barely credible that a woman who was an ardent evangelist and deeply committed to the cause of religious reform should secretly have resorted to sorcery.

It is also possible that the King's talk of sortileges may have sprung purely from crushing disappointment rather than premeditated conviction, for although Anne would in time to come be charged with heinous crimes, she was never accused of witchcraft, although that may well have been implicit in one of the articles of her indictment. Yet if Henry truly believed her guilty of sorcery, that most feared and sacrilegious of crimes, why did he not proceed against her immediately? It might therefore appear that the King spoke of witchcraft only in anger and frustration, or was bitterly casting about in his mind for any pretext to extricate himself from this unsatisfactory marriage.

There may be another explanation. According to Chapuys, Henry had confided his suspicion of witchcraft to an unnamed person, yet it was another anonymous person, someone high up in the court, who reported this to the Exeters (both partisans of Katherine and Mary), who in turn reported it to Chapuys. Thus the information that the ambassador received was fourth-hand, and it came from two unnamed sources. It is not even clear if the person Henry allegedly spoke to actually told the high-ranking courtier what he had said, or if the courtier had overheard Henry, or had heard the person to whom the King uttered those words talking about what he had said. It is therefore possible that what Chapuys heard was somewhat garbled, or even made up; such information always had its price, and this was the kind of thing that both Exeter and the ambassador would have wanted to hear. Then again, what Henry said, or was supposed to have said, was so sensational that one might not expect those recounting it to get it substantially wrong.

Whether or not Henry sincerely believed that Anne had snared him by witchcraft, and aside from the fact that he was seemingly now convinced that she would never bear him an heir, there were good reasons for ending their marriage, the most compelling being his genuine fear that God was displeased by it, a fear that has even been described by some writers as panic, and upon which Anne's enemies would no doubt make play to their advantage in the weeks to come. The King was perhaps wondering if severing himself from Anne would restore his credit with the Deity, put an end to much political opposition, pave the way for a new, uncontroversial and fruitful marriage, and provide a solution to the problem of the Lady Mary.[9] He may already have had these factors in mind when he had made tentative enquiries about an annulment some time prior to Katherine's death. Certainly, from the time of Anne's miscarriage, many people believed that the King was planning to free himself from her.

It seemed like poetic justice to some when, on the very day of Katherine's funeral, Anne lost the son who would have ensured her safety. The Imperialists in Europe would rejoice when they heard what had befallen her: 'This is news to thank God for,' Dr Ortiz wrote. 'Although the King has not improved in consequence of his fall, it is a great mercy that his paramour miscarried of a son.'[10]

It may be that it was the stress of her insecure situation alone that caused Anne to miscarry,[11] but her contemporaries believed that there was more to it than that, and there was rampant speculation at court. Chapuys reported on 10 February that 'some think it was entirely owing to a defect in her constitution, and her utter inability to bear male children, others imagine that it was caused by the fear that the King would treat her as he treated his late Queen, which is not unlikely, considering his behaviour towards a lady of the court named Mistress Seymour, to whom, as many say, he has lately made valuable presents'.[12] Given that Henry had already set aside one wife in order to marry her maid-of-honour, there was every reason for Anne to worry that he might do it again, although Chapuys would for some time be dismissive of rumours that Henry actually wanted to marry Jane.

When news of the Queen's miscarriage spread, the rumours multiplied. On 10 February, Chapuys also reported: 'There are innumerable persons who consider that the Concubine is unable to conceive, and say that the daughter said to be hers and the abortion the other day are supposititious.'[13] He meant that people thought Elizabeth to be a changeling, rather than the fruit of adultery; this was not the first, or the last, time that the blood of an English royal heir had been impugned – John of Gaunt's political enemies had called him a changeling in the fourteenth century, and the Catholic James II's son, Prince James Francis Edward Stuart, the so-called 'warming-pan baby', would suffer the same calumny in the seventeenth. In September 1534, Anne Boleyn had had to admit to the King that her announcement of a pregnancy had been too premature,[14] so it is hardly surprising that those who had not seen the dead foetus did not believe in its existence. The Bishop of Faenza, in a letter to the Vatican, reported that 'that woman' had not been with child at all, and had had much trouble concealing the fact, so 'to keep up the deceit, she would allow no one to attend upon her but her sister'. There is, however, no evidence that Anne's sister, Mary Boleyn, was in attendance; she had been banished from court after an ill-advised marriage in 1534. Soon, it was widely believed abroad that Anne had not been pregnant at all. Dr Ortiz wrote illogically on 22 March that 'La Ana feared the King would leave her, and it was thought that the reason of her pretending the miscarriage of a son was that the King might not leave her, seeing that she conceived sons.'[15]

In 1989, Retha Warnicke put forward the startling theory that Anne's fall came about for 'the sole reason' that she had borne a deformed foetus, which in the Tudor period was associated with witchcraft, and that this had raised in the King very real fears of God's displeasure, and had moved him to get rid of her. In 1585, the Jesuit Nicholas Sander, the source of so many unfounded calumnies about Anne Boleyn (including the assertion that she was Henry VIII's own daughter), claimed that the foetus had been deformed and that Henry had convinced himself that it was not his, yet there is no contemporary evidence for any of this; had there been, Chapuys would surely have found out about it, as he had clearly been asking questions and states that what Anne delivered on 29 January 'seemed to be a male child'; he makes no mention of any deformity in his reports. On the contrary, Lancelot de Carles heard that Anne had miscarried 'a beautiful son, born before term'.

That foetus would have been examined very closely to determine its sex and the fact that it was of about fifteen weeks' gestation. And had there been any abnormality, it would surely have been used as evidence against Anne, for people then believed that deformity was a judgement of God on both parents, especially in cases where conception took place outside marriage; such evidence could have bolstered charges of adultery, and indeed incest, which was thought even more likely to be responsible for deformity.[16] Warnicke attempted to reinterpret several sources in order to bolster her unfounded theory, but a closer reading and understanding of them shows that she was inferring far too imaginatively, and most historians[17] have rightly discounted her findings. The lack of any evidence, and the fact that the birth of a deformed foetus was never used against Anne, effectively demolishes Warnicke's arguments.

Yet Chapuys might have been right about Anne having a 'defective constitution' and being unable to bear children, although the possible nature of her problem was unknown to sixteenth-century medical science, for it was not identified until 1940. Anne's first pregnancy had resulted in a healthy child, but her three subsequent pregnancies had ended in stillbirths, one at full term. Could it be that she was one of the few women who are rhesus negative?

Problems can arise when a man's blood is rhesus positive and his partner's is rhesus negative. They do not occur in a first pregnancy, but during that labour, tiny amounts of the baby's blood can cross the placenta into the mother's bloodstream, and if the baby is rhesus positive, the mother becomes sensitised to these harmful antibodies. In succeeding pregnancies, the mother's antibodies will pass through the placenta into the baby's blood and, recognising it as 'foreign', will try to break down its red blood cells. Nowadays, the condition can be diagnosed and treated by blood tests and transfusions, but in Anne Boleyn's day, it would invariably have resulted in stillbirths. Worse still for Henry and Anne's dynastic hopes, if she *had* had this condition, she could never have borne another living child.

Anne had many enemies, at court and in the country at large. Mention has been made of Eustache Chapuys, the Imperial ambassador, who had arrived in England in 1529 and since proved himself to be one of Katherine and Mary's most staunch champions. Chapuys, now forty-six, was a cultivated and sophisticated native of Savoy, a canon lawyer by profession, a former ecclesiastical judge, a humanist and a friend of the great scholar Erasmus. He was able, astute and unafraid to speak his mind. He spoke excellent French, Spanish and Latin, but was less fluent in English, and when he had first arrived in England, he had had to rely on a secretary to translate for him. His command of the language had improved immeasurably over the seven years he had been resident, yet he still may not have fully understood English idioms, which might account for the occasional vagaries in his dispatches.

These dispatches are heavily prejudiced in favour of Katherine of Aragon and the Lady Mary. Chapuys deplored the way in which the former Queen and her daughter had been treated by the King and 'this accursed Anne', and he fought their corner zealously, far exceeding his instructions from the first, and repeatedly urging his master to invade England in support of Katherine's cause. Anne Boleyn was his *bête noire*. She had supplanted the Emperor's aunt and cruelly treated the Lady Mary, Charles's cousin, and in the eyes of the Imperialists, she was nothing but a whore, a heretic and an adventuress. Acting on Charles V's orders and his own inclinations, Chapuys, who openly deplored Anne's 'abominable and incestuous marriage', had never acknowledged her as queen. Chapuys' stance made him a constant irritation to Henry VIII, and earned him both the distrust of the King's advisers and the hatred of the Boleyn faction. It is no great surprise to find him writing, on 17 February 1536, that Anne 'bears me no good will'.[18]

Chapuys' diplomatic reports are among the most important sources for this crucial period, and for generations historians have relied heavily – and perhaps too trustingly – upon them. Henry's secretary, Sir William Paget, had a poor opinion of the ambassador: 'I never took [Chapuys] for a wise man, but for one that used to speak without respect of honesty or truth, so it might serve his turn. He is a great practiser, tale-telling, lying and flattering.' Paget, of course, was biased, but it is apparent that Chapuys did sometimes repeat gossip or rumour as fact, and saw himself as something of a crusader in the cause of Katherine and Mary, so was unable to view affairs from any other viewpoint. Despite being astute and observant, he sometimes unwittingly relied on information that was deliberately fed to him for political reasons. Moreover, being based around London and with little knowledge of the further reaches of the realm, he vastly overestimated the lengths to which Henry's subjects would go to uphold the cause of Katherine and Mary. For over a century, modern historians have questioned the veracity of Chapuys' testimony, and it has been suggested that he was not as close to events as has been hitherto thought, and that he was therefore an unreliable witness.

Yet that is not entirely true. Chapuys had a difficult role. He did not like England or the English, yet he was obliged to exercise his diplomatic talents in that kingdom during one of the most tumultuous periods of its history. It has been asserted that he rarely attended court functions, yet it is clear that he enjoyed frequent access to Henry VIII, and to his ministers, with whom he often dined; he also had numerous contacts and informants, many of them close to the King, and operated an efficient spy network in the royal household. He was not just an eyewitness of many of the events he describes, but a shrewd observer. Henry appears to have liked him, although Chapuys angered and irritated him at times; Henry even confided in the ambassador now and then, or deliberately fed him information. Theirs was a sparring relationship, given that the King was aware of the ambassador's disapproval of many aspects of his policy, not least his marital adventures; but there was respect on both sides. The Boleyn faction, of course, hated Chapuys.

Although at this stage there was no cohesive anti-Boleyn faction, Chapuys' hatred of Anne Boleyn was shared by many, both at court and in the kingdom at large. Those who would become his natural allies in his continuing and relentless campaign to bring down Anne Boleyn and her faction were Sir Francis Bryan; Sir Nicholas Carew; the Seymours; members of the 'White Rose' families who were descended from the Yorkist kings of England, most notably the Courtenays, led by the Marquess of Exeter, and the Poles, headed by Lord Montagu, whose brother Geoffrey would express the view that the King 'had been caught in the snare of unlawful love with the Lady Anne';[19] the humanist courtier Sir Thomas Elyot, former ambassador to Charles V, friend to the late Sir Thomas More, and a secret sympathiser with Queen Katherine; Catholic right-wingers, who resented the reforming Anne and her supporters; and anyone else who cherished a secret sympathy for Katherine and for Mary, who was regarded by many as Henry's rightful heir.[20] And, of course, Mary herself.

The influential courtier Sir Francis Bryan had no good opinion of Anne, and was perhaps one of the first people to view Jane as a means of toppling her from her throne. The one-eyed Bryan was nicknamed by Cromwell 'the Vicar of Hell'; the subjective Sander says he was called this on account of 'his notorious impiety', yet it may be that he earned this name because of his plotting against Anne Boleyn.[21] He was no rake – as the nickname might suggest – but a Renaissance scholar and close friend of the King, and had long been a gentleman of the Privy Chamber. His mother, Margaret Bourchier, Lady Bryan, who was half-sister to Anne Boleyn's mother, had been governess in turn to the Lady Mary and the Princess Elizabeth. Bryan, ever the pragmatist, had been one of the earliest supporters of his 'cousin' Anne, and later a leading member of her faction, but had since come to hate and resent her.

Bryan was related to the Seymours and probably hoped to profit by his kinswoman's affair with the King. He seems to have had a special affection for Jane Seymour. It was he who had secured her a place at court as maid-of-honour to Katherine of Aragon, back in the 1520s, and he who had later placed her with Anne Boleyn.[22] Both his sympathies, and Jane's, had secretly remained with Katherine and her daughter Mary. In 1534, in order to distance himself from the Boleyn faction, he had deliberately picked a quarrel with Lord Rochford.[23] Although Bryan was absent from court for much of the early part of 1536,[24] he was to do his best to undermine Queen Anne's power by encouraging her rival, Jane Seymour, notwithstanding the fact that his mother held a position of high honour as governess to Anne's daughter.[25]

The Courtenays, a noble family headed by Henry Courtenay, Marquess of Exeter, were descended from the House of York – Exeter's mother and the King's had been sisters – and had become somewhat marginalised at court, thanks largely to their closeness in blood to the throne, their support for Queen Katherine and their religious conservatism, which naturally made them objects of suspicion. The Marquess himself – a cousin of the King, a member of the Privy Council, and one of the two noblemen of the Privy Chamber (the other being Lord Rochford) – had told Chapuys that he 'would not be among the laggards' to shed his blood for the fallen Queen and her daughter. His wife, Gertrude Blount, had long been active in using Chapuys as a channel for imparting news to those ladies, and she was a good source, given how well placed her husband was to obtain inside information about the King and his doings.[26] Lady Exeter had been a supporter of Elizabeth Barton, the 'Nun of Kent', who had been hanged in 1534 for her dire prophesies against the marriage of Henry VIII and Anne Boleyn.

The Poles, cousins of the Courtenays, were another White Rose family. Margaret Pole, Countess of Salisbury, a niece of Edward IV and Richard III, had been a friend to Katherine and governess to the Princess Mary, but had long since been dismissed from the court for her loyalty to them. She and Katherine had once cherished a plan to marry Mary to the Countess's son, Reginald Pole, who was even now in Italy, writing a virulent treatise against the divorce. These so-called 'White Rose' families, who had long been under government surveillance, were the enemies of Anne Boleyn, and therefore willing to be allies of Chapuys.

Chapuys referred, in April 1536, to the Countess of Kildare

being among those who united against Anne Boleyn. She was Elizabeth Grey, the Dowager Countess, first cousin to the King – they shared a common grandmother in Elizabeth Wydeville, queen of Edward IV.[27] With her White Rose connections, it is unsurprising that the Dowager was hostile to Anne Boleyn.

Another unexpected ally and friend of Chapuys was Bryan's brother-in-law, the hitherto pro-French Sir Nicholas Carew, Master of the Horse and an accomplished diplomat, whose sympathy for Katherine and Mary had been covertly growing since 1529; he and his wife had for some time secretly been in touch with Mary, assuring her of their support and keeping her informed of what was happening.[28] Carew was friendly too with the Marquess of Exeter, and his wife, Elizabeth Bryan, was the daughter of Margaret, Lady Bryan.

A champion jouster and experienced diplomat, Carew was close to the King also, having been brought up with him from the age of six, and a powerful force in the Privy Chamber. He had at first been one of Anne's partisans – they were cousins – but by 1532 she had alienated and angered him not only by her overbearing ways and her abuse of her position, but also by her unjust treatment of his friend, Charles Brandon, Duke of Suffolk, and his brother-in-law, Sir Henry Guildford. Carew privately disapproved not only of her marriage, but also – being a conservative in such matters – of the religious changes that had come in its wake, so he was now more than willing to be complicit in her downfall and advance the fortunes of her rival, Jane, and the Lady Mary.

Mary Tudor herself, now twenty, had more reason than most to loathe Anne Boleyn. Her happy childhood, spent basking in the love of both her adored parents, had been brought to a brutal end by the rift between them. Katherine of Aragon had all along staunchly refused to agree that her marriage was incestuous and unlawful, and would never do anything to prejudice her daughter's rights. As she grew older, Mary had supported her in her brave stand, insisting that she would accept no one for queen except her mother, but in so doing, she had incurred the wrath of her father and the malice of Anne Boleyn.

After her mother's marriage was declared invalid in 1533, Mary was branded illegitimate. She lost her title, her status in the European marriage market and her place in the succession, and was supplanted by the infant Elizabeth as their father's heiress. When Elizabeth was assigned her own household in December 1533, Anne vindictively insisted that Mary be made to wait on her, and a protesting Mary found herself treated little better than a servant. The household was in the charge of Sir John and Lady Shelton, the latter being another Anne Boleyn, the fifty-year-old sister of Thomas Boleyn, Earl of Wiltshire, the Queen's father. The Sheltons, the parents of six children, had both sat for the painter Hans Holbein in 1528.[29]

When Mary refused to acknowledge her half-sister as the King's heir, and openly – and very vocally – set herself up as a focus of opposition to the new Queen, Anne urged a reluctant Lady Shelton to make her do as the King required of her, and if she resisted, to give her 'a good banging on the ears, like the cursed bastard she was'.

It must be said in Lady Shelton's favour that, initially, she tried to mitigate Mary's lot, earning a reprimand from Lord Rochford and the Duke of Norfolk for treating the girl 'with too much respect and kindness' instead of the abuse deserved by a bastard. Lady Shelton had stood up for herself, insisting that, whatever Mary's status, she 'deserved honour and good treatment for her goodness and virtues'.[30] Mary, however, continued to demand her rights as a princess and as the King's heir, and it was probably to protect the teenager from her outspoken self that Lady Shelton took to locking her in her room and nailing the windows shut whenever visitors came. From where Mary was standing, this must have looked like cruelty. By 1534, when the passing of a new Act of Succession made it a capital crime for Mary to continue refusing to recognise Anne Boleyn as queen and Elizabeth as Henry's heir, Lady Shelton's treatment of her had become harsher, partly because Mary was so hostile, and probably because the governess feared for her own neck, especially after the King sent to command her to tell his daughter that she was 'his worst enemy'.

Once when Mary defied the Privy Council, Lady Shelton angrily took her by the shoulders and shook her, and when Mary fell seriously ill in 1535, she told the miserable girl she hoped she would die. That summer, Lady Shelton brought in an apothecary whose pills made Mary very sick, which led both the princess and Chapuys, who already believed that Anne Boleyn was plotting to do away with Mary, to believe they had even more cause for suspicion and alarm,[31] although it seems unlikely, in the face of the evidence, that Mary actually had been poisoned.

Nevertheless, Lady Shelton was certainly remorseless and unrelenting. 'If I were in the King's place,' she told the defiant princess, 'I would kick you out of the King's house for your disobedience!' Only the day before, she continued brutally, the King had threatened to have Mary beheaded for disobeying the laws of the realm.[32] And when the tragic news came of the passing of Katherine of Aragon, she 'most unceremoniously and without the least preparation' bluntly told Mary that her beloved mother was dead.[33] Yet, given her protective attitude towards Mary in the beginning, it is likely that the governess's cruelty resulted chiefly from pressure being brought to bear on her by the King, the Queen and the Boleyn faction. Moreover, being guardian to the truculent and difficult Mary was a horrendous responsibility, especially since the girl was acting in defiance of the law. As early as 1534, Lady Shelton had been reduced to tears just thinking of the possible consequences of any lack of vigilance on her part.[34]

But now, with Katherine dead, and his latest hopes of an heir dashed, the King began treating Mary more kindly, ceasing to demand that she acknowledge Queen Anne and the Princess Elizabeth, and sending her a substantial sum of money. When

Anne tried belatedly to extend the hand of friendship to the bereaved Mary, inviting her to court and offering to be 'like another mother' to her; Mary, ill with grief, snubbed her, saying that to agree to that would 'conflict with her honour and conscience'.[35] Chapuys noted that Lady Shelton 'does not cease with hot tears to implore the Princess to consider these matters', but to no avail.[36] An exasperated Anne then wrote to Lady Shelton and told her that what she had done had been 'more for charity than because the King or I care what course she takes'.[37]

It may be that, in the wake of the Queen's miscarriage, a perspicacious and worried Lady Shelton had taken stock of her position and begun to think of the future; for if her niece fell from favour, Mary might well be restored to it. It was at this time that the governess began taking bribes from Chapuys, in return for her allowing his servant to visit Mary – herself being present – in defiance of the King's orders, something she had never permitted before. Despite his doubt as to its veracity, Chapuys also thought fit to inform Lady Shelton of the fourth-hand report he had received that the King was thinking of taking another wife, probably in the hope that this might spur Lady Shelton to treat her charge with even less severity. And indeed, from now on, that lady ceased being so harsh towards Mary.[38]

Deprived of her mother, her beloved governess Lady Salisbury, and her chance to make a good marriage, unkindly treated and suffering from numerous chronic and psychosomatic ailments, Mary was isolated and miserable. She clung to the staunch religious faith nurtured in her by her devout mother, and was deeply disapproving of Anne Boleyn's reformist leanings and Anne's influence over the King in this respect. Yet, against all the odds, she had conceived a strong affection for her half-sister Elizabeth, and lavished on the child all her frustrated maternal instincts. It is to her credit that she never, in these difficult years, visited her enmity for Anne on Anne's innocent daughter.

If Chapuys is to be believed – and it was a constant theme in his dispatches – Anne had 'never ceased, day and night, plotting against' Mary, and had relentlessly, but fruitlessly, urged Henry to have his daughter and her mother executed for their defiance under the provisions of the Act of Supremacy of 1534. The ambassador heard that she had repeatedly threatened that, if the King were to go abroad and leave her as regent, she would have Mary starved to death, 'even if she were burned alive for it after'; and by 1534, Chapuys, having heard of Lady Shelton warning Mary how Henry had threatened to have her beheaded if she continued to defy him, had come to believe even that the King 'really desires his daughter's death'.[39] But Henry was probably bluffing, for the French ambassador noticed that, when the King complained to him of his daughter's obstinacy, he also praised her with tears in his eyes.[40]

Henry was in a difficult position: he could not be seen to be allowing his own daughter to defy him, or the law of the land, and since she continued to do so, he could not see her. In the circumstances, he was being remarkably lenient. But Anne was relentless; pregnant for the fourth time, she wrote menacingly of Mary to Lady Shelton: 'If I have a son, as soon I look to have, I know what then will come to her.' We may read into Anne's malice her fear of her own increasingly insecure position, and her desperate need to protect the rights of her daughter.[41]

But Anne, Chapuys and others believed, went further than threats. After Katherine died, and the 'bowelling and cering'[42] of a *post-mortem* revealed that her heart was 'black and hideous' both inside and out, with 'some black round thing which clung closely to the outside' – which, according to modern medical opinion, was probably due to cancer (a secondary melanotic sarcoma)[43] or a coronary thrombosis – the examining physician pronounced that he was afraid there could be no doubt as to the cause of her death, for 'the thing was too evident'. Mary herself was told by this same doctor that a 'slow and subtle poison' had been mixed with a draught of Welsh beer that had been given to her mother just prior to her final relapse.[44] The doctor's suspicions convinced Chapuys – and the wider world – that Katherine had been murdered through the malign efforts of 'that she-devil of a Concubine' and her brother, Lord Rochford, and that Mary would follow her to the grave shortly; and so he formulated a plan to spirit the princess abroad to the safety of the Emperor's dominions. Mary was all ready to go, but Charles V hesitated – if she went into voluntary exile, it might be seen as tantamount to relinquishing her rights – and the moment was lost.[45]

Even though there is no evidence that Anne actively had tried to poison Katherine, Mary had no cause to love her stepmother, and the animosity was entirely mutual. The princess had the sympathy and support of Chapuys, the White Rose families, the Seymours, the Bryans, Carew, the Emperor Charles V himself, and all who wanted to see her restored to the succession, and with her mother dead, she had automatically – and willingly – become the focus of opposition to Anne Boleyn.[46] The King could easily restore her rights even without impugning his second marriage, for there could be little doubt that his first had been made in good faith and that consequently Mary should be regarded as legitimate. If Henry could be brought to acknowledge this, Mary would be able to take precedence over Elizabeth in the succession,[47] and Anne would find it difficult to contest that. With this firmly in mind, Chapuys set to work on Thomas Cromwell, aware that Cromwell had for some time been advocating a strengthening of diplomatic relations with Charles V, and that a new alliance could only benefit Mary's cause, while discountenancing – and hopefully unseating – the Boleyns. With Katherine dead, the time was now ripe for action.

Chapuys knew very well that, with the people of England at large, Anne was deeply unpopular. She and her faction were perceived to be responsible for the harsh and rigorously enforced laws that had been passed in recent years, for promoting heresy and radical religious change, for the deterioration of England's relations with other European powers and for the slump in her hitherto-lucrative trade with the Empire.[48] Many of the King's subjects, especially women, resented this 'goggle-eyed whore' usurping the place of the much-loved Queen Katherine. In 1531, a mob of seven thousand had descended on the London house in which Anne was dining, and had she not made a rapid escape by barge, they would probably have lynched her.[49]

Anne had been hissed at in several villages whilst accompanying the King on a progress, and had at length been obliged to turn back.[50] By 1532, some MPs had taken to meeting at the Queen's Head tavern, just off Fleet Street, to plot ways of opposing the King's plans to marry her.[51] When she first appeared as queen, going in state to chapel at Easter 1533, there was dismay and consternation at court and a torrent of public protests;[52] one London congregation, when asked to pray for this woman who was 'the scandal of Christendom', walked out in disgust 'with great murmuring and ill looks', while a priest who preached in favour of the marriage in Salisbury 'suffered much at the hands of women' for doing so. A parson in Lancashire indignantly asked, 'Who the devil made Anne Bullen, that whore, queen?'[53] People in general were 'greatly agitated' at Anne's elevation to queenship, and a priest, Ralph Wendon, who had been hauled before the justices in 1533 for calling her 'a whore and a harlot'[54] was only voicing the opinions of many. Some people were even calling for the 'common stewed whore' to be burned at Smithfield.[55] At her coronation in June 1533, Anne passed in procession through largely silent, hostile crowds, while some sneered 'Ha! Ha!' when they saw the entwined initials of Henry and Anne on the decorations.[56] In 1534, the Act of Succession made it treason to impugn the King's marriage to Anne and their issue.

It did not silence her critics. In October 1534, the French ambassador, Jean de Dinteville – who appears (left) with Georges de Selve, Bishop of Latour, in Holbein's famous double portrait,

'The Ambassadors' – informed Francis I that 'the lower people are so violent against the Queen that they say a thousand ill and improper things against her, and also against those who support her in her enterprises'.[57] Chapuys was more happy than most to be able to report evidence of Anne's unpopularity, but although he was biased, he was probably not exaggerating, for throughout the years 1533 to 1536, official records and other sources contain numerous instances of people being arrested for uttering opprobrious words about the Queen.[58] In 1535, the unpopular Anne was perceived to be responsible for the executions of the much-respected Sir Thomas More, John Fisher, Bishop of Rochester, and several Carthusian monks, all of whom had refused to acknowledge the validity of her marriage;[59] this was the final straw for many conservatives.

Early in February 1536, an Oxfordshire midwife, Joanna Hammulden, on being told by a grateful patient that 'she was worthy of being midwife to the Queen of England', said that she would be pleased to serve a queen 'provided it were Queen Katherine, but she was too good for Queen Anne, who was a harlot'. She added that 'it was never merry in England when there were three queens in it' – a pointed reference to Jane Seymour, whose dalliance with the King was now evidently known beyond the court – and she trusted 'there will be fewer shortly'. For uttering these words Joanna Hammulden was imprisoned.[60] Her slander was typical of the crimes that the authorities were now dealing with on a fairly regular basis. Opposition to Anne could not be silenced.

Over the years, Anne had managed to alienate several of the King's friends and nobles, among them her own uncle and former supporter, Thomas Howard, Duke of Norfolk, whose sister was Anne's mother, Elizabeth Howard. Norfolk was now sixty-three, 'small and spare of stature, and his hair black'. His portrait by Holbein depicts a granite-faced martinet, but his contemporaries thought him 'liberal, affable and astute', 'a man of the utmost

wisdom, solid worth and loyalty'. As Earl Marshal of England and
the realm's leading peer, the Duke was one of the foremost
members of Henry VIII's Privy Council, having 'great experience
in the administration of the kingdom', an admirable grasp of affairs
and ruthless ambition.[61]

There was no love lost between Anne and Norfolk: two strong
characters, they had quarrelled too often, and in 1531, the Duke
had predicted that she would be 'the ruin of all her family'.[62] By
1533, they were barely on speaking terms, and Norfolk had taken
to comparing her unfavourably to Queen Katherine;[63] in 1535,
Anne's former suitor, Henry Percy, Earl of Northumberland (whose
marriage to her had been prohibited by Cardinal Wolsey in 1523),
'began to complain of the wickedness of this King's woman, saying
that lately she used more insulting language to Norfolk than one
would to a dog, such that he was obliged to leave the room, and
moved to heap abuse on the said Lady. One of the least offensive things he called her was "great whore".'[64]

Six months later, Chapuys wrote that Anne did not 'cease day
and night to procure the disgrace of the Duke of Norfolk, whether
it be because he has spoken too freely of her, or because Cromwell,
desiring to lower the great ones, wishes to commence with him'.[65]
Norfolk had not profited as he might have hoped to from his
niece's elevation; he was further disadvantaged by his traditional
Catholic views. Ten years later, in the Tower and facing execution himself (although the King did not, in the end, sign the
death warrant), he reminded the lords of the Council 'what malice'
his niece, 'as pleased the King's Highness to marry, did bear unto
me', saying it 'was not unknown to such ladies as kept [her] in
this house' – he meant during her imprisonment in the Tower.[66]

Norfolk was one among the many enemies Anne had made
at court. 'There is little love for the one who is Queen now, or
for any of her race,' Jean de Dinteville reported.[67] Anne, whose
father was one of the 'new men' who had made their fortunes
at the Tudor court, had been insolent towards the older nobility,

who detested her;[68] the Imperialists hated her because she was the staunch friend of the French, had supplanted Katherine of Aragon, deprived the Lady Mary of her rights, and entertained what they regarded as heretical views. She had become a target for political opposition, for she had also made enemies of those whose influence she had overridden, or who were opposed to the radical religious reforms she had enthusiastically promoted. Alexander Aless, the Scots reformist, was to tell Elizabeth I in 1559 that, because Anne had pushed Henry towards an alliance with the German Lutherans, 'all the bishops who were opposed to the purer doctrine of the Gospel, and adhered to the Roman Pontiff, entered into a conspiracy against your mother'. Given Aless's friendship with Cranmer, he was in a position to know.

Abroad, in Catholic Europe, Anne's reputation was dismal; she was the subject of obscene propaganda, and was frequently reviled as a whore, an adulteress and a heretic. There would be few to champion this unpopular Queen in her hour of need.

'Having thus so many, so great factions at home and abroad set loose by the distorted favour of the King, and so few to show themselves for her, what could be?' asked George Wyatt, with mournful hindsight. 'What was otherlike but all these lighting on her at once should prevail to overthrow her?'

As early as 8 January, the day after Katherine of Aragon's death, the King took the first significant step towards renewing his former friendship with Katherine's nephew, the Emperor. On that day, Thomas Cromwell, the King's principal Secretary, wrote a letter to Sir John Wallop and Stephen Gardiner, Bishop of Winchester, England's envoys at the Imperial court, informing them that, 'considering the death of the Lady Dowager, and as the Emperor has now no occasion of quarrel' and might seek Henry's friendship, they were to try to 'hasten agreement before the King is pressed by the Emperor' and seek advantageous terms. The King commanded Cromwell to add a postscript telling the ambassadors

that, now that Katherine was no more, they need not be so accom-
modating towards the French King – who had, of course, long
showed himself friendly towards Anne Boleyn.[69]

Henry also told Chapuys he was eager for an alliance 'now
that the cause of our enmity no longer exists'. Cromwell, who
was the King's chief and most trusted minister, and who was to
play a crucial part in Anne Boleyn's downfall, had for some time
been anxious to promote a new Anglo-Imperial pact.[70]

Cromwell, the son of a Putney blacksmith,[71] was a former
mercenary who had travelled in Italy in his youth, and there
conceived an admiration for the political ideas of Machiavelli. He
had been (in his own words) 'a ruffian'[72] before he settled down
and became a merchant and property lawyer, in which latter
capacity he had come to the notice of Cardinal Wolsey, the King's
former chief minister, who found him to be vigorously hard-
working and 'ready at all things, evil or good'.[73] He had remained
in the Cardinal's employ until Wolsey's fall in 1529.

Cromwell then rose rapidly to political prominence, impressing
the King with his efficiency, and undertaking 'to make him the
richest sovereign that ever reigned in England'.[74] He had been
preferred to the Privy Council in 1531, then made Chancellor of
the Exchequer in 1533; he was also Master of the Jewel House
and Master of the Rolls, and such was his grasp of affairs and
administration that in April 1534 he was appointed principal
Secretary to the King, an office that – thanks to his abilities and
machinations – would soon become of supreme political importance; effectively, he became Henry's chief adviser, having 'risen
above everyone, except it be the Lady . . . Now [wrote Chapuys]
there is not a person who does anything except Cromwell.'[75] It
is clear, though, that Cromwell was not yet as powerful as he
would later become, especially within the Privy Chamber, where
the King's favoured intimates had the sovereign's ear and controlled
patronage.

Hans Holbein's portrait of Cromwell shows a burly, black-haired man with watchful, porcine eyes, and betrays none of the personal charm or conviviality that won Master Secretary a circle of admiring friends. Chapuys found him 'a person of good cheer, gracious in words and generous in actions'. But while Cromwell was known for his affability, there was steel beneath the charm. He was clever, resourceful, intelligent and able, an administrative and financial genius, knowledgeable, pragmatic, hard-headed and ruthless, all qualities that were much admired by – and useful to – the King. Cromwell adhered to Machiavelli's principle that a prince may publicly be above reproach but might privately do evil or cruel things in order to maintain the stability of the state and ensure the greater good. George Cavendish, who had been his fellow servant in Wolsey's household, thought Master Secretary one whom 'all others did excel in extort[ing] power and insatiate tyranny'.[76] Alexander Aless saw Cromwell as 'the King's ear and mind, to whom he entrusted the entire government of the kingdom'.

Cromwell now wielded authority by exercising his formidable talents, charming people into his confidence, or intimidating them with threats, overtly or by implication. Even though Henry VIII is now thought to have been the driving force behind the break with Rome and the revolutionary legislation of the Reformation,[77] Cromwell was instrumental in implementing these changes and the propaganda of the New Monarchy, while the efficient spy network he had established – a web of paid informers and numerous grateful clients anxious to do him a service – would become a model for future governments, and brought him a wealth of confidential and sensitive information.

Controlling access to the King and occupying a position of enormous influence made Cromwell equally envied and resented, and while the nobles disdained him for his humble origins, they, like most people, feared him. But it was important to have such a powerful operator on one's side. The Boleyns had wasted no time in cultivating him, and he had risen to power with their support, to the extent that, in 1533, Anne Boleyn had referred to

Cromwell as 'her man'. As proponents of the Reformation and the royal supremacy, and advocates of religious reform, both shared, for a time, common aims.

Cromwell, a fellow reformist, had originally been Anne Boleyn's staunch supporter, and had done all in his power to facilitate the annulment of the King's first marriage; he agreed with Anne that the Lady Mary's precarious position was her own fault,[78] and he had been active in enforcing the King's persecution of Katherine of Aragon; he told Chapuys in 1534 that a lot of trouble would have been avoided 'if God had taken to Himself the Queen'.[79] It was Cromwell who relayed orders from Henry and Anne to their daughter's nurse, Lady Bryan; Cromwell, whose duties now encompassed such diverse responsibilities as the running of the royal nursery and the preliminary preparations for the wholesale dissolution of the monasteries.

But, as Retha Warnicke has convincingly demonstrated, the notion of a political alliance between Anne and Cromwell has been largely overstated by modern historians, who have relied too heavily on the dispatches of Chapuys, and inferred too much from them. Nor is there any hard evidence to suggest that Queen and Secretary were allied in a court faction for the purpose of furthering reform. In fact, there are remarkably few known instances of their acting together; on the contrary, the evidence shows them usually to have operated independently of each other. By the summer of 1535, they were moving, crucially, in different directions, and Cromwell's attitude towards Anne had changed, probably because she resented the more radical direction in which his planned closure of the monasteries was taking him: he was pushing for their wholesale dissolution, while she appears to have favoured their reform.

Perhaps Anne had also come to resent – or even fear – Cromwell's growing power as a threat to her own influence. She was a Francophile, while his instincts, honed by his good relations with the merchants of London, were beginning to lean towards the Empire, where they had their markets.[80]

In consequence of these fundamental differences, Cromwell and Anne – far from working together for a common aim – had become rivals for power. That was evident as early as June 1535, when Cromwell, bent on smoothing relations with the Emperor, had discussed with an astonished Chapuys the desirability of restoring Mary to the succession, since she was loved by the people and would have a better chance of holding the throne than the young Elizabeth. He told the ambassador that, if Anne learned of this, 'she would live to see his head cut off'. But he remained unruffled. 'I trust so much on my master that I fancy she cannot do me any harm,' he said comfortably, although his complacency would turn out to be misplaced. Chapuys could hardly believe what he was hearing. 'All I can say,' he observed incredulously, 'is that everyone here considers him Anne's right hand.' He could only conclude that Cromwell desired 'to lower the great ones', and assumed that he might begin with the Queen's estranged uncle of Norfolk.[81]

Despite his earlier interest in a Protestant German alliance, Cromwell was now moving towards an Imperial one; in the wake of Katherine of Aragon's death, the councillors had been increasingly pushing for that, and Master Secretary had no desire to put himself in an isolated position, and every reason to distance himself from the Queen. On the evening of 29 January, the day Anne miscarried, he had a secret meeting with Chapuys to broach the subject of an Imperial alliance, and even said that Katherine's death had been beneficial to relations between Henry and Charles. Cromwell had already anticipated that Anne might well prove an insurmountable obstruction, and the ambassador obviously felt the same, for at that meeting he told Master Secretary that the world at large would never acknowledge her as the King's lawful wife, although it might well be prepared to acknowledge any other lady whom Henry might marry.

Cromwell was aware of Anne's continuing support for an alliance with the Lutheran princes; the English delegation was still at

Wittenberg (it would not return until after May). She had good cause to oppose a pact with the Emperor, which was one reason why she was pushing Henry in the other direction. Alexander Aless, who had himself visited Wittenberg and embraced the doctrines of Martin Luther and Philip Melanchthon, held the biased opinion that Anne's zeal for an alliance with German heretics was the reason why her enemies united against her, for there was always a risk that the King might succumb to her persuasions.

Cromwell knew it would be useful to have Chapuys on his side. We do not know if Chapuys told Cromwell what Henry had reportedly said about having been seduced into his marriage by witchcraft, and taking another wife. But whether he did or not, the tenor of their conversation would have led both men to the unspoken conclusion that it would be in everyone's interests for Henry to rid himself of his unpopular queen.

3

'The Frailty of Human Affairs'

When Henry VIII left Greenwich early in February to go to London for the Shrovetide celebrations and the final session of the Reformation Parliament, which opened on the 4th, he left Anne behind to recover and 'to her own pursuits'.[1] Chapuys believed he was still angry with her, still hardly speaking to her, and that he had 'shown his sentiments by the fact that, during these festive days, he is here, and has left her in Greenwich, whereas formerly he could not leave her for an hour'.[2]

Certainly that was how the situation must have appeared outwardly, yet Parliament's business was exceptionally important, and Henry always made a point of being near at hand when crucial matters were being debated,[3] while Anne would have needed time to recover from her miscarriage: this was, after all, an age in which women were expected to lie in bed for two weeks after parturition, so she could not have been expected to accompany the King to London just days after losing a baby of fifteen weeks' gestation. Indeed, Henry would surely have preferred her to be with the court – and would indeed summon her back as soon as she had recovered – because he could not see Jane Seymour otherwise. For, since the Queen was remaining at

Greenwich, he was obliged, for propriety's sake – his own house-hold being an exclusively male preserve – to leave Jane there too.

Yet, proving that Anne was not entirely out of favour, Parliament passed legislation assuring the manors of 'Hasyllegh', Essex, and Collyweston, Northamptonshire, to the Queen.[4] Collyweston had once been the property of Henry's grandmother, Margaret Beaufort, and latterly it had been in the hands of his bastard son, Henry FitzRoy, Duke of Richmond; the King must have approved Richmond giving Queen Anne that manor and palace in exchange for Baynard's Castle and Durham House in London.[5] This indicates that Henry was still determined outwardly to support Anne, that she yet exerted some hold over him, and that Jane Seymour was, for the moment, just another passing fancy, like Mary Boleyn and Madge Shelton.

For all that, Anne must have been deeply unhappy at this time, mourning for her lost baby and fearing that she had lost her husband's favour. Isolated at Greenwich, her only companions were her ladies and 'her Grace's woman fool'.[6] Anne was no dunce: having leisure to reflect on what had happened, she was probably wondering if Henry would abandon her. On 6 March, Dr Ortiz, the Emperor's ambassador in Rome, would report to the Empress Isabella that 'La Ana fears now that the King will leave her to make another marriage.'[7] There may have been more of wishful thinking and garbled rumour in this than well-founded truth, but it was possibly not far off the mark.

The presence of Jane Seymour was a constant trial to Anne. If Chapuys' sources were correct, a number of 'valuable presents' and loving messages had arrived for Jane from York Place (soon to be known as Whitehall Palace), where the King – who was said by Cromwell on 4 February to be 'merry and in perfect health'[8] – was residing. Chapuys mentioned the presents on 10 February, the first time he referred to Jane by name in one of his dispatches. Anne evidently was upset to learn about the presents and tormented by jealousy. She watched Jane continually, and 'there was often much scratching and by-blows between the Queen and her maid',[9] it being the prerogative of any mistress whose servant gave offence to resort to slaps. Thomas Fuller, in his *History of the Worthies of England* (1662), records a tale of how Anne, seeing Jane wearing a new jewelled pendant about her neck, asked to see it; when Jane showed herself unwilling, Anne lost control of her temper and ripped the locket from Jane's neck with such force 'that she hurt her hand with her own violence; but it grieved her heart more when she perceived in it the King's picture'. Fuller could have had access to sources lost to us, or his story may be apocryphal, but it is credible within the context of contemporary testimony.[10]

As soon as Anne had fully recovered, Henry sent for her to join him in London. She had left Greenwich for York Place by 24 February, on which day she and the King celebrated the feast day of St Matthias there. Chapuys reported that Henry had been sufficiently moved by Anne's distress over his affair with Jane to forsake the latter's company for hers on this occasion. It was on the following day that Chapuys wrote: 'I have learned from several persons of this court that, for more than three months, this King has not spoken above ten times to the Concubine.'[11] But it would seem that Chapuys was rather overstating the matter, or that Henry had now thawed a little, for relations between him and Anne were on the mend, as would be borne out over the coming weeks. On 28 February, Anne felt confident enough to intercede with him on behalf of Joyce, the former Prioress of Catesby, offering him 2,000 marks (£235,000) so that the priory could escape dissolution; however, he did not immediately give her 'a perfect answer' because the Prioress had also appealed to Cromwell, who told the King that the nuns could no longer support themselves, at which Henry quite reasonably turned down Anne's request.[12]

It was at this time that the University of Cambridge wrote to the Queen to thank her for using her influence in persuading the King to remit their dues of first fruits and tenths.[13] Late in April, Henry, Lord Stafford, wrote to Cromwell and the Earl of Westmorland, soliciting their support for his petition to the Queen in respect of his being granted Ranton Priory, Staffordshire.[14] So clearly Anne's influence was still considerable, and perceived to be so.

Anne was perhaps also occupying herself with her charitable works, as well as with dressing up her daughter. Between 19 February and 28 April, she spent lavishly on garments for the two-year-old Elizabeth, whom she loved intensely.[15] Her purchases included purple, white and crimson satin caps with cauls of gold; crimson satin and fringe for the Princess's cradle head; 'fine pieces of needle ribbon to roll her Grace's hair'; and a fringe of gold and silver 'for the little bed'.[16] Agnes Strickland, the Victorian author of *The Lives of the Queens of England*, describes Anne being very melancholy during these weeks, and withdrawing from 'the gaieties of the court' to the peace of Greenwich Park, or one of the palace courtyards, where she sat silently for hours, playing with her dogs, but Strickland does not state where she obtained this information.

By February 1536, the fragile alliance between the Emperor and King Francis I of France was breaking down, with the French threatening Imperial interests in Italy. That, and the death of Katherine of Aragon, had conveniently paved the way to an alliance between Charles V and Henry VIII, a circumstance of which Cromwell now took full advantage. With Pope Paul III on the brink of promulgating the bull of excommunication that had been drawn up by his predecessor, Clement VII, which would deprive Henry VIII of his throne, and the implications that would have for England's future in a largely Catholic Europe, the friendship of the Emperor would be a highly desirable asset. Given the instability of England's relations with France during the past year, it offered the greatest hope for the future security of the realm, for it would also reduce the risk of France and the Empire coming to terms and leaving England dangerously isolated.

On 25 February, Cromwell asked Chapuys to meet him in secret at the church of the Augustine friars, which lay between the ambassador's London residence and the fine house that Master Secretary was building for himself. He told Chapuys 'he wished to speak to me himself, and not by command of the King'. At their secret meeting, as Chapuys reported to Charles V, Cromwell revealed 'that he considered continually night and day how to cement' an alliance between the King and the Emperor. He emphasised that Henry 'desired nothing more earnestly' than the Emperor's friendship', and that his councillors, including some of the formerly pro-French Boleyn faction, were 'strongly urging' him in that direction, hoping that, now that Francis I had moved closer to the Pope, the Emperor would be their friend. They had heard that Charles, desperate to prevent Henry setting aside Anne and making a marriage alliance with France, and eager to mend the breach with England, had recently prevailed upon the Pontiff not to issue his bull against Henry, and was even ready to persuade him to recognise Henry's marriage to Anne in return for Henry acknowledging Mary's legitimacy on the grounds that she had been born of a marriage entered into in good faith.[17] Having a half-Spanish princess as next in line to the English throne augured well for the future of Anglo-Imperial relations and could only benefit both powers.

Cromwell did stress to Chapuys that he spoke of his own accord, and that he had no power to make any overture regarding an alliance – that would have to come from the Emperor himself. 'He thought the King his master would do all that your Majesty wished,' Chapuys informed Charles V.

Cromwell made it plain that he was unhappy about the negotiations that were proceeding in Germany. 'He was ready to forfeit his head if it were found that anything had been treated to the prejudice of your Majesty,' and he made out that those negotiations were of little moment, which Chapuys thought to be untrue, but he forbore to say anything.

He asked instead if the King would be prepared to return to obedience to Rome, to recognise Mary as his legitimate heir, and to ally himself with the Emperor against France and the Turks, who had been encroaching on the eastern borders of the Habsburg Empire. Cromwell told Chapuys that Henry would certainly agree to the alliance, and might be persuaded to reinstate Mary, but would not be as amenable to acknowledging the supremacy of the Pope.[18] This was indeed the issue on which Henry VIII would prove immovable.

Four days after this meeting, on 29 February, Charles V informed Chapuys that it was now possible, and indeed necessary, to negotiate a new rapprochement between himself and Henry VIII against their common enemy, the French, and instructed the ambassador formally to open negotiations. This alliance, he added, would be the best means of improving the situation of the Lady Mary.

The Boleyn faction was still dominant at court, still entrenched at the centre of a web of patronage. But on 3 March, an official inventory was begun of all grants to Anne's father, Thomas Boleyn, Earl of Wiltshire, and her brother, George Boleyn, Lord Rochford, since April 1524.[19] This has been seen by some historians as ominous, in the light of what was to come, suggesting that the Boleyns' fall was already forecast, and that a list of the spoils was being drawn up in anticipation of the annulment of the King's marriage to Anne. That is unlikely, for no move was ever made to dispossess Wiltshire, and that very same day, he had his lease of Crown property at Rayleigh, Essex, with its associated lordships and manors, extended with a rebated rent for the term of thirty years, his son Rochford being brought in as joint tenant. On 19 March, one George Browne, seeking promotion in Ireland, was in no doubt that it would be advantageous to canvas Rochford's support.[20] On 14 April, the King would grant Wiltshire the town of King's Lynn along with two redundant abbeys, the dissolution of the monasteries having begun in March that year.[21]

But the power of the Boleyns was coming under threat, for by 18 March, according to Chapuys, Jane Seymour had become 'a young lady whose influence increases daily', and her family had begun to benefit. The ambassador reported that day: 'The new amours of the King with the young lady of whom I have before written still go on, to the intense rage of the Concubine, and the King fifteen days ago put into his [Privy] Chamber the young lady's brother', Sir Edward Seymour. Chapuys praised Jane to his master as someone of great virtue and kindness, whose sympathies lay with the Lady Mary. But he also sounded a note of caution, for he had sensed that her demure façade concealed less admirable qualities. It was to be hoped, he wrote, 'that no scorpion lurks under the honey'.[22]

Jane's brothers, Edward and Thomas Seymour, were men of ambition, who had no doubt anticipated from the first that Henry VIII's pursuit of their sister might, in the event of her becoming his mistress, lead to their own advancement. Now, in the wake of Queen Katherine's death and Queen Anne's miscarriage, the focus of their ambition began to shift to greater things and, envisaging future glory for their sister, and power, status and riches for themselves, they were only too eager to coach Jane in the art of virtuously snaring a king. The fact that they pushed forward Jane as a viable alternative to Anne shows that the Seymours and others had reason to suppose that the latter's position was now untenable.[23]

Sir Edward Seymour's rise to a position of influence was impressively swift: now a gentleman of the Privy Chamber, he was shortly to be made Master of the Horse; both offices brought him into daily contact with the King, with whom he now stood in high favour and enjoyed increasing influence. He was a cold, greedy, ruthless and cunning man, whose later nickname – 'the Good Duke' – was largely undeserved.[24] Given that his brother

Thomas would also prove to be greedy, ruthless and cunning, we might wonder if their sister shared the same character traits.

For Mary's supporters, and those who wanted to stem the floodtide of religious reform, Jane's elevation to queenship appeared to offer the best chance of restoring the princess's rights. Jane was known to be a friend to Mary, and Mary was certainly warm towards the Seymours, and would remain so all her life.[25] Of course, in the long term, the Seymours' ambitions were chiefly for themselves: they wished to see Jane married to the King and the mother of a son who would displace Mary from the succession to which they were now working to restore her.[26] No one, even Mary herself, then doubted that a male ruler would be preferable to a female one. What mattered at this point was that the Seymours were sympathetic to Mary and ready to stand up for her rights.

Sir Nicholas Carew, the Exeters and their friends were active in advising Jane on how to get her man. 'The young lady has for the most part been well-taught by those intimate with the King, who hate the Concubine,' Chapuys wrote. They instructed her to keep Henry tantalisingly at arm's length, stress her virtue, and hold out for the ultimate prize: 'she must by no means comply with the King's wishes except by way of marriage, in which she is quite firm. She is advised to tell the King how boldly his marriage is detested by the people, and none consider it lawful', and when she raised such matters, she was to do so in the presence of 'titled persons, who will say the same if the King put them on their oath of fealty'. On 1 April, Lady Exeter, Chapuys' informant, sent him a note asking for his backing for Jane and suggesting that it would be a good idea if he himself endeavoured to be present on these occasions, so that he could endorse the opinions of those lords. He assured Lady Exeter that he would speak up in support of Jane whenever possible.[27]

Coached by her ambitious family and the anti-Boleyn faction, Jane was becoming formidable competition. She evidently aimed to profit by following Anne's earlier tactics of holding her royal lover at bay and denying him the ultimate favour. For all her outward meekness, she seems willingly to have colluded in a calculated campaign to snare her mistress's husband, and to have been, beneath the meek and demure exterior, a determined woman who wanted to be queen. To be fair to her, though, as a partisan of Katherine and Mary, she probably did not regard Anne as the King's true wife,[28] and no doubt hoped to use any influence she could exert on Mary's behalf.

On 1 April, Chapuys reported the incident that suggests that Jane had begun to conduct herself in such a manner as to manoeuvre the King into marriage – there would be no more dallying on his knee where they could be observed. Chapuys had got his information from Lady Exeter, a 'Mr Gelyot' (possibly Sir Thomas Elyot) and a servant of Jane's whom he had taken into his pay.[29] 'The King being lately in London, and the young lady, Mistress Seymour, whom he serves, at Greenwich, he sent her a purse full of sovereigns, and with it a letter.' On the evidence of Henry's love letters to Anne Boleyn, the latter is more likely to have contained the importunings of the eager swain than a summons to the royal bed, as has been suggested. Either way, Jane was having none of it. She had so far expressed no scruples about accepting her lover's expensive presents, but money was another matter entirely. It was time to show a little maidenly reluctance and remind Henry how a virtuous woman should be treated. 'The young lady, after kissing the letter, returned it unopened to the messenger and, throwing herself on her knees before him, begged the said messenger that he would pray the King on her part to consider that, by her prudence, she was a gentlewoman of good and honourable family, without reproach, and had no greater treasure in this world than her honour, which she would not injure for a thousand deaths. If the King should wish to send her a present of money, she begged it might be when God should send her some honourable match.'[30]

Lady Exeter added that the King was entranced by this calculated display of maidenly decorum, and that 'his love and desire towards the said lady was wonderfully increased'. He declared that 'she had behaved most virtuously, and to show her that he only loved her honourably, he did not intend henceforth to speak with her except in presence of some of her kin'.[31]

Just how honourable were Henry's intentions? Did they extend to marriage, and was he seriously contemplating ridding himself of Anne at this stage? It would certainly appear so, for the only other 'honourable' position he could offer Jane was that of acknowledged mistress in the courtly sense, which allowed her mastery over his affections and did not oblige her to grant him the physical favours that time-honoured convention permitted him to entreat. This was all above board and an accepted game at court and, conducted in the presence of Jane's kinsfolk, it would not compromise her reputation; but surely Henry wanted more from her than mere courtly flirtation? It may not have escaped his attention that she came from a fertile family, being one of ten children.[32] Henry's determination from 'henceforth' to see Jane only in the presence of her relatives strongly suggests that he was indeed thinking of marriage, and that, given that she might become his queen, he was determined to treat her with respect and decorum. He ceased trying to seduce her, and instead took care to prevent any hint of scandal from attaching itself to her reputation.

When he returned to Greenwich in March, he obliged Cromwell to vacate his chambers, 'and lodged there' Jane's brother, Sir Edward Seymour, and his wife, Anne Stanhope, 'in order to bring thither the same young lady'. The King could access these chambers from his own apartments 'by certain galleries, without being perceived', and pay his addresses to Jane in the presence of her relatives, who now found themselves enjoying even greater influence with their sovereign. But the new arrangement wasn't *that* discreet: Chapuys knew of it by 1 April.[33] This arrangement perhaps suggests that an anti-Boleyn alliance between Cromwell and the Seymours was already in existence.[34] Finding out that her rival had been installed in lodgings so near to the King's can only have aggravated Anne's enmity towards Jane, and her fears.[35]

The Emperor was becoming increasingly anxious to conclude the proposed alliance with England as soon as possible, for early in March, war had broken out between Spain and France, and on the 28th, needing Henry's support, Charles again instructed Chapuys to negotiate a new accord. Anne did not know it, but her situation was now more precarious than ever, with Chapuys at this time regarding her removal as a matter of crucial import- ance. Chapuys did not receive his master's instructions until 15 April, but Cromwell was there ahead of him: on 31 March, he would tell Chapuys that 'the King was more inclined than ever' to reach an understanding with Charles, 'and likewise those of his Council'.[36]

By then, Anne had fallen out with Cromwell; she was prob- ably furious with him for so readily giving up his rooms to the Seymours; it was not long, after all, since she had regarded him as 'her man'. But increasingly, the main issue between them was their diverging aims in regard to the dissolution of the monas- teries, which, as Vicar General, Cromwell was managing on the King's behalf. A vast survey, the *Valor Ecclesiasticus*, had shown many religious houses to be redundant in terms of numbers, income and morals, whereupon a bill for the dissolution of the monasteries had been passed in March; yet while there is no doubt that monasticism had been declining rapidly in England for well over a century, the Henrician dissolution was chiefly a pretext for sweeping away institutions that were potential hotbeds of popery, and – more to the point – whose riches and resources could be used to augment the declining wealth of the King and utilised to buy the loyalty of those who supported the Reformation.

Up to a point, Anne and Cromwell had shared similar religious convictions, but Anne now made it plain that she was fiercely opposed to the wealth of the doomed monasteries being sold off wholesale to individual men of influence in return for their support for the royal supremacy. Instead, she – along with other reformists, including her almoner, John Skip – was determined that the confiscated riches should be used for educational and charitable purposes that would benefit everyone,[37] and she was bent upon persuading Henry to agree with her.

According to Chapuys, Anne was still 'the person who manages, orders and governs everything, whom the King does not dare to oppose'. Cromwell, on the other hand, was not yet as powerful as he would one day become, and he would have foreseen her policy spelling disaster for the revolutionary legislation that was being pushed through Parliament, for not only did the King need the wealth of the monasteries to replenish his empty treasury, but, without popular support – which could be bought by bribes or sales of monastic property – there was the alarming possibility that the dissolution might provoke reactionary anger or worse, and put the Reformation and the royal supremacy itself at risk – and that could well rebound on Master Secretary.[38]

It seems, too, that the Queen had openly confronted Cromwell. If Alexander Aless is to be believed, she had effectively accused him, along with the up-and-coming Thomas Wriothesley, the coroner and attorney of the King's Bench, of corruption. Both 'hated the Queen because she had sharply rebuked them and threatened to inform the King that, under the guise of the Gospel and religion, they were advancing their own interests, that they had put everything up for sale and had received bribes to confer ecclesiastical benefices upon unworthy persons, the enemies of the true doctrine'. Whether they were guilty or not is another matter, but Anne appears to have been convinced of it.

Chapuys learned of the animosity between Anne and Master Secretary late in March, when he hosted a dinner for the

Marquess and Marchioness of Exeter, Lord Montagu, Sir Thomas Elyot and the Dowager Countess of Kildare – none of them friends to the Queen. The fact that Anne's enemies were gathered around the table on this occasion supports the theory that they had for some time been intriguing with Chapuys to bring her down.

It was Montagu who told Chapuys 'that the Concubine and Cromwell were on bad terms, and that some new marriage for the King was spoken of'. Chapuys himself had recently received a report from France that the King 'was soliciting in marriage the daughter of France', and that seemed to bear out what Montagu had said,[39] but Montagu may merely have been reiterating the rumours that had been circulating for some weeks. Chapuys had also just been made aware of Henry's newly honourable intentions towards Jane Seymour.

Cromwell spoke of the enmity between him and the Queen to Chapuys when they met a day or so later, after dinner on 31 March, and conversed in a window embrasure.[40] Chapuys had confided to him 'that I had for some time forborne to visit him, that he might not incur suspicion of his mistress, well remembering that he had previously told me she would like to see his head off his shoulders. This I could not forget for the love I bore him, and I could not but wish him a more gracious mistress than she was, and one more grateful for the immense services he had rendered the King.' He stressed that Cromwell 'must beware of enraging her', and mischievously expressed the hope that the Secretary's 'dexterity and prudence' would save him from the fate of Cardinal Wolsey, who, having incurred the King's displeasure for failing to procure an annulment, had narrowly escaped the axe by dying in his bed in 1530.

This was all part of a clever diplomatic game intended to topple the hated Concubine. Chapuys was strongly hinting that she should be replaced. His fulsome solicitude for Cromwell's future safety was a ploy to secure the latter's co-operation.

With masterful understatement, Chapuys took care to point out that if it was true what he had heard, that 'the King was treating for a new marriage, it would be the way to avoid much evil' and the best means of 'preserving [Cromwell] from many inconveniences'. Such a marriage could only be 'of much advantage to his master, who had hitherto been disappointed of male issue, and who knows quite well, whatever they may say or preach, that this marriage would never be held as lawful'. Despite this, Chapuys himself would welcome the birth of a son to succeed the King, even though it would affect the Lady Mary's prospects. He added – startlingly – that he bore no hatred for Anne Boleyn.

Such words, uttered by an English subject, might well have been construed as treason, but 'Cromwell appeared to take all this in good part, and said it was only now that he had become aware of the frailty of human affairs, especially of those of the court, of which he had before his eyes several examples that might be called domestic'.

It has been argued that these words suggest that Cromwell had already begun plotting Anne Boleyn's fall, and that his later admission to Chapuys that he himself thought up the plot on 18 April was just a smokescreen to hide its true origins, namely that the King had ordered him to make a case against her,[41] but they are far more likely to reflect his own fears as to the extent and consequences of Anne's enmity towards him, of which he had only recently been made aware. Is it likely that Cromwell, that clever and devious strategist, would even have hinted at such sensitive proceedings to a foreign ambassador, who might spread gossip that would forewarn the Queen? His use of the word 'domestic' suggests the personal animosity between Anne and himself; this was, after all, the subject under discussion. It might also refer to the tensions arising as a result of Henry's interest in Jane Seymour.

Cromwell added piously that 'if fate fell upon him as upon his predecessors, he would arm himself with patience and leave the rest to God'. But 'then [he] began to defend himself, saying he had never been the cause of this marriage, although, seeing the King determined upon it, he had smoothed the way; and notwithstanding that the King was still inclined to pay attention to ladies, yet he believed he would henceforth live honestly and chastely, continuing in his marriage'. Master Secretary's cool tone, and the fact that he was leaning back against the window and cupping his hand over his mouth so as to conceal a smile, led Chapuys 'to suspect the contrary'. His suspicions seemed to be confirmed when Cromwell, contradicting himself, went on to say that 'the French might be assured of one thing, that if the King his master were to take another wife, he would not seek her among them'.[42] This was what the Emperor and the Imperialist faction at court had feared, and a relieved Chapuys seems to have taken it to indicate that Henry was indeed planning to marry Jane Seymour.

Chapuys, whom Cromwell begged on parting to accept the gift of a fine horse, came away from their interview feeling that he had achieved much. Cromwell had implied that there were plans afoot to remove the hated Concubine, and also that he would not support her if that happened, and the ambassador was gratified that he had at last been able to do something constructive on Mary's behalf. He wrote telling the Emperor that he would 'inform her of what is going on, and with her advice, will act in such a manner that, if we cannot gain, at least we shall lose nothing'.[43]

He also informed Charles how Jane had rejected the King's overtures, revealing that she had been 'well-tutored and warned' of how easily he might discard her were she to surrender to his advances. His next comment to his master shows him to have had no great opinion of Jane's virtue or of her chances of surviving as queen: 'You may imagine whether, being an Englishwoman, and having been long at court, she would not hold it a sin to be still a maid,' he opined cynically to the Emperor, anticipating that this might be to the King's advantage in the future. 'He may marry her on condition she is a maid, and when he wants a divorce, there will be plenty of witnesses ready to testify that she was not.'

From now on, Chapuys would use all his powers of diplomacy to bring to fruition the mooted alliance. Over the course of the next few days, he would meet again with Master Secretary and with the Imperialists at court.[44] The latter welcomed the intim- ation that the King intended to set Anne aside and remarry. They happily – and naively, as it turned out – anticipated that the dis- solution of his marriage would mean the acknowledgement of the validity of his union with Katherine of Aragon and the restoration of the Lady Mary to the succession, with priority over Elizabeth. It was fortuitous that the negotiations in Wittenberg were now flagging; on 30 March, Melanchthon had written, 'Everybody thinks that the English ambassadors are stopping here too long.' He supposed they would leave after Easter, for no agreement had been reached on the divorce question or crucial articles of doctrine; and they did, departing for home in April.[45]

Chapuys was striving to unite all Anne's enemies in a co- hesive anti-Boleyn faction. Jane now found herself the focus of Imperialist ambitions, flattered and courted by Anne's enemies. It was probably in April – when he was briefly at court[46] – that Sir Francis Bryan sent word to Sir John and Lady Seymour that soon 'they should see his niece well-bestowed in marriage'.[47] His sending such a message at this time shows that Bryan's support for Jane was no new thing, and that he was confident of Anne's ruin.

Cromwell's fears that Anne hated him and wanted him executed appeared to be borne out on 2 April, Passion Sunday, when she had John Skip, her almoner, preach a disapproving sermon in the King's chapel on the text 'Which among you accuses me of sin?' (John, 8:46). In the presence of the King and Queen, Skip mounted his pulpit and 'explained and defended the ancient ceremonies of the Church'. He made clear Anne's views on the dissolution of the monasteries by stoutly 'defending the clergy from their defamers and from the immoderate zeal of men in holding up to public reprobation the faults of any single clergyman as if it were the fault of all'. He 'insisted on the need of a king being wise in himself and resisting evil counsellors who tempted him to ignoble actions', and spoke against 'evil counsellors, who suggested alteration in established customs'. He insisted upon the example of the Biblical Persian King Ahasuerus (also known as Xerxes), who was moved by a wicked minister to destroy the Jews. He urged that a King's councillor 'ought to take good heed what advice he gave in altering ancient things' and 'lamented the decay of the universities and insisted on the necessity of learning'.[48]

His words left his congregation in no doubt that his references to evil counsellors were aimed at Cromwell, and that there was a comparison to be drawn between Master Secretary and Haman, the 'wicked minister' of King Ahasuerus. An educated court audience would have known that Haman had also tried to bring down Ahasuerus's queen, Esther, and that, after Esther had exposed his plot and thus saved the Jews from persecution, Haman found himself facing death on the seventy-five-foot-high scaffold he had had built for his rival, the Queen's protector, Mordecai; there were at least four sets of tapestries depicting the story hanging in the royal palaces.[49] There could be no doubting that Anne was represented in the almoner's sermon by Esther, 'a good woman, which this gentle King Ahasuerus loved very well, and put his trust in, because he knew she was ever his friend'.[50]

Skip even went so far as to embellish the story and assert that Haman had assured Ahasuerus that eliminating the Jews would result in ten thousand talents being appropriated for the royal treasury, and for the King's personal gain.[51] The subtext to the sermon was clear: that the Crown, misled by evil counsel, wanted the Church's property. Anne was throwing down the gauntlet, publicly setting herself up as a leader of opposition to Cromwell's policies. Possibly she believed she had much to fear from him, and suspected him of plotting her overthrow with the Imperialists, which would fatally undermine the cause of reform that she had so avidly espoused. But it is clear also that she was determined to outwit him. The swords were unsheathed; there could be but one victor in this deadly battle.

That this sermon was seen as controversial at the time is suggested by the fact that there are several written copies of it. It would seem that Anne, who had almost certainly heard talk of the King taking another wife, had a message for her husband also, for Skip 'cited the example of Solomon to show that he lost his true nobility towards the end of his life by sensual and carnal appetite in the taking of many wives and concubines'.[52] Henry VIII had been compared to Solomon before; just two years past, his painter, Hans Holbein, had personified him as that king in a miniature, and the comparison was so well established that, four years hence, Henry would again appear as Solomon in a stained-glass window in the chapel of King's College, Cambridge. So there could have been little doubt in anyone's mind that the Queen's chaplain was making, at her bold behest, a thinly veiled reference to the King. Clearly Anne was determined to go down fighting.

Henry VIII and Cromwell were greatly angered by the sermon, and Skip was interrogated and censured for 'preaching seditious doctrines and slandering the King's Highness, his counsellors, his lords and nobles and his whole Parliament'.[53] We may imagine that Henry was furious with his wife also. Effectively she had publicly upbraided him for seeking to replace her.

Undaunted, Anne stuck to her principles. At her instigation, the reformist Hugh Latimer preached his next sermon before Henry VIII on the parable of the tenants who refused to pay rent to the owner of a vineyard. Latimer's subtext was that, once the tenants had been evicted, the vineyard would pass to more worthy persons.[54] The allusion to the dissolution of the monasteries was blatant, and its purpose was to persuade the King to 'convert them to some better use'.[55] Anne also seems to have enlisted the support of Archbishop Cranmer in her mission to thwart Cromwell's plans; he wrote to Master Secretary in support of her views on 22 April.[56]

Given that Parliament had granted the King the right to reprieve some religious houses from closure, Anne had some leeway for further opposing Cromwell's plans for wholesale dissolution. She had already intervened on behalf of Catesby Priory, and had since been asked to save the convent of Nun Monkton in Yorkshire. William Latymer states that, after the Dissolution Act was passed, a delegation of abbots and priors came to her, asking for protection.[57] Clearly she was, and was perceived to be, an adversary to be reckoned with – but only for as long as her influence with the King lasted. If her enemies could subvert that, she was doomed. Later, Henry VIII would warn Jane Seymour – after she in her turn spoke up for the religious houses – that she should 'attend to other things, [for] the last Queen had died in consequence of meddling too much in state affairs'.[58] No fool, Henry knew exactly what had brought about Anne's downfall.

Anne, who performed her customary queenly function of distributing money to beggars and washing their feet on Maundy Thursday, 13 April,[59] must surely have heard the continuing rumours about her husband's affair with Jane Seymour and possibly whispers of his intention of marrying her. She must have wondered, with mounting dread, if Henry did mean to set her aside, and if so, what would happen to her and Elizabeth. Her inner turmoil, and her fears, may easily be imagined.

On 14 April, Parliament was dissolved. It has often been suggested that a plot against Anne had been hatched before then, in the knowledge that, with Parliament no longer sitting, she would effectively be prevented from appealing to it as the supreme court in the land. However, this would only later be regarded as an advantageous circumstance, for – as Cromwell would confide

to Chapuys in June[60] – it was not until 18 April that he resolved
that the Queen must be eliminated by a more effective and perma-
nent means than the annulment of her marriage, which was, so
the surviving evidence suggests, the most that the King was at
present contemplating.

In fact, the dissolution of the Reformation Parliament, which
had sat for seven tumultuous years as the compliant instrument
of the King's will, can be viewed as virtually conclusive proof
that Henry himself was not seriously considering getting rid of
Anne at this time, for her title and the rights of her issue were
enshrined in the 1534 Act of Succession, and Henry would have
needed Parliament to reverse that.[61]

On 15 April, Chapuys received the Emperor's instructions of
28 March, in which a hopeful Charles V had urged him to press
for four crucial things: the reconciliation of England to Rome;
the restoration of the Lady Mary to the succession with precedence before the Princess Elizabeth; English aid in Charles's war
against the Turks; and a declaration of hostilities towards the French.
Chapuys was also to seek out Anne Boleyn's views, for matters
would proceed far more smoothly with her consent. It is evident
that he had acquainted his master with Anne's precarious situation, for Charles had written:

It is quite clear that the King can have no issue from the
Concubine that can hereafter dispute the right of the Princess
[Mary] to the succession, [but] should the Concubine not
be satisfied with the proposal that Mary should be legitimated – a proposal which, after all, she and all her adherents
ought to welcome as a means of escape from the fear and
danger in which they now continually are – and should she
claim more for her daughter, or for the children she may
still have, the negotiation must not for that be broken off.
If you find her demands too exorbitant, you may use

Cromwell's help. And if perchance the King of England should wish to marry anew, you are not to dissuade it.[62]

The English alliance was now so important to the Emperor that he was prepared to recognise the young Elizabeth's claims too, although Mary's must take precedence. And, now that his aunt was dead, he was ready to be even more conciliatory and pragmatic, to the extent of stating that he was, in the last resort, willing to accept 'the continuation of this last matrimony or otherwise'; for with Henry safely married to Anne, he could not seek a marriage alliance with France. However, Charles's recognition of Anne was conditional upon the Lady Mary being declared legitimate and recognised as Henry's true heir. To this end, the Emperor ordered Chapuys to make cautious overtures to the Boleyn faction, in the hope of bringing about a rapport between England and Rome and restoring Mary's rights. Charles V's demands in regard to Mary were communicated to Henry himself, in a letter sent on 14 April from Richard Pate, his ambassador at the Imperial court.[63]

Early on Easter Sunday, 16 April, when Chapuys sought out Cromwell to request an audience with the King to discuss the proposed alliance, Cromwell showed himself delighted and eager, and hinted that his master would soon be ready to conclude an *entente* with the Emperor.

Henry VIII, in fact, was far less than enthusiastic. The Emperor's demands were unacceptable on every count, and he was in no great hurry to meet with Chapuys to discuss them. Excusing himself on the grounds that it was Easter Sunday, he told Cromwell he would see the ambassador two days hence, on Tuesday, 18 April. Already, word of the Emperor's friendly approaches had circulated at court, and the Boleyn faction were aware of his specific proposals; Anne herself was pressing for the alliance. She must have felt confident that the King would circumvent the Emperor's demands.

Not so long ago, Henry, disappointed of a living son, had perhaps been contemplating the annulment of his union with Anne, but now he was determined to secure Charles V's recognition of her as his lawful wife, which would effectively be an acknowledgement that he had been right all along to set aside Katherine and marry her. With the Emperor endorsing the marriage, the Pope would surely think twice about excommunicating Henry.

Chapuys was delighted to receive a communication from Cromwell on 17 April to say that he had shown the King the Emperor's letters 'and reported all our conversations, with which the King had been much pleased, and desired that I would come to court next day, Easter Tuesday, about six in the morning, and that I should have an answer which he doubted not should please me'.[64] Chapuys was now expecting to hear Henry say that he had approved the terms of the proposed alliance, but Henry had no intention of doing that; his primary purpose in summoning the ambassador was to afford him every opportunity of publicly paying his respects to the Queen, whose hand he had until now refused to kiss. This became clear when, on 18 April, Chapuys was greeted at the gates of Greenwich Palace very cordially by the lords of the Council, and in particular by George Boleyn, Lord Rochford, Anne's brother. Gritting his teeth, no doubt, Chapuys listened as Rochford declared his fervent desire for an alliance between England and the Emperor; the ambassador returned the pleasantries, taking care not to touch on the subject of Rochford's regrettable heretical opinions during their conversation.

Cromwell wasn't far behind, with a message from Henry VIII inviting Chapuys to visit Anne and kiss her hand – a great honour that was conferred only on those in high favour. Chapuys was assured that, although this 'would be a great pleasure to the King', Henry had left the decision up to him. With studied tact, the ambassador declined on the grounds that he ought to wait until after he had discussed the Emperor's proposals with the King; until then, paying such a courtesy to Anne was 'not advisable, and [he] begged Cromwell to excuse it, in order not to spoil matters'. Cromwell concurred with this, and went away to confer with the King, then came back to say that his master 'had taken it all in good part' and was satisfied with Chapuys' answer, and that, after dinner, the ambassador would have an opportunity to speak with Henry at leisure.

Chapuys spoke again of his hopes for a happy resolution to the negotiations, and 'just after this, the King came out and gave me a very kind reception, holding for some time his bonnet in his hand, and not allowing me to be uncovered longer than himself'. Henry enquired most courteously about the Emperor's health, and spoke of Charles's recent visit to Rome, but when Chapuys hinted at what he really wished to speak of, the King said, 'Well, we shall have leisure to discuss all matters,' and departed to Mass.[65]

Chapuys was conducted by Lord Rochford to the service in the Chapel Royal. He must have gone with some dread, because he knew he would no longer be able to avoid the woman whose marriage he had for so long refused to recognise; and 'another thing made me unwilling, that I was told she was not in favour with the King', and that it would profit him little to pay court to her.[66] Had it been Cromwell, Anne's enemy, who had said this? Cromwell who had agreed that it was best for Chapuys to wait before going to kiss her hand? If the Emperor were to recognise Anne, she might end up in a stronger position, and Cromwell certainly did not want that.

When Henry and Anne entered the chapel, they seated themselves, as was customary, in the royal pew in the upstairs gallery that overlooked the nave where their households worshipped. Chapuys reported that 'there was a great concourse of people, partly to see how the Concubine and I behaved to each other when they [i.e. the King and Queen] descended to the altar to make their offerings'. Anne, entering the body of the chapel from the staircase, espied Chapuys standing behind the lower door, and seeing her emerge before him, he could do no other than bow to her. 'She was courteous enough, for she turned back to make me a reverence like that which I made to her,' he wrote afterwards. He then went further and handed her two candles to use in the altar ceremonies, commenting afterwards (on 24 April) that politeness had required such a courtesy. 'If I had seen any hope of the King's answer, I would have offered not two but two hundred candles to the she-devil.'[67]

Anne was jubilant, for Chapuys had never paid her such courtesies before, and she emerged from the chapel triumphant. At last, after all these years, Charles V's representative had recognised her as queen. That day, she could be heard loudly proclaiming that she had abandoned her friendship with King Francis and was sorry that France and Spain were at war, but that she was now on the side of the Emperor. 'It seems that the King of France, tired of life on account of his illness [syphilis], wants to shorten his days by going to war,' she opined scornfully.[68] Her brother's warm reception of Chapuys earlier is evidence that the Boleyn faction were aware that their former hopes of a new *entente* with France or the Lutheran princes were better forsaken in favour of a rapprochement with the Emperor.

But Chapuys' acknowledgement of Anne was a victory for the King as much as for the Queen. It was Henry who had manoeuvred the ambassador into making that bow, because he wanted the Emperor to acknowledge that he had been right all along in putting away Katherine and marrying Anne. It was nothing less than a public endorsement of his marriage. And that would shortly be underlined by Henry when he at last got to speak to Chapuys.

After Mass, as was his custom, the King went to dine in the Queen's apartments with honoured guests, and Anne was confidently anticipating that Chapuys would be present, so that she could cement her new rapport with him. But, as Chapuys explained to the Emperor, 'everybody accompanied [the King] there except myself', and Anne was disconcerted to see that he was not among the group of foreign envoys waiting at her door to be received.

'Why does not Monsieur Chapuys enter, as do the other ambassadors?' she asked Henry, obviously perplexed.

'It is not without good reason,' Henry answered.[69] He knew very well that Chapuys' courtesy towards Anne had excited much comment at court, and was probably already aware that the Imperialists had reacted with anger and astonishment when they were told of the deference he had paid to the Queen. The Lady Mary would send Chapuys a cold note conveying her disapproval, as he was to report on 24 April: 'the Princess and other good persons have been somewhat jealous at the mutual reverences required by politeness, which were done at the church', even though Chapuys had not kissed 'that woman' or spoken to her.[70] Ashamed to think that people might believe he had betrayed Mary and his allies, the ambassador had resolved never to speak to Anne again. Instead of attending the dinner she was hosting, he had supped with Lord Rochford and the chief nobles of the court in the King's presence chamber.

Thither Henry went after dinner. It was time for his audience with Chapuys. His initial approach was as friendly as it had been that morning, and taking the ambassador by the hand, he led him into his privy chamber, where only Cromwell, the Lord Chancellor, Sir Thomas Audley – 'Cromwell's creature'[71] – and, significantly, Sir Edward Seymour were present, and there sat down with him in a window embrasure, apparently ready to listen to the Emperor's proposals. But the King's mood quickly became irritable and cantankerous, and it became glaringly obvious that his enthusiasm for the alliance had either evaporated, or been overstated in an attempt to induce Charles to be a suitor to him, rather than the other way about[72] – or, worse still, had been largely a figment of Cromwell's wishful thinking. It was not long before Chapuys realised that Henry's affection for the Emperor 'was not

sincere', while the King had similar suspicions of Chapuys: in a
letter sent on 25 April to his envoys at the Imperial court, he
confided his belief that the ambassador was merely 'pretending a
wish to renew the old treaties' and had other aims entirely.[73] In
fact, as Norfolk was to tell Chapuys the next day, 'whatever overture the Emperor might make, things would not be other than
they have been hitherto'[74] – in other words, Henry would not
agree to acknowledge Mary as his heir or concede to any of
Charles's other demands. Contrary to a popular misconception,
it was these things, rather than Anne Boleyn, that were the major
stumbling blocks to any accord.

Seated in that window, the King bluntly rejected all idea of an
alliance with the Emperor against France, and refused to make
any concessions; nor had he any intention of returning to the
Roman fold. 'He was not a child,' he told Chapuys, 'and they
must not give him the stick and then caress him.' Launching a
tirade, he ranted against the Emperor's ingratitude for the friendship he had shown him, declared himself on the side of the French
in their disputes with Charles, and insisted that the latter acknowledge himself to have been at fault throughout and recognise Anne
as queen – all in writing. At the very least, Charles should insist
on the yet-to-be-promulgated sentence of excommunication being
entirely revoked. As for Mary, Henry declared he would not
tolerate any interference: she was his daughter, he would treat her
as she deserved, and 'nobody had anything to do with that', for
'God, of His abundant goodness, had not only made us a king
by inheritance, but had also therewithal given us wisdom, policy
and other graces in most plentiful sort.'[75]

Henry now summoned Cromwell and Audley to join him, and
made Chapuys repeat the Emperor's terms. Then Chapuys withdrew so that they could discuss them, and 'made some acquaintance
with the brother of the young lady to whom the King is now
attached';[76] this encounter appears to have marked the beginning
of his collaboration with the Seymours. But he was watching the

three in the window closely, and soon became aware that 'there was some dispute and considerable anger between the King and Cromwell'.[77] There can be little doubt that Henry was furious with Cromwell for exceeding his authority and showing himself so eager for the alliance, and angry at the demands Charles had made; yet it is also likely that, in rejecting them out of hand, the King was cunningly hoping to wrest the concessions he wanted from the Emperor,[78] for already he was doing his best to persuade Francis I to put pressure on Charles in that respect. But Francis, who had obtained a copy of the Papal bull, was determined to publish it if Henry made a pact with the Emperor.[79] No wonder Henry was showing little enthusiasm for an Imperial alliance.

Cromwell must have been listening to his master in mounting consternation, even alarm: he had worked hard for a rapprochement and rightly feared that, in consequence of this stalemate, neither Henry nor Charles would ever agree to each other's terms. It appeared that Henry even saw Cromwell's diplomatic overtures as a betrayal, which could only undermine Cromwell's credibility and his influence. Worse still, with Henry demanding Imperial recognition of his marriage, it now looked very much as if Anne had recovered her ascendancy over the King: Anne, whose repudiation many believed Henry recently had been contemplating; Anne, who was now Cromwell's open enemy and was doing her best to wreck his carefully nurtured plans and schemes; Anne, who had made it clear that she would bring him down – and worse – if she could, and would surely capitalise on this latest calamity, and take full advantage of his having fallen foul of the King.

Cromwell must have known that, although Henry and Anne had fallen out on many occasions, Anne knew well how to rule her husband, and it now looked very much as if she had exercised her wiles once more to good effect and re-established her command of him – as she had done many times before. Why else would Henry resolutely have forced Chapuys to acknowledge her at last? In her battle with Cromwell, Anne, it seemed, might very well win.

Chapuys watched as, 'after some considerable time, Cromwell, grumbling, left the conference in the window where the King was, excusing himself that he was so very thirsty and quite exhausted – as he really was with pure vexation – and sat down upon a coffer out of sight of the King'. Henry now beckoned to Chapuys and told him that he must put his proposals in writing, otherwise he himself could not lay them before his Council, 'or make me any reply', but when Chapuys answered evasively, Henry 'insisted wonderfully on having the said writing, and several times said very obstinately that he would give no reply' if he did not receive it. But he reiterated, 'confusedly and in anger', that his dispute with the Pope was none of the Emperor's concern, that 'the Princess was his daughter and he would treat her according as she obeyed him or not, and no one else had a right to interfere' – and much more in an irritable vein. All he would agree to was that, the next day, he would look over the treaties he had with the Emperor 'and inform me of what they determined' with a view to ratifying them once more.

The audience thus terminated, Chapuys returned later to take his formal leave of the King, whom he found in a slightly more gracious mood, and left the court. By then, word of what had taken place had already spread, and many courtiers took it upon themselves to accompany him to the palace gates, saying how sorry they were to hear of it.[80]

After Chapuys had withdrawn, Cromwell attempted to remonstrate with his sovereign. It did him no good, for Henry showed himself so angry and obstructive that Cromwell decided it would be unwise to press him further.[81] Soon afterwards, Henry wrote to Richard Pate, his ambassador at the Imperial court, and made very clear his intention of ignoring Charles V's demand that Mary be restored to the succession.[82] The next day, the Duke of Norfolk told the Bishop of Tarbes, the French ambassador, that, whatever the Emperor might offer or propose, the King would never with-draw from his alliance with France.[83]

It was after that fraught confrontation with his master in the window embrasure that Cromwell, out of favour, angry and in considerable turmoil, and fearful lest Anne Boleyn should seize her chance and exploit the situation, 'thought up and plotted' her downfall.[84]

The next morning, Cromwell sought out Chapuys and they 'expressed their mutual regret' over what had happened. Cromwell was in despair, and 'hardly able to speak for sorrow; he had never been more mortified in his life'. He had far exceeded his remit in showing himself enthusiastic for the alliance – in itself suffi-cient cause to fear for his future – and now he had to explain himself to the ambassador. 'He declared to me [reported Chapuys] that although he had all the time dissembled and made me believe that what he said to me was his own private view of the affair, not the King's, he could assert – nay, swear – that he had done or said nothing without his master's express commands.' Chapuys asked what had happened to alter the King's opinion, but Cromwell could give no answer. He merely observed that 'princes were endowed with qualities of mind and peculiarities unknown to all other people', and that 'whoever trusts in the word of princes (who one day say one thing and on the next retract it), relies on them, or expects the fulfilment of their promises, is not a wise man'.[85]

That same day, the Council assembled, and – as Cromwell would tell Chapuys – 'there was not one of them but remained long on his knees before the King, to beg him, for the honour of God, not to lose so good an opportunity of establishing a friendship so necessary and advantageous; but they had not been able to change his opinion'. The next day, Thursday, Cromwell reported all this to Chapuys and 'thanked him on the part of the King for the good office I had done', begging him to continue and to obtain a letter of credence from Charles V, as Henry had demanded. Backtracking furiously, Cromwell again explained that 'although he had always pretended that what he said to me was of his own suggestion, yet he had neither said nor done anything without express command from the King', but it was easy for Chapuys to detect 'his dissatisfaction at the strange contradictions of his master'. Despite all he had seen and heard, Chapuys was still 'in hope of good issue'.[86]

Later that day, 20 April, Cromwell resolved to feign illness and retire from court, seeking refuge at the Great Place, his house by St Dunstan's Church at Stepney Green, east of London. Chapuys reported on the 21st that Cromwell had 'taken to his bed from pure sorrow'.[87] In fact, he was plotting the Queen's ruin.

4

'Plotting the Affair'

The fall of Anne Boleyn has long been seen by many as the direct result of a marital breakdown, what Agnes Strickland called 'the royal matrimonial tragedy', but that is too simplistic an interpretation. 'A mere estrangement', such as may have occurred between the King and Queen in the early months of 1536, 'cannot explain either the suddenness or the vehemence of Henry's reaction'.[1] The evidence therefore strongly suggests that it was Cromwell, rather than Henry VIII, who was the prime mover in the matter.

Cromwell was to tell Chapuys on 6 June that, 'owing to the displeasure and anger he had incurred upon the reply given to me [Chapuys] by the King on the third day of Easter [18 April], he had thought up and plotted the affair (*il a fantasier et conspirer l'affaire*) of the Concubine, in which he had taken a great deal of trouble'[2] – as would become clear. Of course, misleading or even false information could be fed to ambassadors, but the cynical Chapuys was no novice at the game, and he accepted what Cromwell said as the truth. Furthermore, it is supported by the other evidence.

What Cromwell was ambitiously plotting was no less than the

removal of the Queen and the purging of her powerful faction in the Privy Chamber, men who were close to the King and had served him for years, and who could be counted on to fight for Anne's rights if Cromwell moved against her alone. He would build his case on the King's obsessive fear of treason and the Queen's flirtatious nature.[3] By totally annihilating the Boleyn influence, Cromwell could pre-empt all risk of its resurgence and its power to bring him down. His words to Chapuys were crucially significant, as they prove that it was Cromwell's determination, rather than any evidence, that brought about Anne's fall,[4] and that it was Master Secretary who instigated the political coup that has been called 'one of the most audacious plots in English history'.[5]

What Cromwell told Chapuys must, once and for all, lay to rest the oft-repeated myth that Henry VIII, tired of Anne, disappointed of a son and eager to marry Jane Seymour, ordered Cromwell to find incriminating evidence that would send his queen to her death. For there is absolutely nothing to support the theory that Henry VIII 'passed on to Cromwell the task of finding the quickest and most effective way of getting rid of her'.[6] That is the traditional, and now discredited, view, exemplified by Strickland's sweeping assertion that 'Henry's vindictive purpose against [Anne] was evident from the beginning'.

More than a century ago, the eminent historian, James Anthony Froude rightly asked if Henry VIII, his hands full with the crucial issue of European alliances that would impact in one way or another on England's future, and determined to assert his independence in the face of the great Catholic powers, would have initiated a domestic scandal that would distract himself and his ministers from the tough and demanding negotiations with which they were heavily preoccupied.[7] No, the King was forced to accept a case that other men had constructed for him;[8] he was 'not seeking a way to dispose of a wife of whom he had tired'.[9] He did not need to. He now had total command of the Church of England and could call upon the services of bishops and propagandists to push through and justify an annulment;[10] getting rid of Anne by this means would not have been difficult, and indeed *was* not, as time would prove.[11] And because Catholic Europe did not recognise the marriage, there would have been no diplomatic repercussions, as there had been with Katherine.[12]

Paul Friedmann, Anne's Victorian biographer, thought that an annulment would have been out of the question because it would have given the impression that the King, upon entering both his marriages, had been careless of any impediments, which would have cast doubts on his scruples of conscience. It is a theory that gives the historian pause for thought, but the fact remains that Henry did ultimately have his marriage to Anne annulled on the grounds of an existing impediment of which he was aware at the time.

It has also been argued, by several historians, that Henry did not go down the route to annulment because Anne would never have accepted his repudiation of their marriage or the bastardising of her child. Yet incontrovertible grounds for a nullity suit did exist, as would shortly be proved, and Anne did in the event acquiesce without protest. It is true that she was *in extremis* at the time, and that she was probably offered significant inducements, but that strongly suggests that earlier on, being aware of the precariousness of her position, she would have been susceptible to persuasive or bullying tactics, rather than risk the further consequences of Henry's displeasure.

The King cannot but have been aware that Anne was widely unpopular and that her removal would meet with public approval – after all, he had signed the Act criminalising her critics. There would be no political backlash, as there had been with Katherine. Asserting that a displaced Anne might well have allied with her brother Rochford and 'some devoted friends' to form an opposition party dedicated to restoring her[13] fails to take into account the fact that Anne had few friends and many enemies, and that rejected royal wives were likely to be abandoned by those who wished to remain in the King's favour, as the history of Katherine of Aragon had proved.

If Henry had wanted to get rid of Anne, he could have done so without the assistance of her enemies. The fact remains that, having perhaps toyed with the idea of annulling their marriage, he had taken no evident steps to pursue it. Is it likely that, bent on ridding himself of her in the wake of her miscarriage, and desperate for a son in his middle age, he would have waited three months to move against her? Furthermore, if he had been working secretly to destroy her, why did he insist, almost up to the time of her arrest, on the Emperor acknowledging her as queen? In taking such a stand in secret expectation of her imminent fall, on charges of immorality, Henry would knowingly have been setting himself up for a monumental loss of face, as Catholic Europe metaphorically turned round to him and said, 'We told you so!' Why go through such a pantomime when he could have acted on the 'evidence' and proceeded against her without further delay? It was not as if Anne were a foreign princess with powerful relatives, as Katherine had been. There was no need for him to stand up for the rights of a woman who would soon be branded a 'public strumpet', for he would have known that the way would soon be clear for him to marry a wife whom the whole world could acknowledge.

In recent years, it has increasingly been recognised that what has been called 'the most rapid and bloody political crisis of the century'[14] originated with Cromwell, who had good cause to believe that Anne's influence with the King posed a threat to his policies and to his very life.[15] As David Starkey has pointed out, Anne was 'a brutal and effective politician' who had already brought even the great Cardinal Wolsey to ruin.[16] The threat was real: Cromwell had urgent cause for concern. Political rivalries at court could be deadly, as he was to find out four years hence, after arranging Henry's fourth marriage, to Anne of Cleves, having persuaded the King that an alliance with the German princes would counterbalance his isolation after France and the Empire had united against him in the wake of his excommunication. But Henry took a violent dislike to his bride and the marriage was dissolved after six months, not without a lot of diplomatic shuffling and embarrassment. In the meantime, the threat of invasion had passed. As a result of this debacle, Cromwell's enemies were able to pounce, and with the King willing to believe their calumnies, he was sent to the block on a trumped-up charge of heresy, the victim of his own policies.

Cromwell himself had been instrumental in bringing about the political executions of Sir Thomas More and John Fisher, Bishop of Rochester, in 1535; he knew how easy it was for a great man to fall from favour, and he knew too that Anne had threatened to have him executed. Chapuys had taken her threat seriously, and Chapuys' acknowledgement of the danger in which Cromwell stood must have been preying on the latter's mind, alongside his own fears. Anne's enmity and intentions had been made plain enough to the whole court on 2 April in that sermon preached at her behest, and now there was Cranmer's letter (see p. 73 above), which reached Cromwell around this time, and which must have convinced Master Secretary that she was not going to yield an inch, but would continue to defy him. Above all, Anne, it had just become alarmingly obvious, still wielded considerable influence over the King, and might well gain ascendancy in what looked set to be a bitter power struggle with Cromwell. And Henry was suggestible, as Cromwell must already have known.

In entertaining the Emperor's uncompromising terms for an alliance, with all that they implied for Anne and her daughter, Cromwell had laid himself open to censure and worse, for it had now been made plain that the King was reluctant to enter into a new compact with Charles V; and who knew how Anne, already angry with Cromwell, might react were she to hear of his discussions with Chapuys? She and her faction in the Privy Chamber,

which exercised influence and patronage independent of Master
Secretary, would show no mercy, that much was certain.[17] Against
their power and malice, Cromwell knew himself alarmingly
vulnerable.

It has been said that Cromwell moved against Anne because
her marriage was 'an impediment to diplomatic progress'.[18] But
Charles V had made it clear that, if it came to it, he would recognise that marriage, while Anne herself was in favour of an Imperial
alliance. It was Charles's other conditions that were a barrier to
it. Anne was not the major issue in negotiations. Nevertheless,
were Anne to be removed, the path to a rapprochement with the
Emperor would obviously be far smoother.

Crucially, Cromwell and Anne were pulling in different directions over religion. In defying him, and in re-exerting her influence
over the King, she had showed herself to be an obstacle that
needed to be removed.[19] He knew now that he might wait for
ever for Henry to proceed with a nullity suit, and that, if Anne
was to be eliminated, other means must be found to force Henry
to abandon her. Never mind that Cromwell had once supported
her and smoothed the way for her marriage, for their interests
had now dangerously diverged, and he had come to the stark
realisation that she was now his enemy, and that she and her influential supporters at court were seeking to bring him down and
even compass his death. That must be pre-empted at all costs. So
Cromwell, who had learned a bitter lesson during the past few
days, was ready to take the initiative, as he had, to disastrous effect,
over the Imperial alliance – only this time, with the stakes much
higher, there must be no possibility of failure.

It has been asserted that Cromwell discounted a second royal
divorce because that would have left 'the nucleus of a powerful
party in Anne and Rochford, with their fortunes intact and a
great body' of reformist friends,[20] although that, as we have seen,
is highly unlikely. Moreover, he now evidently believed that the
King had moved away from the idea of an annulment and that

Anne had reasserted her influence. He, by contrast, was now in some disgrace. The only option left to him was to discredit and ruin her once and for all. It was an almighty gamble, but Cromwell may have felt that, in presenting her to the King as a monster of depravity hell-bent on his destruction, and in rescuing Henry from that danger, he himself would win his master's undying gratitude and be restored to favour.

According to what he told Chapuys, and his own account of events, written in a letter dated 14 May 1536 to the English ambassadors in France,[21] Cromwell and other privy councillors had already become aware of salacious gossip about Anne. He told Chapuys that 'one of the things that had aroused his suspicion and made him inquire into the matter was a prognostic [i.e. an indication or forecast] made in Flanders threatening the King with a conspiracy of those who were nearest his person'.[22] This could just have been a mere prophecy that was inflated for Cromwell's own purposes into something more sinister, and utilised accordingly. But Alexander Aless also claimed that some of the evidence against Anne came from abroad, stating that, at the time when the English embassy had been dispatched to Wittenberg the previous year, Stephen Gardiner, Bishop of Winchester, had been ambassador to France (having arrived there in November 1535), and had written to his friends at the English court 'to the effect that certain reports were being circulated in the court of the King of France, and certain letters had been discovered, according to which the Queen was accused of adultery'.

Much of this could have been mere gossip, but certainly Anne had enjoyed close links with the court of France, had patronised French scholars and imported controversial religious tracts, so it is not beyond belief that she had committed to writing certain indiscretions, open to misconstruction, in letters sent across the Channel.

It is more likely that Aless, the friend of Cranmer and Cromwell, was not entirely in their confidence and had made assumptions, misconstruing what he had learned and mistaking – with the benefit of hindsight – accusations of political interference and incompetence with accusations of adultery; and that the truth chimed more harmoniously than he knew with his theory that Anne's fate was the direct consequence of that embassy to Wittenberg. While Gardiner was in Paris, Henry VIII wrote asking for his opinion on the German proposals for the formation of a Protestant league with England, a project that would have won Anne's approval. But Gardiner lambasted the idea, writing to Cromwell that the King in his realm 'was emperor and Head of the Church of England', and if he bound himself to the German Lutherans, he 'would be able to do nothing without their consent'.[23] Henry sat up and took notice, which sounded the death knell to the negotiations, and also to the Queen's hopes of influencing her husband in favour of the Protestants, and it laid her open to the machinations of her hard-line Catholic enemies. Aless says that Henry 'was angry with the Queen' at the failure of this embassy that he had sent at her instigation, because 'the princes would not enter into a league with him against the Emperor unless for the defence of the [Lutheran] doctrine. They demanded more money than he was willing to give, and the King was exceedingly indignant because the Princes of Germany doubted his faith.' It was all, clearly, Anne's fault.

Aless states that Gardiner's letter from France was delivered by his steward, Thomas Wriothesley – who was soon to become one of the King's four secretaries, and, as we have seen, had already incurred the enmity of the Queen – and that it was he who showed it to Cromwell. But Cromwell apparently had other sources of information closer to home.

The assertion that Cromwell's report of 'the judicious sequence of suspicion, investigation, evidence and arrest' was a lie[24] cannot be substantiated because we cannot be certain if Cromwell's suspicions had already been aroused by the gossip and the warnings before he decided to make use of them and proceed against Anne, or whether he deliberately set about making a case against her after 18 April. Telling Chapuys that he had 'thought up and plotted' that case suggests that the whole plot was Cromwell's idea from the first. Yet one might wonder what prompted the idea of accusing Anne of sexual crimes. Was Cromwell acting on testimony already laid or snippets of gossip his spies had already brought him? Probably his spies picked up court gossip, which their master seized upon and 'threaded together into an unseemly chronicle'.[25]

Some of that gossip was perhaps based on things Anne herself had said; she had a habit of being indiscreet. Lancelot de Carles asserts that it was because the Queen 'did not leave off her evil conversation' that she was 'at length brought to shame'. As the historian A.F. Pollard later wrote, 'her conduct must have made the charges plausible'.

There must have been many salacious allegations on which Cromwell could act, given the Queen's unpopularity and the treasonable things that we know had been said about her; several people had called her a whore or a harlot, which implied that people might not have any trouble in believing that she was promiscuous. Certainly Cromwell would make good use of the one factor that the King, above all others, would understand: Anne's appeal for men, and her ability to inspire passion and sexual desire. That could be employed to good advantage, to construct a case against her that was sufficiently convincing – and shocking – to persuade an appalled Henry that she had betrayed him in the basest manner and made a fool of him.

It is possible therefore that Master Secretary was telling the truth, with perhaps a little embroidery and exaggeration, when he wrote to the English ambassadors on 14 May, informing them that 'the Queen's abomination, both in inconvenient living and other offences towards the King's Highness, was so rank and common that her ladies of her privy chamber and her chamberers could not contain it within their breasts, but, detesting the same, had so often consultations and conferences of it, that at last it came so plainly to the ears of some of his Grace's Council'.[26]

If this is true, then being discovered gossiping about such dangerous matters must have been initially a terrifying experience for the ladies and servants concerned because, since 1534, it had been high treason to make any statement slandering the King's marriage and his issue, and since this gossip clearly concerned the Queen's morals, it might cast some doubt on the legitimacy of her daughter. And if such unsubstantiated slanders reached the ears of the Queen or the King's councillors, the consequences could be dire.[27]

But whereas Cromwell had until recently been zealous in punishing those who had offended against the statute of 1534, he was now prepared to overlook such subversions in the interests of bringing down the Queen, and no doubt to assure those who assisted in his enquiries of their immunity from prosecution.[28] Possibly these ladies of the Queen's household were sufficiently cozened or intimidated by Master Secretary to dredge up all the gossip they could think of and tell him what he wanted to hear, which was what would be described at Anne's trial as 'bawdy and lechery'.[29]

We know very few details of the initial investigations, but one thing seems likely. John Husee, a gentleman of the King's retinue in Calais and the attorney of Henry VIII's uncle, Arthur Plantagenet, Lord Lisle, Governor of Calais, was in London when, on 23 May, he wrote to Lady Lisle of the recent sensational events that had rocked the court, and informed her that 'the first accuser' of the Queen was 'the Lady Worcester, and Nan Cobham, with one maid more; but the Lady Worcester was the first ground'. Two days later, Husee reiterated to Lady Lisle, 'As to the Queen's accusers, my Lady Worcester is said to be the principal.'[30] In corroboration, Lancelot de Carles also describes her as the initial witness. This would appear to bear out what Cromwell told the ambassadors, that he and the Privy Council acted on evidence laid before them.

*   *   *

Elizabeth, Countess of Worcester, the daughter of Sir Anthony Browne, was married to Henry, the second Earl, the son of Charles Somerset, Earl of Worcester, an illegitimate descendant of the Beauforts and, through them, cousin to the King.[31] The Countess, whose tomb effigy survives in St Mary's Church, Chepstow,[32] was one of the Queen's ladies-in-waiting and evidently close to her, despite her half-brother, Sir William FitzWilliam, treasurer of the King's household, being (according to Chapuys) 'a man of sense and a good servant' of the Lady Mary.[33] FitzWilliam, who had once been Cardinal Wolsey's 'treasure' and had no love for the woman who had brought down his old master,[34] was to be instrumental in bringing about Anne's fall, while the Countess's brother, the younger Sir Anthony Browne, would openly rejoice at it. This might suggest that, aside from acting as was required of them on their allegiance to the King, they both felt they were justified in doing so.

Lady Worcester had attended the Queen at her coronation banquet in 1533, and seems to have been in her confidence, as can be inferred from the fact that, on 8 March 1537, ten months after Anne's fall, the Countess was to confide to Cromwell that she had borrowed £100 (£34,900) from her mistress without telling her husband. He responded by reassuring her that she need not trouble to pay it back as it had been given out of the former Queen's privy purse. 'On that matter I most heartily thank you,' Lady Worcester replied, 'for I am very loath it should come to my husband's knowledge. I am in doubt how he will take it.'[35] As will be seen, Anne was certainly under the impression that the Countess was a good friend: Elizabeth Browne was pregnant in the spring of 1536, and Anne was to attribute the fact that the baby 'did not stir in her womb' to the sorrow that the Countess suffered on account of her mistress's misfortunes.[36] But Anne may have been harbouring a false impression.

At some point in the spring of 1536, according to Lancelot de

Carles, a 'lord of the Privy Council, seeing clear evidence that his sister loved certain persons with a dishonourable love, admonished her fraternally. She acknowledged her offence, but said it was little in her case in comparison with that of the Queen, who did more than she did, and was accustomed to admit some of her court to come into her chamber at improper hours.' She then declared that, 'as he might ascertain from Mark [Smeaton]', a court musician and member of the King's Privy Chamber, Anne was 'guilty of incest with her own brother', and added 'that Smeaton could tell much more'.

This passage appears to refer to Lady Worcester. There is another version of this tale in the Lansdowne MSS in the British Library, in which the brother's name is given as 'Antoine Brun', but since the Countess's half-brother, FitzWilliam, was a member of the Privy Council, and her brother, Sir Anthony Browne, a member of the Privy Chamber, was not, it is more likely that she confided in FitzWilliam. It has been claimed that there is no evidence for her being promiscuous[37] but, equally, there is none that she was not, although the theory that she was pregnant by Cromwell does not bear serious scrutiny.[38]

Since most sources agree that the only evidence for incest would rest upon the testimony of Jane Parker, Lady Rochford, it appears that Lancelot de Carles had got some of his facts mixed up, and that Lady Worcester revealed to her kinsman only that the Queen was promiscuous and that Mark Smeaton could testify to that.

Nan Cobham has never been conclusively identified,[39] but she was clearly one of the Queen's maids, and was perhaps the 'Mrs Cobham' who had been the recipient of a royal gift at New Year 1534,[40] and/or the Anne Cobham who in May 1540 was granted the advowson of Warminghurst, Sussex, with remainder to Edward Shelley, who died in 1554 and was buried in the church there.[41] She may perhaps credibly be identified with Anne Braye, the wife of George Brooke, Lord Cobham, who was among the peers who would sit in judgement on Anne Boleyn. It is highly unlikely that she had acted as midwife during Anne's last confinement, as has been suggested,[42] for she was probably a lady of rank, although she may have been present.

The 'one maid more' who was the third of the first three accusers mentioned by Husee has been identified as Mistress Margery Horsman,[43] who was quite an important mover and shaker in the Queen's privy chamber. Mrs Horsman, who had arranged for a kirtle to be delivered from Anne's wardrobe as a royal gift to a grateful Lady Lisle in March, was highly influential and would end up serving every one of Henry VIII's six wives.[44] However, on 3 May, Anne's chamberlain, Sir Edward Baynton, would reveal in a letter that he had not managed to extract any information from Mrs Horsman, who was behaving 'strangely' towards him, probably (he thought) because she was a friend of Anne's;[45] and furthermore, she was clearly too important to be a mere maid-of-honour, so it is unlikely on both counts that she had been one of the first witnesses.

Although we do not know what it was, one of the most damning pieces of evidence against Anne came from someone who claimed to have spoken to Bridget Wiltshire, Lady Wingfield, before that lady's death in 1533.[46] The daughter and heiress of Sir John Wiltshire of Stone Castle, Kent, Bridget had married the courtier, diplomat and substantial Huntingdonshire landowner, Sir Richard Wingfield of Kimbolton Castle, around 1513, and borne him ten children before his death in 1525. Thereafter she was married twice more, to Sir Nicholas Harvey of Ickworth, who died in 1532, and by whom she had four sons, and to Sir Robert Tyrwhitt of Kettleby, who long outlived her. She had last received a New Year's gift from the King in January 1533,[47] and probably died later that year.[48]

It has been suggested that Lady Wingfield's revelations, which were possibly made on her deathbed, were conveyed to Cromwell by her stepson, Sir Thomas Harvey,[49] the son of Sir Nicholas by his first wife, Elizabeth, who was a sister of William FitzWilliam. This theory rests on the grounds that Harvey, who had been born before 1512 and acted as FitzWilliam's executor on the latter's death in 1542, apparently fled abroad on the accession of Anne Boleyn's daughter Elizabeth in 1558, and remained there until his death in 1577. But Harvey was a life-long Catholic, and had served Mary I as Knight Marshal; his going into voluntary exile could equally have been to ensure his freedom to practise his religion unmolested. However, the FitzWilliam connection could be significant.

Lady Wingfield's hearsay testimony was mentioned by Sir John Spelman, a justice of the King's Bench and a member of the jury that would try the Queen and her alleged lovers. He recorded in his Commonplace Book: 'Note that this matter was disclosed by a woman called the Lady Wingfield, who had been a servant to the Queen and shared the same tendencies; and suddenly the said Wingfield became ill, and a little time before her death she showed the matter to one of those etc.'[50] Whatever Lady Wingfield had confided, if she had in fact said anything at all, it could only have related to the period prior to her death in 1533,[51] and whoever repeated her words had kept these revelations to him- or herself for at least two years. That is perhaps understandable, for during that period the law had come down heavily on anyone who spoke ill of the Queen. But once word had got out that her conduct was the basis for an investigation, that person – who might have been Thomas Harvey, Lady Worcester, Nan Cobham or the 'one maid more' referred to by Husee – may have felt obliged to speak out.

Some historians have wondered if Lady Wingfield should be identified with the Privy Councillor's sister of dubious morals referred to by Lancelot de Carles, yet there is no record of a brother with the surname Wiltshire among the lords of the Privy Council, so the reference in the poem must have been to

FitzWilliam or, less probably, Anthony Browne.

Various writers have also speculated that Lady Wingfield was in possession of sensitive information about Anne Boleyn, and even that she had once tried to blackmail her. At least four years earlier (between December 1529 – when Anne's father had become Earl of Wiltshire and she began using his subsidiary title of Viscount Rochford as a surname – and September 1532, when she was created Lady Marquess of Pembroke),[52] Anne had written to Lady Wingfield, who still lived at Stone Castle, twenty miles north of the Boleyns' castle at Hever:

> Madam, I pray you, as you love me, to give your credence to my servant, this bearer, touching your removing, and any thing else that he shall tell you of my behalf, for I much desire you to do nothing but that shall be for your wealth. And Madam, though at all times I have not shown the love that I bear you as much as it was in deed, yet now I trust that you shall well prove that I loved you a great deal more than I made fair for. And assuredly, next mine own mother, I know no woman alive that I love better; and at length, by God's grace, you shall prove that it is unfeigned. And I trust you do know that I will write nothing to comfort you in your trouble but I would abide by it as long as I live. And therefore, I pray you, leave your trouble, both for displeasing of God, and also for displeasing of me, that doth love you so entirely. And trusting that you will thus do, I make an end, with the ill hand of your assured friend during my life.
>
> Anne Rochford.[53]

We might infer from this that Anne's relations with Lady Wingfield, whom she had evidently known for many years and was fond of, had not always been congenial. There is no clue as to what Lady Wingfield's 'trouble' was; she might have been mourning the death of her second husband, Sir Nicholas Harvey, in August

1532,[54] or the loss of one of her children, yet Anne would hardly have thought to comfort someone newly bereaved by urging her to 'leave your trouble' because it was displeasing to God and herself. In saying effectively that she would stand by any advice she gave her and exhorting Lady Wingfield to pull herself together, she was perhaps telling her that she was worrying unnecessarily about something.

Excessive courtesy was common in Tudor letters, so it would be unwise to read too much into Anne's fulsome protestations of affection. It is hard to infer from this letter that Anne was being blackmailed, which is one recent theory.[55] In October 1532, after it was written, Henry VIII and Anne Boleyn stayed the night with Lady Wingfield at Stone, *en route* for Calais,[56] and the following January that lady was the recipient of royal New Year's gifts, as she had been the year before[57] – all of which suggests that relations were congenial. The fact that the letter ended up among Cromwell's papers may only prove that he asked to see any correspondence that his informants could produce, and could have no more significance than that.

Yet there *is* a hint of compulsion in this letter, almost a threat that, if Lady Wingfield does not take Anne's advice, she will get no sympathy from her, or the friendship might be tested to the limit, but this suggests that it was Anne who had the upper hand in the relationship. The first sentence implies that she is constraining Lady Wingfield to do something which that lady is reluctant to do. To sweeten the pill, Anne is laying on the flattery, and perhaps trying to comfort her friend in her trouble by reassuring her of her own affection, of which she might not always have been aware.

The letter is probably a 'red herring', of which too much has been made. However, Lady Wingfield may privately have spoken out against Anne. Her third husband, Sir Robert Tyrwhitt, was a staunch supporter of the Lady Mary, while she herself was related to both the Duke of Suffolk and Sir William FitzWilliam, who were no friends to the Queen. Even if she had been friendly with Anne earlier, she might have been persuaded that it was not in her interests to continue it, and she may thereupon have divulged what she knew – if, of course, she divulged anything at all.

It seems to have been the initial testimony of these ladies that led Cromwell to construct the criminal process against Anne.

Anne had failed to give the King a son. She had proved unstable and unfit in many people's eyes to be a queen, with her strident tantrums and her immoderate behaviour. She had not been a meek and submissive wife. Despite her conscious efforts to portray herself as virtuous, and her genuine devotion to the reformist cause, she was known to be pleasure-loving and flirtatious, and to enjoy the admiration of the men in her circle. Prior to her marriage, her reputation had been notorious, which in sixteenth-century eyes was irrevocably damning: she had encouraged the advances of a married man, and there had been frequent allegations that she had lived with the King out of wedlock; indeed, from the autumn of 1532, these were justified, for her daughter Elizabeth was born only seven months and thirteen days after her parents' secret marriage. It would not be difficult for people to credit that a woman who had indulged in premarital intercourse could also indulge in extramarital affairs. Earlier still, Anne had spent years at the French court, which was a byword for promiscuity; after marrying her, Henry had discovered that she had been corrupted there and become quickly disillusioned. Cromwell probably realised that charges of immorality would stick because people would believe in them.

Later commentators, writing in the reign of Anne's daughter Elizabeth I, evolved their own spin on Anne's reputation. William Latymer, who had been one of Anne's chaplains during the last months of her life, wrote a eulogistic chronicle of her that was dedicated to Queen Elizabeth, and in it asserted that, after she became queen, she had endeavoured to set a high moral standard for her household, instructing her officers to set a godly 'spectacle' to others, to attend Mass daily and to display 'a virtuous demeanour'. If any person employed by the Queen was caught brawling, swearing or frequenting brothels, they risked instant dismissal and 'utter shame'. That these rules were enforced is suggested by the testimony given by Jane Wilkinson, Anne's former silkwoman, to John Foxe, the Protestant author of the famous *Book of Martyrs*, also published in Elizabeth's reign: Jane claimed that she had never seen 'better order amongst the ladies and gentlewomen of the court than in Anne Boleyn's day'. George Wyatt mentions the Queen's lavish charitable donations, and asserts that her ladies were required to be pious and above reproach, and had to devote hours of their time to sewing garments for the poor, yet it is clear from contemporary accounts that these strictures did not preclude them from having illicit affairs.

Latimer, Foxe and Wyatt were all eager to rehabilitate the memory of the mother of the Virgin Queen, and to stress her reformist virtues, so their accounts are naturally biased in Anne's favour, and they are somewhat at odds with what we know of social relations within her court. According to the poet Sir Thomas Wyatt, Henry's courtiers worshipped 'Venus and Bacchus all their life long'. There is ample testimony to the merry 'pastime' that went on in the Queen's chamber: in 1533, Anne's own vice-chamberlain, Sir Edward Baynton, wrote that, 'if any man had gone away leaving at court a lady who might mourn at parting, I can no whit perceive the same by their dancing and pastime they use here'.[58] Anne's was a court primarily bent on pleasure; there was nothing but 'sporting and dancing', as Sir Thomas More's daughter Margaret was to report in 1535.[59] To that, she might have added gambling.

Given that there were probably fewer than a hundred women among the court's population of between eight- and fifteen-hundred persons (depending on the season), it is hardly surprising that a hothouse atmosphere prevailed when it came to interaction between the sexes. George Wyatt refers to 'those that pleased the King in recounting the adventures of love happening in court'. The gentlemen of the King's Privy Chamber would flock to the Queen's apartments knowing that she appreciated witty, stimulating conversation, and that there would be opportunities aplenty for flirting with her ladies. Nor was Anne above joining in the repartee, as her own accounts of her banter and familiarity with these gentlemen vividly show.[60] Thanks to her upbringing at the French court, she was familiar and free-and-easy in her manner and her social relationships.

Her flirtations were probably innocent; they were an accepted aspect of the game of courtly love that had been a tradition in European courts since the twelfth century. A knight might pay his ardent addresses with all seemliness to a mistress who was above him in rank and might even be married; he could wear her colours at a tournament, write songs and poems for her, sigh and languish for one sign of favour, or even pursue her with greater intent. The theory was that she was unattainable, and that this behaviour was acceptable so long as it did not go beyond the bounds of propriety and lead to seduction or the breaking of marriage vows.

Of course, such courtly relationships *were* often an excuse for sexual dalliance or adultery, and there is much evidence to show that this was commonplace at Henry VIII's court. But Caesar's wife had to be above reproach, and by indulging in the flirtatious games and light-hearted innuendo of courtly love, the Queen of England ran the risk that her behaviour might be misconstrued – perhaps by Lady Worcester and other people who testified against her – while actual adultery was another matter entirely, for any gentleman who thus ventured to compromise her honour would have been guilty of high treason. The Statute of Treasons of 1351 provided for the prosecution of any man who 'violated the King's companion' – the word 'violated' being used in its widest sense – and the punishment was hanging, drawing and quartering.

For it was not honour alone that was compromised, but the succession itself: as William Thomas, Henry's apologist, was to point out in 1546, 'adultery in a king's wife weigheth no less than the wrong reign of a bastard prince'.[61]

The Statute of Treasons, however, did not provide for a queen to be accused of high treason for adultery, only the man who had violated her. It was not until 1542, in the wake of the fall of Katherine Howard, Henry VIII's fifth wife, that the definition of treason was extended specifically to embrace adultery on the part of a queen.[62] But in 1534, Parliament, seeking to protect Queen Anne from her enemies, had passed an act widening the definition of treason to all who 'do maliciously wish, will or desire, by words or writing, or by craft imagine' the King's death or harm, and to anyone who impugned the King's marriage to Anne or his issue.[63] Perversely, this same statute was to prove Anne's downfall, for committing adulterous acts was construed as treason on the count of impugning the King's issue, and thus justified a capital charge. But an even worse accusation was to be levelled against Anne, of a crime that was treason by any legal definition. According to Cromwell, who had mentioned those reports from abroad, 'there brake out a certain conspiracy of the King's death', and that, he said, left him and his colleagues quaking in their shoes.[64]

Cromwell stayed away from court, perfecting his case against the Queen, until 23 April. By then, his plans were well advanced; various councillors had been taken into his confidence, and the support of Chapuys, the Seymours, Bryan, Carew, Exeter and other partisans of the Lady Mary enlisted. This may have been put in place before Cromwell even left court to feign sickness.

This unlikely – and, indeed, temporary – alliance between the conservatives at court and the reforming Cromwell would previously have been unthinkable, but both sides now shared a common aim in working for the elimination of the Queen and her faction, while Cromwell – despite his ongoing support of Lord Lisle in a property dispute with Sir Edward Seymour[65] – had realised that supporting Jane Seymour, and exploiting the Imperialist network of support that had formed around her, offered him his best chance of political survival.

Hitherto, the Imperialists had naively envisaged that an annulment of the King's marriage to Anne would be sufficient to get rid of her. Cromwell had disabused them of that idea – had the King not just insisted upon Chapuys and Charles V acknowledging her as Queen? – and rapidly secured their backing for his more radical solution.[66] It was Chapuys who obtained the Lady Mary's qualified approval of the plot to remove Anne.[67] He was happy to work with anyone who 'could help in its execution', believing they did 'a meritorious work, since it would prove a remedy for the heretical doctrines and practices of the Concubine, the principle cause of the spread of Lutheranism in this country'.[68]

Of course, what the court conservatives did not know was that there was no intention for the removal of Anne to lead to reconciliation with Rome and the reinstatement of the Lady Mary,[69] which they fondly expected would happen. But Cromwell, who would immediately distance himself from them once his goal was achieved, was not about to disillusion them. Not yet.

Anne's every move was probably being observed by Cromwell's spies and informants. Speed was of the essence: the King – who had fallen out with Anne many times, yet remained in thrall to her – must not be allowed time for scepticism, sentimental feeling or the residue of passion to overtake the shock of hearing that his wife had not only been unfaithful with several men, but had planned to kill him. That would surely be sufficient to alienate the insecure and suspicious Henry, and preclude another reconciliation.

The ruthlessness with which the Queen was brought down was indicative of the extent to which Cromwell and others feared her.[70] What they were afraid of was not so much her ability to command support from an affinity of adherents − which was unlikely, as she was so unpopular − as the power she undoubtedly wielded over the King, which had just been demonstrated so alarmingly.

Events now moved forward swiftly. We have Cromwell's own account of what happened next, in his letter of 14 May. On his return to court on 23 April, he saw Henry VIII and although there is no record of what passed on that occasion, it was probably then that he and other privy councillors, 'with great fear, as the case enforced, declared what they had heard' of the Queen's conduct; they told the King that 'we that had the examination of it quaked at the danger his Grace was in' and realised that, 'with their duty to his Majesty, they could not conceal it from him'. On their knees, they 'gave [God] laud and praise that He had preserved him so long from it'.[71]

Alexander Aless makes it clear in his account of the period leading up to Anne's arrest that Henry VIII was made aware of the suspicions of Cromwell and others before ordering further investigations, and that it was only after these had been carried out that they reported back to him (probably on 30 April). Thus it is likely that Cromwell approached the King as soon as he returned to court. Many historians have remarked upon the speed with which the investigation progressed, but it would only have needed a few days to arrange and conduct the interrogation of members of the Queen's household.

Lancelot de Carles states that, prior to this audience, the Privy Councillor − almost certainly FitzWilliam − to whom the Countess of Worcester had confided her suspicions of the Queen 'did not know what to do, and took counsel with two friends of the King, with whom he went to the King himself, and one reported it in the name of all three. The King was astonished, and his colour changed at the revelation, but he thanked the gentlemen.'

Although, according to Carles, this evidence was supposed to have been revealed to the King at the end of April, on the same day the decision was made to proceed against the Queen, the Lisle letters make it clear that the first evidence had been laid by Lady Worcester, and that had probably been some time before 18 April, so it almost certainly formed the basis of the councillors' revelations to Henry, which internal evidence suggests were disclosed to him before 24 April. It is obvious that very few people were aware of what was really going on behind the scenes, and that Carles was relying on gossip and hearsay. Yet some of it perhaps was based on fact, and his poem may reflect what actually happened when Henry VIII was first informed of his councillors' suspicions, with FitzWilliam consulting with Sir Anthony Browne, his kinsman, and Cromwell, and acting as spokesman for them all,[72] bearing in mind that Cromwell was still, to all intents and purposes, out of favour.

Aless, who was in a position to be a reliable source, says that Thomas Wriothesley went with Cromwell to confront the King, so maybe he, rather than Anthony Browne, was the other 'friend of the King' to whom Lancelot de Carles refers. Aless adds that the King 'was furious' when informed of the Queen's misconduct, but quickly 'dissembled his wrath', and ordered Cromwell and the other privy councillors to make further enquiries, 'trusting them with the investigation of the whole business'. It would appear from this that Henry's displeasure with Cromwell had rapidly dissipated in the face of this far more serious crisis, as Cromwell had no doubt hoped it would.[73]

Did Henry think to question the evidence? Contemporary sources suggest that, for a time, the King had been toying purely with the idea of an annulment. It has been asserted that it was Henry's 'egotism and credulity' that brought about Anne's fall;[74] egotism almost certainly played a part, but the King was an intelligent man and well able to exercise his own judgement.

The evidence that had been laid before him must have looked damning on the face of it, and had serious implications for the succession. Yet he did not immediately swallow it whole, nor act impulsively, gleeful that someone had provided him with a pretext for ridding himself of his unsatisfactory queen. Having recently been trounced by Anne for infidelity, and not for the first time, he could have used these accusations of immorality against her to regain the high moral ground and salvage his pride. But he did not, at this stage.

Instead, he prudently resolved to wait and see what further investigation would uncover. We might today look askance at Cromwell's extravagant claim (made to Chapuys in 1533) that Henry was 'an honourable, virtuous and wise prince, incapable of doing anything that was not founded on justice and reason', yet there is no evidence that the King 'personally exerted himself to pervert the course of justice', as the chronicler Charles Wriothesley's Victorian editor put it, while charging Anne with infidelity was almost certainly not his idea. He was an egotistic male who was perhaps touchy about his virility. 'Am I not a man like other men? Am I not? Am I not?' he had angrily rounded on Chapuys in 1533, when Chapuys dared to suggest that he could not be sure of having any more children. 'I need not give proofs to the contrary; you do not know all my secrets,' Henry had snapped.

Is it then likely that the King would have suggested, or approved in advance, charges that would see him publicly branded a cuckold, with hints about him being impotent to boot? Even though, four years and two wives later, he was loudly to proclaim himself impotent with Anne of Cleves in the hope of freeing himself from their marriage, he would instruct his doctors to make sure it was publicly known that, although incapable with her, he was able to perform the sex act with any other woman.

Cromwell would surely never have dared, acting on his own initiative, to instigate an enquiry into the Queen's conduct without first ensuring that he could marshal credible and convincing evidence against her. He would have been aware that such accusations would proclaim his formidable master a cuckold, and irrevocably insult the Queen of England – for there was always the risk that Henry would take Anne's part. Cromwell knew he had to make the most convincing case against Anne and present it to Henry as *fait accompli* – the King, it has been said, was 'bounced' into a decision[75] – but he would have known also that, in doing so, he was risking all. This was one of the rare occasions on which Cromwell, backed by the conservatives, forced Henry's hand.[76] Certainly Henry could not have ignored the things that people were alleging against Anne without compromising his own honour, and he could never have risked ignoring a plot to assassinate him.[77]

Henry's suspicious nature probably led him to jump to conclusions about his wife,[78] but the things he had been told may retrospectively have struck a chord. He would have been aware of the shifting factions within his court, and that Cromwell had good reason to fear Anne. But he also knew he had married a woman whom many believed had a sullied reputation; he himself had evidently become disillusioned about her for various reasons; and her last miscarriage had been a warning that God did not smile on their union. Now he was being confronted by evidence from members of his wife's household that she had played him false. It is hardly surprising that he wanted this investigated further.

We will never know Henry's true role in Anne's fall.[79] Traditionally, it has often been assumed that, enamoured of Jane Seymour, he was desperate to get rid of Anne and seized the opportunity of doing so. This is the facile explanation that has been accepted by so many over the years, and the answer may be as simple as that. The assertion that the King, shocked at the birth of a malformed foetus and unable to accept that it could be his, 'had his Master Secretary search for men, especially those with lecherous reputations, who could be charged with having committed sexual crimes with his consort'[80] falls on the simple fact that there is no evidence whatsoever that the child Anne miscarried was deformed, and can therefore be rejected.

There is, of course, the possibility, which cannot lightly be dismissed,[81] that Anne was guilty as charged, and that Cromwell had no trouble in finding evidence against her, and had indeed acted on genuine information laid before him. Had she been driven by her desperation for a son, and her fear that Henry would abandon her, to seek solace and the quickening of her womb in the arms of other men? How foolhardy that would have been, for there was every chance that either Henry, who was inordinately suspicious by nature, or one of her enemies might have guessed what was going on. And logistically, it would have been difficult for Anne to have illicit affairs. A queen was rarely alone and enjoyed little privacy. Had she indulged in a succession of amorous intrigues, there would surely have been witnesses. The lives of royalty were played out in public; kings and queens nearly always had attendants about them, even when they were in bed or on the close stool; their doors were guarded, and servants slept on pallets inside and outside their bedchambers. The only time they were alone was when they were making love, and even conjugal visits were conducted with due ceremony, with the King going in a torchlit procession to his wife's bedchamber, the getting of royal heirs being a matter of state business. So it is hard to see how the Queen of England could have managed to keep any extramarital affairs a secret.

It is also barely credible that Anne would have taken such risks. She was keenly aware that she was being watched – in February 1535, at a court banquet, looking strained and nervous, she had begged a French envoy to persuade the reluctant French King to consent to the marriage of his son to her daughter Elizabeth, 'so that she may not be ruined and lost, for she sees herself very near to that, and in more grief and trouble than before her marriage'. Looking anxiously at the King, she whispered that 'she could not speak so amply to me as she would, for fear of where she was and of the eyes that were watching her countenance, not only of her husband, but of the lords with him. She told me she did not dare express her fears in writing, that she could not see me, and could no longer talk with me. I assure you that the lady is not at her ease.' This was made manifest when she abruptly ceased speaking and walked away.[82] Furthermore, Anne knew she was unpopular, and that all that stood between her and her enemies was the powerful presence of the King. It is hard to believe that she would have undermined her own security by cuckolding Henry, nor risked her crown and even her life for the sake of casual sex with a string of lovers. One false step, and she would be ruined.

But desperate people do desperate things. The charges against Anne were to be so grossly overstated and in parts so manifestly invented, as to suggest that she was framed, but who is to say that they were not based on a modicum of truth? Or that Henry VIII, an intelligent and shrewd man, was not duped by the lies of Cromwell and others into abandoning and destroying his wife, but was devastated by what appeared to be highly compelling evidence against her?

The King 'dissembled his wrath', wrote Aless, but there were warning signs. On 23 April, the day of Cromwell's return to court and his interview with Henry, there took place at Greenwich the annual chapter meeting of the Order of the Garter, which was attended by the King and many lords, including the Duke of Norfolk; the Earl of Wiltshire, Anne's father; Henry Percy, Earl of Northumberland, whom she had once hoped to marry; and Henry FitzRoy, Duke of Richmond, Henry VIII's bastard son. A vacancy had arisen for a new Garter knight, and Anne had asked that her brother Rochford be preferred, but to the latter's 'great disappointment', Henry chose instead Sir Nicholas Carew, Anne's known enemy and the man who had been mentoring Jane Seymour. According to Chapuys, 'the Concubine has not had sufficient influence to get it for her brother'. The ambassador interpreted this as a sign that the Boleyns were falling from favour, even though the King's bastard son, the Duke of Richmond, had voted for Rochford,[83] and it was only five days later that Henry, Lord Stafford, was thanking the Earl of Westmorland 'for furthering my suit with the Queen',[84] which suggests that Anne's influence was still perceived to be considerable. Furthermore, Henry had earlier promised Francis I that he would 'remember' Carew when a Garter vacancy arose, so he perhaps felt bound to honour that.[85] Nevertheless, Carew's appointment amounted to – and was seen as – a public snub to Anne.

The very next day, 24 April, at Westminster, the Lord Chancellor, Sir Thomas Audley, a man who was very much under the influence of Cromwell,[86] appointed two special commissions of oyer and terminer, which was a legal procedure for hearing and judging pleas of the Crown, in use since the thirteenth century. Each set of commissioners and jurors constituted a grand jury, and in this case they were required to set up courts to make diligent inquiry into all 'betrayals, concealment of betrayals, rebellions, felonies, murders, homicides, riots, unlawful assemblies, insurrections, extortions, oppressions, offences, misprisions [of treason], falsehoods, deceptions, confederacies, conspiracies and misdemeanours' committed in the counties of Middlesex and Kent, and to hear and determine the same according to law.[87] In other words, their function was to determine if there was a case and whether it should proceed. Such commissions were rare, and were only instituted in serious cases, of which there were only seventeen in Henry VIII's reign.[88] That in itself, together with the citing of the counties in which the Queen's alleged offences were said to have been committed, shows that this commission was specifically appointed to examine the evidence against her.

In most cases of oyer and terminer, a commission was only issued after the accused had been arrested. In this case, however, it was issued beforehand, probably to avoid the usual delay of about eleven days, which suggests that Cromwell, fearing (with good reason, given Henry and Anne's past history) that the King might succumb again to his 'great folly' over his wife and dispute the evidence, was aware of the need to secure a speedy conviction.[89]

It was the duty of the sheriff of the county to select the jurors, but the list of those chosen on this occasion suggests that Cromwell had brought some pressure to bear on officialdom.[90] These commissions were 'virtually a death warrant for Anne'.[91]

The names of the worthies who served on these grand juries are preserved in the National Archives in the *Baga de Secretis* (Bag of Secrets), the collection of records of the King's Bench and of state trials. These jurors were men of standing, sworn to uphold justice, who were no doubt resolved to do what was expected of them. To avoid bias, instructions were issued that no juror should be related to the defendants.[92] The inquiry was not made public, nor were the persons most nearly concerned – the suspected traitors – made aware of it. All was to be kept secret until sufficient evidence to justify a prosecution had been gathered.[93]

The Middlesex commission was addressed to Lord Chancellor Audley and others, the Kent one to the Duke of Norfolk and others. Audley's name appears only on the former, but both commissions consisted of Cromwell himself; Anne's uncle, the Duke of Norfolk; the Duke of Suffolk; Anne's own father, Thomas Boleyn, Earl of Wiltshire; John de Vere, Earl of Oxford; Ralph Neville, Earl of Westmorland; Robert Radcliffe, Earl of Sussex; William, Lord Sandys; Sir William FitzWilliam; Sir William Paulet; Sir John FitzJames; Sir John Baldwin; Sir Richard Lister; Sir John Port; Sir John Spelman; Sir Walter Luke; Sir Anthony FitzHerbert; Sir Thomas Englefield; and Sir William Shelley, who may have been associated with 'Nan' Cobham. The jurors of Middlesex comprised eight esquires entitled to bear arms, and forty gentlemen, while those of Kent were three soldiers, six esquires and sixteen gentlemen. All were described as 'discreet and sufficient persons'.[94] Several had been with the King at the Garter chapter the previous day.[95]

Given the choice of commissioners, how likely was it that this investigation would be impartial? The Lord Chancellor was a staunch King's man from first to last. Anne had long since alienated Norfolk by her arrogance, and Norfolk may have had ambitions of his own; his daughter, Mary Howard, was married to the King's bastard son, the Duke of Richmond, and there had been serious moves in the past to have Richmond legitimated and declared Henry's heir. If Anne were to be put away and Elizabeth bastardised, then Norfolk's daughter might yet be made a queen.[96]

Suffolk was the King's brother-in-law and close friend, and Anne's enemy. Oxford was also a friend of the King, as was FitzWilliam, who was much of an age with Henry and had been brought up with him, and had since served him faithfully ever since; as we have seen, FitzWilliam was instrumental in orchestrating Anne's fall, and was related to several people who were closely concerned. In 1537, he would be created Earl of Southampton and made Lord High Admiral in recognition of his services to the King.

Wiltshire, Anne's father, is not known to have attempted to defend either of his children, and was probably living in fear for his own neck at this time. Westmorland, a privy councillor who attended to matters of law, had a long record of loyal service to Henry VIII, as did Sussex, who had received his earldom for supporting the King in the divorce, and long enjoyed his master's confidence. Lord Sandys was a great favourite of Henry. Paulet, a man much trusted by the King, was to serve the Crown faithfully through four reigns.

Of the judges on the commission, FitzJames, a former Attorney General, had been Chief Justice of the King's Bench and Chief Baron of the Exchequer, offices that were now held by his fellow commissioner, Sir Richard Lister. FitzJames had conducted the prosecution of the Duke of Buckingham in 1521, and had been one of the judges who condemned More and Fisher in 1535, as had Baldwin, who was Chief Justice of the Common Pleas and enjoyed a similarly distinguished legal career. Port was a justice of the King's Bench, who had served on the commission of oyer and terminer that brought More and Fisher to trial. Sir John Spelman, whose Commonplace Book offers unique insights into the legal process against Anne Boleyn, was another judge of the King's Bench, and had also been one of the commissioners who tried More and Fisher. A discreet courtier, he was held in esteem by Cromwell, and in April 1537, in return for his service on the Grand Juries, he was granted the manor of Gracys in Norfolk.[97] Sir Walter Luke was also a justice of the King's Bench. FitzHerbert, Englefield and Shelley were justices of the Court of Common Pleas and the former had also been a member of the tribunal that condemned More. Shelley, no reformist, was not one of Cromwell's favourites, but nevertheless took part, on the Crown's behalf, in all the important state trials of the period.

Of the Kent jurors, Edmund Page, the MP for Rochester, had opposed the Act of Restraint of Appeals, one of the crucial landmarks of Reformation legislation, which had been aimed at preventing Katherine of Aragon from appealing her case to Rome, so he was not likely to be sympathetic to Anne Boleyn. Nor, surely, were two Middlesex jurors, Giles Heron, Sir Thomas More's son-in-law, and Sir Giles Alington, who had married More's stepdaughter.[98] Alington was under government suspicion because of his link to More, and his presence on the Grand Jury suggests that his loyalty was being tested.

No one could say that these men were not competent to examine the evidence against the Queen, for they included among their number the premier lords and chief judges of the land. Yet all had prospered under Henry VIII and enjoyed his favour, or needed to prove their loyalty, and therefore not one was likely to risk his prosperity and status by incurring his displeasure. Moreover, the jurors were no doubt in some awe of the nobles and law lords on the commission, and anxious to take their cue from them. Nearly every petty juror was a servant of the Crown, a creature of Cromwell, and no friend to Anne.[99] Yet for all that, the outcome of the inquiry was by no means a foregone conclusion; had it been, and had there been any really damning evidence at this stage, it is highly unlikely that the King would have appeared in public with Anne at the Greenwich jousts on 1 May. And there is no evidence that the jurors had any knowledge of the King's will in this matter, or that they were suborned into submission.

The appointing of such commissions was routine, and although the opening words announced that 'our lord the King has entrusted this case' to his 'most esteemed and faithful' lords and 'relatives' named in these documents, it has been suggested that Henry VIII may not have been privy to what was afoot.[100] He was not at Westminster on the day the commission was appointed, but at Greenwich.[101] His signature was not needed and the necessary documents could be issued by the Chancery in his name on the instructions of the Lord Chancellor. Yet Henry *had* authorised Cromwell to investigate further, and several of the highest-ranking nobles in the land had been appointed to the grand juries. The institution of such a commission was a significant event.[102] With a compelling vested interest in the outcome, it is highly unlikely that Henry VIII would not have been aware of what was going on.

Outwardly, though, Henry – a notoriously great dissembler – was still giving every impression that he intended to continue in his marriage. He was planning to take Anne with him to Dover and Calais (then an English possession) at the end of the month, the trip having been arranged some weeks earlier, with a view to the King inspecting the new harbour and fortifications at Dover.[103] At this time, he was preoccupied with making a decision as to whether to ally himself with Charles V or Francis I, and on 25 April, in a letter sent to Richard Pate, to his ambassador in Rome, and to Gardiner and Wallop, his envoys in France, he instructed them to oppose the demands of the Emperor because of 'the likelihood and appearance that God will send us heirs male [by] our most dear and most entirely beloved wife, the Queen'.[104] Taken at face value, this suggests that Henry was still sleeping with Anne, and it could even imply that he thought she was pregnant again, which is highly unlikely.[105] We should not read too much into him publicly referring to her in such affectionate terms, because he was merely using the conventional style employed by royalty when writing of their spouses.

On 25 April, when that letter was composed, the Council sat all day and late into the night, almost certainly discussing the crisis over foreign alliances, and perhaps debating the fate of the Queen.[106]

Anne had her daughter with her at Greenwich; among the final entries in her household accounts, relating to 28 April, were payments for silver and gold fringe and gold and silver buttons for a saddle for the King, two leading reins 'with great buttons and long tassels' for the Princess Elizabeth, and – the last entry of all – 'a cap of taffeta with a caul of damask gold'.[107] But such innocent and normally enjoyable pleasures were undoubtedly overshadowed by a sense of impending disaster, for the Queen, her wits sharpened by worry and fear, had already somehow sensed or learned that something sinister was afoot. With her household being closely interrogated, how could she, with her clever, sharp mind, have failed to suspect what was going on? And of course, if she were guilty, or feared that she had somehow compromised herself, there was even more cause for apprehension. Her father, Wiltshire, had perhaps got wind of something ominous at meetings of the Privy Council,[108] or maybe, in private, the King had given her cause to be fearful.

That Anne already feared that something ill might befall her, and had realised that Elizabeth would be left in a very vulnerable position,[109] is clear from her seeking out, on or soon after Wednesday, 26 April ('not six days before her apprehension'), her chaplain of two years, Matthew Parker. Parker was thirty-two and one of a group of Cambridge reformists that included the future Protestant martyr, Hugh Latimer. He was a moderate man, a great evangelical preacher and an independent thinker who despised religious intolerance, and those qualities had earned him the admiration of the like-minded Anne Boleyn, whose chaplain he had reluctantly become a year or so earlier. The King liked him too – he would, in 1537, make Parker one of his own chaplains – and that is probably why Anne felt there was some hope of Parker being able to carry out her wishes. What he stood for and believed in was what she wanted for her daughter.

Anne charged Parker with the care of Elizabeth, should anything happen to her. She did not reveal what it was she feared, but it is likely to have been that, in the event of her marriage being annulled, she might be forbidden to see her child, or Elizabeth might be bastardised. She can have had little premonition of what actually would befall her.

Her plea made a profound impression on the chaplain. Years later, when Elizabeth was queen and he had become her first archbishop of Canterbury, he would dedicate himself to her service and tell her secretary William Cecil that 'he would fain serve his sovereign lady in more respects than his allegiance, since he cannot forget what words her Grace's mother said to him not six days before her apprehension'.[110] Unfortunately for posterity, he did not say what those words were.

On 27 April, writs summoning Parliament – and a letter commanding the Archbishop of Canterbury from his palace at Knole – were issued,[111] paving the way for any legal process against the Queen to be formally endorsed.[112] It was reported to Lord Lisle the following day that 'the Council has sat every day at Greenwich', while Chapuys says that on Tuesday, 25 April, the councillors 'assembled in the morning till nine or ten at night'; their business was said to have been connected 'upon certain letters brought by the French ambassador',[113] although again, it is more than likely that the matter of the Queen was also extensively discussed.

Chapuys was to reveal, on 29 April, that Dr Richard Sampson, Dean of the Chapel Royal, 'has been for the last four days continually with Cromwell. One of his servants has told me he is to be sent as ambassador to the Emperor, which I do not believe, as Cromwell has said nothing about it.'[114] Dr Sampson was one of the leading experts on canon law, and Cromwell may have been discussing with him possible grounds for annulling the King's marriage to Anne Boleyn. Sampson would be appointed Bishop of Chichester in June 1536, possibly as a reward for the advice he had given Cromwell at this time,[115] and for acting as the King's proctor when the case went before Thomas Cranmer, the Archbishop of Canterbury.

On 28 April, at dinner, Chapuys was told by Geoffrey Pole, the younger brother of Lord Montagu, that someone – possibly Cromwell – had asked John Stokesley, Bishop of London, 'if the King could abandon the Concubine' – i.e. have their marriage annulled. Stokesley was close to the King: he had long been a councillor and chaplain to Henry, had productively supported him in the annulment of his first marriage and the establishment of the royal supremacy, and had christened the Princess Elizabeth in 1533. But his reply was dismissive: 'he would not give any opinion to anyone but the King himself,' he said, 'and before doing so, he would know the King's own inclination'. Chapuys thought he meant 'to intimate that the King might leave the Concubine, but that, knowing his fickleness, he would not put himself in danger', presumably of public scandal and disapprobation. The ambassador added that, although 'the Bishop was the principal cause and instrument of the first divorce, of which he heartily repents, he would still more gladly promote this, since the said Concubine and all her race are such abominable Lutherans'. But as it was uncertain which way the wind was blowing, 'the Bishop would not risk the effects of the Concubine's displeasure if there were a chance of her remaining in favour'.[116]

Speculation about a nullity suit was rife. On 2 May, Chapuys reported that the King, 'as I have been for some days informed by good authority, had determined to abandon [Anne]; for there were witnesses testifying that another marriage passed nine years before had been made and fully consummated between her and the Earl of Northumberland, and the King would have declared himself earlier, but that someone of his Council gave him to understand that he could not separate himself from the Concubine without tacitly confirming not only the first marriage, but also what he most fears, the authority of the Pope'.[117]

Anne *had* had an affair with the Earl of Northumberland – of which more later – and the possibility of a binding precontract between them was without doubt raised at this time, and was perhaps connected in some way with Bishop Stokesley being asked to comment on the King's prospects of securing an annulment; for Chapuys would not otherwise have known of Anne's affair with the Earl, which had ended in 1523, six years before he arrived in England. But it had happened thirteen years earlier, not nine, and there had been no marriage, so his source was probably not someone who was as well informed as, say, Cromwell would have been.

The fact that an annulment was being discussed at this stage perhaps suggests that the King and his advisers were by no means certain that there would be sufficient evidence to prosecute the Queen, and that some felt that a divorce might be an easier means of removing her. However, it is more likely, in view of what was shortly to transpire, that Cromwell, and possibly the King himself, anticipating that Anne would soon be a convicted traitor, were looking for means to have her marriage dissolved and her daughter disinherited.

As he was to reveal to the Emperor on 2 May, Chapuys wrote to the Lady Mary at this time, informing her of this momentous development and claiming that he himself had been instrumental

in bringing it about, telling her that he hoped to bring the matter
to a successful conclusion. He added that Elizabeth would almost
certainly now be excluded from the succession, and that Mary
herself might be restored, albeit after any children that Jane
Seymour might bear the King. Mary wasted no sympathy on the
woman who had for so long cast a malign shadow over her life,
and replied to Chapuys that it was her wish that he should help,
and not hinder, any divorce proceedings: he was to 'promote the
matter, especially for the discharge of the conscience of the King
her father. She did not care a straw whether her father had lawful
heirs or not, though such might take away her crown, nor for all
the injuries done either to herself or the Queen her mother,
which, for the honour of God, she pardoned everyone most
heartily.' All Mary cared about now was that Anne be got rid of.
Guided by her, Chapuys 'used several means to promote the
matter, both with Cromwell and with others', with a view to
securing Anne's removal and making Jane queen.[118]

Sir Nicholas Carew in particular was proving indefatigable. The
ambassador observed, 'It will not be the fault of this Master of
the Horse if the Concubine, although his cousin, be not
dismounted. He continually counsels Mistress Seymour and other
conspirators to make an assault; and only four days ago, he and
some persons of the [Privy] Chamber sent to tell the Princess
[Mary] to be of good cheer, for shortly the opposite party would
put water in their wine, the King being already as sick and tired
of the Concubine as he could be.'[119] We might infer from this
that Carew was aware of the formal proceedings against Anne.[120]
Sir Francis Bryan too, by his own admission in June 1536, was
often involved at this time in secret discussions with Mary's
supporters in the Privy Chamber about a new marriage for his
master the King; among them were Sir Anthony Browne and Sir
Thomas Cheyney, both of whom were to be proactive in bringing
down Anne Boleyn. Bryan also at this time visited a fellow scholar,
Henry Parker, Lord Morley, the father of Lady Rochford, travel-

ling to Morley's house at Great Hallingbury, Essex, possibly in a bid to seek his support. Morley was on friendly terms with Cromwell,[121] and his young kinsman, another Henry Parker, was one of Bryan's servants.[122]

Outwardly, though, life was going on as normal. The King was still planning to take the Queen with him to Calais on 4 May,[123] departing for Dover (where Anne was expecting Lady Lisle to receive her) immediately after the jousts that were planned for May Day. On their previous visit to Calais, in October 1532, three months before their marriage, Henry and Anne had just become lovers and had had interconnecting bedchambers at the Exchequer Palace. Did Anne dare now to hope that, on revisiting that palace, Henry's former love for her might be rekindled?

If so, it was a vain hope. By 29 April, as preparations for the visit were going ahead, the Privy Council had formally been informed of the planned judicial proceedings against the Queen, and rumours of her imminent disgrace had begun circulating at court.

5

'Unlawful Lechery'

Meanwhile, Cromwell and his colleagues had been carrying out their master's orders. Spies were already at work in the Queen's household, 'watching her privy apartments night and day' and 'tempting her porter and serving men with bribes; there is nothing which they do not promise the ladies of her bedchamber. They affirm that the King hates the Queen because she has not presented him with an heir to the realm, nor was there any prospect of her so doing.'[1]

'In most secret sort, certain persons of the Privy Chamber and others of [the Queen's] side were examined.'[2] The inquiries that were made in the Queen's household must by now have alerted several of those questioned to what was going on, and it may be that some of those who served Anne had old scores to settle.

In the course of these investigations, the councillors questioned 'many other witnesses',[3] including Lady Rochford, Anne's sister-in-law; 'in which examination[s],' Cromwell later wrote, 'the matter appeared so evident, that besides that crime with the accidents, there broke out a certain conspiracy of the King's death, which extended so far that all we that had the examination of it quaked at the danger his Grace was in'.[4] Anne, it was alleged, had not only taken lovers, but had conspired with them to murder Henry VIII so that she could marry one of them and rule England in her infant daughter's name.

Plotting the death of the King was high treason, the most heinous of all crimes, for the sovereign was the Lord's anointed, divinely appointed to rule. 'Kings of England,' Henry VIII once told his judges, 'never had any superior but God.' The royal prerogative was regarded as the will of God expressing itself through the will of the King. Thus anyone who offended against the King was punished with the greatest severity. Here was the indisputably capital charge that Cromwell needed, yet its very incongruity argues that it was merely a device for getting rid of Anne. For it is patently clear that Anne revelled in being a queen, a rank she had aspired to for many years, and it is therefore highly unlikely that she would ever have contemplated throwing away her status, her greatness and her power in order to marry a man who was far below her in rank and could give her nothing on a par with what the King had to bestow. Never mind the fact that the unpopular Anne was hardly likely to have intrigued to murder the King, who was her chief protector and defender – the death of Henry would have been 'absolutely fatal' to her.[5]

Since 1536, there has always been a strong suspicion that Cromwell threw everything he could against Anne Boleyn, including the useful ploy of character assassination, in order to get rid of her. It is probably no coincidence that her alleged crimes were so heinous as to inspire universal shock and revulsion, which would preclude anyone taking up her cause. That way, the King would emerge from this the victim of a woman's wickedness rather than a man who changed wives at a whim; and as such, he would earn the sympathy of all.

Master Secretary now constructed what was almost certainly a convincing case against the Queen, in which she would be charged with adultery with five men – one her own brother, another a lowly musician – and conspiring regicide.

*   *   *

The five men who would, over the next few days, be arrested for committing treason with the Queen were George Boleyn, Viscount Rochford, Sir Henry Norris, Sir Francis Weston, Sir William Brereton and Mark Smeaton.

George Boleyn was probably the youngest of the three surviving Boleyn siblings, having been no older than twenty-seven when he was preferred to the Privy Council in 1529, the year his father was created Earl of Wiltshire and he himself was given the courtesy title Viscount Rochford.[6] His sister's connection with the King had brought him royal favour, rapid preferment, lucrative offices, including those of Gentleman of the Privy Chamber (1528), Constable of Dover, Lord Warden of the Cinque Ports and Master of the Buckhounds, and a career as a leading diplomat, as well as the palace of New Hall, which Henry VIII had renamed Beaulieu, in Essex; and he was not only one of the two noblemen of the King's Privy Chamber, but also the foremost member of Queen Anne's court. Both before and after her marriage, she had gathered around her young people with wit, charm and intelligence, who could be relied upon to ensure that life was never dull, and Lord Rochford was at the core of this inner circle. There was a close bond between Anne and George, who shared – amongst other things – a love of poetry, George having 'the art in meter and verse to make pleasant ditties'.[7] The poet Richard Smith wrote admiringly that 'Rochford clamb the stately throne which muses hold in Helicon'.[8]

Brother and sister were also fervent for religious reform – George's views, inferred from the French literature he imported, were bordering on the heretical – and both hated and despised the Lady Mary. When Katherine of Aragon died, George had said 'it was a pity' that the Lady Mary 'did not keep company with her mother'.[9]

George Boleyn had been at court since his early teens, if not before. He married Jane Parker, daughter of Henry, Lord Morley, late in 1524. In looks he was an Adonis,[10] in character promiscuous.

George Cavendish, Wolsey's former usher, who had no love for the Boleyn faction that had brought his master to ruin, wrote candidly of Rochford's 'sensual appetite':[11]

> My life not chaste, my living bestial;
> I forced widows, maidens I did deflower.
> All was one to me, I spared none at all,
> My appetite was all women to devour,
> My study was both day and hour,
> My unlawful lechery, how I might it fulfil,
> Sparing no woman to have on her my will.

This strongly implies that Rochford omitted even to stop at rape, and – there is no other interpretation that can be placed on Cavendish's use of the word 'bestial' – that he indulged in buggery too.[12] Cavendish also refers to Rochford being unable to resist 'this unlawful deed', while

> . . . to declare my life in every effect,
> Shame restraineth me the plains to confess,
> Lest the abomination would all the world infect:
> It is so vile, so detestable in words to express,
> For which by the law condemned I am doubtless,
> And for my desert, justly judged to be dead.

This points at something far worse to contemporary eyes than the lechery to which Rochford, as personified in these verses, *had* openly confessed, or the crime of treasonable incest for which he would publicly be condemned; it may of course refer to the 'lewd adultery' that Cavendish's Rochford asks people to take example from, yet it is also likely that Cavendish is alluding to illegal sexual practices such as buggery (with women or men) and even homosexuality, then regarded as odious sins against God, with both being capital crimes.[13] Rochford himself, in his dying speech, was to confess he had sinned more shamefully than could be imagined, and that he had known no man so evil.[14] As he had stoutly denied charges of incest, the likelihood is that he was referring to other sexual practices then regarded as perversions.

Rochford's reputation – and possible unlawful sexual predilections – made him an easy target for Cromwell, who would have realised that any accusations of criminal congress would appear entirely credible, and who was well aware that it would take such serious charges to bring down the formidably powerful Rochford.[15]

Rochford's other notorious vice was his insufferable pride. 'Hadst thou not been so proud,' the poet Wyatt would write after George's fall, 'for thy great wit, each man would thee bemoan.'

Sir Henry Norris was the second son of Sir Edward Norris by Frideswide, daughter of Francis, Viscount Lovell, a close friend of Richard III, the last Yorkist king. Sir Henry, a discreet, level-headed man of proven integrity, was Groom of the Stool to Henry VIII, and had held this office since before 1529. In this capacity, he was not only the Chief Gentleman of Henry's Privy Chamber, which was the King's private household, but its most trusted member and the 'best-beloved of the King',[16] whom he had served faithfully for twenty years.[17]

There were just twelve Gentlemen of the Privy Chamber, and there was rampant competition for places, for these men were closer to the monarch than any other. They had the right of entry to his private chambers, attended on him in shifts and provided him with daily companionship. They were in a highly privileged and powerful position, able to advise and influence the King, control access to his presence, and exercise patronage. Some were in office simply because Henry liked them, some because of their usefulness, but all were expected to be loyal and trustworthy. Norris's office of Groom of the Stool obliged him to be present when the King performed his basic natural functions, so he was unavoidably more intimate with his master than most. Yet there was more to his role than that, for any who wished to present a petition to the King had to lay their request before Norris, rather than Cromwell, something that Cromwell may rather have resented.

Norris's other posts reflected Henry's confidence in his abilities. The King 'extended his benignity with wealth, worship and huge abundance';[18] in 1531, he had made Norris Chamberlain of North Wales, and since then, thanks to the favour of Henry and Anne, Norris had been appointed Keeper of the King's Privy Purse, Master of the Hart Hounds and of the Hawks, Black Rod in the Parliament House, 'graver' of the Tower of London, collector of subsidy in the City of London, weigher of goods in the port of Southampton, High Steward of the University of Oxford, and keeper or steward of many castles, manors and parks. His modest annual Privy Chamber income of £33.6s. 8d (£11,650) was boosted by fees and annuities of £400 (£139,700) from other offices, and rents from lands he had been granted or leased.[19]

Norris was not only 'a man in very great favour with the King'[20] but had also been a supporter of the Boleyn faction since at least 1530. So trustworthy was he accounted that he had been one of the few witnesses to the secret marriage of Henry VIII and Anne Boleyn in 1533.[21]

Norris's first wife, Mary Fiennes, the daughter of Lord Dacre, had died before 1530, leaving behind three young children, and he had recently become betrothed to the Queen's cousin, Madge Shelton, who had briefly been the King's mistress in 1535. Norris owned a house at Greenwich, which Henry VIII generously maintained.

That Anne should have betrayed the King with someone so close to him would have appeared shocking in the extreme. Cavendish believed that ambition blinded Norris and drove him to commit a grave 'misdemeanour' against the master whose bounty had been so generous:

My chance was such I had all thing at will,
And in my wealth I was to him unkind,
That thus to me did all my mind fulfil,
All his benevolence was clean out of mind:
Oh, alas, alas, in my heart how could I find
Against my sovereign so secretly to conspire,
That so gently gave me all that I desire?[22]

Cavendish is here referring to the treasonable crimes of which Norris would shortly be accused.

Sir Francis Weston was twenty-five, and also – since 1532 – a gentleman of the Privy Chamber; he had served Henry VIII there as a page since at least 1525. The son of Sir Richard Weston, former Under-Treasurer of the Exchequer, by Anne Sandys, one of Queen Katherine's gentlewomen, he came from an old and honourable family whose seat was Sutton Place, a beautiful Tudor house near Guildford in Surrey; it had been granted to Sir Richard by Henry VIII in 1521.

Francis was a talented lute player and a first-class athlete – 'in active things, who might with thee compare?'[23] – who was described by the poet Wyatt as a 'pleasant' young man, and 'well-esteemed'. He had been 'daintily nourished under the King's wing',[24] and over the years had received a number of grants and pensions.[25] In 1533, at Anne Boleyn's coronation, he had been dubbed a Knight Companion of the Order of the Bath. He was much liked by the King ('who highly favoured me and loved me so well'),[26] the Queen and Lord Rochford; he played cards with them all, beating the King at nearly every game, and partnered Henry at tennis and bowls.[27] At night, the King often chose him as one of those gentlemen who would sleep in his bedchamber and be on call to attend to his needs.[28]

When Weston had married Anne, the daughter and heiress of Sir Christopher Pickering, in May 1530,[29] Henry had presented him with ten marks (£1,200) and wished him better fortune than he himself had found in marriage. A fine oak marriage cupboard, bearing the carved portraits of Francis and Anne in relief, is now in the museum at Saffron Walden, Essex. A sixteenth-century portrait at Parham Park in Sussex, of one 'Weston Esq. of Sutton [Place], Surrey', may be a likeness of Francis. He and his wife now had an infant son, Henry, born in 1535.

Despite this apparent marital felicity, the biased Cavendish refers to 'Weston the wanton . . . that wantonly lived without fear or dread, . . . following his fantasy and his wanton lust'; he castigates Weston for his 'unkindness against [his] sovereign lord', for Weston, thanks to Henry's favour, had had his 'will and lust in every thing'. In this young man, Cavendish avers, wilfulness and 'hot lust kindled the fire of filthy concupiscence', and, 'having no regard to princely disdain', finally that 'lust presumed to the Queen'.[30] Yet Weston seems to have been generally popular prior to that, for he 'was young, and of old lineage and high accomplishments'.[31]

Sir William Brereton (or Bryerton) of Aldford, who came from a leading Cheshire family, was another member of Anne Boleyn's inner circle, and, like Norris and Weston, a Gentleman of the King's Privy Chamber, who had been promoted from groom, a position he had held since at least 1521.[32] In 1531, there is a record of him delivering jewels to Anne Boleyn.[33] Brereton, like Norris, was so trusted and liked by Henry and the Boleyn faction, whose staunch adherent he became, that he had been invited to witness Henry's secret wedding to Anne in January 1533.[34] That same year, he was involved in some dealings with Lord Rochford.[35]

Despite being a noted seducer of women,[36] Brereton was married to the King's cousin, Elizabeth Somerset, sister of the Earl of Worcester, and was thus highly placed at court and 'flourishing in favour'.[37] He had given Anne her beloved greyhound, Urian, who was named after Brereton's brother, a groom of the Privy Chamber. William often accompanied the King and Anne on hunting expeditions, and enjoyed the patronage of Henry's bastard son, the Duke of Richmond, whose steward he was in the Welsh Marches,[38] and of Anne's uncle, the Duke of Norfolk.[39]

Thanks to royal grants of extensive estates and Crown offices worth £1,200 (£401,850) a year,[40] and the backing of Richmond, Norfolk and Queen Anne, Brereton exercised virtually autonomous territorial power in Cheshire and North Wales, where he served as Richmond's deputy, becoming notorious as an over-mighty subject 'both in town and field, readily furnished with horse, spear and shield'.[41] Cromwell seems to have viewed Brereton's power in the Marches as a threat to his planned administrative reforms, through which he intended to replace feudal control in Wales by the establishment of English-style shires; these plans were well advanced by March 1536.[42] The elimination of Brereton, and the breaking of his alliance with Richmond and Norfolk, would certainly remove significant barriers to these reforms.[43]

At nearly fifty, Brereton could hardly be cast in the guise of court gallant,[44] but his reputation was such that people would not find it difficult to believe him a villain. He was a constant irritant to the Privy Council.[45] George Cavendish paints a picture of him as a persecutor of the innocent, an administrator whose justice was rigorous and driven by personal animosity. He refers to the shameful hanging in 1534 of a Flintshire gentleman, John ap Griffith Eyton, whose death Brereton had contrived through sheer malice, 'by colour of justice', and in defiance of Cromwell's attempts to save the man. Brereton believed that Eyton had killed one of his own retainers, and it made no difference to him that Eyton had already been acquitted of that by a court in London.[46] The contemporary Welsh chronicler, Ellis Gruffydd, states that Anne Boleyn helped Brereton to secure Eyton's rearrest, which would not be surprising, given the growing rift between Anne and Cromwell, and it may have been one of the things that caused them to fall out. Later, Cavendish has Brereton lamenting his own ruin, reflecting that he 'who striketh with the sword, the sword will overthrow', and seeing his fall as divine punishment for his multitude of crimes and sins:

> Lo, here is the end of murder and tyranny!
> Lo, here is the end of envious affection!
> Lo, here is the end of false conspiracy!
> Lo, here is the end of false detection
> Done to the innocent by cruel correction!
> Although in office I thought myself strong,
> Yet here is mine end for ministering wrong.[47]

Brereton's disregard for the niceties of the law had become apparent as far back as 1518, when Cardinal Wolsey and other councillors had examined him in the Star Chamber court about his 'maintaining and comforting' the murderers of a Master Swettenham, whose brains had been spilled whilst playing bowls. Brereton and two other men had been accused of preventing Swettenham's family from obtaining justice and helping the killers – one of whom was Brereton's relative, another his servant – to escape arrest. For this, Brereton got off relatively lightly with a fine of 500 marks (£52,150), and suffered no loss of office or influence, which might explain why he was still disturbing the peace in Cheshire in the 1530s.[48]

In 1534, Brereton was supposed to be investigating bribery and corruption at Valle Crucis Abbey, near Llangollen in North Wales, but was himself probably as compromisingly involved as the Abbot.[49] The next year, Cromwell's agent in the area, Rowland Lee, Bishop of Coventry and Lichfield, alluding to Brereton's dubious activities as Richmond's steward, disapprovingly remarked that it was not to the young Duke's honour to have his badge and livery 'worn upon strong thieves' backs'. Again, Brereton was suspected of protecting murderers from trial and execution, this time, somewhat audaciously, in Richmond's name.[50] In May 1536, only days before his arrest, and evidently blithely unaware of Cromwell's hostility, Brereton was pressing Master Secretary to grant him the spoils of dissolved abbeys in Cheshire.[51] There were therefore several good reasons why Cromwell should have plotted his elimination. Even so, Brereton clearly had no idea of what was imminently in store for him.

Brereton's wife happened to be sister-in-law to the Countess of Worcester, the first person allegedly to lay evidence against the Queen, and there has been speculation that the relationship between these ladies was too close for coincidence,[52] and that the Countess may have got her information from Lady Brereton. However, that is unlikely, for, as will become clear, there can be no doubt that Elizabeth Somerset believed in her husband's innocence.

These four gentlemen – Rochford, Norris, Weston and Brereton – had all been members of the powerful Boleyn faction for some years. Yet the humble Mark Smeaton, the most remarkable inclusion among those who were accused of criminal association with the Queen, was to be the subject of greater scandal and comment than all the rest put together, for few were able to comprehend how Anne could so far have forgotten herself as to take this lowly musician to her bed.

Mark, a 'very handsome' young man,[53] and 'one of the prettiest monochord players',[54] had been appointed a Groom of the Privy Chamber in 1529,[55] so the suggestion that he was perhaps little older than twenty in 1536 cannot be correct.[56] He was not of gentle birth, for his father was a carpenter

> . . . and laboured with his hand,
>   With the sweat of his face he purchased his living,
>   For small was his rent, much less his land;
>   My mother in a cottage used daily spinning.
>   Lo, in what misery was my beginning.[57]

A sixteenth-century Italian chronicler, Lodovico Guicciardini, who had spent many years in the Low Countries and wrote a history of Europe covering the period 1529 to 1560, referred to Smeaton, when writing about Anne Boleyn's fall, as 'Mark the Fleming, her keyboard player'.[58] But Smeaton was not Anne's keyboard player; he was employed by the King. His Flemish surname may have been de Smet or de Smedt, and he probably changed it to Smeaton (or Smeton) when he came to England;[59] this would explain how he knew French. It is possible that he was talent-spotted by, and came to England under the auspices of, Philip van Wilder, the celebrated Dutch lutenist, who was in charge of all the musicians of the Privy Chamber.[60] It was perhaps Wilder who brought him to the attention of Cardinal Wolsey.

Mark owed his position at court to his musical talent, for he was skilled at playing the lute, the virginals and the portable organ, as well as being a gifted singer and 'the deftest dancer in the land'[61] – abilities that were all rated highly at Henry's court, and which were admired by Cardinal Wolsey, himself of lowly parentage, who recruited the young Smeaton for his choir. Cavendish knew him in those days as 'a singing boy'.[62]

After the Cardinal's fall from favour in 1529, the youth had transferred to the Chapel Royal, a preferment that would not have come his way unless he had had an outstanding voice. 'Being but a boy, [he] clamb up the high stage, that bred was of nought, and brought to felicity.'[63] Yet not everyone was full of praise for his talents. The French reformist scholar and poet, Nicholas Bourbon, who admired Anne Boleyn and spent two years at the English court, 'granted' that Mark wrote good songs, but complained that he rendered them tedious by 'so assiduously singing them; anything overdone is unwelcome. Even honey, if taken too much, becomes bitter.'

Despite Smeaton's promotion to the Privy Chamber, where his duties would have included entertaining the King, he was still low down in the court pecking order, which is apparent from people addressing him only as 'Mark'. But Henry VIII obviously thought highly of him: his Privy Purse expenses show that he supported Smeaton financially, gave him special rewards each Easter and Christmas and, from 1529, himself provided him with shirts, hose, shoes and bonnets, so that he could present himself smartly. 'Young Master Weston', described as a lutenist, was given festive gifts along with Smeaton,[64] which reveals that Francis Weston was one of his colleagues and played music with him in the Privy Chamber, all members of which were expected to turn their hands, when required by the King, to music-making, singing, dancing or acting.

It was not long before the musician was befriended by Lord Rochford, who drew him further into the Boleyn circle. Rochford owned a manuscript of two poems, 'Les Lamentations de Matheolus' and 'Le Livre de Leesce' (or 'Le Résolu en Mariage'), by the fifteenth-century French writer Jean Lefèvre. It is inscribed above the text in his own hand: *This book is mine. George Boleyn 1526*, but Smeaton's signature – *A moy, M. Marc Sn* ('*a moi*' meaning literally 'to me', but effectively 'mine') – appears at the bottom. The emphatic inscription suggests that Rochford had given the manuscript to Smeaton.[65] It has recently been suggested by Retha Warnicke that Smeaton was one of Rochford's homosexual lovers. In fact, Warnicke suggests that all the men accused with Anne had indulged in illegal sexual practices and were thus easily framed, but much of the evidence is purely inferential, and her theory has been dismissed by most historians.[66] However, she may have had a point where Rochford was concerned, as has been discussed.

A choir book now in the collection of the Royal College of Music in London was probably once owned by Anne Boleyn, and it has been suggested that it was perhaps compiled by Smeaton.[67] This theory rests on the grounds that the handwriting on it is similar to his signature on the Lefèvre manuscript. This book contains a collection of motets and chansons, and bears an initial letter illustrating what is supposed to be a falcon, Anne's armorial badge, attacking a pomegranate, the badge of Katherine of Aragon; however, the badge in the picture is very unlike Anne's. Nevertheless, the music book does carry the motto of her father, Thomas Boleyn, and her name, 'Mrs. A. Bolleyne', but the use of the title 'Mistress' dates the book to the period prior to Thomas Boleyn being created Earl of Wiltshire in 1529 (after which Anne used the courtesy title Lady Anne Rochford) – too early for it to have had any connection with Smeaton.[68]

Despite Smeaton's 'poor degree',[69] he appears to have enjoyed enviable status, to have kept horses at court and had servants who wore his livery. He had also become very grand – 'I knew not myself, waxed proud in my courage, disdained my father, and would not him see'[70], which may have prompted him to discourage the use of his surname, for he is frequently referred to in the sources as Mark, Marc or Marks.[71] A contemporary life of Henry VIII known as the 'Spanish Chronicle' – not always a reliable source – speaks of his overbearing manner and his insolence to his fellow courtiers. His comfortable financial status is attested to in a list of prisoners in the Tower of London in May 1536, detailing the charges of their maintenance, which shows that all, including Smeaton, the only one who was not of gentle birth, 'had lands and goods sufficient of their own'[72] to pay for their keep.

That Smeaton's career had advanced steadily is obvious from the fact that at Christmas 1530, he had received 40s (£750) from the King, yet on 6 October 1532, he got £3.6s.8d (£1,250).[73] He may have been in Henry's suite for the state visit to Calais that began five days later. Sadly, the King's Privy Purse accounts for the years 1533–6 are lost, so we have few means of charting Smeaton's later career.[74]

Of all the men who would be accused with Anne, Smeaton was to be the only one to persist in his admission of guilt, which proved to some appalled contemporaries that he was no gentleman. Cavendish, of course, thought him guilty, and that he died 'like a wretch' for his 'presumption':

> Lo, what it is, frail youth to advance
> And to set him up in wealthy estate,
> Ere sad discretion had him in governance
> To bridle his lust, which now comes too late.[75]

Other Catholic writers would make much of Anne's supposed intrigues with Smeaton, which proved to be rich fodder for the scandalmongers of Europe.

If Cromwell contrived this plot against the Queen – and on his own admission he did – why did he select these particular men to be her partners in crime? One obvious answer is that he had good reason to believe that they were guilty of treasonable misconduct with her because they had been identified by witnesses as men who were suspiciously close to her.[76] Yet the surviving evidence, both documentary and circumstantial, does not generally support that contention.

Certainly he chose them for shock value. Just one accomplice should have been enough to make a charge of adultery stick,[77] but Cromwell wanted Anne's reputation irrevocably ruined, and for this and other reasons he chose to accuse her of criminal intercourse with five lovers.

Rochford was Anne's brother, and incest was probably as great a taboo then as it is now, although it was not illegal in Tudor times and did not become a misdemeanour until 1908, when the Incest Act was passed. Nevertheless, Strickland, writing before then, called it 'a crime of the most revolting nature', which was probably how most people viewed it in the sixteenth century. Norris, Brereton and Weston were long-standing intimates of the King, so to betray him with them rendered Anne's infidelity all the more heinous. Smeaton was of humble birth: that the Queen of England could have brought herself to stoop so low to satisfy her lusts only served further to blacken her reputation.

It is almost certain that Professor Eric Ives's theory that these men were 'victims of a faction battle' at court is correct.[78] Certainly, Anne, with Rochford and Norris, by virtue of their influential positions in the Privy Chamber, 'made a formidable trio'.[79] The 'Spanish Chronicle' has Anne declaring that her brother's fall was plotted alongside hers 'so that none should be left to take my part', and although these words are probably apocryphal, they are apposite, for Rochford was a very powerful man. Norris, too, had the King's ear, and he also could be counted upon to defend her. Brereton and Weston, being close to Henry, enjoyed considerable influence too.

Retha Warnicke at one time shared Professor Ives's view on the faction battle,[80] but later developed the theory that all the men were closet sodomites and homosexuals and therefore obvious and vulnerable targets, homosexuality being a capital offence. The evidence for this is purely inferential. All we can say for certain is that these men were known to be promiscuous – they themselves admitted to leading sinful lives – so people would have found it credible that they could rashly commit criminal intercourse with the Queen, unless, of course, it was known that they preferred members of their own sex (which seems unlikely).

Certainly, if Anne were to be removed, influential members of her faction would have to perish with her, to eliminate all opposition. The powerful Rochford was her staunch supporter. Norris and Weston were known to be close to her, and when Cromwell uncovered useful, if insubstantial, evidence that could be used to link them to her criminally, he did not shrink from sacrificing them. He also wanted his own man in Norris's prominent place in the Privy Chamber, in order to extend his influence into the inner sanctum of power. The removal of Brereton, another of the Queen's affinity, would excise a long-chafing thorn in Master Secretary's side. It is possible that Sir Anthony Browne, who was active behind the scenes in destroying Anne, also found it convenient to have Brereton removed, for Brereton held in receivership lands belonging to Browne.[81] As Cavendish later observed, Brereton was brought down 'shamefully, only of old rancour'. Smeaton was of little account and expendable anyway.

Others, like Bryan and Carew, who had once supported Anne, were not targeted because they had become disaffected and had worked to bring about her fall. Her father, Wiltshire, was spared; he was now fifty-nine, an old man in Tudor terms, who was probably expected to be sufficiently intimidated by the proceedings against his children to connive at their fate, which is just what he did do. The purge would be extensive and terrifying enough to deter anyone else from speaking out for the Queen.

What is surprising is that no woman was arrested for aiding and abetting the Queen in her alleged crimes.[82] When Katherine Howard was accused of adultery in 1541, Lady Rochford was apprehended for acting as go-between, and lost her head for it. Yet, as the Katherine Howard affair would prove, it would have been impossible for Anne to have conducted a succession of liaisons with courtiers without the collusion of at the very least one trusted female attendant; perhaps significantly, however, none were targeted, which might in itself argue that the case against her was spurious. On the other hand, they may simply have turned King's evidence.[83]

It has often been argued, in Anne's favour, that there is very little evidence of her being especially close to any of these men, apart from her brother Rochford; that there is hardly anything to connect her with Brereton, in particular. Unfortunately, we cannot rely on that lack of evidence as proof of her innocence, because there is so little surviving information about what went on in her chamber, and in the court, on a daily basis.

Anne was certainly close to her brother, and she knew all the other men, with the exception of Mark Smeaton, very well, yet prior to April 1536, there is no evidence to suggest that she knew them too well. Nor is there any evidence to support the assertion that, in order to win Henry back after her miscarriage, she began 'flaunting her sexuality';[84] significantly, in this respect, none of the charges that would be brought relate to 1536.

For Cromwell, speed and surprise were now requisite. The Boleyn faction was not to be permitted any chance of regrouping and fighting back. In less than three weeks, it would be utterly annihilated.

The evidence against Lord Rochford was said to have been laid solely by his wife of twelve years, Jane Parker; she is described by Henry VIII's seventeenth-century biographer, Edward, Lord Herbert of Cherbury, as the 'particular instrument' in the ruin of her husband and his sister;[85] Cherbury based his account on the lost journal of Anthony Anthony, a witness at the trials of George and Anne Boleyn.

Jane was the daughter of the erudite humanist scholar Henry Parker, Lord Morley; her mother, Alice St John, was a distant cousin of the King through his Beaufort connections. Jane had been 'brought up in the court' from a 'young age',[86] accompanied it to the Field of Cloth of Gold in 1520 as one of Queen Katherine's gentlewomen,[87] and had become one of its youthful stars by 1522, when – inappropriately, as it proved – she had danced the role of 'Constancy' in a pageant with Anne Boleyn and others.[88] She was for years a member of Anne's circle, and had served her as a lady-in-waiting from 1533. At Anne's coronation, Jane had been assigned a prominent place in the proceedings, in the company of the Countess of Worcester and other great ladies.[89]

George Cavendish, who had known Jane personally[90] but had no love for the Boleyns and wrote with the benefit of hindsight, had no great opinion of her character. She had been reared, he asserted, speaking as Jane,

> Withouten bridle of honest measure,
> Following my lust and filthy pleasure,
> Without respect of any wifely truth,
> Dreadless of God, from grace also exempt,
> Viciously consuming the time of this my youth.[91]

We know that Lady Rochford had a talent for intrigue, for she was complicit in Katherine Howard's adulterous affairs in 1541, acting as facilitator and lookout. She was not new to the game. Chapuys reported, in October 1534, that Anne Boleyn had involved her in 'a conspiracy' to get one of the King's mistresses replaced by Madge Shelton, the Queen's cousin. But Henry found out, and Jane was dismissed from her post of lady-in-waiting and banished from court. We do not know when she returned.

In October 1535, while the King and Queen were away on a progress, the Bishop of Tarbes (who had just returned to France) reported to the Bailly of Troyes that, when the Lady Mary had lately removed from Greenwich, 'a vast crowd of women, wives of citizens and others, unknown to their husbands, presented themselves before her, weeping and crying that she was princess, notwithstanding all that had been done. Some of them, the chiefest, were placed in the Tower, constantly persisting in their opinion.'[92] In the margin by that sentence, the words 'Millor de Rochesfort and milord de Guillaume' (Lord Rochford and Lord William Howard) appear, and from this it has been credibly inferred that their wives, Lady Rochford and her aunt-by-marriage, Lady William Howard (the former Margaret Gamage, who had only recently married Lord William), were among the demonstrators who ended up in the Tower.[93] Both these ladies would be arrested with Lord William Howard some years hence, in November 1541, for abetting and concealing the adultery of Katherine Howard, Henry VIII's fifth wife, and the Howards would be found guilty of misprision of treason, while Jane Rochford would be convicted of treason. Their later collusion perhaps suggests that Lady Rochford and Lady William Howard might have intrigued together on that earlier occasion.

It is naïve to claim that speaking out in favour of Mary would be uncharacteristic of Jane, and that she knew her destiny lay with the Boleyns.[94] As we have seen, quite a few movers and shakers attached to their party – Bryan, Carew, Norfolk and, most notably, Cromwell – had become disaffected, alienated by

Anne's overbearing influence; and if – as the evidence strongly suggests – Jane was jealous of her husband's closeness to his sister the Queen, then her defection is explicable. If you were not for the Boleyns, then you had to be against them, batting for the opposition – the Lady Mary.

Sir Francis Bryan's visit to Jane's father, Lord Morley, at the time when he and his allies were working to destroy Anne Boleyn, and his employment of Morley's kinsman, has already been noted. Bryan's private visit to Morley may have had a dual purpose, for by then the investigations against the Queen were well advanced, and the well-informed 'Vicar of Hell' may have gone to inform Morley of his daughter's allegations against her husband and the Queen, and in the hope of enlisting the support of the outraged father on behalf of the Lady Mary and Jane Seymour. In fact, Bryan probably already knew or suspected that Morley's sympathies lay with Mary.

It may be significant that Morley, despite his overriding loyalty to the King, his friendly relations with Cromwell, and his avoidance of embroilment in political matters (which was probably the reason why Bryan had visited him at home), had by Whitsunday, 4 June 1536, demonstrated that he was on close and friendly terms with the Lady Mary. With his wife and one of his two daughters – possibly Lady Rochford herself – he was to visit her at Hunsdon on that date, when they discussed only 'things touching to virtues'.[95] It is certainly significant that Morley's family visited the princess with Anne, Lady Hussey, the partisan wife of Mary's chamberlain; Lady Hussey had managed to smuggle several gifts with coded messages to Mary during the years in which the latter was out of favour, and the fact that Lord Morley came in her company suggests that he shared her devotion and faithfulness.

Morley was to praise Mary most chivalrously in various manuscripts he gave her in the two decades that followed. After her accession in 1553, he spoke of 'the love and truth that I have borne to your Highness from your childhood'.[96] This proves that his loyalty to Mary long predated that visit in June 1536.

Maybe Jane Rochford had been in some way influenced by her father's sympathetic attitude towards the princess. It has been convincingly argued that she was in fact Mary's friend and hoped to see her restored to the succession.[97] Having been brought up at court in the household of Katherine of Aragon, she would have known the princess well. According to one of the manuscripts Morley gave to Mary, he had held up Mary as a model of virtue and learning to his family.[98] It is easy to see how Jane Parker could have grown up revering Mary Tudor.

There is an even more credible reason why Jane Rochford switched her allegiance to Mary Tudor in 1535.[99] Her father had spent some years in the household of Mary's great-grandmother, the Lady Margaret Beaufort, who had acted as regent for her seventeen-year-old grandson, Henry VIII, for a short time after his accession in 1509, until he attained his majority. On 22 June 1535, the Lady Margaret's great friend, John Fisher, Bishop of Rochester, was publicly beheaded for refusing to acknowledge either the King as Supreme Head of the Church of England or his marriage to Anne Boleyn. Sir Thomas More suffered a similar fate early in July, but apart from the outrage that these executions provoked, Morley and his family had special reason to be grieved, for Fisher had been the Lady Margaret's confessor, and Morley had been present in 1509 when she died during a Mass celebrated by the Bishop. Public opinion laid the blame for Fisher's execution firmly at the door of the Boleyn faction, and it is likely that Lord Morley and his family did too. Morley was to tell Mary Tudor that he had been with Fisher – 'so good a man and so divine a clerk' – shortly before the old man went to the block.[100] It seems that the Parkers, like so many who had been of the Queen's party, had become disaffected and decided to distance themselves from Anne and place their hopes for the future in the Lady Mary.

Julia Fox, Jane Parker's recent apologist, is almost certainly overstating her case when she claims that the Rochfords' marriage was successful and that there is no reason to suppose it anything but happy; romantically, she imagines George and Jane 'snuggling up' in bed together. The traditional – and sounder – view is that the marriage was an unhappy one; it may be significant that it produced no children – George Boleyn, Dean of Lichfield in Elizabeth I's reign, is more likely to have been Rochford's bastard than his son by Jane. But, sadly for romantics, the surviving evidence convincingly shows that Jane did testify to her husband having committed incest with his sister, and that she also confided to her interrogators some highly sensitive – and probably false – information.[101]

Possibly the marriage had foundered early on. Rochford's possession of 'Les Lamentations de Matheolus', Lefèvre's cynical satire on women and wedlock, perhaps mirrored his own views on his wife and their marriage; he had acquired it, according to his own inscription, in 1526, within two years of their wedding. It is hardly likely that such a book would have been a wedding gift, as has been suggested,[102] for the writer dates the beginning of his nuptial torments to the day he was wed.

It may be that Rochford had subjected Jane to sexual practices that outraged her – cause enough for enmity. Another, less convincing, theory is that Jane sought revenge on her husband after discovering that he was involved in a homosexual liaison with Mark Smeaton.[103] If that was true, why take it out on Anne, her sister-in-law?

Primary evidence for Jane's testimony appears in a dispatch of Chapuys and in the anonymous Portuguese account of 10 June 1536, which refers to 'that person who, more out of envy and jealousy than out of love towards the King, did betray this accursed secret, and together with it the names of those who had joined in the evil doings of the unchaste Queen'.[104] George Wyatt states that in 'this principal matter [of incest] between the Queen and her brother, there was brought forth, indeed, witness, his wicked wife, accuser of her own husband, even to the seeking of his blood. What she did was more to be rid of him than of true ground against him.' There is no reason to dismiss this just because it is a later account, since much of Wyatt's exhaustively researched information came from people like Anne Gainsford, who had been in Anne Boleyn's household, or others who had known her.

Bishop Burnet, writing one hundred and fifty years later, and basing his work on extensive original sources, wrote that Lady Rochford 'carried many stories to the King, or some about him, that there was a familiarity between the Queen and her brother beyond what so near a relationship could justify'. Peter Heylin, the seventeenth-century Oxford academic historian, also asserted that Jane was jealous of Rochford. That may be very near the truth: perhaps she was inordinately jealous of the close bond between her husband and her sister-in-law, or of Anne's influence over Rochford, who must have spent far more time at court with his sister than at home with his wife during the months of Jane's banishment. Possibly Jane was also bitterly resentful of Anne for involving her in the plot that led to her disgrace; she is even more likely to have been alienated by the latter's perceived responsibility for Fisher's death.

Maybe Jane, realising that the Boleyns were on a headlong course to disaster, pragmatically followed the example of the other ladies of the Queen's household in laying evidence against their mistress. And she had more cause than they, for she would have needed to do something radical to distance herself from the crumbling Boleyn faction to which she was so closely attached, in order to avoid being sucked into the maelstrom of their destruction. Weighed against the prospect of future penury, with her husband convicted of treason and his life and goods declared forfeit, saving her own skin might have seemed the preferable option. This way, she might salvage something through the gratitude of the King and Cromwell.

A third possibility was that Cromwell, knowing that Jane stood in a precipitous position, put pressure on her to lay evidence against the Boleyns, and that she had no choice but to co-operate in the hope of saving her own neck.

A letter that Lady Rochford wrote to Cromwell later in 1536, in which, after referring to her late husband, she added, 'whom God pardon', has been seen as proof that Jane believed George to have been guilty of incest.[105] Yet this was no more than a customary form used in those days when speaking of the departed, and alludes only to the general sinfulness of mankind and the hope of redemption.

Whatever Lady Rochford's involvement, the charge of incest – 'undue familiarity' – was no doubt laid in the knowledge that it would irretrievably malign Anne's reputation and create a scandal of epic proportions.

6

'Turning Trust to Treason'

On Sunday, 30 April, Henry VIII was still urging his envoys abroad to press the Emperor to agree to an alliance without unpalatable conditions attached; even with the investigations into Anne's conduct going on, he was determined that Charles should acknowledge the validity of his second marriage. He also signed a demand for Francis I to abandon his alliance with the Pope unless the latter agreed to revoke all actions against England, actions that had been aimed against the divorce and the Boleyn marriage.[1] He was bent on forcing the European powers and the Roman Church to admit that he had been right to put away his first wife and take a second. That Anne was under a cloud of suspicion was beside the point.

Alexander Aless, who was 'at this time in attendance upon Cromwell in the court, soliciting the payment of a stipend awarded to me', says it was 'not long after' the investigation began that 'the persons returned who had been charged with the investigation of the rumours which had been circulated', and indicates that it was on that same day, 30 April, that Cromwell and his colleagues, 'with everything having been arranged to their entire satisfaction', laid before the King further evidence of the Queen's immorality, alleging that she had seduced several members of the Privy Chamber including her own brother and Mark Smeaton.[2] Aless gives details not mentioned elsewhere, which he can only have gleaned from Cromwell – whom he was visiting at that time – or Cranmer, with whom he 'was on intimate terms'. He says the investigators 'assured the King that the affair was beyond doubt; that they had seen the Queen dancing with the gentlemen of the King's Chamber, that they could produce witnesses who would vouch to the Queen having kissed her own brother, and that they had in their possession letters in which she informed him that she was pregnant.'

All this appears to have been entirely innocent. Dancing was not evidence of adultery, nor was it a criminal act to kiss one's brother or tell him the glad news of a pregnancy, unless of course the implication was that he was the father, which it obviously was in this case. Aless's account certainly does not reflect the full force of the evidence laid before Henry VIII, which was sufficient to convince him that Anne had a case to answer. He does not mention the most serious accusation, that Anne was said to have plotted regicide, the ultimate crime, with the intention of marrying one of her lovers and ruling as regent for Elizabeth.

This was all more than enough to arouse fury in any husband, let alone an egotistical monarch who was also Supreme Head of the Church of England, and Henry's reaction was that of a man who believed what he was hearing, which convinced him that he had nourished a viper in his bosom, that Anne had betrayed and humiliated him, both as a husband and a king, and that, by her misconduct, she had put the royal succession in jeopardy. Worse still, it seemed she had wanted him dead. As Cavendish put it, Anne had 'turned trust to treason' and 'changed [Henry's] lust to hatred'.[3] In the coming weeks, his behaviour would be that of a betrayed husband who was genuinely convinced of his wife's guilt, and struggling to come to terms with it and save face. And indeed, he had good reason to take at face value the evidence Cromwell had laid before him. After all, Anne had deceived him about saving her virtue for marriage, and he must have been aware of her provocative banter and flirtations with admiring male courtiers. How could he have forgotten the effect she had had on *him* during the protracted torture of their long courtship?

Aless makes it clear that it was at, or just after, the meeting on 30 April, that 'it was decided and concluded that the Queen was an adulteress and deserved to be burnt alive'. That same day, an angry and outraged Henry sanctioned the arrest of Mark Smeaton and summoned the Council[4] urgently to debate the evidence against the Queen and her other alleged accomplices. After this, Anne's accusers moved against her with such speed and ruthlessness as to suggest that they were unsure of their case, fearful of her influence over the King and the possibility of another reconciliation, and above all determined to bring her down.

As a simmering Henry was closeted with Cromwell at Greenwich, 'the Queen, meanwhile, took her pleasure unconscious of the discovery, watching dogs and animals that day fight in [Greenwich] Park',[5] probably as Cromwell was laying before the Council his evidence against Anne and her supposed lovers. According to the 'Spanish Chronicle', he had received a letter from Sir Thomas Percy, brother to the Earl of Northumberland. Percy, whom it would appear had been watching Mark Smeaton with suspicion, had been involved in a violent altercation with him, and complained to someone in authority about his conduct. Queen Anne, hearing of this, sent for Percy and ordered him to make his peace with Smeaton. Begrudgingly he did so, but at the same time he wrote to Cromwell, telling him what had happened and confiding his misgivings. He wrote:

It is hardly three months since Mark [Smeaton] came to court, and though he has only an hundred pounds [£34,900]

a year from the King, and has received no more than a third,
he has just bought three horses that have cost him five
hundred ducats, as well as very rich arms and fine liveries
for his servants for the May Day ridings, such as no gentleman
at court has been able to buy, and many are wondering
where he gets the money.

The implication was that he had been given it by Anne in return
for sexual services.

According to the author of the 'Spanish Chronicle', Anne was
guilty of adultery with all her supposed 'minions', having 'osten-
tatiously tried to attract the best-looking men and the best dancers
to be found'; above all, she was passionately in love with Smeaton,
having fallen for him after hearing him play and finding him to
be a good dancing partner. That is all at variance with her own
testimony.

Despite the fact that Smeaton had been at court since 1529,
and not for just three months, the salary quoted sounds realistic,
as a page of the Privy Chamber could be paid £100 'during pleasure'. It was substantial remuneration: mere musicians got about
£6 (£2,100) a year; Lucas Horenbout, the King's painter, received
£33 (£11,550) a year, while his successor, the great Hans Holbein,
earned rather less. But even earning that kind of money, having
received a third of his salary, and allowing for the fact that a gold
ducat was then worth about 9s.4d (£150), Smeaton could hardly
have afforded the £70 (£24,450) that those horses would have
cost, or the rich liveries.

Cromwell had allegedly responded by asking Percy secretly to
keep an eye on Smeaton, which he had done; and on 29 April,
he reported that, that very morning, he had seen Smeaton emerging
from the Queen's apartment.[6]

Whether this account was true or not, the Crown acted on
information that apparently corroborated the testimony of Lady
Worcester and others, and Smeaton was arrested on Sunday,

30 April and taken to Cromwell's house in Stepney for questioning. Since Cromwell is known to have gone there too on that day, perhaps with Smeaton in his custody, it is likely that he himself conducted the interrogation.[7]

'In the evening, there was a ball' at court, at which 'the King treated [Anne] as normal'.[8] However, she was probably preoccupied with her concerns about a conversation she had had sometime that Sunday with Sir Henry Norris.

As she was to reveal only three days later to one of Cromwell's spies, she had asked Norris 'why he went not through with his marriage, and he made answer he would tarry a time'. It may be that Norris was employing delaying tactics because he was worried about allying himself with the Boleyn faction,[9] but Anne had interpreted his words to mean that he was reluctant to marry Madge Shelton because he had feelings for her, the Queen – and possibly Norris had given her cause in the past to think this.

'You look for dead men's shoes,' she told him provocatively, 'for if aught should come to the King but good, you would look to have me.' Norris was probably shocked, because the conventions of permissible courtly dalliance dictated that the lover importune the mistress, not the other way about, and he denied it, protesting that 'if he should have any such thought, he would his head were off'. He was aware that this was a dangerous conversation – for to refer to the King's demise, even in jest, was no light matter, since the Statute of Treasons of 1351 covered imagining and compassing the death of the sovereign, while it had more recently been enacted that even to talk of such a thing could also be treasonable – and his words must have brought home to them both the serious implications of what they were discussing, for Anne pointedly told Norris that 'she could undo him if she would, and therewith they fell out'.

At some point, they both realised that their remarks had been overheard and might be misconstrued – which was what in fact happened. The Queen of England had to be above suspicion in every respect, but on this occasion Anne's rash words were open to a more serious and dangerous interpretation: people might (and indeed would) think that she had flirted outrageously, gone way beyond the accepted rules of courtly banter, been overfamiliar with Norris, at the very least, or was even actively plotting the King's assassination. Indeed, her remarks gave rise to the worst possible scenario, for they would be seen as damning evidence of treason – and actually appear to have been among the Crown's most compelling pieces of evidence; moreover, they showed that she was ready to initiate a dangerous flirtation. It followed that, in her indictment, her accusers were able convincingly to portray her as a female seductress who at every opportunity incited her lovers to criminal acts. Anne, all unwittingly, had given Cromwell evidence he needed to bring her down. Her exchange with Norris could not have been more timely.

Anne was sufficiently concerned about what she and Norris had been heard to say that she bade him go to her almoner, John Skip, and 'swear for the Queen that she was a good woman'. That, as it was to prove, was a fatal mistake, for Skip's suspicions were immediately aroused, and he confided the matter to Anne's chamberlain, Sir Edward Baynton, who also took a dim view of the exchange, possibly because this was not the first time that Anne had said compromising things to Norris – she herself would shortly reveal that there had been another conversation between them on 25 April, the details of which are not clear.[10] The almoner and the chamberlain discussed the matter, and Skip urged Baynton to go to Cromwell and Sir William FitzWilliam, who was heavily involved in the investigation against Anne, to 'plainly express' his opinion, which he did.[11]

Given the suspicions to which the conversation between Anne and Norris gave rise, even in John Skip, who hitherto had been a supporter of the Queen, we might conjecture whether Anne, fearing the consequences (for she was a prisoner in the Tower at the time), reported it in its entirety, and that what Norris said to

Skip was more compromising. This is not to suggest that it was necessarily evidence of criminal intercourse, or even a serious flirtation, but that there was perhaps more sexual innuendo than Anne could bring herself to admit to, or, which is perhaps more likely, the exchange about Norris looking for dead men's shoes was more explicit and open to an even worse interpretation.

The strange thing is that Anne was never charged with offences involving Norris at this time, only with inveigling the men to treason in November 1535, and compassing the King's death on 8 January 1536 *and on various dates thereafter* (author's italics). It is evident that her accusers were intent on alleging that this was a long-established – and therefore more dangerous – conspiracy, and that she was so wicked that she had not scrupled to plot regicide when she was carrying the King's child. There is no record of the conversation with Norris being mentioned at Anne's trial, or in the written testimony of witnesses (none of which survives), but the records and eyewitness accounts are incomplete. Nevertheless, it clearly was regarded as crucial evidence, and seems to have been the basis for some of the Crown's allegations.

Sometime that day, or the next morning, Aless witnessed the King and Queen arguing. He wrote an account of what he had seen in 1559 in a letter to Elizabeth I:

> Never shall I forget the sorrow I felt when I saw the most serene Queen, your most religious mother, carrying you, still a little baby, in her arms, and entreating the most serene King your father in Greenwich Palace, from the open window of which he was looking into the courtyard when she brought you to him. I did not perfectly understand what had been going on, but the faces and gestures of the speakers plainly showed the King was angry, although he could conceal his anger wonderfully well.

The cause of the quarrel is not known, because Aless could not hear the words that passed between the royal couple. It is possible that Anne, fearful that Henry would get to hear of her conversation with Norris, sought to pre-empt his anger by trying to explain herself, taking Elizabeth with her for maximum emotional appeal;[12] or that Henry had already heard about it, and that she was trying to defuse his wrath. It has recently been suggested that Anne was pleading with him for mercy,[13] which is very likely, but it begs the question of what she had heard exactly. Was it divorce she feared? Or did her fears go deeper? Certainly they had been mounting over the past weeks. Whatever it was, we can assume that Henry refused to divulge what was going on – he was a man who preferred to keep his secrets to himself, and once said that if his cap knew what he was thinking he would throw it in the fire[14] – and that Anne's appeal for enlightenment or understanding failed.

The Council sat until eleven o'clock that night. By then, conjecture had spread about the nature of the urgent business being debated, and a throng of people, Alexander Aless among them, had gathered at Greenwich to speculate as to what was going on. 'From the protracted conference of the Council (for whom the crowd was waiting until it was quite dark, expecting that they would return to London), it was most obvious to everyone that some deep and difficult question was being discussed. Nor was this opinion incorrect.'[15] When the meeting broke up, an announcement was made that the planned trip to Calais would be postponed for a week.[16] No reason for the sudden change of plan was given. 'The King's journey is prolonged,' Lord Lisle was informed by John Granfield, his man in London. 'My brother Diggory will bring you the certainty of the King's coming.'[17]

This sudden decision to cancel the Calais trip in itself strongly suggests that the evidence against the Queen had only been recently laid, and that the outcome of the investigations had thrown everything into disarray. Contrary to what has recently been claimed,[18] it cannot in any way be seen as proof that Henry had known all along of Cromwell's plot to destroy Anne.

The 'Spanish Chronicle' asserts that, when Smeaton arrived at Cromwell's house, 'two stout young fellows were called, and the Secretary asked for a rope and a cudgel. The rope, which was filled with knots, was put around Mark's head, and twisted with the cudgel until he cried, "Sir Secretary, no more! I will tell the truth. The Queen gave me the money."'

He then, according to this chronicle, made a confession, saying that after he had entered the Queen's service (which is incorrect, because he was in the King's service), she had singled him out for special notice, asking her ladies, 'Does not the lad play well?' Then one morning, she had sent for him as she lay abed, and he had been ordered to play so that her ladies might dance. Watching him, she resolved to seduce him and began scheming to get him discreetly into her bed, no easy thing with all her ladies about, and with Smeaton too lowly to be expected to make the first move. So she took into her confidence an old waiting woman called Margaret, who slept every night in the antechamber of the Queen's bedroom, the other ladies sleeping beyond, in the gallery.

In the antechamber there was a cupboard in which were stored sweetmeats, candied fruits and conserves. One night, when all was quiet, Margaret, acting on Anne's instructions, hid a very nervous Mark behind the royal bed-curtains; then, when her mistress called out from her bed, 'Bring me a little marmalade!' Margaret took him by the hand and pulled him into view, saying – for the benefit of anyone who might be within earshot – 'Here is the marmalade, my lady.'

'Go along, go to bed,' Anne is said to have replied, and after Margaret had gone, she 'went to the back of the bed and grasped the youth's arm, who was all trembling, and made him get into bed. He soon lost his bashfulness, and remained that night and many others.' In reward for his services, Anne gave him money, which enabled him to become 'smart and lavish in his clothes'. He was aware, though, that both Sir Henry Norris and William Brereton were rivals for her favours.[19]

This account is probably largely apocryphal, either the invention of a hostile Spaniard or based on the rumours that were circulating in the City of London at this time. The chronicle further asserts that Margaret was arrested and put on the rack, where she incriminated Norris and Brereton, but swore that Sir Thomas Wyatt – who was not yet in Cromwell's sights, so far as we know – was innocent; then she is said to have been burned at the stake under cover of darkness within the Tower. There is no evidence to corroborate these statements. The account is littered with errors, with Rochford being referred to as a duke and Weston's name being omitted entirely, while 'Margaret' cannot be identified, although it is possible that the writer confused her with either Lady Wingfield or Margery Horsman.

Someone else thought that Smeaton was perhaps tortured, although not in the manner that the 'Spanish Chronicle' describes. One of the best contemporary sources for this period is George Constantine, William Brereton's former school-fellow and long-standing friend, who was now Sir Henry Norris's body servant and later became registrar of the bishopric of St David's. Constantine had long been a zealous Protestant and trafficker in forbidden books, and in 1531 had narrowly escaped burning at the hands of the former Lord Chancellor, Sir Thomas More, having saved himself only by betraying his associates and fleeing abroad. Thanks to the reforming influence of Anne Boleyn, he had been able to return to London under the protection of Norris, bringing with him, for Anne, a copy of Miles Coverdale's translation of the Bible into English. Given his sympathies, Constantine at first 'could not believe' that the Queen was guilty.[20]

Three years later, Constantine wrote a memorial of these events for Cromwell.[21] According to this, 'the saying was that [Smeaton] confessed, but he was first grievously racked, which I could never know of a truth'.[22] It is easy to see how Constantine imagined that torture was routine in such interrogations, for, according to his own explanation of why he had betrayed his friends five years earlier, he himself had been subjected to the most dreadful torture.[23] It is hardly conceivable that there was a rack at Cromwell's house, but there was certainly one at the Tower, even though torture was officially illegal in England. Although all the sources imply that the hapless musician's confession was obtained at Stepney, it is of course possible that he was racked soon after his arrival at the Tower on 2 May; but if he was tortured thus, he must have given in before too much unbearable pressure was brought to bear, for there is no evidence that his bones were dislocated, and he was able, only days later, to stand trial and walk to his execution without anyone commenting on him being in evident pain or in any way disabled, while no observer mentions any visible injuries consistent with the rope torture, which is almost certainly a lurid fabrication. In 1546, when the heretic Anne Askew was racked, with the then Lord Chancellor, Thomas Wriothesley, himself turning the wheel, people knew about it, not least because she was carried in a chair to the stake.[24] Moreover, Lancelot de Carles states that, although 'Mark was forced to answer the accusation against him, without being tortured, he deliberately said that the Queen had three times yielded to his passion'. So probably the tales of Smeaton being tortured were based on unfounded rumours and assumptions. The fact that he was not 'well-lodged' in the Tower until ten o'clock at night on 2 May[25] certainly suggests that he was again interrogated, probably for several hours, but he certainly did not suffer 'twenty-four hours of fierce torture', as one historian has recently claimed.[26]

The fact that he was initially questioned for at least twenty-four hours suggests that Smeaton did not willingly divulge any information. Yet in the end, racked or not, he finally admitted 'that he had been three times with the Concubine'[27] in the spring of 1535 – a confession that (as will be seen) was at variance with Anne's own independent recollections of her dealings with him, in which she stated she had only spoken to him twice, and then just briefly.[28]

Having confessed to the adultery, Smeaton threw himself on the King's mercy,[29] but he was adamant that he was not guilty of abetting the Queen in compassing the King's death, and desired to be tried by a jury on that charge. This rather reinforces the view that he was not tortured, otherwise he surely would have capitulated on all counts, the penalty being the same for violating the Queen as it was for plotting regicide: a traitor's death. It does, however, raise the question of why he admitted the adultery. Did he mistakenly think it was a lesser charge? Or was he – and by implication, Anne – in fact guilty? Or was 'psychological pressure'[30] brought to bear on him? He was perhaps told, as Norris would be, that he could save his life by confessing; or he could have been informed that, since it was known that he had committed treason and must suffer the penalty anyway, he might be rewarded with a quicker death than that usually meted out to traitors in return for his co-operation, a choice that would be offered to Anne herself; this would explain why Smeaton was allowed to die like a gentleman.

Cavendish states that 'by his confession, he did them all accuse'.[31] The well-informed contemporary printer and annalist, Richard Grafton, in his extension of Edward Hall's *Chronicle*, says that Smeaton was 'provoked' to incriminate himself, the Queen and others 'by the [future] Lord Admiral [Sir William FitzWilliam, the King's treasurer], that was later Earl of Southampton, who said unto him, "Subscribe, Mark, and see what will come of it."' It sounds as if names were put to him, and that pressure was exerted to make him incriminate them.

Lancelot de Carles asserts that Sir Anthony Browne – acting perhaps on information gleaned from his sister, Lady Worcester

– also cited Norris, and laid evidence that Norris had promised to marry Anne after the King's death. It may therefore have been Browne who overheard the conversation between Anne and Norris. But Browne was the half-brother of Sir William FitzWilliam, who was to play an important role in Anne Boleyn's downfall, and to whom Sir Edward Baynton had confided his suspicions about Norris, so it is also possible that Carles confused Browne with FitzWilliam.

FitzWilliam was a loyal and dependable King's man. He had grown up with Henry from the age of ten and was consequently one of those closest to him; he also had a long and distinguished record of service in warfare, diplomacy and the royal household. He was a solid individual who trimmed his sails to the prevailing wind and for the most part kept aloof from the factional politics that divided the court. As will be seen, he was plainly willing to do his very best to secure the conviction of the Queen and her alleged lovers, and became so deeply involved in building a case against them that he would later confess to having neglected all his correspondence 'since these matters begun'.[32] Because of the paucity of evidence, the extent of his involvement in Anne Boleyn's fall will never be fully understood, but it is clear that he was at the centre of the investigations from the first.

Smeaton had not only confirmed the allegations of Lady Worcester, Lady Rochford and others, but had told 'much more', as Lady Worcester had said he would. Cromwell now had all the information he needed to proceed against the Queen, and he hastened to lay it before the King.

At the May Day tournament at Greenwich, Anne was disconcerted when Henry got up and left without a word to her, yet she can have had no idea that she would never see him again.

Lancelot de Carles says that, during the jousts, Henry loaned Norris his own horse, knowing 'that he could not keep it long', and that he showed kindness to Norris, Weston and Brereton, 'concealing their forthcoming ruin', but it is unlikely that the King had been made aware before the tournament of the results of Smeaton's interrogation. His abrupt departure was prompted by a message he was given, which was almost certainly to inform him that Smeaton had confessed to adultery with the Queen and had incriminated Rochford, Norris and Brereton, and perhaps Weston also, confirming what the King and his ministers probably already suspected about Rochford and Norris. The 'Spanish Chronicle' asserts that Cromwell sent his nephew Richard Williams (who adopted the surname Cromwell) to the King with Smeaton's actual confession, as well as the forged confessions of Anne and Rochford – which is patently untrue; and that when Henry had read them all, 'his meat did not at all agree with him'. When learning that Smeaton had confessed to having violated Anne, he cried, enraged, 'Hang him up, then! Hang him up!' The tale is probably apocryphal.

Lancelot de Carles, who may have been repeating the official line that was fed in secret to the French ambassador, claims the councillors told Henry that 'when you retire at night, she has her darlings already lined up. Her brother is by no means last in the queue. Norris and Mark would not deny that they have spent many nights with her without having to persuade her, for she herself urged them on, and invited them with presents and caresses.' It sounds suspiciously like the wording of the indictments that would soon be drawn up against the Queen.

The historian S. T. Bindoff, writing about Anne Boleyn's fall, asserted, 'Where a Borgia would have used poison, a Tudor used the law.' It is worth noting that it was only after being informed of Smeaton's confession that Henry resolved upon proceeding against Anne and her alleged lovers. He had no choice, for he could not afford to ignore such evidence. He had known for a week that there was cause for suspicion, yet had not acted precipitately; instead, he had waited to see if there was any further evidence to support his councillors' allegations. He was to show a like restraint five years later when similar unsubstantiated claims were made against his fifth wife, Katherine Howard. His immediate response would be to reject them out of hand as being malicious accusations – which suggests he was by then well aware of how Anne Boleyn had been brought to grief[33] – and order an investigation, and it was only when incontrovertible evidence was laid before him that he ordered any arrests. On that latter occasion, he wept in council, his grief warring with a surge of anger so bitter that it had him crying out for a sword with which to slay Katherine.

Since being informed of his councillors' suspicions concerning Anne Boleyn's conduct, his mood – on the available evidence – had been angry rather than grieved, but his relations with Anne had been deteriorating for some time, whereas when Katherine Howard's misconduct was disclosed to him, he had just publicly given thanks for the happy life he was leading with her, his 'rose without a thorn'. Yet there can be little doubt that some vestiges of his grand passion for Anne remained – witness his keeping her company on St Matthias's Day, his insistence that Chapuys pay court to her, and his remarks about her bearing him a prince in the near future – and when he was confronted with what looked like convincing evidence of her treachery, he must have been plunged into a turmoil of emotions. It does seem that he was greatly shaken and shocked by the reports that had been brought to him, and his sudden departure from the jousts must be viewed in this context. He may well have felt that he could not bear to set eyes on Anne again, or might not have trusted himself to refrain from violence.

Had Henry VIII been instrumental in bringing about Anne's ruin, he would surely not have been so obviously angry. Yet it is hard to explain why he accepted at face value evidence that many people, including even Chapuys, Anne's enemy, were to regard as flimsy. Maybe it was all too easy to believe such things of a wife of whom he had tired, the marrying of whom, he now apparently believed, had incurred God's displeasure. Possibly the very fact that his councillors had dared to lay such damning evidence against her was enough to convince him that it was all true, and, having been publicly humiliated by these sordid revelations, he was too angered and hurt by her betrayal of him, both as a man and as the King, to give her, or the men accused with her, the benefit of any doubt. Cromwell was no fool – what he had laid before his master would have had to have been pretty watertight, or the consequences for Master Secretary could have been horrific. It should also be remembered that Chapuys' view of the evidence, although clearly shared by some other observers, was not that professed by the majority of his contemporaries, who – until Anne's daughter ascended the throne – behaved as if they accepted the Queen's guilt without question.

'Immediately after the tourney', when 'the jousts were over and they were disarming', 'archers were ordered to arrest Norris, and were much astonished and grieved, considering his virtue and intimacy with the King, that he should have committed disloyalty'.[34] 'The Captain of the Guard came and called Master Norris and Master Brereton, and said to them, "Sirs, the King calls you."'[35]

It would appear that Norris was arrested on the King's orders while Brereton was detained for questioning; he would not be arrested for another three days. 'Before [Norris] went to prison, the King desired to speak to him.'[36] Constantine says that Henry 'rode suddenly to Westminster, and all the way, as I heard say, had Norris in examination', accusing him of committing adultery with Anne as far back as 1533. It was almost unheard of for the King himself to question a suspected traitor; as an anointed sovereign, he would always distance himself from those accused of treason, and indeed would never have anything to do with anyone tainted even by the suspicion of it, so it is probably correct to say that Henry's interrogation of Norris was 'the action of a man taken by surprise'.[37] He had been very close to Norris, and was evidently

outraged at what he believed to be the betrayal of a friend whom
he had thought utterly loyal. It is hard to believe that Henry
would have been a party to sacrificing the faithful Norris, knowing him to be innocent, merely as a means of ridding himself of
Anne.

Norris was aghast to hear that he was accused of criminal intercourse with the Queen. But Henry 'promised him his pardon [if]
he would utter the truth'.[38] Cavendish, who believed Norris guilty,
imagined him looking back with bitter regret on this interview:

> His [Henry's] most noble heart lamented so my chance,
> That of his clemency he granted me my life,
> In case I would, without dissimulance,
> The truth declare of his unchaste wife,
> The spotted Queen, causer of all his strife;
> But I most obstinate, with heart as hard as stone,
> Denied his grace – good cause therefore to moan.[39]

Carles also states that the King offered 'to spare [Norris's] life and
goods, although he was guilty, if he would tell him the truth'.
Maybe this offer was meant genuinely and Henry was indeed
prepared to be lenient with Norris, although that is by no means
certain. But, Constantine says, 'Mr Norris would confess nothing
to the King.' 'Being told the accusation, [he] offered to maintain
the contrary with his body in any place'[40] – that is, submit to
trial by combat. Far from being reassured by this, Henry appeared
determined to believe the worst, and he 'authorised and commissioned' Cromwell 'to prosecute and bring to an end the
Concubine's trial', as Master Secretary was to inform Chapuys.[41]
Norris's determination to maintain his innocence in the face of
the King's offer of pardon suggests either that he believed that
to be an empty promise, or that he was innocent.

On arriving at York Place, Norris was placed in the custody
of Sir William FitzWilliam,[42] who was among the councillors who

examined him at York Place later on 1 May, at a special meeting of the Privy Council summoned by the King 'to treat of matters relating to the surety of his person, his honour, and the tranquillity of the realm'.[43] Norris's chaplain told George Constantine that, during this interrogation, Norris did confess to something, although he did not say what, and Norris would later declare that he had been deceived into making his confession by FitzWilliam's trickery. This is the second independent account of FitzWilliam coercing the Queen's alleged lovers into incriminating disclosures. Chapuys later informed Dr Ortiz, the Imperial ambassador in Rome, that 'two of the five [who would be arrested] confessed their guilt'.[44] Contrary to what is often stated, it may not have been the case that Smeaton alone confessed.

Cromwell was to write to Stephen Gardiner, the King's envoy in Rome, that the Queen's lovers – note the plural, suggesting again that Norris too confessed – disclosed under interrogation things 'so abominable that a great part of them were never given in evidence, but clearly kept secret'.[45] He could have been implying that they had indulged in forbidden sexual practices with Anne. In an age in which even marital intercourse was not supposed to take place on holy days or during pregnancy or menstruation, and oral sex and masturbation were seen as utterly sinful, to hint at such things was effectively to accuse Anne and her lovers of unbridled depravity. Yet the question remains, why were these things not made public, thus bolstering the Crown's case? Was it to protect the King's honour from further scandal? Or was it that these men had confessed to homosexual activity, which was punishable by death? If so, that could hardly have been alleged against them, given that they were supposed to have been repeatedly committing adultery with the Queen; it would substantially have undermined the whole case. The other, more likely, possibility, of course, is that they had confessed to nothing of the kind, and that Cromwell was merely bolstering his case with fabrications.

★   ★   ★

At dawn the next morning, Norris was taken under guard to the Tower.[46] On entering his prison, he was permitted to see his chaplain, and told him he had never betrayed the King, reiterating, 'I would rather die a thousand deaths than be guilty of such a falsehood.'[47]

Around the same time, Mark Smeaton was also committed to the Tower.[48] George Constantine, Anthony Anthony and the 'Spanish Chronicle' all give the date of his arrest as 1 May, Constantine saying that Mark was brought to the Tower in the morning and Anthony claiming that he was taken there at six p.m. Anthony was Surveyor of the Ordnance at the Tower, and should have been in a position to know when Smeaton arrived, but it seems that he was mistaken, because Chapuys, writing on the 2nd, states that Smeaton had been taken to the Tower early that morning, and that Lord Rochford followed after dinner (which was served at court between ten a.m. and one p.m., depending on one's rank and where one ate), 'more than six hours after the others'. This was to be corroborated by Anne herself referring to the fact that accommodation was not found for Smeaton in the Tower until ten o'clock on the evening of the 2nd.[49]

Rochford, who had followed the King back to York Place,[50] had been arrested and conveyed downriver to the Tower[51] apparently without having been subject to any interrogation.[52] According to Lancelot de Carles, he was heard to remark that 'he had well-merited his fate', but that information sounds suspiciously as if it had been 'leaked' to the French embassy by official sources. Rochford's arrest was so discreetly accomplished that few, least of all the Queen, knew he had gone. Even Chapuys had no inkling of what was to happen next.

7

'To The Tower'

Anne spent part of the morning of 2 May watching a game of tennis. Her champion won, and she was regretting not having placed a bet on him[1] when a gentleman messenger came and bade her, 'by order of the King', present herself before the Privy Council at once.[2] For a queen to be thus summoned was strange and portentous indeed, and Anne must have felt deep trepidation as she entered the council chamber, especially as her most powerful protector, the King her husband, had gone to Westminster. Contrary to the traditional version of her story, which shows her as being taken completely unawares by the events of 2 May, it is more than likely that she had been half expecting something ominous to happen. Why else would she have entrusted Elizabeth to Matthew Parker's care, or tackled Henry with Elizabeth in her arms? If the crowds of courtiers who had huddled in speculation at Greenwich the night before had been aware that something momentous was afoot, Anne must have been too, and she surely had cause to suspect that it concerned herself.

There were three grave-faced men present in that council chamber, who all respectfully rose to their feet. They were her uncle, the Duke of Norfolk; Sir William FitzWilliam, who had that morning returned to Greenwich from London, after committing Norris to the Tower; and Sir William Paulet, the King's comptroller. Norfolk, as we have seen, had long since fallen out with Anne, and she could not expect him to be sympathetic towards her now. Even so, in the days to come, the Duke would betray some distress at her plight. Nevertheless, his overriding sense of self-preservation, and his relentless ambition, were forcing him to be complicit in her destruction.

Without preamble, these lords informed Anne of the powers granted to the royal commissioners, accused her of 'evil behaviour', and formally charged her with having committed adultery with Sir Henry Norris, Mark Smeaton and one other whom they did not name, and told her that both the named men had already admitted their guilt.[3]

Anne denied the charges,[4] but it did her no good. Cavendish says she protested that she was the King's true wife and that no other man had ever touched her. She would have realised that the crimes laid against her were grave, and it must have been immediately obvious that her enemies were determined to destroy her. Worst of all, she can have been in no doubt that the King her husband had ordered her arrest.

The lords were very severe with her. Four days later, she was to complain, 'I was cruelly handled at Greenwich with the King's Council, with my lord of Norfolk, that he said, "Tut, tut, tut." As for Master Treasurer,' she went on, 'he was in the forest of Windsor.' 'You know what she means by that,' Sir William Kingston, Constable of the Tower, was later to comment to Cromwell, from which we may infer that 'the forest of Windsor' was a euphemism for something else. It has erroneously been assumed that 'Master Treasurer' was the Earl of Wiltshire, Anne's father, and that he was hunting at Windsor,[5] but FitzWilliam had replaced him in that office in 1525, and was clearly present at the Queen's interrogation and arrest. Her remark may have been a reference to Sir Brastius, one of the knights in Sir Thomas Malory's *Morte d'Arthur*, a book that was very popular at this time, and well known at court. Sir Brastius became a hermit in the forest of Windsor, and because hermits lived silent, solitary lives, Anne may have been implying that FitzWilliam had been uncommunicative when she was before the Council. There is no evidence that she was 'cruelly handled' physically by Norfolk and FitzWilliam;[6] their cruelty, as she saw it, was probably verbal. She received better treatment from 'Master Comptroller', Sir William Paulet, whom she called 'a very gentleman'.[7]

After charging her, the lords had her escorted back to her apartments and left her there under guard while her dinner was served. The meal was a dismal affair,[8] with Anne distressed when the King's waiter did not arrive to wish her, on her husband's behalf, 'Much good may it do you,' as he customarily did. She also noticed the ominous silence of her ladies, and her servants struggling to conceal tears, which further unnerved her. The cloth had only just been removed, and she was still at table, seated under her canopy of estate, and wearing a sumptuous gown of crimson velvet and cloth of gold, when Norfolk returned at two o'clock with Cromwell, Lord Chancellor Audley, John de Vere, Earl of Oxford, William, Lord Sandys, the Lord Chamberlain, and several lords of the Council. With them, according to the 'Spanish Chronicle', was the captain of the King's guard, who had come to Greenwich 'with a hundred halberdiers in the King's great barge'. The writer of this chronicle could not have been an eyewitness to many of the events he describes, and his account of Anne's fall is often inaccurate, melodramatic and mostly fabricated, but he lived in London and may well have seen those halberdiers going to Greenwich in that barge. He also had contacts in the Tower itself, and may have got some of his information from them.

Norfolk had in his hand a scroll of parchment – the warrant for the Queen's arrest. Anne rose to her feet and asked the lords 'why they came'. Norfolk replied 'that they came by the King's command to conduct her to the Tower, there to abide during his Highness's pleasure'. (This gives the lie to the editor of the 'Spanish Chronicle's assertion that Anne at first believed she was being taken to York Place to see the King.) She could have been in no doubt that her situation was serious, but at that time, the Tower cannot have appeared quite as menacing a place as it later did, for no royal personage had as yet been executed there.

'If it be his Majesty's pleasure, I am ready to obey,' Anne answered, calmly enough, and then, 'without change of habit, or anything necessary for her removal, she committed herself to them'.[9] She was not given time to pack clothes or personal possessions, say goodbye to her child, or summon her women, but was informed that money would be provided for her needs while she was in the Tower; the fact that the Constable would be allocated £25.4s.6d (£8,800) for her food shows that she was served as befitted a queen during her imprisonment.[10] Her household, however, was left behind at Greenwich.[11]

The councillors conducted Anne to the waiting barge.[12] It was usual for state prisoners to be conveyed to the Tower under cover of darkness, but Anne Boleyn made the journey 'in full daylight',[13] under guard, accompanied by Audley, Norfolk, Cromwell, Sandys, Oxford and Sir William Kingston, Constable of the Tower.[14]

Kingston, who was to have custody of the Queen during her imprisonment, was now, as he put it that year, 'in the midst of mine age'[15] (he was to die in 1540), but he had been 'a very tall, strong knight' in his triumphant jousting days, when he had tilted against the King.[16] He was a soldier courtier who had served as a yeoman of the Chamber as far back as 1497, being promoted to gentleman usher by 1504. Since then, he had enjoyed a distinguished military and diplomatic career, as well as the King's favour over many years, and had held the office of Constable of the Tower since 1524.

Described by a Venetian ambassador in 1519 as a 'creature' of

Wolsey's, Kingston had supported Henry VIII's nullity suit against Katherine of Aragon and played an official role at Anne Boleyn's coronation in 1533. Yet Chapuys thought him wholly devoted to the late Queen Katherine and her daughter, and he may indeed secretly have sympathised with them, for he once referred to Anne as being 'unjustly called Queen'.[17] Yet, whatever his private opinion, and for all his professed belief in her guilt, he was to behave towards her, while she was in his charge, with courtesy and humanity – as he had to Cardinal Wolsey at the time of the latter's arrest in 1530 – and would come to feel admiration for her courage.

As they sat in the barge, Norfolk repeated to Anne, with a good deal more sanctimonious tut-tutting, that 'her paramours had confessed their guilt', but he got no satisfaction of it, for she disdained to reply. Strickland says she passionately protested her innocence and begged to see the King, but Norfolk just replied, 'Tut Tut.' Anne thereupon declared with desperate bravado that 'they could not prevent her from dying their queen', and made a gesture towards her neck. Again the tale comes from one of the later sources consulted by Strickland, and may be apocryphal. The news of Anne's arrest had spread rapidly, and large crowds were to be seen flocking to the river banks to see her conveyed to prison.

'About five of the clock at night, the Queen, Anne Boleyn, was brought to the Tower of London.'[18] Today, it takes thirty minutes by river bus to get there from Greenwich; Anne had been arrested around two o'clock and had been made to leave her lodgings immediately,[19] so even allowing time for walking through the palace to where the barge was waiting at the privy stairs, which were flanked by stone statues of heraldic beasts, three hours seems a long time for such a short journey. It is possible that the Queen had had to be held under guard at Greenwich until the tide changed.

The oarsmen steered the vessel towards the Byward Tower,

then known as the Tower by the Gate,[20] and Anne 'came to the Court Gate'.[21] It is often incorrectly stated that she entered the Tower through the water gate below St Thomas's Tower, which later became known as Traitors' Gate, but in the fifteenth and sixteenth centuries it was usual for kings and queens to use the Court Gate in the Byward Tower, the private entrance to the Tower of London from Tower Wharf, this entrance having originally been built by Edward I in the thirteenth century, although the gate through which Anne passed (which survives today) had been constructed in the fifteenth. The Court Gate led on to Water Lane, the thoroughfare in the Outer Ward that runs parallel with the River Thames, and it was just a short walk along there, past the rear of the Lieutenant's House on the left, to the entrance to the palace, where the Queen was to be lodged.

Alexander Aless, returning home from Greenwich, had scarcely crossed the Thames and reached London when the cannon on Tower Wharf 'thundered out', announcing to the world the incarceration of a 'person of high rank'. He was told that 'such is the custom when any of the nobility of the realm are conveyed to that fortress, there to be imprisoned'.[22] The cannon fire must have given rise to much excited speculation in London.

Waiting to greet the Queen at the Court Gate was Kingston's deputy, the Lieutenant of the Tower, Sir Edmund Walsingham, he who famously reminded the imprisoned Sir Thomas More that 'orders is orders', and who infamously consigned one of his own servants to the notorious Little Ease – a cell so small that anyone confined in it could neither stand up nor lie down – for attempting to help a prisoner escape. Anne was to be fortunate insofar as her dealings with the Tower officials were limited to the more sympathetic Constable.

Faced with the stark reality of her situation, the Queen's composure was disintegrating; there is no evidence that she started screaming, as at least one historian has asserted, although she seems already to have been in a fragile state: it was only three months since she had miscarried,[23] and during that time she had suffered increasing anxiety and fear, culminating in her arrest. After disembarking at the privy steps at the Court Gate and 'entering in' the Tower, she 'fell down on her knees before the lords' on the cobblestones, 'beseeching God to help her as she was not guilty of her accusement'.[24] She must have looked a pitiful sight, 'her soul beaten down with afflictions to the earth',[25] for she would have been aware that it was rare for anyone accused of treason to escape condemnation and death. The councillors made no comment but formally committed her to the custody of the Constable. As they made to depart, Anne got to her feet and 'desired the said lords to beseech the King's Grace to be good unto her; and so they left her there, prisoner'.[26]

Kingston reported to Cromwell the next day that, after Norfolk and the councillors had departed to their barge, he 'went before the Queen into her lodging'. The 'Spanish Chronicle' has him taking her by the arm, and her saying to him, 'I was received with greater ceremony the last time I entered here,' recalling how she had come in triumph before her crowning in 1533. The Constable himself later reported that she asked fearfully, 'Mr Kingston, do I go into a dungeon?'

'No, Madam, you shall go into your lodging that you lay in at your coronation,' the Constable told her. He was referring to the Queen's apartments in the royal palace, which had been refurbished for her at great expense three years earlier.

'It is too good for me!' Anne cried. 'Jesu, have mercy on me!'

This was a strange observation for a woman who had just protested that she was not guilty of the crimes of which she had been accused. If she were indeed innocent – and that had to be presumed until she was condemned – then she deserved to be accorded the respect due to her rank and to be comfortably housed as queen. Moreover, the news that she was to be held in such state, and not in a dungeon, might have been cause for optimism and an uplifting of spirits. Anne's assertion that it was too good for her might suggest that she knew herself to be guilty of something. But maybe she was just too hysterical to know what she was saying, for after uttering these strange words, Kingston reported, she 'kneeled down weeping a great pace, and in the same sorrow fell into a great laughing, and she hath done [so] many times since'.

Kingston must have applauded the decision to lodge Anne in the Queen's apartments, since his wife was to be in attendance on her, and it would make things easier for that lady to be accommodated in comfort. It is unlikely that this decision had been made by the Constable;[27] the orders had probably been relayed through Cromwell. Anne was still the Queen of England, and not as yet convicted of any crime, and even when she was, she would still be honourably housed in the Tower. She was never treated as a common prisoner.

Kingston now conducted her to her lodgings, which lay on the east side of the inner ward between the Lanthorn Tower and the Wardrobe Tower, and had been largely rebuilt three or four years earlier.[28] Although the Tower palace had been a favoured royal residence for centuries, it had become outdated by the Tudor period, and Anne had only stayed there once, with the King, on the two nights before her coronation. In 1532–3, in anticipation of that triumph, Cromwell, on Henry's orders, had spent £3,500 (£1,276,000) on repairs and improvements, so that Anne might be lodged in suitable splendour. The walls and ceilings were decorated in the 'antick' Renaissance style, and the luxurious apartments comprised a 'great' (presence) chamber, a closet leading off that appears to have been used by Anne as a private oratory, a dining chamber embellished with a novel 'mantel of wainscot with antick', and a bedchamber with a privy. Since Anne had left these rooms for her coronation in June 1533, they had lain deserted. By the end of the sixteenth century, they would be uninhabitable,[29] and at the end of the eighteenth, they would be dismantled.[30]

★　★　★

Kingston had instructions from Cromwell to record anything of significance that Anne said. For this reason, those appointed to wait on her were to be forbidden to speak with her unless Lady Kingston was present.[31] Master Secretary was evidently hoping that she would incriminate herself out of her own mouth, and thus bolster the case that was being drawn up against her. Kingston was faithfully to obey his orders, and his reports are preserved in the Cotton MSS in the British Library; they were damaged in the fire that swept through the Cottonian Library in 1731, but they had been seen and largely transcribed before then by the antiquary John Strype, who printed them in his *Ecclesiastical Memorials of the Church of England under King Henry VIII* in the eighteenth century. These letters give vivid insights into Anne's imprisonment, and her state of mind while she was in the Tower.[32]

The ladies and servants who had been chosen to attend the Queen were waiting to greet her in the presence chamber. Anne's old nurse, Mrs Mary Orchard, had been chosen as one of her two chamberers (domestic servants) – an unexpected kindness, this – along with the 'Mother of the Maids', Mrs Stonor, the former Margaret (or Anne) Foliot, who was married to Sir Walter Stonor, he being the King's sergeant-at-arms and a prominent courtier; Mrs Stonor later became a maid-of-honour to Katherine Howard, Henry VIII's fifth wife.

Anne had also been allocated two menservants (probably grooms or ushers) and a boy. But the Queen could not have been pleased to see the four ladies selected to wait on her, who were clearly spies chosen by Cromwell to watch and report on the prisoner. There was her aunt, Elizabeth Wood, Lady Boleyn, the wife of her father's younger brother, Sir James Boleyn of Blickling Hall in Norfolk, who, despite being chancellor of Anne's household, had – perhaps pragmatically, seeing his niece heading for ruin – switched his allegiance to the Lady Mary.[33] Another aunt had also been set to spy on Anne: her father's sister, Lady Shelton, she who had helped to make life a misery for the Lady Mary.

We might pause here to consider if Lady Shelton was the more willing to spy on Anne and work for the downfall of Norris and Weston on account of their cavalier treatment of her daughter Madge. In February 1535, reasoning that if the King had to have a mistress it should be someone sympathetic to herself, Anne had manoeuvred Madge Shelton into his path. The brief affair that ensued soon petered out, but not before it had caused Anne bitter pangs of jealousy and sullied the Shelton girl's reputation; by 1536, Madge Shelton was betrothed to Sir Henry Norris, but clearly (as will be seen) Sir Francis Weston thought she was fair game. Anger at the compromising of her daughter may well have turned Lady Shelton against Anne and her faction.

Yet Lady Shelton had perhaps been nursing another grievance against Anne for some time. As we have seen, she had been forced to follow the Queen's instructions and make the Lady Mary's life a misery, the which ill-treatment only served to reinforce the girl's suspicion that the Boleyn faction was trying to do away with her. Yet although Anne's letters to Lady Shelton reveal that she placed great trust in her, and there is no hint of any falling out between them, it is possible, even likely, that Lady Shelton resented the role she had been forced to play, and that remorse had bred in her a desire to be revenged on the niece who had driven her to such cruelties, and to distance herself from them.

There may also have been a third reason for Lady Shelton's defection. Her son, John Shelton, was married to Margery Parker, the sister of Lady Rochford,[34] and it is possible that the Sheltons were disposed to be sympathetic to Jane Rochford's complaints against her husband, even to the extent of believing in her allegations of his incest with the Queen, and viewing Jane as a deeply wronged woman. If so, it is hardly surprising that Lady Shelton was willing to co-operate with Cromwell. On the other hand, she – and Lady Boleyn – may well have felt that, above all other considerations, it was politic to do so, since the Boleyn faction was hurtling headlong to destruction. Whatever her motives, Lady Shelton had learned from Anne how to treat a disgraced royal lady, and she now had the opportunity of putting that knowledge into practice once more.

The other two chief attendants who were to be employed as spies were Mrs Margaret Coffin and Mary Scrope, Lady Kingston, Sir William's second wife, who perhaps was not enjoying good health at this time, for her husband had described her as 'my sick wife' the previous January;[35] she had served Katherine of Aragon and was a friend of the Lady Mary, so cannot have been sympathetic towards Anne. Margaret Dymoke, Mrs Coffin (or Cosyn), was the wife of William Coffin, who was the Queen's Master of Horse and one of the King's long-favoured Gentlemen of the Privy Chamber, and resided – when not at court – at Haddon Hall in Derbyshire. He would be knighted the following year, by which time his wife was in the service of Jane Seymour.[36] The Coffins were related by marriage to the Boleyns. Mrs Coffin was 'a gentlewoman appointed to wait upon the Queen here, and that lay on her pallet bed';[37] it was normal practice for a servant to share a royal bedchamber and attend to any needs of their master or mistress during the night.

Anne viewed these ladies with dismay; by her own later admission, she had never liked any of them, and she was perhaps aware that the feeling was mutual; above all, she was angry with Henry for appointing them,[38] and she must surely have guessed why they were there. Cromwell was no doubt hoping that, with a little baiting and pressure, she would give rein to her notoriously indiscreet tongue and incriminate herself.

As was customary with prisoners of rank, Anne was to take her meals with her custodian, Sir William Kingston. That first evening in the Tower – Kingston wrote on the 3rd that 'all these sayings was yesternight' – Anne, who was evidently aware of her peril, and of the need to proclaim her innocence, desired Kingston, perhaps while they were at table, 'to move the King's

Anne Boleyn, as she probably looked at the time of her fall
'There is no one who dares contradict her, not even the King himself.'

Henry VIII

His 'blind and wretched passion' for Anne had long since abated.

Jane Seymour

'The new amours of the King go on,
to the intense rage of the Concubine.'

Sir Nicholas Carew

'It will not be the fault of this Master of the
Horse if the Concubine be not dismounted.'

The Lady Mary

'When I have a son,'
Anne Boleyn wrote, 'I know what
then will come to her.'

Henry FitzRoy, Duke of Richmond

His father the King told him he was
lucky to have 'escaped the hands of
that accursed whore'.

Thomas Howard, Duke of Norfolk

He referred to Anne, his niece,
as 'the great whore'.

Thomas Boleyn, Earl of Wiltshire
He connived at his children's fate, and even sat in judgement on them.

Signature of George Boleyn, Lord Rochford

Signature of Mark Smeaton

Henry Parker, Lord Morley
He had instilled in his daughter Jane, Lady Rochford, such loyalty to the Lady Mary as would prove fatal to the Boleyns.

Thomas Cromwell,
'Master Secretary'

'He thought up and plotted the
affair of the Concubine.'

Sir William FitzWilliam

'A good servant' of the King, he was
instrumental in bringing Anne to ruin.

Elizabeth Browne,
Countess of Worcester

She was 'the first accuser' of the Queen.

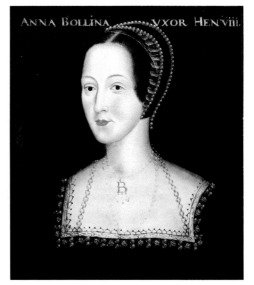

Anne Boleyn
She had clearly overstepped the conventional bounds of courtly banter between queen and servant, man and woman.

The Indictment against
Anne Boleyn and Lord Rochford
'She incited her own natural brother to violate her.'

Greenwich Palace, where Anne Boleyn was arrested.
'I was cruelly handled at Greenwich with the King's Council.'

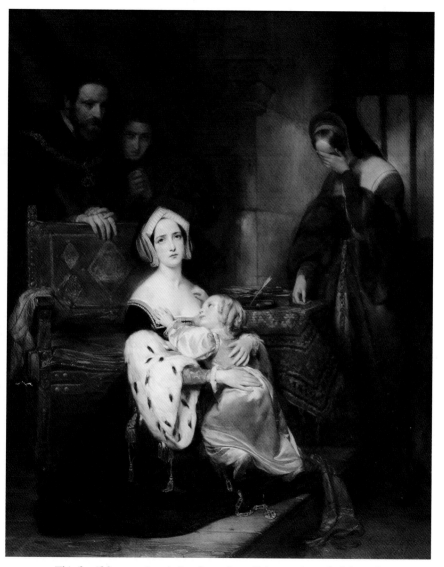

This fanciful, romantic painting shows Anne Boleyn saying a final farewell to her daughter, the Princess Elizabeth.

'Never shall I forget the sorrow I felt when I saw the most serene Queen, your mother, carrying you, still a little baby, in her arms.'

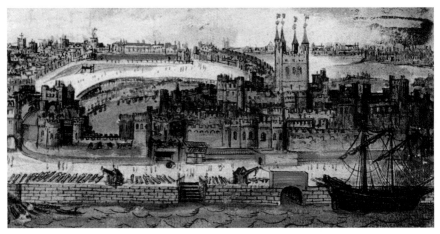

The Tower of London.

The King's Hall, where Anne Boleyn was tried, can be seen behind the wall fronting the river; the Queen's Lodgings, where she was held, can just be seen to the far right, stretching between the wall and the White Tower. The scaffold on Tower Hill, and the guns on the Tower wharf, are also visible.

Another romantic view: Anne Boleyn at the Queen's Stairs
'Mr Kingston, do I go to a dungeon?'

Highness that she might have the Sacrament in the closet by her chamber, that she might pray for mercy'. Certainly arrangements were immediately made for her to take Holy Communion that evening, because on 7 May she would recall, 'I knew of Mark's coming to the Tower that night I received the sacrament; it was ten of the clock ere he were well lodged, and I knew of Norris going to the Tower.' Evidently this was the first she had heard of these arrests. She did not, as yet, know that her brother had been taken.

She was anxious to make it clear to the Constable that there was no reason why she should not receive the Sacrament. 'My God, bear witness there is no truth in these charges,' she declared to him, 'for I am as clear from the company of man as from sin, [and] as I am clear from you; and am the King's true wedded wife! Master Kingston, do you know wherefore I am here?'

'Nay,' Kingston replied, doubtless as he had been told to do. Cromwell was no doubt working on the premise that the less Anne knew, the more she might reveal.

'When saw you the King?' Anne persisted.

'I saw him not since I saw him in the tiltyard [on May Day],' the Constable told her.

'Master Kingston, I pray you tell me where my lord my father is,' Anne demanded to know.

'I saw him afore dinner in the court,' Kingston replied. Working herself up into what Cavendish called 'the storms of deep desperation',[39] she cried, 'Oh, where is my sweet brother?' – which, in the circumstances, probably sounded pretty damning.

'I said I left him at York Place,' Kingston reported, 'and so I did.' Anne did not at this stage know of the shameful charge that was soon to be laid against her and her brother, and she was perhaps hoping that Rochford would speak to the King on her behalf and stoutly defend her. She must also have imagined his distress when he heard of her arrest – and, of course, there is always the remote possibility that she had indeed committed incest with him, and knew that there was much to fear. Her next words, coming immediately after her question about her brother, suggest that the awful truth might have been dawning on her.

'I hear say that I should be accused with three men,' Anne said, 'and I can say no more but nay, without I should open my body.' And so saying, 'she opened her gown', spreading her skirts in a dramatic and symbolic gesture, saying, 'Oh, Norris, hast thou accused me? Thou art in the Tower with me, and thou and I shall die together.' Her words reveal her awareness of the fate that might well await her, and her reference to dying together supports the theory that she was close to Sir Henry, but not necessarily in an intimate way, although her enemies would see it in that light.

Then her thoughts turned to the other named man accused with her. 'And Mark, thou art here too,' she said, becoming agitated again. 'Oh, my mother, thou wilt die for sorrow,' she wept, 'with much compassion', as it struck her how badly the news of her arrest, with all its dread and shocking implications, would affect that lady, for just two weeks earlier, Elizabeth Howard, Countess of Wiltshire, had been described by one of Lady Lisle's correspondents as being 'sore diseased with the cough, which grieves her sore'[40] – and indeed, she was to die just two years later. Anne would have been aware of how ill she was.

Maybe the thought of her mother was too much to bear, for she quickly changed the subject and 'much lamented my lady of Worcester, because her child did not stir in her body'. The Countess of Worcester, of course, had been the first person to lay evidence against Anne.

'What should be the cause?' Lady Kingston asked.

'It was for the sorrow she took for me,' Anne told her, referring perhaps to her miscarriage, or to the fear and misery she had suffered over the intervening weeks, which she had perhaps confided to the Countess. It might also have been remorse over having been pressured into betraying her mistress; and as a consequence of that, there would be even more cause for Elizabeth

Browne to feel sorrow and guilt, because her sister-in-law, Elizabeth Somerset, was married to William Brereton,[41] who had been named by Smeaton as one of the Queen's lovers.

Then Anne turned to the Constable. 'Master Kingston, shall I die without justice?' she asked.

'The poorest subject of the King hath justice,' he replied, provoking bitter laughter in the Queen, who knew very well that persons accused of high treason were rarely acquitted, especially if it were known that the King wanted them condemned. She must have been aware that her enemies were out for her blood – and she knew that her husband was the most suggestible of men. She would have known also that her protestations of innocence would avail her little, for the law did not allow her access to any lawyer or adviser, or any legal representative who could speak for her in court.[42]

Anne was already doomed. There was no way that Henry VIII or his advisers were going to risk a repeat performance of what had happened when the King had tried to set aside Katherine of Aragon. She had not gone quietly, but had held her ground and stood up for her rights for nine tortuous years, maintaining – even after he had had their marriage annulled and married Anne – that she was the King's true wife and her daughter his lawful heir. Anne might be unpopular, but she still had a number of powerful relatives and supporters of the reformist persuasion, who might make trouble on her behalf. The way had to be cleared for the King to make a third, undisputed marriage, and that could only be achieved literally over Anne's dead body.[43]

By nightfall on 2 May, most people at court had learned of the Queen's arrest. Never before had a queen of England been charged with adultery and imprisoned in the Tower. Chapuys was almost jubilant, and at once penned a somewhat self-congratulatory letter to the Emperor:

Your Majesty will be pleased to recollect what I wrote to you early in the last month touching the conversation between Cromwell and myself about the divorce of this King from the Concubine. I accordingly used several means to promote the matter, both with Cromwell and with others, of which I have not hitherto written, awaiting some certain issue of the affair, which in my opinion has come to pass much better than anybody could have believed, to the great disgrace of the Concubine, who, by the judgement of God, has been brought in full daylight from Greenwich to the Tower of London, conducted by the Duke of Norfolk, the two chamberlains, of the realm and of the Chamber, and only four women have been left to her.

Chapuys was convinced that the Almighty had ordained Anne's fall in vengeance for the wrongs she had inflicted on the late Queen Katherine and the Lady Mary, and he felt no pity whatsoever for her. He went on:

The report is that it is for adultery, in which she has long continued with a player on the spinet of her chamber, who has been this morning lodged in the Tower, [along with] Master Norris, the most private and familiar body servant of the King, for not having revealed these matters.

Chapuys obviously did not as yet know that Norris had also been accused of adultery with the Queen, but he had heard that

the brother of the Concubine, called Rochford, has also been taken to the Tower, but more than six hours after the others, and three or four hours before his sister.[44]

The ambassador had no doubt at this stage that Anne was guilty as charged; this dramatic — and fortuitous — new development only served to confirm his low opinion of her. He had guessed that her days as queen were numbered.

> Even if the said crime of adultery had not been discovered, this King, as I have been for some days informed by good authority, had determined to abandon her.

He then went on to inform the Emperor of the abortive plan to have the union annulled on the grounds that Anne had secretly married the Earl of Northumberland some years earlier.

> These news are indeed new, but it is still more wonderful to think of the sudden change from yesterday to today, and the manner of [Anne's] departure from Greenwich to come hither [i.e. to the City of London, where Chapuys had his house], but I forbear particulars not to delay the bearer, by whom you will be amply informed.[45]

This dispatch shows that Chapuys, for all his connections at court and his efforts to further Imperialist interests and befriend Cromwell, was not quite at the centre of affairs, and was certainly not kept informed of everything that was going on in the privy apartments and the council chamber. Yet he had been able to discover, or had been fed, certain information, such as that which concerned Northumberland's possible precontract with Anne.

Sir Francis Bryan was to reveal in June that, 'upon the disclosing of the matter of the Queen', Sir Nicholas Carew, Sir Anthony Browne, Sir Thomas Cheyney, Knight of the Body to the King, 'and the rest of his fellows of the Privy Chamber [were heard] saying that they rejoiced that the King had escaped this great peril and danger, and that the issue the King might have, if he took another wife, should be out of all doubt'.[46] Out of all doubt also, in their minds, was the Queen's fate.

Most people appear to have agreed with Chapuys and Bryan

that Anne was guilty, including the populace at large. Her dismal progress along the river had drawn much interest, while Cromwell's agents may have been at work spreading the official version of events, and very soon – within a matter of hours – the sensational news of her arrest and imprisonment was all around London. 'The City rejoiced on hearing the report, hoping that the Princess would be restored.'[47]

That the story became somewhat garbled and embroidered in the process, and that there was little doubt of what the outcome would be, is clear from a letter written from London on 2 May by a panic-stricken Roland Buckley (or Bulkeley), a poor lawyer of Gray's Inn, to his brother, Sir Richard Buckley, Norris's friend, who enjoyed some influence with the King, but who, in his capacity as Knight-Chamberlain of North Wales and deputy to Norris, had made an enemy of the powerful Brereton:

> Sir, ye shall understand that the Queen is in the Tower, the Earl of Wiltshire, her father, my Lord Rochford, her brother, Master Norris of the King's Privy Chamber, one Master Mark of the King's Privy Chamber, with divers other sundry ladies. The cause of their committing there is of certain high treason committed concerning their Prince, that is to say that Master Norris should have ado with the Queen, and Mark and the other [be] accessories to the same. They are like to suffer, all there, more is the pity, if it pleased God. Otherwise I pray you make you ready in all the haste that can be, and come down to your Prince, for you yourself may do more [i.e. to intercede for the accused] than twenty men in your absence; therefore make haste, for ye may be there ere only a word be of their death. When it is once known that they shall have died, all will be too late, therefore make haste!

Some details reported by Buckley were incorrect: Anne's father had not been arrested, nor had any ladies. It is often assumed that

Buckley, anticipating that rich pickings would be had in the wake of the arrests, wanted to ensure that Sir Richard got his share, but it is more likely that he was urging Sir Richard to hasten to London in order to use his influence on behalf of Norris; Cromwell evidently thought that to be his purpose, for Buckley's courier was halted at Shrewsbury, relieved of his letter and clapped into gaol. The letter was forwarded to Cromwell, and Sir Richard never knew how nearly he was embroiled in the political drama that was being acted out in London. Within three months he would have attached himself to the Seymours.[48]

Had Roland Buckley been obeying a chivalrous impulse to champion Anne's cause, or that of the men accused with her, his would have been virtually a lone voice, for Anne had never been popular; she had few powerful friends in England or abroad to speak up for her, and now hardly anyone was prepared to make any protest at her arrest. Most people appear to have believed – or to have affected to believe – that Anne was capable of the crimes of which she had been accused, and even that it had been her 'full intent lineally to succeed to this imperial crown'.[49]

From the time of Anne's committal to the Tower, Henry VIII's behaviour was typical of a man who has been confronted with appalling evidence of his wife's infidelity, and whose masculine pride has been deeply wounded. He avoided parading his humiliation in public, and remained incommunicado until all was over.[50]

Henry was apparently ready to believe anything of Anne. He would shortly manifest the conviction that she was a monster not only of lechery but also of cruelty. The latter was, to him, probably entirely credible. She had hounded Wolsey nigh unto death; she had repeatedly urged Henry to send Katherine of Aragon and Mary, his own daughter, to the scaffold; she had been ruthless against her enemies. Five years earlier, rumour had placed her faction behind an attempt to poison John Fisher, Bishop of Rochester, an outspoken and upright opponent of the Boleyns;

and only a couple of months ago, it had been bruited that Katherine of Aragon had been poisoned, and that Anne was the culprit. Now it appeared that she had plotted to do away with the King himself, her own husband. That certainly gave Henry a jolt, and his imagination began to run riot. When his bastard son, the seventeen-year-old Henry FitzRoy, Duke of Richmond, came on the evening of 2 May to receive his father's blessing before retiring for the night, 'the King began to weep, saying that he and his sister [the Lady Mary] were greatly bound to God for having escaped the hands of that accursed whore, who had determined to poison them'.[51] These tears were the only ones that Henry is known to have shed in connection with Anne Boleyn's fall,[52] while his tirade betrayed his conviction that she was guilty of far worse than adultery, and the sharp-minded Chapuys picked up on this: 'From these words, it would appear the King knows something about it.'[53]

When Richmond unexpectedly died the following month of what was probably a suppurating pulmonary infection (rather than the tuberculosis that has traditionally been blamed for his demise), that would no doubt have reinforced the opinions of Henry and others, who 'thought he was privily poisoned by the means of Queen Anne and her brother, Lord Rochford, for he pined inwardly in his body long before he died. God knoweth the truth thereof.'[54] In fact, Richmond's final illness was short and unexpected, and developed far too late to have been the consequence of poison.

8

'Stained in Her Reputation'

As soon as they heard of her arrest, Anne's family and supporters sought to distance themselves from her, and effectively abandoned her to her fate. Aless recalled reactions in London:

> Those who were present well know how deep was the grief of all the godly, how loud the joy of the hypocrites, the enemies of the Gospel, when the report spread in the morning that the Queen had been thrown in the Tower. They will remember the tears and lamentations of the faithful, who were lamenting over the snare laid for the Queen, and the boastful triumph of the foes of the true doctrine. I remained a sorrowful man at home, waiting for the result, for it was easy to perceive that, in the event of the Queen's death, a change of religion was inevitable.

One influential member of her circle who did feel some sympathy for Anne Boleyn, and shock at her fall, was Thomas Cranmer, Archbishop of Canterbury since 1533, when he had controversially declared Queen Katherine's marriage null and void, and Anne's valid. A former chaplain to the Boleyns, and a closet

Protestant, he had done much to promote reform within the Church of England, a cause very dear to Anne's heart and his own.

On the day of the Queen's arrest, Cromwell sent a letter to Cranmer, who was then at his palace at Knole in Kent, informing him that his former patroness was in the Tower and that the King wished him to go to Lambeth Palace, the London residence of the archbishops of Canterbury, there to await his pleasure. Henry intended for Cranmer to find grounds for the annulment of his marriage to Anne. It was unthinkable that he could have lawfully been married to such a woman, and unthinkable too that the office of Queen of England should be brought into such disrepute, but on a more practical level, Anne's daughter Elizabeth, whose right to succeed to the throne was enshrined in the Act of Succession of 1534, could not be allowed to stand in the way of any heirs that Jane might bear Henry. Thus Henry wanted Archbishop Cranmer to find a pretext for dissolving this marriage that he had found to be good and valid just three years earlier, and for declaring Elizabeth – like her half-sister Mary before her – a bastard.

No one thought – or dared – to point out (as Bishop Burnet did one hundred and fifty years later) that the two concurrent lines of proceedings against the Queen – the one to prove marriage unlawful and invalid, the other to prove her adultery – were incompatible.[1] It would have made little difference to the outcome, however, for there remained that charge of plotting the King's death, which was high treason by anyone's reckoning.

Cranmer was shocked to hear the news of Anne's arrest. He returned to Lambeth at once, as he had been instructed, but he knew – because Cromwell had told him so – that it was pointless trying to obtain an audience with the King. So he did the next best thing. On 3 May, in evident distress – not only on Anne's account but also, probably, because he feared that, with her influence removed, Henry might proceed no further in the cause of religious reform, or even abandon it – he wrote cautiously to the King to express his astonishment at the Queen's crimes, his forlorn hope that she would be proved innocent, and his loyalty to his master – and to soothe Henry's wounded ego. His opening words – the first of which strangely presage the eloquent Liturgy in his future *Book of Common Prayer* – suggest he was aware that his master was distressed by the recent revelations regarding the Queen, which is perhaps further evidence that Henry had taken them seriously:

> I dare not presume to come to your presence, in accordance with the Secretary's letters, but of my bounden duty I beg you somewhat to suppress the deep sorrows of your Grace's heart and take adversity patiently. I cannot deny that you have great causes of heaviness, and that your honour is highly touched. God never sent you a like trial.

Cranmer did not attempt to dispute the charges, although clearly he found them hard to believe, having served as household chaplain to the Boleyns, and having known Anne very well since 1529.[2] Nevertheless, he wrote on the premise that they were justified:

> If what has been reported openly of the Queen be true, it is only to her dishonour, not yours. My mind is clean amazed, for I never had better opinion of woman, but I think your Highness would not have gone so far if she had not been culpable. Next unto your Grace, I was most bound unto her of all creatures living, which her kindness bindeth me unto, and therefore beg that I may with your Grace's favour wish and pray for her, that she may declare herself inculpable and innocent. Yet if she be found guilty, I repute him not a faithful subject who would not wish her punished without mercy. And as I loved her not a little for the love which I judged her to bear towards God and the Gospel, so if she

be proved culpable, considering your Grace's goodness towards her, and from what condition your Grace of your only mere goodness took her and set the crown upon her head, and as I loved her not a little, there is not one that loveth God and His Gospel that ever will favour her, but must hate her above all other; and the more they favour the Gospel, the more they will hate her, for there was never creature in our time that so much slandered the Gospel; and God hath sent her this punishment, for that she feignedly hath professed his Gospel in her mouth, and not in heart and deed. And though she have offended so, that she hath deserved never to be reconciled unto your Grace's favour, forasmuch as your Grace's favour to the Gospel was not led by affection unto her, but by zeal unto the truth.

Cranmer had all but finished this letter when he was summoned to the Star Chamber, a tribunal distinct from the King's Council, being comprised of privy councillors and judges, their functions being to hear petitions, try offences against the Crown, and ensure that justice was fairly enforced against the high-born and the powerful. This court took its name from the ceiling decoration of the chamber in the Palace of Westminster where it sat. Cranmer met there with Audley, Sandys, Oxford and Sussex. Their purpose was to show the Archbishop the evidence that had been laid against the Queen and pre-empt him from speaking out on her behalf. It seems that they managed to convince him of her guilt, for on his return to Lambeth he added a postscript to his letter to the King:[3]

I am exceedingly sorry that such faults can be proved by the Queen, as I heard of their relation, but I am, and ever shall be, your faithful subject.[4]

He was to demonstrate that in the dark days to come, in which it would become clear that his affection and admiration for Anne counted for little against his desire to please the King, his sense of self-preservation, and his zeal for reform. But Cranmer was in a difficult position. He must have been well-aware that the Queen's fall might impact on him, the man who had facilitated her marriage to the King, and that the cause that he and she had espoused so dearly might well suffer if he chose to champion her, which might prove fatal for him as well as for her. With Jane Seymour being courted by the Imperialists, Cranmer needed to survive to fight for the cause another day. Anne would have to be abandoned. He had no choice.

Chapuys also wrote a letter of condolence to Henry VIII at this time. He enclosed a copy of it with his dispatch of 6 June, and forwarded it to the Emperor, explaining that he had sent it to the King 'a little after the arrest of the Lady', having beforehand shown it to Cromwell, who altered nothing. The King, he declared, was pleased with it.[5]

Kingston had received specific orders from Cromwell, who had 'commanded me to charge the gentlewomen that give their attendance upon the Queen, they should have no communication with her unless my wife were present'. However, it had become clear on Anne's first night there that it would be impossible to enforce this rule, as he reported to Master Secretary the next morning: 'And so I did it, notwithstanding it cannot be so, for my Lady Boleyn and Mistress Coffin lie on the Queen's pallet and I and my wife at the door without [presumably also on pallet beds], so that they must needs talk that be within; but I have everything told me by Mistress Coffin that she thinks meet for you to know, and together two gentlewomen lies without me, and as I may know the King's pleasure in the premises, I shall follow.'[6]

Kingston's words about Mrs Coffin undermine the theory that 'Cromwell had not expected to get anything incriminating out of the Queen after her arrest'.[7] Mrs Coffin had clearly been well briefed, her sinister purpose being to extract whatever she could from Anne, who, in her agitated state, was inclined to be garrulous and indiscreet. Mrs Coffin had been instructed to question her about the conversation she had had with Sir Henry Norris the previous Sunday, 30 April, and on the morning of 3 May, 'as minding to inquire of her concerning the occasion of her present trouble', she asked Anne how it had come to pass that Sir Henry Norris 'did say unto the Queen's almoner that he would swear for the Queen that she was a good woman. Madam, why should there be any such matters spoken of?'

'Marry,' said Anne, 'I bade him do so.' She then recounted her conversation with Norris, patently anxious to set the record straight and clear herself of any suspicion of treasonable intentions. Kingston's report is damaged, and this section ends with just fragmentary details of something that Anne had 'said on Whitsun Tuesday', 25 April, '. . . that Norris came more . . . -age and further'.[8] Maybe she had had more than one encounter with Norris that could possibly be held against her.

Mrs Coffin now disclosed – as she had doubtless been told to do – that Sir Francis Weston was being questioned by the Privy Council about his relations with the Queen. Anne 'said she more feared Weston', for Weston knew about Norris's feelings for her – of which, patently, she herself and others in her circle had also been aware. She recounted to Mrs Coffin a conversation she had had with Weston on Whit Monday, 24 April,[9] when she had had occasion to reprove him for flirting with Madge Shelton, Norris's betrothed, and wondered aloud to him why Norris had not yet married her. Weston confided to Anne that Norris 'came more to her chamber for her than for Madge'.[10]

Anne need not have worried that Weston would testify against her, for he protested to the Council that day that he was innocent of any criminal congress with the Queen. It would not save him from arrest, though.

Later that day – Kingston reported it in a postscript to his first letter to Cromwell, written 'from the Tower this morning' on the 3rd – Anne told Mrs Coffin that she had teased Weston 'because he did love her kinswoman Mrs [Madge] Shelton, and that she said he loved not his wife', to which Weston had daringly 'made answer that he loved one in her house better than them both'. 'Who is that?' Anne had asked. 'It is yourself,' Weston replied, whereupon Anne 'defied him', as she told Kingston.[11] Such exchanges were typical courtly repartee, and probably meant very little, but these conversations 'were now twisted to their worst meaning'.[12] Taken literally, as Cromwell and others would choose to interpret them, these and Anne's other flirtatious remarks made to Norris were to prove highly damaging to her, for they enabled Master Secretary to construct a stronger case against her.

The atmosphere at court was understandably tense as people wondered what might happen next. Anne's receiver-general, George Taylor, and her sewer, Harry Webb, were in fear for their lives, lest they should be accused next; and when all was over, Taylor was visibly relieved.[13] Even Bryan, once the Queen's supporter, apparently came under suspicion. He had left court in April, but now received a 'marvellous peremptory command-ment' to return 'on his allegiance', and was questioned by Cromwell. Satisfied as to his disaffection from Anne, Master Secretary wrote to Stephen Gardiner, Bishop of Winchester, informing him that the 'Vicar of Hell' had abandoned her.[14] After that, Bryan was one of the few privileged persons who were allowed to see the King.

Cromwell had a substantial number of persons bound over under the threat of heavy fines to present themselves before him or the Privy Council should they be so required, thus adding to the climate of fear and suspicion that now pervaded the court. It may be that the councillors did suspect that others were impli-cated in the Queen's treasonable activities, and that they were spreading their net of investigation wider. Some of their targets may have been people whom Cromwell believed could be prevailed upon to furnish evidence against Anne; or perhaps he meant to intimidate those who might have spoken up for her into fearing that they too would be arrested, and thus to ensure their silence and that of anyone else who was thinking of protesting at the treatment being meted out to her.[15]

Further evidence of Sir William FitzWilliam's involvement in the investigations against Anne appears in a mutilated (and therefore incomplete) letter sent to him on 3 May by Anne's chamberlain, Sir Edward Baynton, obviously in response to one that FitzWilliam had sent him. Baynton was in charge of the Queen's Privy Chamber, her personal household, and all those who served in it, and after he had gone to FitzWilliam and Cromwell with his suspicions about Anne's conversation with Norris on 30 April, he had evidently been enlisted to gather evidence against his mistress, and was clearly eager to distance himself from her by assisting zealously in the investigation against her. His letter reveals that he had in fact discovered nothing further:

Mr Treasurer,
      This shall be to advertise you that here is much communication that no man will confess anything against her, but alonely Mark of any actual thing. Wherefore (in my foolish conceit) it should much touch the King's honour if it should no further appear. And I cannot believe but that the other two be as fully culpable as ever was he. And I think assuredly the one keepeth the other's counsel. As many conjectures in my mind causeth me to think specially of the communication that was last between the Queen and Master Norris. Mr Almoner [John Skip, the Queen's confessor] told me as I would I might speak with Master Secretary and you together [to] more plainly express my opinion . . . if case be that they have confessed like wret[ches?] . . . all things as they should do than my n . . . at a point. I have mused much at the conduct of Mistress Margery which hath used herself

strangely toward me of late, being her friend as I have been. But no doubt it cannot be but that she must be of counsel therewith, there hath been great friendship between the Queen and her of late. I hear further that the Queen standeth stiffly in her opinion that she would not be convicted, which I think is in the trust that she hath in the other two [i.e. Norris and Rochford]. But if your business be such . . . not come, I would gladly come and wait . . . ke it request.

From Greenwich . . . morning.[16]

Baynton's observation that it would greatly touch the King's honour if only Smeaton confessed to adultery with Anne has incorrectly been interpreted as meaning that it was the adultery that impugned the King's honour[17] rather than the failure of the inquiries into the conduct of the Queen to unearth any better evidence than this. Asserting that Baynton's remarks only make sense if they are taken to refer to the deformed foetus that Warnicke supposes Anne to have delivered three months earlier is stretching credibility too far.[18]

What survives of Baynton's letter suggests that 'Mistress Margery' was a lady who had lately grown very close to the Queen, and that she had been advised or warned to be wary of Sir Edward's investigations; it is likely that this was Margery Horsman. Court gossip about that lady might have given rise to the tale of the 'Margaret' referred to in the 'Spanish Chronicle', who had supposedly brought Mark Smeaton to the Queen's bed.

Baynton clearly thought that Margery Horsman had been the Queen's confidante in the latter's illicit affairs, but if so, she was never arrested. In fact, she would go on to serve Anne's successor, Jane Seymour,[19] so it is almost certain that Baynton was mistaken.

Baynton evidently believed Norris and Rochford had made a pact not to admit to anything under questioning, and had kept to it; and he knew that Anne was protesting her innocence. He may not have known that Norris had already made a confession of sorts; his reference to there being 'much communication' in the Queen's household that Smeaton alone had confessed reflects only what people were saying, not what he knew. Clearly he himself had been questioned, and now felt it his duty to report every little bit of gossip and opinion that might prove useful.

Throughout the time that Anne was in the Tower, the King did not appear in public, and saw only his closest advisers and intimates. Cranmer's remark in his letter about not daring to come into the royal presence 'in accordance with the Secretary's letters' suggests that access to Henry was being strictly controlled by Cromwell.[20] Alexander Aless would recount how a servant of Cromwell later told him that the King had given orders 'that none but the councillors and secretaries should be admitted' to his presence, 'and that the gate of the country house in which he had secluded himself should be kept locked'. Probably Henry – and certainly Cromwell – wanted to pre-empt those who might dare to speak up on the Queen's behalf,[21] but there were probably other reasons why the King wanted privacy at this time.

For fourteen days, from 5 to 19 May, 'his Grace came not abroad, except it were in the garden, and in his boat at night, at which times it may become no man to prevent him'.[22] But that was not the whole of it: Chapuys reported on the 19th that 'the King has shown himself more glad than ever since the arrest of the Concubine, for he has been going about banqueting with ladies, sometimes remaining after midnight, and returning by the river. Most part of the time he was accompanied by various musical instruments and, on the other hand, by the singers of his chamber, which many interpret as his delight at getting rid of a thin, old and vicious hack in the hope of getting soon a fine horse to ride.' The 'hope of change', he added, 'is a thing specially agreeable to this King'.[23] Chapuys did not believe those who informed him that the King had said publicly 'that he has no desire in the world to marry again'.

The ambassador also wrote that reports of these jaunts 'sounded ill in the ears of the people',[24] and Henry's behaviour at this time has since earned the condemnation of historians, who deem it in bad taste, but the King may have been driven by embarrassment, shame, self-deception and self-pity, rather than by guilt or callousness. All the evidence suggests that he accepted the charges against Anne without question, but doing so meant that, for the first time in his charmed life, he would be publicly branded a cuckold. For a man of his vanity, reputation and status, that must have been humiliating in the extreme, however pragmatically one looked at it. How could he have faced his subjects in such circumstances, especially with speculation rife about the Queen's infidelities? It may have taken him several days to come to terms with her betrayal. In the meantime, he was doing his best to bolster his pride and give the impression of rampant virility as best he knew how, in surrounding himself with a bevy of beautiful women – but only at a distance from his subjects.

It is hardly likely that Henry's bashfulness was informed by guilt. He was the King, he did not need to justify his actions before his people, and since Parliament had named him Supreme Head of the Church of England under Christ, he had become increasingly self-righteous and sanctimonious. The evidence suggests that the charges against Anne had been laid before him unheralded, and that he believed them; and even if he had been the prime mover in the plot to bring Anne down, then probably he felt that his actions had been justified by what Cromwell had uncovered.

It may be that Henry felt uncomfortable about destroying the woman whom he had once loved to distraction and who was the mother of his child, and that he was seeking refuge in pleasure jaunts in order to distract himself; or that his merrymaking with a bevy of ladies by night was intended to deflect public interest from Jane Seymour, the real object of his intentions.[25]

In Tudor times, most people would have agreed that a queen who had committed such crimes as were imputed to Anne Boleyn

unquestioningly deserved death. But Henry clearly felt that people
might be more convinced of her guilt if Jane Seymour were not
in evidence. On 4 May, Chapuys reported from London that the
King, 'to cover the affection which he has for the said [Jane]
Seymour ['Semel'], has lodged her seven miles hence in the house
of the Grand Esquire', Sir Nicholas Carew.[26] This was Beddington
Park in Surrey. Carew's offer of accommodation for Jane at a
discreet distance from London shows that he was manoeuvring
alongside Bryan, Cromwell, Chapuys and others to make her
queen. Beddington Park[27] was a magnificent house built around
1500 and sited in a large park. Its great hall – on which the
impressive hall at Hampton Court is said to have been modelled
– still survives today. The fact that it was inconveniently situated
for a king who was avoiding appearing in public suggests that
the decision to move Jane there was a rushed one. Beddington
was some seven miles from the Thames at its nearest point in
Fulham, and thus inaccessible by barge.

We might wonder what part Jane Seymour had played in
bringing Anne down. Nothing is known of her involvement, if
any, in the plot against her mistress, apart from the fact that, since
late March, encouraged and endorsed by her supporters, she had
been actively poisoning Henry's mind against Anne. When Henry
made it clear that he wanted to marry her, she must have known
that the Queen's removal would be necessary. Yet even when it
became clear that this would be by more brutal means than the
annulment of a marriage, Jane apparently did not flinch from her
chosen course, nor betray any trace of guilt.

Of course, it could be argued that she would have been
powerless in the face of the King's will, but Jane was not without
ambition or a streak of ruthlessness. She had embarked on her
campaign to snare Henry knowing fully what she was doing, and
she was clearly convinced of the rightness of it. For Anne, she seems
to have had no pity whatsoever: to Jane, as to all the Imperialists,
Anne was the woman who had been the chief cause of the

sufferings of the late Queen Katherine and the Lady Mary. Probably Jane had no difficulty in believing the charges against Anne, and regarded the proceedings against her as justified. Yet it must have occurred to her that the laying of such charges was all too conveniently timely.

Chapuys was apparently in touch with Jane and her friends at this time. He was certainly aware that she was anticipating becoming Henry's wife, for he had heard that, 'even before the arrest of the Concubine, the King had spoken with Mistress Seymour of their future marriage'. This could have been at any time after Jane was installed in her brother's apartment at the end of March, but – since the King would have made himself ridiculous by forcing Charles V and the Pope to recognise Anne and then abandoning her for someone else – it is likely to have been far more recently, after Henry had seen compelling evidence of Anne's misconduct. Resolving to marry again 'on the rebound' was perhaps, for him, a way of saving face, apart from being a dynastic necessity.

Chapuys added that, on this occasion, Jane had bravely brought up the touchy subject of the Lady Mary, and told Henry that when she was queen, she hoped to see Mary reinstated as heiress to the throne. This hit Henry on a raw nerve and he became terse and imperious, telling her that she was a fool who 'ought to solicit the advancement of the children they would have together, and not any others'. Undeterred, Jane answered that she did think of them, but also of Henry's peace of mind, for unless he showed justice to Mary, Englishmen would never be content.[28] It sounds as if she had been groomed to speak up for Mary in this way, even though she must have shared these sentiments, while to venture what amounted to criticism of the King's policy towards his daughter took some courage. 'I will endeavour by all means to make her continue in this vein,' Chapuys wrote. 'I hope also to go and speak with the King within three days, and with members of the Council in general. I think the Concubine's little bastard

Elizabeth will be excluded from the succession, and that the King
will get himself requested by Parliament to marry.'[29]

In speaking up for Mary, Jane would win through in the end,
but not before Henry had exacted from his daughter a humiliating apology for her defiance. That lay weeks in the future,
though, and by then, Anne Boleyn would be history.

On the afternoon of 4 May, the day after Jane arrived at
Beddington, Sir Francis Weston was arrested, probably as a result
of Anne's indiscreet speech, along with William Brereton.[30] The
charges against Brereton were not made public – 'What was laid
against him I do not know, nor ever heard,' Constantine later
wrote – but he would be accused, like the rest, of having had
criminal intercourse with the Queen, possibly on the evidence
extracted from Smeaton; the delay in arresting him may have
resulted from his being away from court. Both men had been
questioned by the Privy Council and, having failed to convince
the lords of their innocence, were incarcerated in the Tower before
two o'clock.[31]

George Constantine, Norris's servant, was haunting the court,
no doubt hoping to pick up any helpful information or gossip.
At nine o'clock that morning, he had spoken to William Brereton
before the latter was taken away, and Brereton confided to him
'that there was no way but one with any matter alleged against
him'. Constantine took him to mean that he was innocent; he
never found out what, if any, evidence was laid against him.

It seems almost certain that the men arrested on the Queen's
account were housed separately in the Tower. The name 'Boullen'
was roughly carved into the stonework of the thirteenth-century
Martin Tower beneath a rose – such as appeared on Anne's falcon
badge – and the letter 'H'; this was possibly the work of George
Boleyn, who, according to tradition, was imprisoned here. This
tradition may be based on fact, as noble prisoners were sometimes allocated a whole tower in order to house their servants,

and the Martin Tower is known to have been used as a prison in Tudor times. Each of its circular floors had a large single room with window embrasures and a stone fireplace; the walls were not panelled until the seventeenth century.[32] Unfortunately, the carving was damaged by fire in the nineteenth century.[33] Anne's falcon badge — minus its crown and sceptre — is the subject of another carving in the west wall of a first-floor cell in the thirteenth-century Beauchamp Tower,[34] suggesting that another of her alleged lovers was held there. It was this carving that perhaps gave rise to the ancient tradition that Anne herself was imprisoned in the Beauchamp Tower.

The next day, Friday, 5 May, saw the final arrests, those of the poet Thomas Wyatt, a privy councillor and diplomat, and Sir Richard Page.[35] Page, who had been knighted in 1529, was a former secretary to Cardinal Wolsey,[36] who had secured his promotion to the Privy Chamber in 1528; this had profited Wolsey little, since the opportunistic Page soon afterwards transferred his loyalty to the Cardinal's enemies, the Boleyns, and later, from about 1530, to the rising star Cromwell. Having been Recorder of York from 1527 to 1533, Page was vice-chamberlain to the Duke of Richmond and clearly well thought of by the King,[37] who appointed him captain of his own bodyguard. His wife, Elizabeth Bourchier, was a cousin to Henry VIII.

Page had been a conspicuous friend to Anne Boleyn, gladly performing several small services for her, which — according to a list of debts owed by her in 1536 — she rewarded with gifts and other marks of favour.[38] Perhaps sensing danger afoot, he had left the court at the end of April for his home in Surrey; his absence probably accounts for his not being committed to the Tower at the same time as the other accused.

Page was of far less significance than Wyatt. Of all the men imprisoned with Anne Boleyn, Thomas Wyatt is the one for whom there is the most evidence of a romantic attachment, several years before, although it appears that his love was unrequited.[39] In *Tottel's Miscellany*, in which his poems were first published in 1557, much is made of the affair, probably exaggerating its importance[40] and giving rise to centuries of speculation. This resulted in Catholic writers hostile to Anne making propagandist capital (much of it obscene) out of her alleged involvement with Wyatt. But what was the truth of the matter?

Cambridge-educated Wyatt, now aged about thirty-two, was an accomplished and intelligent man, a handsome dreamer who charmed women and who later admitted that he had led an unchaste life.[41] Anne must have known Wyatt and his family in childhood; their families lived near each other in Kent, their fathers were long-standing friends, and they would have moved in the same social circles. Anne and her brother George shared a love of poetry with Wyatt, who was to become one of England's greatest poets.

References in some of Wyatt's poems, as well as his grandson George Wyatt's testimony, make it clear that, captivated by Anne's beauty and her witty and graceful speech, he fell in love – or became infatuated – with her before Henry VIII laid claim to her. This must have been around 1525–6, for Henry's interest was rampant by Shrovetide 1526, when he appeared at a tournament wearing a magnificent suit of clothing embroidered in gold with the words *Declare I dare not* – a courtly conceit proclaiming him the humble admirer of a lady who might disdain his advances. Wyatt was also pursuing Anne at this time, but she 'rejected all his speech of love' because he was married, and had been for ten years, albeit unhappily, to a notorious adulteress, Elizabeth Brooke. All the same, Anne did not stoop to scorning him, and Wyatt continued to hope.[42]

Many decades later, George Wyatt wrote that his grandfather had expressed his feelings for Anne Boleyn in his verse, yet today we can find very few overt references to her in his surviving poems, probably because, when the King's jealousy became manifest, the poet destroyed any that were compromising. One riddle about a disdainful mistress has the answer *Anna*, but there is no proof that it refers to Anne Boleyn. Another poem certainly does, and was written after Henry had taken her for his chosen lady and put her beyond Wyatt's – and anybody else's – reach:

> Who list her hunt, I put him out of doubt;
> As well as I may spend his time in vain.
> And graven with diamonds, in letters plain,
> There is written her fair neck round about,
> *Noli me tangere* [do not touch me], for Caesar's I am,
> And wild for to hold, though I seem tame.

Later, when Wyatt had recovered from his loss, embarked on a diplomatic career and taken a new lover, Elizabeth Darrell, who would remain his mistress until his death in 1542, he was able to look back with equanimity on his pursuit of Anne:

> Then do I love again;
> If thou ask whom, sure since I did refrain
> Her, that did set our country in a roar,
> The unfeigned cheer of Phyllis hath the place
> That Brunette had.

Later still, deeming the third line of this poem to be too sensitive, Wyatt changed it to *Brunette, that set my wealth in such a roar*. In 1532, he would look back in verse to a time when he had 'fled the fire that me brent [burned], by sea, by land, by water and by wind'; he was surely thinking back to January 1527, when, seeing that Henry's passion for Anne grew more serious, he had begged to be allowed to join an embassy to Rome.[43] Five years on, as he accompanied the King and Anne, lately become Henry's mistress in every sense, to Calais, he could reflect with equanimity on how his desire for her was 'both sprung and spent'.

George Wyatt relates a tale of Henry VIII's rivalry with Wyatt at the time when they were both pursuing Anne. Wyatt had covertly stolen a jewel threaded on a lace from her pocket, and was cherishing it in his doublet, next to his heart. Soon afterwards, aware of Henry's interest in Anne, he was the King's opponent at bowls; both men believed they had won, and argued the toss, but there can be little doubt that they were really fencing over Anne Boleyn, for Henry had kept 'a watchful eye upon the knight, noting him more to hover about the lady, and she to keep aloof from him'.[44] Wyatt was mortified to see the King pointing to the winning cast with a finger on which was blatantly displayed one of Anne's rings.

'Wyatt, I tell thee, it is mine!' Henry insisted, smiling triumphantly. He was not talking about the cast. Thus provoked, Wyatt rashly pulled out Anne's jewel.

'If your Majesty will give me leave to measure it, I hope it will be mine!' he said meaningfully, and proceeded to measure the distance between casts with the lace, telling the King there was no doubt that he, Wyatt, was the winner.

'It may be so, but then I am deceived!' Henry snapped, and broke up the game. When, soon afterwards, it became clear that the King's intentions towards Anne were serious, Wyatt accepted defeat.

In 1530, when people began noticing that the King's brother-in-law, Charles Brandon, Duke of Suffolk, had been absent from court for 'a long time', Chapuys heard 'people say that he is banished for some time because he revealed to the King that the Lady had found her pleasure with a gentleman of the court who already has been formerly dismissed, and this last time people have avoided him at the instance of the said lady, who has waxed very courageous by him; but at last the King has been interceded to by her that the said gentleman return to court'.

The dubious evidence of later Catholic writers has led several historians to conclude that Chapuys was referring to Thomas Wyatt, but the details in the ambassador's report are at variance with that identification. Wyatt had never been dismissed from court; he had been abroad — at his request — on a prolonged embassy from 1526–7, and had been appointed High Marshal of Calais in 1529, a position of honour. Nor is there any evidence of Anne having an affair with any man then at court, or of a previous sex scandal involving her. And although Henry, having banished the man, is supposed to have given in to her pleas for his speedy return, he was hardly likely to have done this if he believed that she had slept with this courtier; after all, for more than four years, Anne had been holding Henry at arm's length, staunchly protesting her virtue, and telling him, 'Your wife I cannot be, your mistress I will not be.'[45]

George Wyatt asserted that Suffolk did bear 'a perpetual grudge' against the poet, the cause of which he had never uncovered, but he thought that, if Suffolk had said such a thing to the King, 'he did it upon zeal that in his conceit it was true'. That may be correct, for Suffolk had no love for Anne, who had been rude to him, while his wife, Mary Tudor, would have nothing to do with her; it is also likely that Henry would have reacted by banishing Suffolk had the Duke alleged such a thing of Anne. It looks as if Chapuys, in reporting what Suffolk had allegedly said, had relied on embroidered gossip.

By January 1533, when Anne married the King, Wyatt was still a member of her circle, and it was to him that she hinted, in February, in front of a crowd of courtiers, that she might be pregnant.[46] It was logical, given their long-standing association and former romantic connection, for Cromwell to proceed now against Wyatt as one of her adulterous lovers, but Wyatt was not a prominent member of the Boleyn faction and no threat to Cromwell or the Spanish alliance. Indeed, he was on good terms with Cromwell. It is therefore possible that he was the only one of the accused arrested on the King's initiative, Henry remembering jealously that Wyatt had pursued Anne in the past. According to the 'Spanish Chronicle', he had 'sent a message to Cromwell, that he should send for Master Wyatt and question him'.

Recently, the theory has been put forward that it was Lady Wingfield's dying revelations that led to Wyatt's apprehension,[47] because she had been at court in the early 1520s when Wyatt was pursuing Anne and could perhaps testify to what had happened between them then. (This is also the basis for the unfounded theory that Lady Wingfield was at one time blackmailing Anne.) At the time of his arrest, Wyatt himself held the Duke of Suffolk responsible for it. In 1541, he wrote, 'My lord of Suffolk himself can tell that I imputed it to him, and not only at the beginning, but even the very night before my apprehension now last.' It has been seen as significant that Suffolk was friends with Cromwell and the Wingfield family were his clients; Lady Wingfield's brother-in-law, Humphrey Wingfield, was the Duke's man of business.[48] It seems plausible that there could be a connection, but it is unlikely, because, according to Sir John Spelman, Lady Wingfield's evidence was offered at the trial of the four commoners charged with adultery with the Queen, and Wyatt was not among them. Therefore it must have related to the charges against either Norris or Brereton, because the offences said to have been committed by Weston and Smeaten allegedly took place after Lady Wingfield's death. And we might also infer from Wyatt's use of the past tense in 1541 that, while he had at the time blamed Suffolk for his arrest, he had been mistaken, or no longer did so.

Catholic writers, writing with hindsight after Anne's fall, made much of her supposed affair with Thomas Wyatt. The 'Spanish Chronicle', Sir Thomas More's admiring biographer, Nicholas Harpsfield, and the Jesuit Nicholas Sander, all intent on demonising her, assert – sometimes in salacious detail – that she and Wyatt were at one time lovers in the fullest sense.

These three sources all claim that Wyatt, not Suffolk, sought to warn the King that Anne was unchaste. The 'Spanish Chronicle' states that, when he at length was moved to confess all to the King, Henry refused to believe him.

Nicholas Harpsfield claimed to have got his story from the well-informed merchant and banker, Antonio Bonvisi, who had been a business associate of Wolsey and a friend of Sir Thomas More, and who had 'heard [it] of them that were very likely to know the truth thereof'. Clearly, though, the tale had got garbled in the telling. Harpsfield states that Wyatt dared to 'utter [his] own shame' and caution Henry that Anne was 'not meet to be coupled with your Grace . . . Her conversation hath been so loose and base; which thing I know not so much by hearsay as by my own experience, as one that have had my carnal pleasure with her.' Henry, although 'somewhat astounded', merely praised Wyatt for his honesty and charged him 'to make no more words of this matter to any man living'. It is barely credible that Henry VIII would have reacted so mildly to such serious allegations, especially considering that he was set upon making Anne his queen. Harpsfield's tale, though, was written during the reign of Mary Tudor, before Anne Boleyn's reputation had been rehabilitated, and when it was permissible, even desirable, to slander her.

Sander, of course, gave this tale great credence, and embroidered it still further with details that are nowhere else recorded, which suggests that he must have made them up. He represents Wyatt as being afraid 'if the King discovered afterwards how shameless Anne's life had been' and 'that his own life might be imperilled'; 'grievously' troubled by his conscience, he went before the Council and confessed 'that he had sinned with Anne Boleyn, not imagining that the King would ever make her his wife'.

Hearing that 'Anne Boleyn was stained in her reputation', the councillors, concerned for their sovereign's moral welfare and good name, repeated to the King 'all that Wyatt had confessed'. When Henry dismissed 'these stories [as] the invention of wicked men', and declared that he 'could affirm on oath that Anne was a woman of the purest life', Wyatt grew angry at not being believed, and told members of the Council that 'he would put it in the King's power to see with his own eyes the truth of the story, and would bring the King where he might see him enjoy her, for Anne was passionately in love with Wyatt'; there is, as has been shown, very little contemporary evidence for this last assertion. Suffolk was deputed to inform Henry of this preposterous proposal, and still – perhaps understandably – Henry 'believed it not', and 'answered that he had no wish to see anything of the kind', as Wyatt was 'a bold villain, not to be trusted'. Again, this is at variance with Henry's known regard for Wyatt. Sander claimed that Henry revealed all this to Anne, 'who shunned Wyatt' – which also is not borne out by the historical record.

George Wyatt dismissed Sander's tale as 'fiction'; he had learned that it was Sir Francis Bryan, not Wyatt, who had confessed to enjoying one of Henry's mistresses, and that the lady in question was not Anne Boleyn. Henry had pardoned Bryan and 'gave over the lady ever after to him'. George Wyatt was sure that, had Henry had cause to believe that Anne had had sex with Wyatt, he would have 'thrown her off' also. Nor is it likely that he would have allowed Wyatt to remain at court, or made him chief ewerer at her coronation in 1533, or have preferred him to the Privy Council that year. One only has to remember that, when Henry married his sixth wife, Katherine Parr, in 1543, he sent Sir Thomas Seymour, her former suitor, abroad on an extended diplomatic mission, even though he had no reason to think that Seymour had ever been Katherine's lover.

The obvious flaws and discrepancies in these stories, and the fact that they only appear in partisan Catholic sources and are at variance with the evidence in Wyatt's poems, render them highly suspect.

The 'Spanish Chronicle' also gives a detailed account of Wyatt's arrest. Summoned by Cromwell's nephew, Richard (he who had changed his name from Williams to Cromwell), Wyatt rode to

London, to York Place, where the Secretary took him aside and said, 'Master Wyatt, you will know the great love I have and always have had for you, and now I tell you it would grieve me sorely should you be guilty in the matter about which I wish to speak to you.' He then proceeded to tell Wyatt about the arrests of the Queen and her alleged lovers.

Wyatt was astounded, and immediately grasped that he himself was being implicated. Spiritedly, he declared, 'Master Secretary, by the loyalty I owe to God and the King my lord, I have nothing to fear because I have not erred even in my thoughts, for his Majesty the King well knows what I told him before he married.' Cromwell is said to have replied, 'Well, Master Wyatt, you must go to the Tower, and I promise you that I shall be your good friend.' And indeed, he would prove that, which suggests that there is some truth behind this account.

'I shall go readily because I am without stain, have no fear,' Wyatt assured him, then allowed Richard Cromwell to escort him to the Tower, which was done so discreetly that 'nobody suspected that he was under arrest'. When they arrived, Richard said to Kingston, 'Captain, Secretary Cromwell sends to beseech you to treat Master Wyatt with honour.' Kingston 'then put him in a chamber over the gate'.

This account is compatible with the other evidence, apart from the reference to Wyatt warning the King about Anne. It is quite possible that Wyatt was imprisoned where the chronicler describes, either in one of the rooms above the Byward Tower ('the Tower by the Gate') or in one of the old royal chambers above St Thomas's Tower, above the Watergate that later became known as Traitors' Gate. These chambers had been largely rebuilt by Henry VIII to provide accommodation for the Lord Great Chamberlain and the Lord Chamberlain when the court was in residence, which was rare, so they would have been empty. But given that Wyatt was to watch the executions on Tower Hill from a window, it is more likely that he was lodged in the Byward Tower.

According to the 'Spanish Chronicle', Wyatt, on reaching the Tower, wrote a letter to the King, confessing in full the details of his relations with Anne Boleyn in the years before Henry had begun to pay court to her. The chronicler reproduces the exact text of the letter:

Your Majesty knows that before you married Queen Anne Boleyn, you said to me, 'Wyatt, I wish to marry Anne Boleyn; what do you think about it?' And I told your Majesty that you should not do it, and you asked me why, and I said she was a bad woman. Your Majesty, in wrath, ordered me not to appear before you for two years. You refused to ask me my reasons, and since I could not then tell you by word of mouth, I shall do so now in writing.

It happened that one day, when the Lady Anne's father and mother were in the court eight miles from Greenwich, where, as everybody knows, they had taken up residence, that night I took horse and went there. I arrived when Anne Boleyn was in bed and went up to her chamber. When she saw me, she said, 'Lord, Master Wyatt! What are you doing here at such a late hour?' I replied, 'Lady, this heart of mine, which is so tormented, has been yours for so long that for love of you it has brought me here into your presence, thinking to receive consolation from the one who for so long has caused it such suffering.' And I went up to her as she lay in bed and kissed her, and she lay still and said nothing. I touched her breasts, and she lay still, and even when I took liberties lower down, she likewise said nothing. I began to undress, but before I had finished I heard a great stamping above her bedchamber, and straightway the lady got up and put on a skirt [kirtle?] and climbed a staircase that was behind her bed. I waited for her more than an hour, and when she came down, she would not let me approach her . . . And I tell your

Majesty that within a week I had my way with her, and
if your Majesty, when you banished me, had permitted
me to speak, I should have told you what I now write.

The authenticity of this letter is dubious, because if Wyatt's revelations were true, he is unlikely to have been spared the headsman's
axe: Henry was in no mood to make nice distinctions between
what had gone on before he married Anne and what had gone
on after; he certainly did not where Katherine Howard was
concerned. The style of the letter is suspect in itself: in writing
to the King, it would have been usual to refer to his wife as
'Queen Anne', not 'Queen Anne Boleyn'; and it is unlikely that
Wyatt would have adopted such a combative tone to the King,
given his precarious situation. There is no record of Henry
banishing Wyatt from court for two years, as we have seen.

Then we have an odd allusion to the court being eight miles
from Greenwich: York Place, then in the possession of Cardinal
Wolsey, was about that distance. The Archbishop of Canterbury's
palace at Croydon and the Bishop of London's palace at Fulham
were also within the same radius, although these two episcopal
residences were rarely visited by the court, so the chronicler was
perhaps referring to York Place; but if so, Wyatt, if he were writing
this letter, would certainly have mentioned such a great and famous
palace by name, whereas a foreigner might not. And the words
'as everybody knows' hardly needed to be uttered to a king who
had invited Anne's parents to take up residence at court. Thus we
can safely conclude that this letter was no more than a figment
of the chronicler's fevered imagination.

Neither Page nor, strangely, Wyatt was to be formally charged
with any crime; both their families petitioned successfully for
their release,[49] and it seems that Cromwell intended all along that
they should be freed, thus perhaps emphasising the 'genuine' guilt
of the rest.

There were now seven men in the Tower on Anne's account.

As if that were not bad enough, from their point of view, they were deemed to have sufficient wealth and lands to meet the charges of their imprisonment, so that the Crown need not be responsible for their maintenance while they were its guests.[50]

9

'The Most Mischievous and Abominable Treasons'

Kingston's letters to Cromwell are mostly undated, and it is not obvious in every case when they were written. His second and third letters, which were clearly scribed on different days, and later than 3 May (the day after Master Secretary had been among the councillors escorting the Queen to the Tower), both refer to Cromwell departing 'yesterday' from the Tower. We can only infer from this that Cromwell made at least two visits to the Tower to see Kingston, ensure that his instructions were being complied with, obtain information that might help his case, and personally monitor Anne's imprisonment. There is no evidence that he saw Anne herself. Cromwell was to remain mainly in London after 6 May, the day on which the King removed to Hampton Court.

Kingston's second report was probably written on the evening of 5 May, for it refers to the arrests of Wyatt and Page. He wrote to Cromwell: 'After your departing yesterday [which would explain why the Constable made no report on the 4th], Greenway, gentleman usher, came to me and [said that] Master Carew and

Master Bryan [had] commanded him in the King's name to my Lord of Rochford from my lady his wife, and the message was now more [to] see how he did; and also she would humbly [make] suit unto the King's Highness for her husband.' There is no record of her doing so; indeed, she had already laid information against him, and was the principal witness in the Crown's case.

There is something very odd about this message. The King himself – or perhaps Cromwell, in his name – had commanded Carew and Bryan to send Master Greenway to Lord Rochford on Lady Rochford's behalf, to find out how he was, and tell him that she would plead with the King for him. Why should either Henry or Cromwell show such consideration to a prisoner in the Tower suspected of treasonable – and shocking – dealings with the Queen? Especially if, as has been claimed, Jane had not laid evidence and her message betrayed genuine concern,[1] in which case it is unlikely she would have been allowed to send it. None of the other prisoners were accorded such consideration, and Weston's family in particular were active on his behalf. Was it that Jane was being sympathetically treated at court because of the invaluable assistance she had afforded the Crown, to the detriment of her marriage vows, and that she took advantage of this to salve her conscience by asking to send a solicitous message to the husband she had betrayed?

His having commanded and authorised that message implies, ludicrously, that the King knew in advance that Jane was going to plead with him for her husband's life. Unless, of course, having received royal permission to write to George, she afterwards, of her own accord, asked Carew and Bryan to assure her husband she would intercede for him with the King – an empty promise at best? Surely she must have known that her words would be reported to Henry by these men, his intimates. In either case, Jane was lying to Rochford. But he trustingly 'gave her thanks' for her message.

Visibly distressed, he asked Kingston 'at what time he should come afore the King's Council', adding, 'for I think I shall not come forth till I come to my judgement'. The prospect was too much for him, and he broke down weeping.[2] There is no evidence that he ever was interrogated by the Council, although he may have been visited by some of its members after the indictments had been drawn up (see p.245 below).[3]

Anne had now been given the dread news of Rochford's arrest by her attendants. Immediately, she sent for Kingston.

'I hear say my lord my brother is here,' she told him.

'It is truth,' he confirmed. It must have been a bitter moment, with all that Rochford's imprisonment implied impacting on Anne.

'I am very glad that we both be so nigh together,' was all she said.

Kingston then revealed that Weston and Brereton were in the Tower too, at which 'she made very good countenance. I also said Master Page and Wyatt was more, then she said, "He hath . . . won his fyst the other day and is here now but ma . . ."' Here, the letter is very badly damaged, and Anne's comments on Wyatt and Page are indecipherable.)

'I shall desire you to bear a letter from me to Master Secretary,' she told the Constable.

'Madam,' he replied, 'tell it me by word of mouth, and I will do it.' She thanked him, saying, 'I have much marvel that the King's Council comes not to me.' She clearly had been wondering why she had not been subject to further examination and, like her brother, was hoping for a chance to explain everything and clear her name. Kingston apparently did not comment. When she prophesied to him that 'we should have no rain till she were delivered out of the Tower', Kingston replied kindly, 'I pray you it may be shortly because of the fair weather.' He added to Cromwell, 'You know what I mean.' He is unlikely to have been referring to Anne's release.

During the evening of the 5th, Anne made plain her antipathy towards her attendants, grumbling to Kingston that 'the King wist

what he did when he put such two about her as my Lady Boleyn
and Mistress Coffin, for they could tell her nothing of my lord
her father nor nothing else, but she defied them all'. Having
digested the news of Rochford's arrest, she evidently feared that
her father's would be next. 'But then upon this, my Lady Boleyn
said to her, "Such desire as you have had to such tales [i.e. intrigues]
has brought you to this."' Evidently she knew her niece-by-
marriage well.

Mrs Stonor then spoke of Smeaton, observing, 'Mark is the
worst cherished of any man in the house, for he wears irons.' She
was referring to manacles or chains.

'That is because he is no gentleman,' Anne replied. She told
her avidly listening attendants that Smeaton 'was never in my
[privy] chamber but at Winchester', the previous autumn. 'There
I sent for him to play on the virginals; for there my lodging was
above the King's.' Interestingly, Smeaton was never specifically
accused of committing adultery with Anne in the autumn of 1535;
his offences were alleged to have taken place in April and May
1534 and April 1535.

'I never spake with him since but upon Saturday before May
Day [29 April 1536],' Anne went on, 'and then I found him standing
in the round window in my chamber of presence; and I asked
why he was so sad, and he answered and said it was no matter.
And then I said, "You may not look to have me speak to you as
I should do to a noble man because you be an inferior person."
"No, no," said he, "a look sufficed me; and thus fare you well."'[4]
This brief conversation may have been witnessed and seen as
suspicious, for it was only the next day that Smeaton was apprehended and taken to Cromwell's house for questioning.

These accounts of the Queen's might suggest that Smeaton
entertained romantic or lustful thoughts of Anne, but John Strype
– who saw the undamaged letters of Kingston – inferred from
the exchange that Smeaton was a haughty person – which is
borne out by other evidence – who thought that Anne did not

accord him enough respect, as their conversation perhaps bears out. Smeaton was excluded by virtue of his humble status from the play of courtly love indulged in by her circle.[5] Strype thought that Smeaton perhaps pursued Anne in order to humble her and show her that he was as worthy as any other man of her notice – for, of course, sex is sometimes a manifestation of control as much as lust. If so, the poor fool little realised that his egotistical power games would cost him his life.

Anne's thoughts were still with the men who had been imprisoned on her account. She asked Lady Kingston 'whether anybody makes their beds'.

'Nay, I warrant you,' that lady answered.

'They might make ballads well now,' Anne suggested, attempting a pun on pallet,[6] 'but there is none but Lord Rochford that can do it.'

'Yes!' disagreed Lady Kingston. 'Master Wyatt.'

'By my faith, thou hast said true,' Anne concurred, but moments later her spirits had sunk again. 'My lord my brother will die!' she wailed. She knew that he was in as great peril as she was.

Anne's conversations in the Tower reveal her to have been indiscreet, both before and after her arrest, and show her entertaining a suspicious interest in the men accused with her. It was also becoming clear, through her own revelations, that she had not kept a proper regal distance between herself and her courtiers, and thus had made herself – and them – vulnerable to accusations of impropriety.[7]

Kingston's letter is charred, so what follows – 'ne I am sure this was as . . . tt down to dinner this day' – is hard to decipher. He begins by saying that at dinner that day, he had sent a plateful of food to Norris along with 'a knave to his priest that waited upon him in the [Tower?]', but then there is a mutilated account of a conversation, probably with Norris, which may perhaps partly be construed as follows: either the knave or the priest referred to the confession he made to FitzWilliam, and '[put i]t unto him, and he answered him again . . . "[If any man wishes to make?] any thing of my confession he is worthy to have [his opinion? . . . But if he believes/accepts?] hyt [it] I defy him"; and also he desireth to have . . . favour if it may be the King's pleasure'.[8]

The writer of the 'Spanish Chronicle' claims that on 6 May, the day after Wyatt's arrest, 'they had the old woman, Margaret [the lady who had allegedly brought Smeaton to the Queen's bed] tortured, and she confessed how Mark and Master Norris and Brereton slept with the Queen, and that she contrived it so that none knew about the others. She was asked about Master Wyatt, and she said that she never saw him speak privately with the Queen, but only in public. And Secretary Cromwell was glad, because he loved Master Wyatt dearly.' That last alone is true, but there is no other evidence of a royal servant called Margaret being tortured at this time; had Margery Horsman been subject to such treatment, people would have known about it. The first recorded instance of a woman being tortured dates from 1546, when a heretic, Anne Askew, was racked in the Tower. And had Margaret been afterwards burned at the stake in the Tower,[9] people would have known about that too. The authorities could not stage a burning, even at night in the Tower, and escape people's notice. The Tower, then as now, was a community in itself, well populated, and people came and went at will.

In the Cotton MSS, in the British Library, there exists a letter headed, supposedly in Cromwell's handwriting, 'To the King from the Lady in the Tower'. First published by Lord Herbert in his *The Life and Raigne of King Henry the Eighth* in 1649, then by Bishop Burnet in 1679, and called by one nineteenth-century editor, Henry Ellis, 'one of the finest compositions in the English language', it is said to be a copy, in Cromwell's handwriting – although the similarities are purely superficial – of an original letter sent by Anne Boleyn to Henry VIII on 6 May from the Tower. Burnet says he himself found it with Sir William Kingston's letters, 'lying among Cromwell's other papers', which were collected after his death in 1540. The letter was damaged in 1731 in the fire that ravaged the Cottonian Library, and its edges remain charred, with the writing worn away in places, but the text is quite legible, and reads:

Your Grace's displeasure and my imprisonment are things so strange unto me that what to write or what to excuse I am altogether ignorant. Whereas you send unto me (willing me to confess a truth and so to obtain your favour) by such a one whom you know to be mine ancient professed enemy, I no sooner received this message by him than I rightly conceived your meaning; and if, as you say, confessing a truth indeed may procure my safety, I shall with all willingness and duty perform your command. But let not your Grace imagine that your poor wife will ever be brought to acknowledge a fault where not so much as a thought ever proceeded. And, to speak a truth, never a prince had wife more loyal in all duty and in all true affection, than you have ever found in Anne Bulen [sic.]; with which name and place I could willingly have contented myself, if God and your Grace's pleasure had so been pleased. Neither did I at any time so far forget myself in my exaltation, or received queenship, but that I always looked for such alteration as I now find. For the ground of my preferment being on no surer foundation than your Grace's fancy, the least alteration was fit and sufficient (I knew) to draw that fancy to some other subject.

You have chosen me from a low estate to be your queen and companion, far beyond my desert or desire; if then you found me worthy of such honour, good your Grace, let not any light fancy or bad counsel of my enemies withdraw your princely favour from me; neither let that stain, that unworthy stain, of a disloyal heart towards your good Grace ever cast so foul a blot on me, and on the infant Princess, your daughter.

Try me, good King, but let me have a lawful trial, and let not my sworn enemies sit as my accusers and as my judges; yea, let me receive an open trial, for my truth shall fear no open shames. Then shall you see either my innocency cleared, your suspicions and conscience satisfied, the ignominy and slander of the world stopped, or my guilt openly declared. So that, whatever God and you may determine of, your Grace may be freed from an open censure; and, mine offence being so lawfully proved, your Grace may be at liberty, both before God and man, not only to execute worthy punishment on me as an unfaithful wife, but to follow your affection already settled on that party, for whose sake I am now as I am, whose name I could some good while since have pointed to, your Grace being not ignorant of my suspicion therein.

But if you have already determined of me, and that not only my death but an infamous slander must bring you the joying of your desired happiness, then I desire of God that He pardon your great sin herein, and likewise my enemies, the instruments thereof, and that he will not call you to a strait account for your unprincely and cruel usage of me at His general judgement seat, where both you and myself must shortly appear, and in Whose just judgement I doubt not (whatsoever the world may think of me) mine innocency shall be openly known and sufficiently cleared.

My last and only request shall be that myself only may bear the burden of your Grace's displeasure, and that it may not touch the innocent souls of those poor gentlemen whom, as I understand, are likewise in strait imprisonment for my sake. If ever I have found favour in your sight, if ever the name of Anne Bulen have been pleasing in your ears, then let me obtain this request; and so I will leave to trouble your Grace any further, with mine earnest prayer to the Trinity to have your Grace in His good keeping and to direct you in all your actions.

From my doleful prison in the Tower, the 6th May,
Your most loyal and ever-faithful wife,
Anne Bulen.[10]

Although Herbert was sceptical, both Burnet and the magisterial Froude were convinced of this letter's authenticity, yet many historians over the years have expressed doubts. Agnes Strickland noticed that the handwriting differed from Anne's. James Gairdner, the Edwardian editor of the encyclopaedic *Letters and Papers of the Reign of Henry VIII*, who studied the original document, was of the opinion that 'the handwriting and style alike indicate beyond reasonable doubt' that 'this letter was not really written or composed by Anne Boleyn'. In his view, it was written decades later, in an Elizabethan hand.[11] Friedmann recorded that it 'is now generally admitted to be a forgery', while Sergeant dismissively wrote that 'all evidence for its authenticity is lacking, neither the handwriting nor the style being Anne's'.

In regard to the handwriting, which is not too dissimilar from Anne's, Henry Savage makes the point that her authenticated letters date from the late 1520s, while this was supposedly written several years later when she was under enormous stress and in great fear of her life. Jasper Ridley, while saying that no one can challenge Gairdner's opinion that the handwriting was not Anne's, thinks that the letter 'bears all the marks of Anne's character, of her spirit, her impudence and her recklessness'.[12] It is just possible that on 6 May, four days after her arrest, she was too agitated to write it herself and dictated it to someone else.[13]

The language used in the letter certainly shows it to have been contemporaneous to the sixteenth century, but it is not very consistent with the style of Anne's authenticated letters, and she normally used the form 'Anne Boleyn' rather than 'Anne Bulen', while the fact that it was allegedly kept by Cromwell is suspicious, for why would Cromwell think it desirable to keep a letter from Anne protesting her innocence? He would surely have preferred to suppress or destroy it. And he would not have referred to her in the heading as 'the Lady in the Tower' but as the Queen. It is possible that Henry had sent a message to Anne urging her to confess and so merit leniency, and that Cromwell – her 'ancient professed enemy' – had conveyed this message when he visited the Tower, although there is no evidence for this in Kingston's reports or anywhere else.

Anne's injured, pious and reproving tone would surely have outraged Henry. 'Every word is a sting, envenomed by the sense of intolerable wrong.'[14] In asserting that her enemies were the instruments of his great sin, and that she was in the Tower on Jane Seymour's account, Anne was effectively saying that he had instigated this plot against her with the sole purpose of marrying Jane. Her provocative remarks about his changeable fancy might have been true, but they were tantamount to accusing him of fickleness and, along with her implication that he might not proceed against her strictly according to law nor allow her an open hearing, her accusation that he had had her imprisoned merely because his affections were set on Jane Seymour, as well as her suggestion that he had already determined that she must die, were an insult to royal justice and guaranteed to arouse his anger, which was surely the last thing Anne would have risked doing at such a time. She was to praise him fulsomely on the scaffold, when she was in far greater extremity than this, so one would expect that, had she indeed written to him from her prison, she would have reined in her sharp tongue in the interests of ameliorating his displeasure.

But Anne had never been afraid to speak her mind, nor even to upbraid or ridicule Henry; she was his wife and had grown used to speaking openly to him. Driven by her fears, her anger and her sense of injury, might she not yet again have let her tongue run away with her, as she already had during her confinement? She may have felt she had nothing left to lose and could freely let Henry know what she thought of him. But there was her child's future to think of, and the threat of repercussions on her family. Would Anne truly have dared to be so provocative at this crucial time? Jasper Ridley is of the opinion that she did so dare, and that this was why an outraged Henry showed her little mercy.

Yet the writer's claim that she had never desired to be queen is certainly untrue. And the signature is odd, as well as the repeated use of the name Anne Boleyn, for Anne would surely have signed herself, as she customarily did, 'Anne the Queen'.[15] However, the final paragraph in which she says that she understands that others are in prison for her sake, rings true, and reflects her perception of the situation as it would have been on 6 May. The question must be, if Anne did not write this letter, then who did? It must have been a person with some detailed knowledge of her imprisonment, someone who had an interest in showing her to be innocent. It may be that one of her Elizabethan apologists, over-zealous in her cause, resorted to forgery. Or, if Jasper Ridley is correct, this letter is indeed a copy — kept for reasons of state — of a letter that Anne wrote herself. But that does not explain its other anomalies, which strongly suggest that it was indeed a forgery.

Just to complicate matters, the antiquarian John Strype, who wrote his *Annals of the Reformation in England* in the early eighteenth century, claimed to have seen another letter written by Anne in the Tower, apparently on a later date than the one referred to above; Strype recorded that, in this second letter, she responded to an invitation to make a full confession of her crimes by saying that she could confess no more than she had already spoken. That rings true, and may refer to the accounts of her conversations with Norris, Weston and Smeaton that she had given to her attendants.

★   ★   ★

Kingston's third letter to Cromwell is undated, but was written no earlier than Sunday, 7 May, since he refers to 'yesterday after your departing', and it is clear from his previous report that Cromwell had not been at the Tower on 5 May.

Kingston began by reminding Master Secretary that 'the Queen hath much desired to have here in the closet the Sacraments, and also her almoner [John Skip], who she supposeth to be devout, for one hour she is determined to die, and the next hour much contrary to that. Yesterday, after your departing, I sent for my wife and also for Mrs Coffin, to know how they had done that day' – presumably Kingston had been closeted with Cromwell and had not had a chance to see the Queen – and 'they said she had been very merry and made a great dinner, and yet soon after she called for her supper, having marvel where I was all day; and after supper she sent for me'.

'Where have you been all day?' she asked him.

'I made answer I had been with prisoners,' he told her.

'So,' she said, 'I thought I heard Master Treasurer.' She was referring to FitzWilliam. Kingston told her – perhaps untruthfully – that 'he was not here'. Then Anne began to talk; it was now that she recalled the way in which the King's councillors had treated her at Greenwich on the day of her arrest, 'shaking her head three or four times'. 'But I to be a Queen and cruelly handled as was never seen!' she lamented, 'but I think the King does it to prove me.' And she 'did laugh withal, and was very merry'. Then her mood suddenly changed.

'I shall have justice,' she declared.

'Have no doubt therein,' Kingston assured her.

'If any man accuse me, I can say but nay, and they can bring no witness,' she replied.

Anne then 'talked with the gentlewomen'. It was in this conversation that she revealed she had known, that first evening in the Tower, of the imprisonment of Smeaton and Norris. She wished she could have made some statement of her innocence: 'if it had been laid [before the Council] she had won'. She then added, 'I would to God I had my bishops' – the ten prelates who owed their sees to her patronage – 'for they would all go to the King for me'. In fact, their silence had been deafening.

Anne went on, somewhat extravagantly, 'I think the most part of England prays for me, and if I die you shall see the greatest punishment for me within this seven year that ever came to England. And then shall I be in Heaven, for I have done many good deeds in my days.' This reveals that Anne was, at heart, true to the faith of her childhood, for had she been secretly of the Lutheran persuasion, she would have hoped to attain Heaven through faith alone rather than good works.

She harked back once more to the subject of her attendants: 'I think [it] much unkindness in the King to put such about me as I never loved.' Kingston reminded her 'that the King took them to be honest and good women', a judgement with which he himself agreed.

'But I would have had of mine own privy chamber, which I favour most,' Anne said plaintively, but in vain. Kingston remained impervious to her complaints.[16]

News of the arrests took several days to reach the outlying shires of the realm. That Sunday, 7 May, Rowland Lee, Bishop of Coventry and Lichfield, and his associates in the Council of the Marches on the Welsh border acknowledged receipt of letters from the Privy Council and expressed their shock: 'As the news in this letter is very doleful to this Council and all the liege people of the realm, God forbid it should be true.'[17]

That same day, the ageing Sir Henry Wyatt, who had clearly not yet learned of his son Thomas's arrest, wrote him a letter from Allington Castle. He considered himself 'most unfortunate that he could neither go nor ride without danger to his life, or do his duty to the King in this dangerous time that his Grace has suffered by false traitors' and 'desired his son to give the King due attendance night and day', adding: 'I trust that ye have so declared yourself that ye are found true to his Grace. His Highness is most bounden to God that he hath given him such grace that this false treason is brought so wisely out. I pray to God give him grace long enough to be with him, and about him that hath found out this matter, which hath been given him of God, and the false traitors to be punished according to justice, to the example of others.'[18] The unwitting Sir Henry's acceptance of the guilt of the as yet untried prisoners reflects the view expressed – and probably held – by the majority of people at that time.

It was a view shared by the highest in the land, and there is evidence that already, the outcome of the affair was expected to be a foregone conclusion. On 7 May, orders were sent in the King's name to the sheriffs of every county, informing them that, 'since the dissolution of the late Parliament, matters of high importance have chanced, which render it necessary to discuss the establishment of the succession in a parliament assembled for that purpose'. The King desired each sheriff to 'declare to the people that the calling of a parliament is so necessary, both for the treating of matters so necessary for their weal and the surety of our person, that they will have cause to think their charge and time, which will be very little and short, well spent'.[19] Given that the annulment of the Queen's marriage had already been discussed, and that Parliament had been summoned on 27 April, before Anne's arrest, what else could this presage but her certain removal by the due processes of Church and State?

On 8 May, one of the Queen's chaplains, William Latymer, returning from Flanders, where he had been about her business, was informed, upon landing in Sandwich, Kent, that 'the Queen and other prisoners were in the Tower', and was then searched, in case he had any incriminating evidence on him. Having shown the mayor and local justices 'the contents of his budget and purse' and the books he had with him, he was allowed to proceed on his way.[20] This incident would indicate that every member of the Queen's household had been subject to questioning.

In Calais, on 8 May, the King's cousin and deputy, Arthur Plantagenet, Lord Lisle, learned of the arrests of the Queen and her alleged lovers, and, not doubting that all would be condemned – if they had not already been – and that their offices, lands and goods would be confiscated along with their lives, which was the fate of convicted traitors, hastened to join the fray of court vultures hoping for rich pickings; as early as 2 May, the day of Norris's arrest, Richard Staverton of Warfield, Berkshire, a landowner and lawyer of Lincoln's Inn (whose wife, Margaret Weston, was probably related to Francis Weston), had written to Cromwell saying he 'shall be glad to have' Norris's rooms and properties near Windsor, 'as I have fourteen children'.[21] On 3 May, an official inventory of Norris's wardrobe stuff had been drawn up, and two days after that, John Longland, Bishop of Lincoln, wrote to Cromwell offering, 'if it is true that Norris has not used himself according to his duty to his sovereign lord', to transfer Norris's stewardship of the University of Oxford to Master Secretary for a small fee.[22] Too late, the Duke of Richmond was to write to the Bishop on 8 May, referring to 'the trouble and business that Mr Norris is now in, the which I think is not to you unknown', and asking, as 'it is presupposed with many men that there is no way but one with him', if he could have Norris's stewardship of Banbury for his servant, Giles Forster; Longland, however, had already promised it to Cromwell.[23]

Not wishing to lose out, Lord Lisle now wrote to Master Secretary:

Right honourable Sir,
    After my hearty commendations, forasmuch as always my full trust and confidence hath been in you, I thought it most requisite to open my mind to you . . . And seeing there are many things now in [the King's] gracious disposition and

hands, by reason of the most mischievous, heinous and most abominable treasons against his most gracious and royal crown and person committed, I wholly trust that his Grace, being good lord unto me, will vouchsafe to employ some part of those same upon me; which I do well know may so much the rather be obtained by your good mediation and furtherance.[24]

In order to expedite the matter, Lord Lisle immediately dispatched to London his attorney, John Husee. Husee carried with him Lisle's letter to Cromwell and also one for the King. Four days later, he was able to tell Lisle that he had given his letter to Cromwell, 'who hath promised to be your very friend' and commanded Husee to deliver the King's letter. But Husee was 'in no wise' permitted to deliver it in person or speak with Henry, and was obliged to entrust Sir John Russell with the task of handing it over. Russell promised to consult with Cromwell, 'and between them both, if they keep promise, I trust something will rise on your Lordship's behalf. But there is no time to make hot suit till time the matters which are now in hand be overblown.'[25] Lisle would just have to be patient.

Speculation at court was rampant; no one knew quite what was going on, and so far there had been no official announcement. At length, on Tuesday, 9 May, the King summoned twenty-two noblemen, and twenty-seven gentlemen of his Privy Chamber, to a meeting at Hampton Court to treat 'of such great and weighty matters as whereupon doth consist the surety of our person, the preservation of our honour, and the tranquillity and quietness of you and all other our loving and faithful subjects'.[26] Among those summoned were men who had long conspired Anne's downfall, notably Exeter and Montagu, as well as Sir William Kingston, William Coffin (whose wife was in attendance on the Queen in the Tower) and Sir William Brereton, who was a relative of one

of the accused.[27] There can be little doubt that the as yet unpublished findings of the commissioners were already known to
the King and Cromwell (who was after all a member of both
grand juries), and that the lords and gentlemen had been
summoned for the purpose of discussing them, and – in the case
of the lords – to try the Queen and Lord Rochford, who had
the right to be tried by their peers. The official summons to the
peers for this purpose would not be issued until 13 May, and to
at least twenty-seven lords, five more than the King summoned
on the 9th; but the fact that Lord Latimer wrote to Cromwell on
the 12th, asking to be excused, proves that they actually had been
called earlier. Since Latimer was at that time staying in his house
at Wyke in Worcestershire, he must have been summoned on
the 9th at the latest, and cannot have been expected to attend the
meeting at Hampton Court on that date.

That day, 9 May, the justices of the King's Bench, sitting at
Westminster, sent their precept for the sheriffs of London to
arrange for the return of the grand juries the following day.[28]
Legal proceedings against the Queen formally began on Wednesday,
10 May, when the Grand Jury of Middlesex assembled in
Westminster Hall before John Baldwin, Chief Justice of the
Common Pleas, and six other judges. There, its foreman, Sir Thomas
More's son-in-law, Giles Heron, announced that the commissioners had found a true bill against the accused on all the charges,
that being the written decision of the jury that it had heard sufficient evidence that an accused person was probably guilty of a
crime and should be indicted.

The decision to proceed to trial by jury, rather than following
the summary and incontestable procedure of the passing of an
Act of Attainder against the accused by Parliament, strongly suggests
that the Crown was confident that it had a sufficiently compelling
case to secure Anne's condemnation. Of course, this confidence
may have stemmed from the knowledge that the King's will in
the matter was known, or had been communicated, to those who

would be sitting in judgement; and in most cases, the King's will prevailed. But clearly Cromwell felt that his case was sound. Had he not, he would surely have opted for attainder, which allowed no possibility of escape for the accused. The decision to go to trial in open court suggests also that the King cared what his subjects thought of this extraordinary process, and that he was aware that, in proceeding against no less a personage than the Queen herself – a move that would undoubtedly cause a sensation – the Crown's case must publicly be seen to be unassailable.

Nevertheless, a guilty verdict, although likely, was not always a foregone conclusion. Only two years earlier, in 1534, Lord Dacre had famously been acquitted of treason, much to the King's disgust, yet although Henry's disapproval was made clear to them, no vengeance was visited upon those lords who had found Dacre innocent.[29] For all that, when the Crown was a party, the chances of a trial being fair by modern standards were remote, and it is true that, of the hundreds of people accused of treason in Tudor times, very few had the bravado to enter a plea of not guilty. When Sir Nicholas Throckmorton was acquitted of treason in Mary I's reign, this was thought to be extraordinary.

Yet the possibility remained that the lords might be reluctant to condemn the Queen of England, for such a conviction was unprecedented. Earlier English queens had been unfaithful, notably Isabella of Angoulême, whose husband King John had ordered her lovers to be strung up and hanged above her bed, and Isabella of France, who unquestionably committed adultery with Roger Mortimer while she was married to the homosexual Edward II; neither of these ladies had met with anything worse than infamy. More seriously, in the twelfth century, Eleanor of Aquitaine had abetted her sons in a treasonous rebellion against Henry II that nearly cost him his throne, and led to her being held under house arrest for sixteen years. And Matilda of Flanders, the wife of William the Conqueror, had also supported a renegade son against her husband, earning little more than a ticking-off. As we have seen, Joan of Navarre, the widow of Henry IV, had been accused (falsely, as it turned out) of witchcraft, for which she was imprisoned for just three years; in 1441, Eleanor Cobham, Duchess of Gloucester, had schemed to predict the death of her nephew Henry VI by witchcraft, but had escaped execution; instead she had been condemned to perpetual imprisonment. No English royal lady, therefore, had ever been sentenced to death for the kind of crimes of which Anne Boleyn was accused.

Nor had this happened in France, where, in 1314, three French princesses, among them the wife of the heir to the throne, had been found guilty of committing adultery; but while their lovers were savagely butchered on the scaffold, they themselves were condemned only to divorce and imprisonment. Given the precedents, Anne could reasonably have expected that to be her fate. Yet it is clear from her recorded utterances in the Tower that she already believed herself to be doomed.

In the indictment drawn up by the Grand Jury of Middlesex for use at the coming trials, the charges against the Queen and her alleged accomplices – already branded as 'traitors' – were enumerated in shocking detail. The original documents survive in the records of the King's Bench in the famous *Baga de Secretis* in the National Archives, along with other records relating to Anne's fall. The two indictments, those of Middlesex and Kent, in which were listed twenty-one specific offences, are likely to have been largely the work of Thomas Cromwell, who sat on both grand juries, and they reflect the scale of his investigations – and perhaps his powers of invention. They constituted a formidable case against the accused.

The Middlesex indictment read as follows:

Record of the Indictment found at Westminster on Wednesday next after three weeks of Easter: that whereas Queen Anne has been the wife of Henry VIII for three years and more, she, despising the solemn, not to mention most excellent and noble marriage between our lord the King and the same lady the Queen, but even at the same time having in her heart malice against our lord the King, seduced by evil and not having God before her eyes, and following daily her frail and carnal appetites, did falsely and traitorously procure by base conversations and kisses, touchings, gifts and other infamous incitations, divers of the King's daily and familiar servants to be her adulterers and concubines, so that several of the King's servants yielded to her vile provocations; viz, on Oct 6th, 25 Henry VIII [1533] at Westminster [i.e. York Place, Westminster], and divers days before and after, she procured, by sweet words, kisses, touches and otherwise, Hen. Norris, of Westminster, gentleman of the Privy Chamber, to violate her, by reason whereof he did so at Westminster on the 12th Oct, 25 Hen. VIII [1533], and they had illicit intercourse, both before and after, sometimes by his procurement and sometimes by that of the Queen.

Also the Queen, 3 Dec. 25 Hen. VIII [1533], and divers days before and after, procured William Brereton, Esquire, late of Westminster, one of the gentlemen of the King's Privy Chamber, to have illicit intercourse with her, whereby he did so on 8 Dec. 25 Hen. VIII [1533] at Hampton Court, in the parish of Little Hampton, and on several days before and after, sometimes by his own procurement and sometimes by the Queen's.

Also the Queen, 8 May 26 Hen. VIII [1534], and at other times before and since, procured Sir Fras. Weston, of Westminster, one of the gentlemen of the King's Privy Chamber, to have illicit intercourse with her, and that the Act was committed at Westminster 20 May 26 Hen. VIII [1534].

Also the Queen, 12 April 26 Hen. VIII [1534], and divers

days before and since, at Westminster, also incited/procured
Mark Smeaton, a performer on musical instruments, a person
specified as of low degree, promoted for his skill to be a
groom of the Privy Chamber, to violate her, whereby he
did so at Westminster, 26 April 27 Hen. VIII [1535].

Also that the Queen, 2 Nov. 27 Hen. VIII [1535] and
several times before and after, by the means therein stated,
procured and incited her own natural brother, George Boleyn,
knight, Lord Rochford, to violate her, alluring him with her
tongue in the said George's mouth, and the said George's
tongue in hers, and also with kisses, presents and jewels,
against the commands of Almighty God, and all laws human
and divine, whereby he, despising the commands of God,
and all other human laws, 5 Nov. 27 Henry VIII [1535],
violated and carnally knew the said Queen, his own sister,
at Westminster, which he also did on divers days before and
after, sometimes by his own procurement and sometimes by
the Queen's.

Furthermore, they being thus inflamed by carnal love of
the Queen, and having become very jealous of each other,
did, in order to secure her affections, satisfy her inordinate
desires; and that the Queen was equally jealous of the Lord
Rochford, and other the before-mentioned traitors that she
would not allow them to hold any familiarity with any other
woman without exhibiting her exceeding displeasure and
indignation. Moreover, the said Lord Rochford, Norris,
Brereton, Weston and Smeaton, being thus inflamed with
carnal love of the Queen, and having become very jealous
of each other, gave her secret gifts and pledges while carrying
on this illicit intercourse; and the Queen, on her part, would
not allow them to show familiarity with any other women
without her exceeding displeasure and indignation; and that
on 27 Nov. 27 Hen. VIII [1535] and other days before and
after, at Westminster, she gave them great gifts to inveigle

them to her will. Furthermore that the Queen and other of the said traitors, jointly and severally, 31 Oct. 27 Henry VIII [1535], at Westminster, and at various times before and after, compassed and imagined the King's death; and that the Queen had frequently promised to marry some one of the traitors whenever the King should depart this life, affirming she would never love the King in her heart. Furthermore, that the King having come within *a short time before* [author's italics] to the knowledge of, and meditating upon, the false and detestable crimes, vices and treasons committed against himself within a short time now passed, took such inward displeasure and heaviness, especially for his said Queen's malice and adultery, that certain harms and perils have befallen his royal body, to the scandal, danger, detriment and derogation of the issue and heirs of the said King and Queen.[30]

On 11 May, Chief Justice Baldwin and his colleagues travelled to Deptford, where the Grand Jury of Kent also found a true bill that was similar in character to the Middlesex indictment, and covered the crimes that had allegedly taken place at 'East Greenwich', that is, Greenwich Palace. However, the original dates cited related to the adultery at Westminster and had to be altered, which may also indicate that some of the charges were fabricated.

The indictment returned by the Grand Jury of Kent was couched in similar terms but related to offences that had allegedly been committed in that county. According to this, Anne was said to have solicited Brereton at Greenwich on 16 November 1533, and to have committed adultery with him there on 27 November; she was also charged with soliciting Smeaton at Greenwich on 12 May 1534 and committing adultery with him on the 19th; soon afterwards, on 6 June, she allegedly solicited Weston at Greenwich, having sex with him on 20 June; then, on 22 December 1535, at Eltham Palace in

Kent, she solicited her brother George, and they committed incest on 29 December. Finally, on 8 January 1536, at Greenwich, Anne, Rochford, Norris, Weston and Brereton compassed the King's death. In every case, the offences were said to have been committed both before and after the dates specified.[31]

The twenty-one specified offences, taken chronologically, can be summed up as follows:

6 and 12 October 1533, with Norris, at Westminster;
16 and 27 November 1533, with Brereton, at Greenwich;
3 and 8 December 1533, with Brereton, at Westminster
   and Hampton Court;
12 April 1534, soliciting Smeaton, at Westminster;
8 and 20 May, 1534, with Weston, at Westminster;
13 and 19 May 1534, with Smeaton, at Greenwich;
6 and 20 June 1534, with Weston, at Greenwich;
26 April 1535, with Smeaton, at Westminster;
31 October 1535, compassing the King's death, at
   Westminster;
2 and 5 November 1535, with Rochford, at Westminster;
27 November 1535, inveigling the men to treason, at
   Westminster;
22 and 29 December 1535, with Rochford, at Eltham;
8 January 1536, compassing the King's death, at
   Greenwich.

It seems barely credible that, with all these intrigues going on over a period of nearly three years, evidence of them had only just come to light. As Ives says, 'quadruple adultery plus incest invites disbelief',[32] while not even the ever-watchful Chapuys, Anne's enemy, who would have relished any opportunity of discrediting her, had ever hinted at any infidelities on her part, although he gleefully reported gossip that the King was unfaithful to her.[33] If the charges relating to adultery were based on fact, then for the greater part of her marriage Anne had not scrupled to hop from bed to bed, slaking her lust with five men, one her own brother.

It has been said that the word 'violate', as used in the indictments, could not have applied to Anne, because she had been the seductress, and that since only the rape of the Queen was treason under the 1351 statute, none of the men should have been indicted for treason on this count.[34] Yet in the sixteenth century, the word 'violation' had a broader meaning (as it does now), and did not just mean rape, but dishonour, transgression, desecration, irreverence or infraction. It is clear that the word is used in these senses in the indictment, while adultery with the King's consort was treason under the 1534 Act of Succession because it impugned his issue; the very words of the 1534 Act were used in the indictments to allege the 'slander, danger, detriment and derogation' of Henry's heirs, and the royal justices ruled that the Queen's offences were treason under that Act.[35]

Anne's conduct was made out to be all the more disgraceful, given that she had been pregnant four times during this period and presumably hopeful of presenting Henry VIII with a living son. The accusation of adultery with Norris in October 1533 might well have been levelled to imply that Norris was responsible for Anne's second pregnancy, which became evident in December that year, and that the guilty pair had compromised the succession; it even prompted some people to wonder if Norris was in fact Elizabeth's father, even though there is no suggestion of this in the indictments.

Similarly, charging Rochford with committing incest with Anne in November 1535 may have been intended to suggest that he had fathered the son of which she miscarried. Warnicke believes that, had that foetus been normal, there would have been no cause to go to such lengths to show that the King could not have been its father, and that the salacious details of Anne inciting her brother and the other men were intended to prove that she was a witch. Yet there is no mention of witchcraft in the indictment, nor of a deformed foetus. These shocking and damning factors would surely have been exploited by Anne's accusers, rather than kept secret, and made the case against her more convincing to contemporary eyes.

The final charge, that of conspiring the death of the King, was the most heinous, for it was high treason of the first order. There could be no doubt that, if guilty, this woman deserved to die.

Certainly the charges were shocking – Strickland was horrified by their 'extravagant and unverified coarseness, which cannot be permitted to sully the pages of any work intended for family reading' – but it would be wrong to take them at face value, especially that of plotting regicide. Such folly would have been barely understandable had it been driven by a grand passion, but Anne could not even have been motivated by love, given that she was alleged to have been bent on marrying any one of her supposed lovers and sleeping with them all at different times.

Jane Dormer later opined that Anne, 'much wanting to have a man-child to succeed, and finding the King not to content her', resorted to taking four lovers, and finally her brother, to achieve her desire. Yet it is highly unlikely that she was motivated in this way, because if Henry were indeed impotent, which is again unlikely, he would surely have known that any child she conceived was not his. No, it would appear that these charges were drawn up with the specific purposes of character assassination and providing a foolproof means for getting rid of her. Describing Smeaton as 'a person of low degree' emphasised how far the Queen had stooped to gratify her desires, and the charge of treasonable incest – graphically enlarged upon in the indictment – was clearly meant to arouse outrage and revulsion.

That, George Wyatt observed, was 'the most odious' of the accusations. 'Partly it is incredible, partly by the circumstances impossible. Incredible, that she had it as her word, the spirit of her mind, that she was Caesar's all, not to be touched of others'

– Wyatt is here echoing his grandfather's famous poem, '*Noli me tangere*' – and yet had been 'held with the foul desire of her brother. Impossible, for the necessary and no small attendance of ladies ever about her, neither could she remove so great ladies, by office appointed to wait upon her continually, from being witnesses to her doings.' Moreover, Anne was aware of the danger in which she stood, and could not have been 'more wary and wakeful, if for none other cause [but] to take away all colour from her enemies, whose eyes were everywhere upon her, and their malicious hearts bent to make some where they found none; as plainly enough as was to be seen when they were driven to those straits to take occasion at her brother's being more private with her'. They feared that 'his conference with her might be for the breaking off [of] the King's new love'.[36]

Close scrutiny of the facts suggests that thirteen out of the twenty-one charges were impossible, and that if, four and a half centuries later, it can be established that only eight were even plausible – which in itself suggests that even these were not genuine offences – then the case against Anne is shaky indeed.[37] Furthermore, allegations that a number of unspecified offences had been committed 'on divers days before and after' the stated dates on which the crimes had purportedly been committed would be difficult to disprove, and Cromwell was doubtless aware of this; it was a 'catch-all guarantee'.[38] It is also evident that Cromwell had not been as thorough as he should have been. In no fewer than twelve instances, either Anne or her alleged accomplice can be shown not to have been in the specified location. For example, she was accused of committing adultery with Brereton on 8 December 1533 at Hampton Court, but the court was at Greenwich on that date.[39] And because it can be shown that quite a few of the dated offences could not have been committed in the places specified, then the rest of the charges are also undermined.[40]

It has, however, been argued that, while the substance of the charges was sound, the details were subject to clerical error or faulty memories, given the lapse in time since the offences were committed, the confusing amount of detail in the indictments[41] and the speed with which they had been drawn up. If Cromwell manufactured these charges, he surely would have taken care to ensure that the details were correct;[42] his political survival, indeed, his very life, would have depended on him concocting a water-tight and credible case against the Queen. So these discrepancies in location cannot be taken as conclusive proof that the charges were fabricated. Yet there are other disturbing aspects to consider.

On all but one of the dates cited, Anne was pregnant. Indulging in sex during pregnancy was scandalous in itself, because inter-course was forbidden until forty days after delivery. For centuries, the Church had enforced the teaching that sex was only for procreation, and that taboo still persisted. But aside from that, in so indulging, Anne had – in sixteenth-century eyes – irrespon-sibly put her unborn children at risk and compromised her chances of bearing an heir.

On the other occasion cited, she was lying in after a confine-ment. She was alleged to have incited Norris to commit adultery on – and even before – 6 October 1533, one month after she had given birth to the Princess Elizabeth. Is it likely that a woman who had recently emerged from her first lying-in, and who was in all probability still bleeding, would have felt like embarking on an adulterous affair, which was allegedly consummated just six days later, and at Westminster, when the court had not left Greenwich?

Furthermore, Anne had not yet been churched following her confinement; this was a public ceremony of blessing and thanks-giving for a woman's recovery from the perils of childbirth, dating from Biblical times, when, following the Levitical law, women were deemed to be unclean after bearing a child and were required to go to the Temple for a ceremony of purification, a ritual observed by the Virgin Mary after the birth of Jesus. In England, mothers were traditionally churched on the fortieth day after delivery, in accordance with the Biblical date of the presentation of Mary and Jesus at the Temple; prior to the Reformation, there remained a strong element of purification, with the woman presenting herself veiled at the church door and being sprinkled with holy water before entering the church itself. Churching signalled a woman's resumption of sexual relations with her husband after a period of ritual seclusion and avoidance. There was a strong social taboo against couples having sex before the wife was churched, and in accusing Anne of committing adultery at this time, Cromwell, who is hardly likely to have been unaware of the date of Elizabeth's birth, was no doubt determined to make her crime appear even more heinous. Yet as far as Anne was concerned, again, it is improbable that she would have been eager or even able to embark upon an adulterous affair at this time, when she was still in seclusion with her women.

At the beginning of December 1533, Anne's family knew she was pregnant again; she was suffering from the tiredness and exhaustion common to that early stage of pregnancy, and from disturbed sleep,[43] yet she was charged with seducing William Brereton during November and December.

In the spring of 1534, when she was supposed to be trying to seduce Weston and Smeaton, Anne's pregnancy was advancing visibly,[44] and she was deeply preoccupied with the defiance of Katherine and Mary, the refusal of Sir Thomas More, Bishop Fisher and others to take the oath to the Act of Succession, which recognised Elizabeth as Henry's heir, as well as the treasonable utterances of Elizabeth Barton, the Nun of Kent, against herself, and the Pope's pronouncement that the King's marriage to Katherine was good and valid. In April and May, the alleged dates of her crimes, she was six to seven months gone with child. It is barely credible that she could have indulged in perilous extramarital affairs at this time – perilous not only because sex was then regarded as a risk to the unborn child, but also because of the danger of being caught. And even if she had indulged, it should be noted that when she was supposed to be cavorting with Smeaton at Greenwich on 19 May and Weston at Westminster on 20 May, she was in fact at Richmond with the King, having gone there on 17 May to keep Whitsuntide. The court remained there until at least 26 May, and then stayed at Hampton Court from 3 to 26 June, so Anne could not have slept again with Weston on 20 June at Greenwich, as was alleged.[45]

The indictment made it clear that Anne was invariably the instigator of adultery. This does not sound like the woman who had held Henry VIII at bay for over six years,[46] but this argument does not of course take into account the fact that a woman's desire can intensify after the establishment of a sexual relationship, or because of hormonal changes. It is not very likely, though, that Anne was desperate to seduce anyone when she was recovering from her confinement.

By February 1535, as we have seen, Anne knew that she was being kept under constant surveillance. Yet two months later, the indictment would have us believe, she persuaded Smeaton, whom she had seduced a year before, to have sex with her again, and this at a time when, once again, she was in the early stages of pregnancy.

In October that year, when she was said to have been plotting the King's death – which was absurd in itself, since Katherine of Aragon was still alive then, and Henry's demise would certainly have prompted a rising in favour of the Lady Mary's right to succeed, or even full-scale civil war and the possible intervention of the Emperor – Anne discovered that she was once more with child, but it was at this time, so the indictment claims, that she seduced her brother Rochford, a crime that was guaranteed to inspire the deepest public revulsion. The implication was, of course – as with the offences in 1533 – that the baby was not the King's.[47] And then, despite her new hope of bearing the son who would ensure her future as queen, she gave gifts to the men who were planning to kill the King on her behalf, one of whom she was allegedly planning to marry. What would it have profited her to ally herself in marriage with any of these men? Not one of them could have satisfied her ambition in the ways that the King had done. Moreover, when she was supposed to have been conspiring against Henry on 27 November 1535 at Westminster, she was at Windsor; again, she was at Eltham on 8 January 1536, when she was supposed to be plotting the King's death at Greenwich. The date of this latter charge may be significant, because it was the day after Katherine of Aragon died; but even with Katherine dead, if Anne had attempted to assassinate Henry in order to rule in Elizabeth's name, she would still have had to contend with the Lady Mary and her powerful supporters, not the least of whom was the Emperor. The illogicality in the charges strongly suggests that they were cobbled together in a hurry, without having been carefully scrutinised.

As for the 'harms and perils' that had befallen the King's body as a result of the stress engendered by discovering his wife's crimes, it is unlikely that this had anything to do with the effects of Henry's jousting accident becoming manifest at this time, as has been suggested, for it was not until the following year, 1537, that he confided to Norfolk's heir, Henry Howard, Earl of Surrey, that 'to be frank with you, which we desire you in any wise to keep to yourself, an humour [has] fallen into our legs'; if he had had this problem at the time of Anne's fall, it cannot have been very severe.

Possibly the 'harms and perils' referred to the fear and paranoia resulting from his lucky escape from his murderous wife, but in mentioning the danger to the King's heirs, it would appear the indictment was implying that he was suffering from sexual impotence, although the latter is unlikely to be true, as will become clear in due course. On the other hand, this might just have been a ploy to win him his subjects' sympathy. Certainly there would be little evidence of Henry suffering any harms and perils in the weeks to come, when he was 'lustily and publicly pursuing Jane Seymour'.[48]

Close analysis of the charges in the indictment against Anne Boleyn suggests that they are intrinsically flawed, although perhaps not as flawed as has hitherto been thought. Many have concluded that they were trumped up. If the Queen was truly guilty, and this had been discovered in the manner that Cromwell described, there should have been sufficient credible evidence against her to support such charges, and no need to manufacture what seems to be a travesty of a case, although we do not have all the documentary evidence. It does seem that a degree of manipulation was at play, in order to ensure a conviction, but that is not necessarily to say that Anne was innocent. Nor should we conclude that justice was maliciously subverted or that her prosecutors knew that the charges were contrived: given the nature of the evidence, the Crown's case seems to have been weak in the detail, even though it might have believed its substance to have been sound. In a word, Anne was probably framed. That has been my position in two earlier books, and to claim, as one author recently did,[49] that I accepted the official charges without question is absurd.

It would be left to later generations to expose the flaws in the indictment. 'Her very accusations speak and plead for her,' opined Wyatt, 'all of them carrying in themselves open proof to all men's consciences of mere matter of quarrel, and indeed of a very preparation to some hoped alteration.' It would have been difficult for Anne to conceal one illicit ongoing love affair, but concealing five would have been an impossibility.[50]

Already people expected the prisoners to be convicted. On 11 May, before any trial had taken place, the Abbot of Cirencester wrote informing Cromwell that he had already promised Sir Henry Norris's stewardship of his abbey to Sir William Kingston, 'when it is void'; it is clear that the matter had been the subject of an earlier communication.[51]

Urgent arrangements had already been put in hand for the

accused to be put on trial. On 10 May, even before the second true bill had been found, the justices had sent a precept to the Constable of the Tower, commanding him to 'bring up the bodies of Sir Francis Weston, knt, Henry Norris Esq., William Brereton Esq. and Mark Smeaton, gent.', all committed to the Tower for high treason by the King's Council, at Westminster for trial 'on Friday next', two days hence. And at the foot of each indictment, in the margin, were afterwards added the words '*Billa vera*' ('True bill'), with a memorandum that the documents had been sent to the Duke of Norfolk, Earl Marshal of England, 'to do all matters concerning the Queen and Lord Rochford' on Monday, 15 May, at the Tower.[52]

The outcome of it all, according to a letter sent on 10 May by Sir John Dudley (who had been among those at the meeting at Hampton Court the previous day) to Lady Lisle, was not in doubt: 'As touching the news that are here, I am sure it needeth not to write to you, for all the world knoweth them by this time,' he wrote. 'This day was indicted Mr Norris, Mr Weston, William Brereton, Markes [*sic*.] and my lord of Rochford. And upon Friday next they shall be arraigned at Westminster. And the Queen herself shall be condemned by Parliament.'[53]

Interestingly, although Wyatt and Page had been in the Tower for five days, they were not mentioned in the indictments. In fact, Cromwell had already written to Wyatt's father to reassure him that his son would not be harmed, which is in itself suspicious, given that none of the accused had yet been tried and that the outcome of their trials was as yet unknown. Overflowing with gratitude, the ageing Sir Henry Wyatt sent him a reply on 11 May, stating that neither he nor his son would ever forget Master Secretary's kindness. Not that Wyatt deserved it, his father thought: in two letters to Cromwell written at this time, he referred despairingly to his son's sexual adventures, and to 'the displeasure he hath done to God'.[54]

Page was also to escape trial. The influence of FitzWilliam, to whom he was related, might have been a factor,[55] but Page and Wyatt were Cromwell's men, indeed his friends, and their incarceration in the Tower may have been intended to show that the investigations into the Queen's misconduct were entirely impartial.

On 11 May, Cromwell visited the King at Hampton Court, where he discussed with him and finalised the arrangements for the coming trials before returning to York Place late in the day.[56] Norfolk, who was to preside over the hearings, was as yet unaware that his fellow commissioners had found a true bill against the Queen, and on the evening of 11 May, Sir William Paulet sent a messenger after Cromwell to let him know that

> my lord of Norfolk showed me that he had no knowledge that the indictment was found, and asked me whether the parties should proceed to their trial or not. I told him I knew not. As to commissioners, he said he knew not how many were required, nor whether they ought to be barons or not. Therefore he could not tell whom to name; and if he knew, he would name no one till he learned of the King's pleasure. So he willed me to advertise you.[57]

This letter does not suggest that Henry interfered a great deal in the proceedings against the Queen.[58] What it does reveal is that Norfolk had been left in the dark as to what was going on and was wary of taking any action without the King's approval. The Duke was not to be kept in ignorance for long, for he would soon receive the documents prepared on behalf of the Crown, and with the two indictments drawn up, the case against the Queen and her alleged lovers could now proceed to trial.

Lancelot de Carles asserts that, before the King gave orders for the trials of the Queen and her alleged lovers to proceed, some lords of the Council visited her in the Tower in the hope of

extracting a confession. But 'the Queen, having no further hope
in this world, would confess nothing. She does not confess
anything, and does not resist strongly, almost wanting to be delivered from living here, to go and live and Heaven, and hope [of
that] is surmounting so much in her that she no longer cares
about dying.' For all this, 'she did not give up her greatness, but
spoke to the lords as a mistress. Those who came to interrogate
were astonished.'

The 'Spanish Chronicle' also asserts that the King sent his councillors – naming Cromwell, Cranmer, Norfolk and Audley – to
examine the Queen, with express orders 'to treat her with no
respect or consideration'. Cranmer is said to have been appointed
spokesman, and to have told her: 'Madam, there is no one in the
realm, after my lord the King, who is so distressed at your bad
conduct as I am, for all these gentlemen well know I owe my
dignity to your good will.' This echoes the sentiments expressed
in Cranmer's letter to the King. But Anne interrupted him.

'My lord Bishop, I know what is your errand!' she said. 'Waste
no more time. I have never wronged the King, but I know well
that he is tired of me, as he was before of the good Lady Katherine.'
This smacks of Spanish bias on the part of the chronicler, although
it is possible that Anne, in her present plight, now felt some
sympathy for Katherine. The use of the title 'Lady' rings true.

Cranmer told her that her 'evil courses' had been 'clearly seen',
and if she desired to read Smeaton's confession, it would be shown
to her. Anne flew into 'a great rage', and cried, 'Go to! It has all
been done as I say, because the King has fallen in love, as I know,
with Jane Seymour, and does not know how to get rid of me. Well,
let him do as he likes, he will get nothing more out of me, and
any confession that has been made is false.'

With that, just as Carles said, the lords 'saw they should extract
nothing from her' and determined to leave, but Norfolk had one
parting shot. 'Madam,' he said, 'if it be true that your brother has
shared your guilt, a great punishment indeed should be yours,

and his as well.' Anne told him he should say no such thing. 'My brother is blameless, and if he has been in my chamber to speak with me, surely he might do so without suspicion, being my brother, and they cannot accuse him for that. I know that the King has had him arrested so that there should be none left to take my part. You need not trouble to stop talking with me, for you will find out no more.' The lords left her, and when they reported her words to the King, he said, 'She has a stout heart, but she shall pay for it.'

There is no other evidence for this interrogation, although that is not to say that it did not take place. The author of the 'Spanish Chronicle' may have embellished his dialogue, but the substance of his account is entirely authentic, and chimes with all the other evidence. No reports from Sir William Kingston survive from this time – there is a gap between his letters of 7 and 16 May. So it is quite possible that, with the indictments drawn up, the councillors had hoped to spare the King the publicity that an open trial would generate by forcing the Queen to admit her guilt. But, realising that Henry was determined on proceeding against her – Chapuys told the Emperor he now meant 'to get rid of' her, regardless of whether her guilt was proved[59] – she knew she had nothing to lose by refusing to confess.

The lords 'afterwards went to Rochford, who said he knew that death awaited him, and would say the truth, but, raising his eyes to Heaven, denied the accusations against him. They next went to Norris, Weston and Brereton, who all likewise refused to confess, except Mark, who had done so already.' After this, 'the King ordered the trial at Westminster'.[60]

10

'More Accused
than Convicted'

As yet, in accordance with the normal procedure in
sixteenth-century treason cases, none of the accused had
been given full details of what was alleged against them in
the indictments that had been drawn up, nor had they been
given any notice or means to prepare a defence. The first time
they would hear the formal charges and any depositions, or
'interrogatories',[1] made by the witnesses was when they were
brought into court, and then they would have to defend themselves
as best they could, without benefit of any legal representation,
which was forbidden to those charged with treason. They could
not call witnesses on their own behalf – it is doubtful if many
people would have dared come forward anyway to dispute a
case brought in the name of 'our sovereign lord the King' – and
there was no cross-examination. All they could do was engage
in altercation with their accusers. The law was heavily weighted
against suspected traitors and the outlook for Anne and the men
accused with her was dismal. As Cardinal Wolsey had once acidly
observed, 'If the Crown were prosecutor and asserted it, justice

would be found to bring in a verdict that Abel was the murderer of Cain.'[2]

It was to the further disadvantage of the accused that the law provided for a two-tier system of justice. Commoners had to be tried by the commissioners of oyer and terminer who had brought the case against them, yet those of royal or noble birth had the privilege of being tried in the court of the High Steward by a jury of their peers. Therefore there had to be two trials, and because of the practical difficulties involved – not the least of which was the fact that the commissioners had to be present at both – they could not be held concurrently. Thus the outcome of the first trial would inevitably prejudice that of the second.[3]

On Friday, 12 May, Anne's uncle, the Duke of Norfolk, was appointed Lord High Steward of England, a temporary office that was only conferred on great lords for the purpose of organising coronations or presiding over the trials of peers, who were customarily tried in the court of the High Steward, which he himself convened. In this capacity, Norfolk would act as Lord President at the trials of the Queen and Lord Rochford.

Norfolk was at Westminster Hall that day as one of the commissioners who assembled there at the special sessions of oyer and terminer at which Norris, Weston, Brereton and Smeaton were to be judged. As commoners, they would be tried separately from the Queen and Lord Rochford, who, by virtue of their high rank, had the right to be tried by their peers. All but one of the judges of the King's Bench had been summoned to court, as well as a special jury of twelve knights, and they were joined by the members of the grand juries who had been appointed on 24 April, among them the Lord Chancellor, who was 'the highest commissioner', and several lords of the King's Council,[4] including Sir William FitzWilliam, who had been instrumental in obtaining confessions from Smeaton and Norris, and the Queen's father, Thomas Boleyn, Earl of Wiltshire.[5] Chapuys heard that he was 'ready to assist with the judgement',[6] probably with an eye to his political survival. It may be significant that Edward Willoughby, the foreman of the jury, was in debt to William Brereton; Brereton's death, of course, would release him from his obligations.

Other members of the jury were unlikely to be impartial. Sir Giles Alington was another of Sir Thomas More's sons-in-law, and therefore no friend to the Boleyns, for many held Anne responsible for Sir Thomas's execution. William Askew was a supporter of the Lady Mary; Anthony Hungerford was kin to Jane Seymour; Walter Hungerford, who would be executed for buggery and other capital crimes in 1540, might well have needed to court Cromwell's discretion; Robert Dormer was a conservative who had opposed the break with Rome; Richard Tempest was a creature of Cromwell's; Sir John Hampden was father-in-law to William Paulet, comptroller of the royal household; William Musgrave was one of those who had failed to secure the conviction for treason of Lord Dacre in 1534, and was perhaps zealous to redeem himself; William Sidney was a friend of the hostile Duke of Suffolk; and Thomas Palmer was FitzWilliam's client and one of the King's gambling partners.[7] Given the affiliations of these men, and the unlikelihood that any of them would risk angering the King by returning the wrong verdict, the outcome of the trial was prejudiced from the very outset.[8]

Legal practice apart, securing the conviction of the Queen's alleged lovers was evidently regarded as a necessary preliminary to her own trial, while such a conviction would preclude the four men, as convicted felons, from giving evidence at any subsequent trial,[9] and the Queen from protesting that she was innocent of committing any crimes with them. Above all, it would go a long way towards ensuring that her condemnation was a certainty. This, more than most other factors, strongly suggests that Anne and her so-called accomplices were framed.

The four accused were conveyed by barge from the Tower to Westminster Hall, where they were brought to the bar by Sir William Kingston and arraigned for high treason.[10] This vast hall had been built by William II in the eleventh century and greatly embellished by Richard II in the fourteenth. Lancelot de Carles, an eyewitness at all the trials, was at pains to describe the process of indictment, and 'how the archers of the guard turn the back [of their halberds] to the prisoner in going, but after the sentence of guilty, the edge [of the axe-like blade] is turned towards their faces'.

There is no surviving official record of the trials that took place on that day, only eyewitness accounts, which are frustratingly sketchy.[11] The accused were charged 'that they had violated and had carnal knowledge of the Queen, each by himself at separate times'[12] and that they had conspired the King's death with her.[13] This was the first time that the charges had been made public, or revealed in detail to the defendants, and the effect must have been at once sensational and chilling.

When the indictments had been read, the prisoners were asked if they would plead guilty or not, but only Mark Smeaton pleaded guilty to adultery,[14] confessing 'that he had carnal knowledge of the Queen three times',[15] and throwing himself on the mercy of the King, while insisting he was not guilty of conspiring the death of his sovereign. In the justices' instructions to the Sheriff of London, to bring his prisoners to trial, which were dated 12 May 1536,[16] Smeaton's name was erased, as if, having confessed, he was no longer thought worthy of examination,[17] so he was probably not subjected to questioning in court. The other three men, Norris included, pleaded not guilty,[18] and the jury was sworn in.

There is no record of the witnesses who were brought into court to testify, and we have Chapuys' statement that, in the case of Brereton, no witnesses were called at all, which suggests that others *were* summoned to give evidence against his fellow accused. This made no difference to Brereton, for according to Chapuys, he was 'condemned upon a presumption and circumstances, not by proof or valid confession, and without any witnesses'. Yet there could have been a valid presumption of culpability, for if the Queen's household servants had known what was going on, then the privileged members of her inner circle could reasonably have been expected to have been aware of it, or to have suspected something, and thus to have alerted the King or his ministers. Their not having done so rendered them a party to treason. And their reported flirtatious banter with the Queen laid them open to further suspicion of complicity and culpability.[19]

Norris protested, 'when his own confession was laid afore him, that he was deceived' into making it by FitzWilliam's trickery, and retracted it, saying that if anyone used it to advantage, 'he is worthy to have my place here; and if he stand to it, I defy him',[20] but that made no difference either. The jury unanimously pronounced all four men guilty 'for using fornication with Queen Anne, and also for conspiracy of the King's death', whereupon Sir Christopher Hales, the Attorney-General, asked for judgement to be pronounced on Smeaton according to his own confession, and on the other three in accordance with the verdict.[21] Lord Chancellor Audley, being the chief commissioner present, read out the grim sentence passed on convicted traitors, that they were publicly to be 'hanged, drawn and quartered, their members [genitals] cut off and burnt before them, their heads cut off and [their bodies] quartered'.[22] Norris had seen at first hand what that dread sentence entailed when, a year earlier, alongside Rochford, he had witnessed the bloody executions of the monks of the Charterhouse for refusing to acknowledge the royal supremacy. Rochford, a nobleman, would probably be spared that agony, but Norris and the rest, as commoners, might well be forced to suffer the full rigour of the law.

'Suddenly, the axe was turned towards them,'[23] but their executions were deferred on account of the impending trials of the Queen and Lord Rochford.

When news of the trial's outcome reached the court, many people expressed sorrow, especially for Norris and Weston, who were widely liked and respected. 'Everyone was moved at their misfortune, especially at the case of Weston.'[24] That day, John Husee, newly arrived in London, wrote to Lord Lisle to report the latest events:

> This day Mr Norris, Weston, Brereton and Mark hath been arraigned, and are judged to be drawn, hanged and quartered. I pray God have mercy on them. They shall die tomorrow, or Monday at the furthest. Anne the Queen and her brother shall be arraigned in the Tower; some think tomorrow, but on Monday at the furthest. And some doth verily think they shall there even so suffer within the Tower, undelayedly, for divers considerations which are not yet known.[25]

It is obvious from this that ordinary people could only speculate as to when the men would be executed, or when the Queen and Rochford would come to trial. But, as has been noted, the date for the latter hearing had already been set on 10 May – for 15 May at the Tower – as Sir John Russell informed Lord Lisle on the 12th: 'Today, Mr Norris and such other as you know are cast, and the Queen shall go to her judgement on Monday next.' He confirmed that he had delivered Lord Lisle's letters to the King, and added a touch peevishly, 'I wonder your Lordship did not write to me, that I might have made suit for you.'[26]

'Neither the whore nor her brother was brought to Westminster like the other criminals,' Chapuys was to observe.[27] State trials were usually held in Westminster Hall or the Guildhall, but clearly the authorities did not want Anne leaving the Tower and perhaps becoming the focus of public demonstrations, for she was not popular. Hence the decision to have her tried within the Tower precincts.

Husee told Lisle on 12 May that Wyatt and Page were still in the Tower, 'but, as it is said, without danger of death; but Mr Page

is banished the King's presence and court for ever'.[28] It has been
suggested that he escaped because his stepdaughter, Anne Stanhope,
had recently married Edward Seymour,[29] but they had actually
been married for more than two years,[30] a circumstance that did
not preclude Page's arrest. No evidence had been laid against
Page, though, nor, evidently did Wyatt have any charges to answer,
although clearly nobody knew for certain.

The next day, Saturday, 13 May, John Husee wrote again to the
hopeful Lord Lisle:

> Pleaseth your Lordship to be advertised that here is no good
> to be done neither with the King ne with any other of his
> Council till such time as the matters now had in hand be
> fully finished and achieved. Also, touching Master Treasurer
> [FitzWilliam], it prevaileth nothing to sue unto him till he
> hath more leisure, for he never read letter since these matters
> begun. If it be as some doth presume, it shall be all rid by
> the latter end of this next week.[31]

This prediction turned out to be accurate. Husee's letter is evidence
that the process against the Queen had brought most government business virtually to a standstill;[32] and it again shows
FitzWilliam right at the centre of affairs.

There was, however, cause for Lord Lisle to be hopeful. A list
of Cromwell's 'Remembrances' written around this time indicates
that the government wasted no time in seizing the condemned
men's assets: 'a remembrance that all Mr Norris's patents be
searched out; Henry Knyvett's letters to Mr Weston, and to young
Weston's wife; Henry Knyvett's bills for the offices and the annu-
ity'.[33] Lists of the convicted traitors' offices and wardships were
drawn up, and assessments would be made of the value of their
lands: Rochford's were worth £441.10s.9d (£154,200), Brereton's
£1,236.12.6d (£431,850) and Norris's £1,327.15s.7d (£463,700).[34]
As Cromwell would write to the ambassadors Stephen Gardiner,

Bishop of Winchester, and John Wallop on 14 May, 'great suit is being made' for the men's confiscated offices and goods; he promised that Gardiner would get £200 (£69,850) of the life pensions worth £300 (£104,750) that Wolsey, in 1529, had forced Gardiner to pay Rochford and Norris out of the revenues of his see. He informed them that 'the third hundred is bestowed of the Vicar of Hell', Sir Francis Bryan, and added, 'And you, Master Wallop, shall not at this time be forgotten, but the certainty of that ye shall have I cannot tell.'[35]

A contemporaneous list of persons newly appointed to offices, written in the hand of Thomas Wriothesley, the future Lord Chancellor, shows that some of these offices, if not all, had belonged to the accused, for it mentions various lordships and stewardships 'as Brereton had the same'; the King's son Richmond was one of the many beneficiaries.[36] The reformer Robert Barnes begged for Rochford's mastership of Bedlam, the hospital for the insane, which was now vacant 'through the death of these false men' and worth £40 (£13,950); he said he would rather have that than a bishopric.[37] Husee listed in his letter some of those who had – even so soon – reaped the spoils of the condemned:

Sir Thomas Cheyney is named Lord Warden [of the Cinque Ports, an office held by George Boleyn from 1533], some saith by Mr Secretary's preferment. My Lord of Richmond is Chamberlain of Chester and North Wales, and Mr Harry Knyvett is Constable of Beaumaris [all offices held by Brereton]. If Mr Secretary keep promise, your Lordship shall have something. Mr [Sir Francis] Bryan is Chief Gentleman of the King's Privy Chamber [in place of Norris], but there is plain saying the King will assign the Groom of the Stool from time to time at his pleasure. I trust your Lordship will remember Mr Secretary with wine and letters.

Weston's family continued to make frantic attempts to save his life. In the same letter, Husee reported the latest rumours:

> Here are so many tales I cannot well tell which to write; for now this day, some saith young Weston shall 'scape, and some saith there shall none die but the Queen and her brother; and some say that Wyatt and Mr Page are as like to suffer as the others; and the saying is now that those which shall suffer shall die when the Queen and her brother goeth to execution. But I think verily they shall all suffer, and in case any do escape, it will be young Weston, for whose life there is importunate suit made.[38]

It is ominous that Husee wrote 'when' rather than 'if', in referring to the Queen and Rochford going to their executions, as if that were not in doubt.

Although many were moved by Weston's plight, 'no one dared plead for him except his mother, who, oppressed with grief, petitioned the King, and his wife, who offered rents and goods for his deliverance'.[39] But they, and his father, Sir Richard Weston, had so far been unsuccessful in obtaining an audience with the King or a meeting with Cromwell, so that they could personally beg for Francis to be spared, for 'the King was determined that the sentence should be carried out. If money could have availed, the fine would have been 100,000 crowns [£8,730,750].'[40]

Husee also wrote on 13 May: 'The rumour is that Harry Webb should be taken in the West Country and put in hold for the same cause. By Wednesday, all shall be known, and your Lordship shall be thereof advertised with speed.'[41] Harry Webb was the Queen's sewer, and – as has been mentioned – he had gone in fear since her arrest; he may even have fled the court. There is no record, however, of him being apprehended on her account.

A letter from John Husee to Lady Lisle, also sent on 13 May, pithily described the wild gossip and speculation that were raging through the court at this time:

> Madam, I think verily, if all the books and chronicles were totally revolved, and to the uttermost persecuted and tried, which against women hath been penned, contrived and written since Adam and Eve, those same were, I think verily, nothing in comparison of that which hath been done and committed by Anne the Queen; which, though I presume be not all thing as it is now rumoured, yet that which hath been by her confessed, and other offenders with her by her own alluring, procurement and instigation, is so abominable and detestable that I am ashamed that any good woman should give ear thereunto.

But there is no evidence that Anne *had* confessed. Indeed, she had throughout protested her innocence, and was to go on doing so to the bitter end. We might infer from this either that it was deliberately being put about at court that she had confessed to the crimes of which she was accused, or that this had been asserted at the trial of her alleged lovers. Whichever it was, Husee was now convinced of her guilt: 'I pray God [he concluded] give her grace to repent while she now liveth. I think not the contrary but she and all they shall suffer.' His next words to Lady Lisle, however, were somewhat at odds with what he had just written: 'John Williams has promised me some cramp rings for you.'[42] The office of blessing rings that were supposedly efficacious in curing cramp belonged exclusively to the Queen of England, so these rings must have been blessed by Anne herself. It seems strange that Husee should think Lady Lisle would want them, given they had been consecrated by one whose reputation was now so irrevocably tainted. Perhaps he was not as convinced of Anne's guilt as he made himself out to be.

By 13 May, the 'heavy news . . . of the imprisonment of the

Queen' had reached Scotland, where it was conveyed by Sir Adam Otterbourne to Henry VIII's nephew, James V, 'to the no small joy of the Scots, especially of the clergy, our capital enemies', as Lord William Howard reported from Edinburgh to Cromwell.[43] James was glad of anything that might discountenance his formidable uncle.

The condemnation of her alleged lovers presaged ill for Anne, and irrevocably prejudiced her own trial, for if they had been found guilty then so, almost for a surety, would she be, and her brother Rochford. That was evidently the King's opinion too, for on 13 May, the day after the men's trial, he ordered her household to be broken up and dissolved, and her servants to be discharged from their allegiance. It was FitzWilliam, the King's treasurer, and Paulet, his comptroller, who went to Greenwich to carry out Henry's orders.[44] On 19 May, John Husee would report that 'the most part of the Queen's servants be set at liberty to seek service at pleasure'.[45] Many were found places in the King's household; others would return later to serve Jane Seymour. It must by now have been obvious to most people that Anne's trial would be a mere formality.

Norfolk's commission of 12 May had appointed him to receive the indictments found against the Queen and Lord Rochford, and to call the accused before him for the purpose of hearing and examining them, and compelling them to answer the charges.[46] Accordingly, on 13 May, the grand juries were commanded to furnish Norfolk with those indictments at the coming trial, and that same day Sir William Kingston was served with a royal writ commanding him to bring Queen Anne and Lord Rochford before the Lord High Steward 'as he shall be required', which was followed hours later by a precept from Norfolk himself, ordering the Constable to bring his prisoners to trial on Monday, 15 May. That same day, 13 May, the Duke of Norfolk, in the King's name, sent another precept to Ralph Felmingham, Serjeant-at-Arms, commanding him to summon at least twenty-seven 'peers of the Queen and Lord Rochford, by whom the truth can be better made to appear'.[47] Obviously, with these trials taking place on the Monday, the executions of the convicted men would have to be postponed, for the Tower officials would be too busy to cope.

On 14 May, Cromwell wrote to Gardiner and Wallop, the English ambassadors in France, formally apprising them of the action taken against the Queen and the judgement on those accused with her. He said he had 'to inform them of a most detestable scheme, happily discovered and notoriously known to all men', of which they may have heard rumours. He 'expressed to them some part of the coming out and the King's proceeding': how Anne's crimes had come to light, the arrests of all concerned, and the condemnation of the men two days earlier. 'She and her brother shall be arraigned tomorrow,' he concluded, 'and will undoubtedly go the same way. I write no particularities, the things be so abominable, and therefore I doubt not but this shall be sufficient instruction to declare the truth if you have occasion to do so.'[48] In this official version of events, Henry VIII was to be portrayed as the grievously injured party.

As news of the arrests spread like wildfire across Europe, the story gained much in the telling. From Paris, on 10 May, the Papal Nuncio, the Bishop of Faenza, reported to the Vatican: 'News came yesterday from England that the King had caused to be arrested the Queen, her father, mother, brother and an organist with whom she had been too intimate. If it be as it is reported, it is a great judgement of God.' The Bishop was still under the impression, on 19 May, that the King had 'imprisoned his wife, her father, mother, brother and friends', and believed that 'that woman will doubtless be put to death'. By 24 May, he had heard a further mish-mash of truth and rumour, and reported: 'It is not true that her father and mother were imprisoned. It is said that the King has been in danger of being poisoned by that lady for a whole year, and that her daughter is suppositious, being the child of a countryman; but these particulars are not known for certain, according to what the King [Francis I] said today. The discovery was owing to words spoken by the organist from jealousy of others.'[49]

In Spain, it was initially believed that 'the mistress of the King of England had been put in the Tower for adultery with an organist of her chamber. Her brother is imprisoned for not giving information of the crime.'[50] On 26 May, John Hannaert of Lyons was to inform the Emperor: 'There is news from England that the so-called Queen was found in bed with the King's organist and taken to prison. It is proved that she had criminal intercourse with her brother and others.'[51] Charles V thought it 'very probable that God has permitted it after her damnable life'.[52]

Dr Ortiz, Charles V's ambassador in Rome, was informed that 'the King of England has imprisoned his mistress in the Tower. Other letters state that, in order to have a son who might be attributed to the King, she committed adultery with a singer who taught her to play on instruments. Others say it was with her brother. The King has sent them to the Tower with her father, mother and other relations.' Ortiz later reported, on 2 June: 'The prayers of the late Queen of England and the Holy Martyrs have prevailed. The King's mistress had six lovers, one being her own brother. Another, a musician, seeing that he was less favoured, discovered the fact to the King, first asking for pardon and his life. Now they are all taken, it is found to be true.' Ortiz recalled the Cardinal of Burgos telling him that it had been prophesied by a martyred saint 'that this Anna would be burned to death'.[53]

In the Vatican, Pope Paul III summoned Gregory Casale, an English government agent, and informed him of what had taken place, declaring that God had enlightened the King of England's conscience, and making it very clear that he would respond gladly to any overture of friendship and reconciliation that the King might make.[54]

On 29 May, in Germany, the Protestant reformer, Philip

Melanchthon, heard the rumours about Anne Boleyn with great sorrow: 'The reports from England are more than tragic. The Queen is thrown into prison with her father, her brother, two bishops and others for adultery.' In June, having obtained more information, he concluded that 'she was more accused than convicted of adultery'.[55] Abroad, some people expressed the opinion that, 'as none but the organist had confessed, the King invented the device to get rid of her'; but many others, convinced that she fully deserved the poor reputation that was hers in Catholic Europe, had no trouble in believing the charges.

Henry VIII had now returned to York Place and, with freedom in sight, had decided that he wanted Jane, his bride-to-be, to be near at hand to receive the news of Anne's condemnation. On Sunday, 14 May, Chapuys reported that the King had that day 'sent for Mrs Seymour by the Grand Esquire [Sir Nicholas Carew] and some others, and made her come within a mile of his lodging';[56] she was installed in the fine house at Chelsea that had once belonged to Sir Thomas More but had reverted to the Crown on his execution the previous summer, and was now in the keeping of Sir William Paulet, comptroller of the royal household and later Marquess of Winchester.[57] Its exact location is uncertain, but it certainly fronted the river, probably where Beaufort Street now lies to the north of Battersea Bridge. This great house boasted a seventy-foot hall, a chapel, a library[58] and twenty-seven acres of beautiful gardens, orchards and parkland, the whole lying in an area that was still largely rural, yet within a half-hour walk of Westminster.

Here, Jane had her first taste of what it would be like to be a queen, finding herself lodged in surroundings of some splendour, 'very richly adorned' in the most sumptuous fabrics and 'served very splendidly by the servants, cooks and certain of the King's officers in very rich liveries'. Her parents, Sir John and Lady Seymour, had come to stay with and support her at this time, and to act as chaperones when the King visited.[59] For all this display of virtue, they, and Jane, were eagerly awaiting the outcome of Anne's trial.

It is clear from Chapuys' dispatches that the Seymours had very quickly taken him into their confidence, and more than likely that the Imperialist party and the Seymour affinity had been lobbying for the death penalty for Anne. The Lady Mary's supporters were convinced that Anne had poisoned Katherine and attempted to do the same to Mary and Richmond, removing all possible rivals to her daughter Elizabeth.[60] They feared that, left alive, she would remain a threat to her successor and any new heirs the King might have. Above all, her death, following on from Katherine of Aragon's, would leave the way clear for a new royal marriage and an undisputed succession. That Anne's execution was widely anticipated is clear from a letter written by Charles V on 15 May, the day of her trial, in which he suggested several possible marriage alliances for Henry VIII, clearly having assumed that she would die.[61]

Throughout the weekend of 13–14 May, the Tower officials were kept busy with hasty preparations for the trials of Anne and Rochford. There was no precedent in England for the trial of a queen, but it was nevertheless felt that it should take place with an appropriate degree of state and ceremonial: it was to be the ultimate show trial, and would be held in the thirteenth-century great hall of the Tower, which was known as the King's Hall.[62] This battlemented building was part of the palace complex, and it stood at right angles to the south end of the Queen's lodging, with one side facing the Jewel Tower and the White Tower, and the other the river. Measuring eighty feet by fifty, the hall had side aisles separated from the central space by two timber arcades with four arches apiece.

The King's Hall had long been neglected, having been used as a storeroom as far back as 1387, and it had had to be repaired and redecorated for Anne's coronation in 1533; these repairs seem to have been purely superficial, for the hall would be falling into ruin by 1559. It was labelled 'decayed' in a plan of the Tower dated 1597,[63] and a temporary canvas roof had to be put in place for the coronation of James I in 1604. In 1641, the hall was converted into an ordnance store. It was finally demolished in or shortly before 1788, when a new store was erected in its place. The Medieval Palace Shop now occupies part of the site.

Anticipating that there would be a high demand by the public for seats, the Constable arranged for a 'great scaffold' or platform to be built in the centre of the hall, 'and there were made benches or seats for the lords', while along the walls were positioned many more benches,[64] so that there would be space for the two thousand spectators mentioned by Chapuys; these benches were still to be seen in the great hall as late as 1778.[65] On the dais at one end of the chamber, the chair of estate – or throne – assigned to the Duke of Norfolk was placed under a canopy of estate bearing the royal arms, for Norfolk, as Lord High Steward, would be representing the King.[66]

On the morning of Monday, 15 May, the Duke seated himself majestically here, holding the long white staff of his office. On a chair at his feet sat his nineteen-year-old son, Henry Howard, Earl of Surrey, grasping the golden staff that symbolised his father's office of Earl Marshal of England. At the Duke's right hand sat Lord Chancellor Sir Thomas Audley; as a commoner, he was not entitled to judge a queen, but was there to offer legal advice to the Duke.[67] At Norfolk's left hand was the Duke of Suffolk, the King's brother-in-law, who had long been Anne's enemy. Now appointed chief of those who had gathered to judge her, he was 'wholly applying himself to the King's humour'[68].

Then were seated, in order of precedence, 'twenty-six of the greatest peers',[69] although the number is also given as twenty-seven,[70] which is in fact the number that had been summoned by Norfolk.[71] Although Constantine claimed that this jury consisted of 'almost all the lords that were in the realm', it in fact comprised fewer than half the entire peerage of sixty-two nobles.[72] Nevertheless, 'the highest peers, marquesses, earls and lords, every one after their degrees', had been 'chosen' to try the Queen and her brother.[73] Friedmann, Anne's Victorian biographer, had no doubt that this panel was 'fairly chosen', but Charles Wriothesley's editor felt that the word 'chosen' lent some credence to conjecture that 'care was taken to select those who could be relied upon to gratify the King's will', as had certainly been the case when Cardinal Wolsey had chosen the lords who had sent the Duke of Buckingham to the block in 1521. George Wyatt heard that the peers who had assembled to judge the Queen were 'men of great honour' but felt 'it had been good also if some of them had not been suspected of too much power and no less malice'. Some were there 'more perhaps for countenance of others' evil than for means by their own authority to do good – which also peradventure would not have been without their own certain perils'.

Given its composition, there was little hope that the panel of peers would be impartial. As one historian has recently written, 'they had much to gain or lose by their behaviour in such a conspicuous theatre'.[74] Ives contends that they had been summoned at such short notice that there can have been little opportunity for the Crown to influence their judgement, but who is to say that it was not made clear to them, directly or indirectly, what verdict was expected?

Among them was Anne's former lover and would-be betrothed, Henry Percy, Earl of Northumberland, whose pursuit of her in 1523 had been halted by Wolsey, acting on the King's orders;[75] Percy had been hustled into an unhappy marriage, and was now an ailing embittered man, whose former love for Anne had long since withered into contempt, especially after she had offended his fellow peer, Norfolk; in 1534, Chapuys had overheard Northumberland saying to a friend that Anne was a bad woman who had plotted to poison the Lady Mary, which effectively demolishes the romantic myth that he loved her till the end of his days. The Earl, having no children, had, the previous January, made the King his heir, describing himself as 'unfeign[ed]ly sick' of 'the debility in my blood'.[76]

The other high-ranking 'lords triers' were Robert Radcliffe, Earl of Sussex, a great confidant of the King, whose name heads the extant list preserved in the *Baga de Secretis*; Henry Somerset, Earl of Worcester, whose wife Elizabeth had laid evidence against the Queen; the Marquess of Exeter and his cousin Henry Pole, Lord Montagu, staunch partisans of the Lady Mary, who were no doubt rejoicing in Anne's fall, for which they had long been scheming; William FitzAlan, Earl of Arundel; John de Vere, Earl of Oxford, another friend of the King; Ralph Neville, Earl of Westmorland, who served Henry VIII loyally in the north; Thomas Manners, Earl of Rutland, and George Hastings, Earl of Huntingdon, both cousins and favourites of Henry's.

The rest of the peers were barons: George Brooke, Lord Cobham, a strong supporter of the King, whose sister Elizabeth was married to Thomas Wyatt, and whose wife was perhaps the 'Nan Cobham' who had given evidence against Anne Boleyn; Henry Parker, Lord Morley, the friend of the Lady Mary, come to sit in judgement on his son-in-law Rochford,[77] and possibly motivated by righteous anger on behalf of his daughter Jane; William, Lord Sandys, the Lord Chamberlain, another long-standing favourite of the King; Thomas Fiennes, Lord Dacre of the South, who had only narrowly escaped being convicted of treason two years earlier, and was not likely to put his neck at risk a second time; John Tuchet, Lord Audley; Thomas West, Lord de la Warr; Arundel's son, Henry FitzAlan, Lord Maltravers; Edward, Lord Grey of Powys, and Thomas Stanley, Lord Monteagle, both of whom were married to daughters of the Duke of Suffolk, the King's brother-in-law and close friend; Edward Fiennes de Clinton, Lord Clinton, who was married to Elizabeth Blount, former mistress to the King and mother of his son, the Duke of Richmond;

Andrew, Lord Windsor, who was very much a King's man; Thomas, Lord Wentworth, whose aunt, Margaret Wentworth, was Jane Seymour's mother; Thomas, Lord Burgh; and John, Lord Mordaunt, a career courtier who served on several treason trials.[78]

The top part of the parchment in the *Baga de Secretis* has perished, and only seventeen names remain on the list of peers. There is a prick-mark beside each, probably made as, one-by-one, the lords took their seats.[79] Notable absentees were the Duke of Richmond, the King's bastard son, who was perhaps excused on account of his youth – he was not quite seventeen;[80] the two female peers; four lords – the Earl of Kent and Lords Dudley, Say and Sele, and Tailboys – who were too poor to attend; three – the Earl of Cumberland, Lord Dacre of the North and Lord Lisle – who were serving as deputies on the northern Marches and in Calais; and several others,[81] among them John Neville, Lord Latimer, the second husband of Katherine Parr (who would become Henry VIII's sixth wife in 1543). Latimer had written to Cromwell on 12 May, begging him 'to have me excused by reason of business in Worcestershire', and protesting, 'I have been at every prorogation and session of the last Parliament since it began, which has been very painful and chargeable to me.'[82]

Alexander Aless was told – by his landlord, who heard it first-hand from people in the crowd that would witness Anne's end – 'that the Earl of Wiltshire, the Queen's father, had been commanded to be an assessor along with the judges, in order that his daughter might be the more confounded, and that her grief might be the deeper'. The account of Anne's trial that is preserved in the Harleian MSS states that Wiltshire 'was among [the peers] by whom she was to be tried', and Chapuys was told that 'the Earl of Wiltshire was quite as ready to assist the judgement as he had done at the condemnation of the other four'.[83] The Bishop of Faenza was to report, on 24 May, that Wiltshire, 'being on the Council, was present at his daughter's sentence',[84] but he is not the most reliable source, and neither is Dr Ortiz, who asserted on 2 June that 'her father approved her condemnation'.[85] In the official record in the *Baga de Secretis*, Wiltshire's name is not included among those who sat in judgement at the trials of his daughter and son, but the list is incomplete. It may be that Wiltshire was the twenty-seventh peer – Norfolk had summoned that number – and that it is time to revise the long-held assumption that he was not among the lords who gathered to try his daughter and his son. Even had he not been, in serving on the jury that had condemned the others, he had effectively colluded in the destruction of his children, for, as Sander's Victorian editor shrewdly pointed out, he 'could not have been ignorant of the effect of the first verdict'.

Conducting the trial was Sir Christopher Hales, the Attorney General and thus the chief prosecutor for the Crown, as well as Sir John Aleyn, 'the Mayor of London with certain aldermen, with the wardens and four persons more of twelve of the principal crafts [guilds] of London'.[86] The French ambassador and other foreign diplomats were permitted to watch the proceedings, but Chapuys was unwell and unable to attend, so had to rely on people who were present for information. Much of what we know of the two trials that were to follow comes from his dispatches.[87] Other eyewitnesses who left records of the proceedings were Sir John Spelman, one of the judges, and the Tower official, Anthony Anthony, Surveyor of the Ordnance, who also owned an inn called The Ship, and served as churchwarden at St Botolph's Church, Aldgate. Unfortunately, his chronicle has not survived, and is known only through the notes on it made by the seventeenth-century writer Thomas Turner, President of Corpus Christi College, Oxford, in his copy of Lord Herbert of Cherbury's life of Henry VIII. Anthony was one of Herbert's sources.

By the King's express command, members of the public were admitted to the trial, and were allowed to stand in the well of the hall behind wooden barriers that had been erected to contain the press of people.[88] George Wyatt gained the impression that Anne's trial was heard 'close enough, as enclosed in strong walls', but Chapuys had the truth of it when he stated that 'the thing was not done secretly, for there were more than two thousand persons present'.[89] The King was determined that justice would be seen to be done, which suggests that he and his advisers felt that they had built a strong enough case against the Queen. Cromwell – as he would tell Chapuys – had 'taken considerable trouble' over the judicial process.[90] This was not to be quite the farcical trial that some historians have claimed it to have been.

The records relating to the legal process against Anne Boleyn and Lord Rochford were long thought to have been suppressed in their entirety, but in fact the Henrician government took unwonted care to preserve some of the official documentation of these proceedings. Nevertheless, crucial papers are missing: the actual trial records, details of the evidence produced in court, the statements known to have been made by Smeaton and Norris, the depositions of all the witnesses who had supposedly been questioned, and transcripts of the interrogations of Smeaton, Norris and the Queen.[91] It was the magisterial Victorian historian, Froude, who first noticed[92] that the records of Anne Boleyn's trial 'survive only in a faint epitome, and we know neither by whom nor why the evidence was done away with'. Yet since the trial had been conducted so publicly, there was really no need for anyone to do away with it. It has been speculated that these documents were destroyed in the sixteenth century, on the orders of either Henry VIII or Cromwell, both of whom perhaps wished to suppress details of dubious evidence or of a scandal that so touched the King's honour, although if that was so, why was not the indictment itself, the very substance of the case, not destroyed too? Cromwell, as Master of the Rolls, would have had control of such documents and the ability to dispose of them, and although it is not unusual for depositions to be missing in such cases, and it is clear from the other documents that depositions were never included with the records in the *Baga de Secretis*,[93] there is a real possibility that, in response to negative comments about the evidence produced at the trial, they were purposely destroyed.

David Starkey has put forward the theory that no depositions ever existed in the first place, and that Cromwell and his colleagues never had all the evidence of which they boasted.[94] In support of this, he cites Rochford's concern – expressed to Kingston probably on 5 May – that he had not yet been summoned before the Privy Council for further questioning, and Anne's marvelling on the same day that the Privy Council had not come to take a deposition from her.[95] But certainly the authorities had Smeaton's confession; there is also good evidence that they had Lady Rochford's testimony, and Sir John Spelman, a judge at the trials of Anne and Rochford, refers to the evidence of the person to whom Lady Wingfield had confided her doubts about Anne, which Starkey does not mention. But even the hostile Chapuys would report that there was no valid proof of Anne's guilt, so it may well be that there were very few 'interrogatories' produced at her trial and that of her brother, and that the Crown relied chiefly on the force and shock value of the indictment and on the prisoners being directly confronted with only the verbal challenges of their accusers.

It has also been suggested, by several writers, that Elizabeth I, Anne's daughter, desirous of suppressing proof of her mother's guilt, destroyed the missing trial documents, although again, that begs the question of why she did not make a more thorough job of it. Furthermore, it seems to have been Elizabeth's policy to leave well alone regarding any matter concerning Anne Boleyn. Quite simply, these papers may have been lost,[96] although considering how crucial and sensitive they were, that is possibly too convenient a theory.

The surviving documents relating to the trials survive in pouches eight and nine of the *Baga de Secretis* in the National Archives. These particular treason trials are among the earliest of which some documentation is preserved. Originally, these papers were kept under lock and key, with only three keyholders: the Lord Chief Justice, the Attorney General and the Master of the Crown Office. This archive consists in each case of an enrolment or summary of the trial and most of the original documents employed in it, including an abstract of the evidence. All have been carefully calendared in the Deputy Keeper's Third Report.

11

'Fighting Without a Weapon'

Jane Seymour did not appear in public on the day of Anne's trial, but stayed indoors with her family at Chelsea. She was agitated about the outcome of the proceedings, and was anxiously awaiting the arrival of Chapuys with news of the verdict. But according to the ambassador, 'one of her relations, who was with her on the day of the condemnation, told me that the King had sent that morning to tell her that he would send her news at three o'clock in the afternoon of the condemnation of the Concubine'. Clearly Henry had made his will in the matter plain, and expected the verdict to be a foregone conclusion.

'On Monday, the 15th of May 1536, there was arraigned within the Tower of London Queen Anne, for treason against the King's own person.' The court being assembled, the proceedings opened with the Crown's commission being read aloud.[1] Then silence was called for and the Duke of Norfolk cried, 'Gentleman Gaoler of the Tower, bring in your prisoner.'[2]

'Summoned by an usher',[3] the Queen was brought forward, having been escorted through the waiting crowds in the Tower precincts and into the great hall by Sir William Kingston and Sir

Edmund Walsingham.[4] 'She walked forth in fearful beauty' and 'seemed unmoved as a stock, not as one who had to defend her cause, but with the bearing of one coming to great honour'.[5] Wearing a gown of black velvet over a petticoat of scarlet damask, and a small cap sporting a black-and-white feather,[6] she advanced attended by Lady Kingston, Lady Boleyn and 'her young ladies'.[7] It would appear that these young ladies, probably four in number, had served as maids-of-honour in the Queen's household, and had been retained to attend her at her trial and afterwards (see p. 333 below).

Beside Anne, according to custom, walked the Gentleman (or Yeoman) Gaoler of the Tower carrying his ceremonial axe,[8] its blade turned away from the prisoner to signify that she was as yet uncondemned. This was not Sir William Kingston, the Constable, but the Tower officer who had overall supervision of the prisoners and their warders and occupied the house on Tower Green that lay between the Lieutenant's Lodging and the Beauchamp Tower.

The Queen 'made an entry as though she were going to a great triumph', carrying herself with calm poise as she was brought to the bar. 'She presented herself with the true dignity of a queen, and curtseyed to her judges, looking round upon them all, without any sign of fear,' wrote Crispin de Milherve, an eyewitness at the trial. 'She returned the salutations of the lords with her accustomed politeness',[9] and even when she saw her father among them, 'she stood undismayed, nor did ever exhibit any token of impatience, or grief, or cowardice'.[10]

Anne's composure was admirable: there was no hint of the hysteria she had shown earlier. Cromwell, by contrast, was tense, concerned lest 'the sense, wit and courage of Anne would go against him'[11] and secure an acquittal – with goodness knew what dire consequences for himself.

A chair had been placed before the bar on the raised platform in the centre of the hall, and Anne now 'took her seat' with notable elegance.[12] Common prisoners stood to hear the charges read, but this was after all the Queen of England, and due ceremony was observed.

'Then her indictment was read before her'[13] in all its embarrassing detail by Sir Christopher Hales, the Attorney General, but Anne's face betrayed no shame as she heard it alleged against her 'that she had procured her brother and the other four to defile her and have carnal notice of her, which they had done often; and that they conspired the death of the King, for she had said to them that she had never loved the King in her heart, and had said to every one of them by themselves that she loved them more than the others, which was to the slander of the issue that was begotten between the King and her, which is made treason by the statute of the twenty-sixth year of the King that now is'.[14]

Anne sat patiently, listening to the indictment. 'Her face said more than words, for she said little; but no one looking at her would have thought her guilty. She defended herself soberly against the charges',[15] and as each was put to her, she put up her hand, pleaded, 'Not guilty',[16] and 'firmly denied' them all, giving to each what Chapuys felt to be 'a plausible answer'.[17]

The Attorney General then argued the case for the Crown, assisted by Cromwell, who was acting as counsel for the King. The substance of their accusations, which were not all grounded in the indictment, was reported by Chapuys on 19 May: 'What she was principally charged with was having cohabited with her brother and other accomplices; that there was a promise between her and Norris to marry after the King's death, which it thus appeared they hoped for; and that she had received and given to Norris certain metals,[18] which might be interpreted to mean that she had poisoned the late Queen and intrigued to do the same to the Princess'[19] – although this was probably the construction that Chapuys himself placed upon that last charge. Dr Ortiz, in far-off Rome, later noted, 'It is said that the process against her states that she poisoned the Queen.'[20] However, there is no charge to that effect in the indictment, and Ortiz may have got his information from Chapuys.

It would appear from Chapuys' report that less emphasis was laid on the more serious charge that Anne had 'conspired the King's death', possibly because the evidence to support it was shaky. Specifying that she had promised to marry Norris, rather than each of her co-accused, as was alleged in the indictment, suggests that a sinister meaning had been deliberately construed from Anne's compromising conversation with Norris on 30 April. It seems the Crown was implying that Anne's relationship with Norris was far more serious than the casual affairs she had supposedly had with the other accused, and that the latter were to be merely accessories to regicide.[21]

Aless reported further details of the evidence, such as it was. 'The Queen was accused of having danced in the bedroom with the gentlemen of the King's Privy Chamber, and of having kissed her brother, Lord Rochford. When she made no answer to these accusations, the King's syndic or proctor, Master Polwarck [Sir Richard Pollard], produced certain letters and bawled out that she could not deny she had written to her brother, informing him that she was pregnant.' The implication, of course, was that Rochford was the father of the child. 'Still she continued silent.'

Chapuys also states that Anne, ludicrously, 'was also charged, and her brother likewise, with having laughed at the King and his dress' and making fun of his poetry, 'which was objected to them as a great crime'; in sum, 'she showed in various ways she did not love the King but was tired of him'.[22] This, of course, was not a crime either, but it was portrayed as shocking in a woman whom the King had honoured with marriage. Dr Ortiz later reported that 'it was proved at the trial that she had behaved in this way before the conception of the child which the King thought to be his'.[23]

Anne put up a spirited defence, and 'made so wise and discreet answers to all things laid against her, excusing herself with her words so clearly, as though she had never been guilty of the same'.[24] 'She positively denied that she had ever been false to the King, but being told that Norris, Weston, Brereton and Smeaton had accused her' – which was substantially untrue, except in the case of Smeaton – 'she said she ought not to conceal certain things which had passed between her and them',[25] which would explain why the Crown had jumped to false conclusions. Among them, probably, were the flirtatious interchanges that Anne had described only days before. She also 'confessed she had given money to Weston, as she had often done to other young gentlemen'.[26] But she insisted, bending the truth, she had maintained her honour and her chastity all her life long.[27] The case against her, it would seem, consisted of what has been described as 'a ragbag of gossip, innuendo and misinterpreted courtliness'.[28]

By all accounts, Anne defended herself with such clarity and good sense that her innocence, which she protested vehemently, seemed manifest to many that heard her, and some began to have doubts and suspicions in regard to the prosecution's case. 'The Queen, sitting in her chair, having an excellent, quick wit, and being a ready speaker, did so answer to all objections that, had the peers given in their verdict according to the expectation of the assembly, she had been acquitted.'[29] Strickland, without identifying the source, claims that Anne, referring to Smeaton's confession, protested 'that one witness was not enough to convict a person of high treason', but was informed 'that in her case it was sufficient'.

The account of the trial in the Harleian MSS states that, after 'the accusers had given in their evidence, the witnesses were produced'. This cannot be accurate, because Chapuys was to state on 20 May that 'no witnesses were produced against her, as it is usual to do, particularly when the accused denies the charge'.[30] What were probably produced were the statements made under examination by those who had testified against Anne, which, as has been noted, do not survive.

Sir John Spelman, a member of the jury and a justice of the King's Bench, later recorded that 'all the evidence was of bawdery and lechery, so that there was never such a whore in the realm' as the Queen. Yet if Anne's conduct had indeed been so blatant as to give rise to such comments, it is strange that there is no abundance of evidence – or, in fact, no evidence at all – for it in other sources.

The Crown certainly stooped to relying on hearsay. Spelman wrote sceptically: 'Note that this matter was disclosed by a woman called the Lady Wingfield, who had been a servant to the Queen and shared the same tendencies; and suddenly the said Wingfield became ill, and a little time before her death she showed the matter to one of those etc.'; as we have seen, this word 'etc.', which has often been incorrectly thought to have been inserted because the page was (perhaps deliberately) torn off here, in fact refers to the witnesses. Lady Wingfield, of course, was the person whose dying words had been repeated to Cromwell by an unidentified informant. Unfortunately, she was now dead and could not confirm her testimony, nor do we know what it was;[31] given that she had probably died by 1534, it perhaps related to offences alleged to have been committed by Norris and Brereton in 1533, or it could even have been to do with something that happened years before, the importance of which had been deliberately exaggerated.[32] In the absence of other witness testimony, it would appear that such evidence as this, along with that of Lady Worcester, Nan Cobham and another maid-of-honour, as well as the Queen's own indiscreet utterings in the Tower, constituted the case for the Crown.

'For the evidence,' wrote George Wyatt, 'as I never could hear of any, small I believe it was. The accusers must have doubted whether their proofs would not prove their reproofs.' That would appear to be corroborated elsewhere.

Following sixteenth-century legal practice, the Queen was not allowed to question any of the Crown's witnesses (had there been any), summon any to speak for her, or give evidence on her own behalf, nor, having been indicted for treason, was she permitted to have any legal counsel for her defence. As her cousin, the fourth Duke of Norfolk, would complain at his trial in 1572, 'I am brought to fight without a weapon.'[33] Nevertheless, Anne had spoken out boldly, stoutly pleading that everything alleged against her was untrue and that she had committed no offence.[34] Yet when it came to the point where she was 'put to the trial of the peers of the realm', the judgement of her peers was unanimous. 'After they had communed together, the youngest lord [the Earl of Surrey] was called first to give verdict, who said *Guilty*, and every lord and earl after their degrees said *Guilty* to the last, and so condemned her.'[35] Against each name on the list of peers appears the abbreviation '*Cul*' for 'culpable', meaning guilty.[36] 'Had the peers given their verdict according to the expectation of the assembly, she had been acquitted; but they, amongst whom the Duke of Suffolk was chief, and wholly applying himself to the King's humour, pronounced her guilty.'[37] It was 'a purely political verdict'.[38]

Excited murmurs were rippling through the assembled spectators at this sensational development, and in the general hubbub, some were unable to tell whether or not the Queen had been found innocent or guilty. Covertly, some of the peers who had condemned her 'did not forbear to deliver out voices that caused everywhere to be muttered abroad that that spotless Queen in her defence had cleared herself with a most wise and noble speech', and this 'was reported without the doors' to the waiting crowds.[39]

Nevertheless, those same peers now told Anne 'she must resign her crown to their hands, which she did at once, without resistance'.[40] This implies either that she was actually wearing a crown at her trial, which is highly unlikely, or that it had been placed at hand in the hall, probably on a cushion. Her being ceremonially divested of it would be dramatically symbolic of her disgrace.

Burnet says that, as she formally gave it up, she protested that she was innocent of having offended against the King.

In Tudor times, crowns were customarily worn at coronations and on the great festivals of the Church. The crown made for Anne Boleyn's coronation in 1533 was of gold studded with sapphires, balas rubies and pearls, with crosses of gold and *fleurs-de-lis* around the rim;[41] probably it had been brought from the Jewel House across the courtyard for her trial, for although queens also wore smaller crowns and coronets on top of their headdresses, as appears in many portraits of the period, Anne is recorded as wearing a cap with a feather for her trial.

'She was then degraded from all her titles, countess [*sic.*], marchioness and princess, which she said she gave up willingly to the King who had conferred them.'[42] Dr Ortiz and the Bishop of Faenza also reported that Anne was sentenced first to be degraded.[43]

Significantly, the title of queen was not mentioned. Wriothesley asserted that after that symbolic act, and the dissolution of her marriage two days later, Anne 'was never lawful Queen of England', and many historians still accept that. Yet for all that she had been ceremonially stripped of her royal insignia, she was never officially deprived of the title of queen, which was hers under the Act of Succession of March 1534, which made her queen by statutory right, and not by right of marriage to the King. This Act was not repealed, only superseded by the 1536 Act of Succession, passed after Anne's death, which just ratified the annulment of her marriage,[44] and left her in the unusual position of being queen without ever having been the King's lawful wife.

That Anne remained Queen of England after her condemnation is clear from the wording of the 1536 Act, in which she is referred to as the 'late Queen Anne', as compared with Katherine of Aragon, who is called merely the 'late Princess Dowager',[45] while Cranmer, when annulling her marriage, called her 'Queen Anne',[46] and Sir William Kingston certainly did so in his letters.

People generally would continue to refer to her as queen, and it was as a queen that Anne Boleyn would go to the scaffold.

It was reported that throughout her trial, Anne had thought herself 'safe from death';[47] her mood had perhaps swung again from pessimism to optimism, and given the precedents, and the humour of the court, she may have been justified in thinking that, at the very worst, divorce and imprisonment would be her fate. She was the Queen of England, and no Queen of England before her had been put to death. But now she was forced to suspend that belief.

A hush descended as the Duke of Norfolk, 'bound to proceed according to the verdict of the peers',[48] pronounced the dread sentence. He and his niece had been estranged for months, but Constantine noted that tears ran down his cheeks as he addressed her, his own sister's child, although of course his tears could have been for his family's lost honour and status, and the jeopardising of his own career, rather than for Anne.[49] He told her gravely: 'Because thou hast offended against our sovereign the King's Grace in committing treason against his person, the law of the realm is this, that thou hast deserved death, and thy judgement is this: that thou shalt be burnt here within the Tower of London on the Green, else to have thy head smitten off, as the King's pleasure shall be further known of the same.'[50] As Spelman noted, burning at the stake was 'the judgement against women in treason, but because she was queen, the Steward gave judgement that she should be burned or beheaded at the King's pleasure'.[51]

On hearing the terrible words spoken by Norfolk, Anne's old nurse, Mrs Orchard, watching from the gallery, 'shrieked out dreadfully'. The ailing Earl of Northumberland 'was suddenly taken ill',[52] and had to be assisted from the hall. Traditionally, it has been assumed that he was overcome by grief for the woman he had once loved, but – as has been shown – that is unlikely. On 19 May, John Husee informed Lord Lisle: 'It is said my lord of Northumberland is dead, but I cannot certify it.'[53] The Earl was in fact mortally ill, and was to die just over a year later.

Chapuys reported that 'when the sentence was read to [Anne], she preserved her composure, saying that she held herself always ready to greet death, but was extremely sorry to hear that others, who were innocent and the King's loyal subjects, should share her fate and die through her. She asked only for a short space for the disposing of her conscience.'[54]

Aless stated that, 'when the sentence of death was pronounced, the Queen raised her eyes to Heaven, nor did she condescend to look at her judges'. Lancelot de Carles wrote that, on hearing her fate, 'her face did not change, but she appealed to God whether the sentence was deserved; then, turning to the judges, she said she would not dispute with them, but believed there was some other reason for which she was condemned than the cause alleged, of which her conscience acquitted her, as she had always been faithful to the King. But she did not say this to preserve her life, for she was quite prepared to die.'

Crispin de Milherve gave a more detailed version of this speech, and his account also shows that Anne believed she was being done away with for reasons other than the crimes alleged against her, and that she knew others were bent on her death.

He too referred to her raising her eyes to Heaven as she declared, 'O Father, O Creator, Thou who art the way, the life and the truth, knowest whether I have deserved this death.' Then she turned to her judges:

My lords, I will not say your sentence is unjust, nor presume that my reasons can prevail against your convictions. I am willing to believe that you have sufficient reasons for what you have done; but then they must be other than those which have been produced in court, for I am clear of all the offences which you then laid to my charge. I have ever been a faithful wife to the King, though I do not say I have always shown him that humility which his goodness to me, and the honours to which he raised me, merited. I confess I have had jealous fancies and suspicions of him, which I had not discretion enough, and wisdom, to conceal at all times. But God knows, and is my witness, that I have not sinned against him in any other way. Think not I say this in the hope to prolong my life, for He who saveth from death hath taught me how to die, and He will strengthen my faith. Think not, however, that I am so bewildered in my mind as not to lay the honour of my chastity to heart now in mine extremity, when I have maintained it all my life long, as much as ever queen did. I know these, my last words, will avail me nothing but for the justification of my chastity and honour. As for my brother and those others who are unjustly condemned, I would willingly suffer many deaths to deliver them, but since I see it so pleases the King, I shall willingly accompany them in death, with this assurance, that I shall lead an endless life with them in peace and joy, where I will pray to God for the King and for you, my lords.

In Chapuys' report of this speech, Anne ended with these words: 'The Judge of all the world, in Whom abounds justice and truth, knows all, and through His love I beseech that He will have compassion on those who have condemned me to this death.' 'Her speech made even her bitterest enemies pity her.'[55]

Various versions of the sentence would be circulated in Europe; on 24 May, the Bishop of Faenza wrote from Paris: 'On the 15th instant, the Queen was degraded, and the following day was to be executed, either burnt or beheaded. But first, her brother, four gentleman [sic.] and an organist, with whom she had misconducted herself, were to be quartered in her presence.' In June, Dr Ortiz, writing from Rome, informed the Empress that Anne was condemned to be 'beheaded and burnt, seeing the others suffer the same death, with the exception of the one who revealed the crime'.[56]

Spelman and his fellow justices were unhappy about the sentence, and 'murmured at this judgement against the Queen, for such a judgement in the disjunctive', meaning that it was unfair to sentence a prisoner to either burning or beheading.[57] However, as would soon become clear, the form of sentence, and the method of execution, had been decided upon beforehand, for the King needed a means of persuading Anne to agree to the annulment of her marriage. All that Norfolk would say to her, in the face of the judges' mutterings, was that, 'according to the old customs of the land she should be burned, but nevertheless it should stand in the King's commandment'.[58]

'The sentence being denounced, the court arose.' Anne curtsied to the peers, then was escorted by Sir William Kingston from the hall, with Lady Kingston and Lady Boleyn following.[59] The Gentleman Gaoler walked alongside, his ceremonial axe now turned towards the prisoner, to show the waiting crowds that she had been condemned to death. Although Lord Rochford's trial was to follow almost at once, Anne and her brother 'did not see each other' as she made her departure.[60]

After the condemned woman had left the court, it erupted in a buzz of conversation as the observers expressed their views on the trial. The Lord Mayor of London openly declared, 'I could not observe anything in the proceedings against her, but that they were resolved to make an occasion to get rid of her at any price.' Even Anne's old enemy Chapuys thought she had answered the charges 'satisfactorily enough' and believed that, like her co-accused before her, she had been 'condemned upon presumption [of guilt] and certain indications, without valid proof or confession'. Norris's servant, George Constantine, later wrote to Cromwell: 'I never heard [that] queens should be thus handled . . . I never suspected, but I promise you there was much muttering of Queen Anne's [being sentenced to] death.' Chapuys reported that Londoners 'spoke strangely' of her trial and the speed of her fall. In a book of hours associated with Anne, next to a picture of Christ before Caiaphas, someone wrote, 'Even so will you be accused by false witnesses.' William Camden, whose life of Elizabeth I was published in 1615, wrote, 'The spectators deemed Anne innocent, and merely circumvented.' It is a view that persists to this day, and with good reason.

It is true that there is no evidence that the Crown had brought pressure to bear to secure a conviction. On the contrary, the letter of the law, as it stood then, had been scrupulously adhered to, and the trial had been superficially fair. Ninety-five jurors, including the commissioners, had found the Queen and her alleged lovers guilty of treason. Yet the composition of the juries had been bound to prejudice the verdicts, and also an awareness of the King's will in the matter. As we have seen, Henry had been expecting a guilty verdict. As soon as news of it came, he sent Sir Francis Bryan 'in all haste' to Chelsea to inform Jane Seymour.[61] 'To judge by appearances,' Chapuys wrote, 'there is no doubt that he will take the said Seymour to wife; and some think the agreements and promises are already made.'[62]

After her condemnation, Anne was 'conveyed back to her chamber', attended by Lady Kingston, Lady Boleyn[63] and her four young ladies. Tradition has long had it that, as an adjudged traitor, she was now moved from the Queen's apartments in the Tower palace to the 'Lieutenant's Lodging', as the Queen's House was called until around 1880; it is now the official residence of the Governor of the Tower and known as the Queen's House or the King's House, depending on the gender of the reigning monarch.

The Lieutenant's Lodging was a medieval house that stood between the Garden (later known as the Bloody) Tower and the Bell Tower. It was ruinous, and there were plans to rebuild it; the first payments had been made in 1533. However, works would not be completed until the 1540s, when the half-timbered house that stands today was erected. The Lieutenant's Lodging faced Tower Green (or East Smithfield Green as it was then known) and the royal chapel of St Peter ad Vincula. Since the 1540s it has been much restored and altered, but two linenfold-oak-panelled first-floor rooms said to have been occupied by Anne Boleyn have been preserved; one, a bedroom fourteen feet square, with a ceiling just eight feet high, boasts a handsome four-poster bed. A rough carving of the name ANNE survives in the stonework of the large fireplace. Originally, the house also boasted a spacious hall two storeys high, the upper part of which later became the Council Chamber.

That carving is probably not contemporary, and there is no other evidence in primary sources that Anne was moved here. It was Elizabeth Benger who, in her *Memoirs of the Life of Anne Boleyn*, published in 1821, incorrectly inferred from Kingston's letters that, since his wife was attending the Queen, the latter was accommodated in the Lieutenant's Lodging, regardless of the fact that Kingston was the Constable, not the Lieutenant; prior to 1821, as Benger states, an unsupported tradition had it that Anne was held in the Beauchamp Tower, where a carving of her falcon badge can still be seen. Benger's misconception was enshrined in William Harrison Ainsworth's enormously popular book, *The Tower of London*, in 1840, and was soon widely accepted as fact. Only gradually are historians rejecting the tradition that Anne was imprisoned in the Lieutenant's Lodging,[64] while it is still believed by the public at large. It is now thought that the rooms alleged to be hers were only built in 1540. Given that Kingston expected Anne to be executed within a day or so of her trial, it was hardly worth the effort to move her and her attendants, while the Lieutenant's half-built house was in no fit state for housing the woman who was still Queen of England: in 1539, among Cromwell's 'Remembrances', is a note to himself about the Lieutenant's Lodging, 'which will fall down'.[65] Since Anne was conveyed 'back to her chamber', she must have returned to the Queen's lodgings after her trial.

'And so she was brought to ward again, and two ladies waited on her, which came in with her at the first, and waited still on her, the Lady Kingston and the Lady Boleyn, her aunt.'[66] At least Anne was now spared the company of the tart and perhaps resentful Lady Shelton, and Mrs Coffin, who had also been dismissed.

'Immediately' after Anne Boleyn's trial,[67] 'the lord of Rochford, her brother, was arraigned for high treason, which was for knowing the Queen his sister carnally, most detestable against the law of God and nature also, and treason to his prince; and also for conspiracy of the King's death'. Having stood at the bar, held up his hand and pleaded not guilty, 'he made answer so prudently and wisely to all articles laid against him, that marvel it was to hear, but never would confess anything, but made himself as clear as though he had never offended'.[68] Lancelot de Carles speaks of 'his calm behaviour and good defence. [Sir Thomas] More himself did not reply better.'

With regard to the main charge, that of treasonable incest, the Crown's case appears to have rested solely on the deposition of Rochford's wife, Jane,[69] and to have related chiefly to an occasion when he had been alone in private with Anne.[70] Burnet says that, in making a request to her, he was said by bystanders to have leaned over her bed and kissed her, but this cannot have been on the occasion when they were alone, so either Burnet's information is apocryphal, or he had access to sources now lost to us. Even so, this was an age in which queens and great ladies would receive guests as they lay on their beds, attired in rich nightgowns in heavy fabrics, and the custom of kissing ladies on the mouth on greeting was widespread in England among all classes, as the humanist Erasmus delightedly noted on his first visit. So Anne's conduct would hardly have been remarkable. The author of the 'Spanish Chronicle', never reliable and inclined to embroider or make up details, claims that Rochford had been espied leaving her bedchamber 'dressed only in his night-clothes' on several occasions.

Spelman and Anthony do not refer to any of this testimony,

but their accounts survive only in part. Chapuys reported that Rochford 'was charged with having cohabited with her upon presumption, because he had once been found a long time with her, and with certain other follies'. He states that Lady Rochford had divulged their 'accursed secret' in a letter.[71] George Wyatt, writing six decades later, refers to this testimony of Rochford's 'wicked wife', but states that she was 'brought forth' to accuse him, a common misconception, for there is no record of her actually being in court, and Chapuys says that, again, no witnesses were called.[72] But Jane's deposition was sufficient, and when it became clear that no one else was to testify, Rochford protested to his judges, 'On the evidence of only one woman, you are prepared to believe this great evil of me!'[73] An anonymous Portuguese observer, whose account was written in May 1536, felt that Lady Rochford, in betraying 'this accursed secret and together with it the names of those who had joined in the evil doings of the unchaste Queen', had acted 'more out of envy and jealousy than out of love towards the King'.[74]

It has been argued that, had Rochford been suspected of homosexual conduct, as Warnicke suggests, political capital would have been made of it at his trial, at which the details would have come out.[75] Yet that argument fails to take into account the fact that a charge of homosexuality would have undermined the main accusation of incest with his sister. Even if Rochford was known to have taken part in homosexual acts, it would not have been in the Crown's interest to draw attention to the fact.

But there were more explosive revelations to come. Chapuys wrote circumspectly to the Emperor:

I would not wish to omit that, among other things that were charged against [Rochford] as a crime, it was also objected against him that his sister the Concubine had told his wife that the King has not the ability to copulate with a woman, for he has neither potency nor vigour. This he was not openly charged with, but it was shown him in writing, with a warning not to repeat it. But he immediately declared the matter, in great contempt of Cromwell and some others, saying he would not in this point arouse any suspicion which might prejudice the King's issue. He was also charged with having spread reports which called in question whether his sister's daughter was the King's child, to which he made no reply.[76]

Why should Rochford have wished to impugn the legitimacy of a royal heir with Boleyn blood?[77] It would not have been in his, or his family's, interests to do so. But that was beside the point. His accusers seem only to have been concerned with branding him a traitor, for to say such things of the sovereign was not only shocking, but also − under the provisions of the 1534 Act − high treason, in that they impugned the King's issue.[78]

There was an accepted medieval belief, still widely prevalent in the sixteenth century, that impotence, temporary or otherwise, was often caused by magic, as was alleged in many requests for marriages to be annulled. This might explain the discreet assertion in the indictment that certain harms and perils had befallen the King's body,[79] which implied that the harm done to the man imperilled both his dynasty and his kingdom. So entrenched in society was the assumption − and awareness − that most cases of impotence were brought about by witchcraft[80] that the fact did not even need to be stated in the indictment. And although this was a far cry from Henry's reported belief that he had been seduced into this marriage by witchcraft, which was why it was barren of sons, it was but a short step from that gossip to the conviction that Anne had taken things a stage further and used magic to prevent her husband from impregnating her. It did not matter that the Queen, in confiding this matter to her sister-in-law − if she ever did so − had perhaps been expressing her fears about not being able to conceive, nor that her very future depended on her bearing Henry an heir. Once she was suspected of witch-craft, people would have been ready to believe anything of her, however irrational; and such a charge would have made sense in the light of her alleged plot to murder the King, marry one of her lovers and rule in Elizabeth's name.

However, it is unlikely that Anne ever made that unguarded remark to Lady Rochford. By the summer of 1535, they had almost certainly fallen out, and Jane had switched her allegiance to Katherine and Mary. If Anne had confided in Jane prior to that date, and her assertions about the King were true, his inca-pacity must have been temporary, for he had begotten a son on her in October that year. It is highly implausible that Anne would have trusted Jane with such sensitive information after their estrangement, and therefore unwise to accept this evidence for Henry VIII's supposed impotency at face value.

It has been suggested that Henry's embarrassment about his poor sexual performance, and his suspicion – or awareness – that Anne despised him for it, may have been a fundamental cause of her fall.[81] Yet there is little evidence to support the widely discussed modern theory that Henry VIII suffered from erectile problems. In 1532, lamenting the fact that he had waited so long to marry Anne Boleyn and still did not have a son to succeed him, Henry himself had told Parliament, 'I am forty-one years old, at which age the lust of man is not so quick as in lusty youth.'[82] This was a strange remark from the man who had been waiting for more than six years to marry Anne, and was supposedly desperate to bed her, but it was probably made to justify the speedy putting away of Katherine of Aragon.[83] Eight years after the King uttered it, even when he had become ill, incapacitated and grossly obese, he was to tell his doctor that he was still having wet dreams twice nightly; at that time – 1540 – he was insisting that he was unable to consummate his marriage to Anne of Cleves, who revolted him in various ways, but that, because of his 'nightly emissions', he felt himself capable of intercourse with other ladies.

It would therefore appear that the King's remark to Parliament in 1532 was merely made to curry sympathy and emphasise the urgency of the situation.

Then there was that touchy response made to Chapuys in 1533, 'Am I not a man like other men? Am I not? Am I not?'[84] though perhaps we should not attach too much significance to that, for it was made in response to the ambassador's suggestion that the King might never have sons. The fact that Anne Boleyn conceived four times in three years, and that Jane Seymour was to become pregnant after only six months of marriage, is proof that Henry VIII functioned sexually as normally as any man of his age.

Whether Anne actually complained of Henry's impotence to Lady Rochford or not is immaterial, for the real purpose of this evidence was probably to reinforce the implication in the indictment that Henry VIII had not fathered the child of which Anne miscarried.[85] What is strange, though, is why the Crown was being so coy about this, and did not openly accuse Anne of impugning the royal succession by foisting a bastard on the King; and why it took a gamble that Rochford would not disobey orders and read out loud what was supposed to be kept secret.

Rochford's answer, followed by his silence, made plain to everyone listening the thrust of the evidence, and its effect was to create a sensation; every foreign ambassador was to report it in gleeful detail.[86] Too late, Rochford protested, 'I did not say it!' No one was willing to listen.

He responded better to the other charges, replying 'so well that several of those present naively wagered ten to one that he would be acquitted, especially as no witnesses were produced against him'.[87] George Constantine told Cromwell that 'there were [those] that said that much money would have been laid that day, and that at great odds, that the Lord Rochford should have been quit'.

Even 'the judges at first were of different opinions, but at last one view overturned the other' and the twenty-six peers (Northumberland being absent) came to a unanimous decision:

when Norfolk 'asked them if he was guilty or not, one (speaking for them all) replied, "Guilty." '[88] The Duke then had to sentence his nephew to the full horrors of a traitor's death: 'that he should go again to prison in the Tower from whence he came, and to be drawn from the said Tower of London through the City of London to the place of execution called Tyburn,[89] and there to be hanged, being alive cut down, and then his members [genitals] cut off and his bowels taken out of his body and burnt before him, and then his head cut off, and his body to be divided in quarter pieces, and his head and body to be set at such places as the King should assign'.[90] Hearing these dread words, Rochford observed that every man was a sinner and that all deserved death.[91] According to Chapuys, he 'said that, since he must die, he would no longer maintain his innocence, but confessed that he had deserved death'. He only 'requested the judges that they would beg the King that his debts, which he recounted, might be paid out of his goods'.[92]

Effectively, unless Chapuys had got it wrong, Rochford had confessed that he was guilty as charged, and that his sister was guilty by implication. It would have been unusual for a man facing imminent divine judgement to confess an untruth, but Rochford may have been referring to his general sinfulness, and perhaps made this declaration with a view to protecting the surviving members of his family, for on the scaffold, he was to protest that he had never offended the King and, according to Chapuys himself, 'disclaimed all that he was charged with'.[93]

Plainly, people did believe him innocent. 'By the common opinion of men of best understanding in those days,' George Wyatt later wrote, Rochford was 'condemned only upon some point of a statute of words then in force'. George Wyatt, like others, was clearly not impressed by Lady Rochford's evidence. 'I heard say he had escaped, had it not been for a letter,' Constantine recorded. He did not specify whether this was his wife's letter detailing his crimes, or the letter produced at the Queen's trial as evidence that he had fathered her child. Had Rochford not been so proud, the poet Wyatt wrote later, every man would have bemoaned his fate, if only for his great wit. But he had made so many enemies through his arrogance that there were few willing to speak up in his favour, however much they had admired his courage during his trial.

'After this, the court brake up.'[94] It had been one of the most momentous days in English judicial history.

Afterwards, news of the verdict was speedily conveyed to the King. On 19 May, Chapuys reported that Henry had 'supped lately with some ladies in the house of John Kite, Bishop of Carlisle'.[95] This would have been on one of the evenings after the trial, perhaps the 15th itself. The Bishop of Carlisle's Inn (later Russell House) stood by Ivy Bridge in the Strand, next to the Savoy Hospital; this house was being currently leased to Sir Francis Bryan.

Bishop Kite told Chapuys the next morning that Henry had 'shown an extravagant joy' at dinner, and was 'heard to say that he believed upwards of a hundred men had had to do with [Anne], and said he had long expected the issues of these affairs, and that thereupon he had before composed a tragedy, which he carried with him; and so saying, the King drew from his bosom a little book written in his own hand; but the Bishop did not read the contents', probably because it was not the occasion for it. Chapuys gained the impression that the book may have contained 'certain ballads that the King has composed, at which the Concubine and her brother laughed as foolish things, which was objected to them as a great crime'.[96] Henry added that Anne had only kept his love through practising her spells and enchantments.[97] His conviction that she had bewitched him was probably genuine, and would go a long way towards explaining his ill-advised passion for her and prevent him from losing face in the light of recent events. Whether Henry really believed that Anne had been rampantly promiscuous with more than a hundred men is dubious: if he had long expected something of that nature, why had he not acted on his suspicions before? No, this was probably another blustering, face-saving remark.

Chapuys sought out Henry that evening to offer his commiserations on the Queen's treachery, upon which Henry observed complacently that 'many great and good men, even emperors and kings, have suffered from the arts of wicked women'. He did not appear to be suffering very greatly. 'You never saw a prince or husband make greater show or wear his horns more patiently and lightly than this one does,' Chapuys observed with irony to the Emperor. 'I leave you to imagine why.'[98]

The reason for Henry's complacency was staying a mile or so along the river, at Chelsea, where Henry had himself rowed after dinner. That night, he stayed up late with Jane, enjoying a supper prepared by his own master cooks. The next day, 16 May, Chapuys noticed that the courtiers were visiting Chelsea in increasing numbers to pay their respects to the woman, whom they expected would soon become their queen. The common people were aware of this too, and crowds were gathering outside the gates in the hope of catching a glimpse of her. Their mood was not entirely approving; at least one defamatory ballad about Jane was already circulating in London, much to the King's annoyance.

The cynical Chapuys was doubtful that Henry's love for Jane would last. 'He may well divorce her when he tires of her,' he opined, doubtless thinking of the King's two failed marriages. But for now Henry was an amorous suitor, as is apparent in this, the only one of his letters to Jane Seymour to survive; it must have been sent around this time, and refers to one of the scurrilous ballads:

My dear friend and mistress,

The bearer of these few lines from thy entirely devoted servant will deliver into thy fair hands a token of my true affection for thee, hoping you will keep it for ever in your sincere love for me. Advertising you that there is a ballad made lately of great derision against us, which, if it go abroad and is seen by you, I pray you pay no manner of regard to it. I am not at present informed who is the setter forth of this malignant writing, but if he is found out, he shall be straitly punished for it. For the things ye lacked, I have minded my Lord [Treasurer] to supply them to you as soon as he could buy them. Thus, hoping shortly to receive you into these arms, I end for the present, your own loving servant and sovereign,

H.R.[99]

12

'Just, True and Lawful Impediments'

At some point between 15 and 17 May – Strickland asserts it was on the 16th – Henry VIII signed the death warrants of the Queen and the men who were to perish on her account. Six years later, when his fifth wife, Katherine Howard, was condemned to death by Act of Attainder, a wooden stamp bearing his signature was impressed on the document, sparing him the pain of signing away the life of a woman he had once loved. But in the case of Anne Boleyn, he had personally to put pen to parchment. In so doing, he was merely complying with the law.[1] There is no contemporary evidence that he took 'a positive delight' in planning her execution, as one historian has written;[2] on the contrary, as will be seen, he was anxious to get it over with, and moved by pity – and pragmatism – to commute the sentence.

On the morning after the trials, Kingston went to York Place to see the King, one of the few privileged persons allowed to do so at this time. Later that day, back at the Tower, he wrote another letter to Cromwell: 'This day I was with the King's Grace, and declared the petitions of my lord of Rochford, wherein I was answered. Sir, the said lord much desireth to speak with you, which touched his conscience much, as he sayest, wherein I pray you I may know your pleasure, for because of my promise made unto my said lord to do the same.' Rochford was fretting about some debts of his that had not been settled, and Kingston had undertaken to raise the matter with Master Secretary.

One of the prisoners was spending his final hours carving Anne's falcon badge on the wall of his cell in the Beauchamp Tower. This carving, which still survives, must date to the days after her condemnation, as the falcon is without its customary crown.

Although the King had informed Kingston that the male prisoners were to die the next day, the Constable had not yet been given a date for Anne's execution, nor been told if she was to be burned or beheaded, and had perhaps not liked to ask Henry face-to-face. Instead, he raised the matter with Cromwell: 'I shall desire you further to know the King's pleasure touching the Queen, as well for her comfort as for the preparation of scaffolds and other necessaries concerning. The King's Grace showed me that my lord of Canterbury should be her confessor, and [he] was here this day with the Queen, and not in that matter.'

Appointing no less a personage than the Archbishop of Canterbury, who knew her well, to look after Anne's spiritual needs was another kindness on the King's part, but there was an ulterior motive involved. Cranmer, perhaps advised by Dr Sampson, had now found grounds for annulling Anne's marriage to the King, but there is no record of what they were, as the case papers documenting his deliberations have disappeared, which has given rise to much speculation. He certainly did not argue – as the Imperialists wanted – that Henry's union with Katherine of Aragon had after all been lawful, not after all the trouble that Henry had gone to in having it dissolved and insisting he had been right to do so; moreover, to have acknowledged that union as valid would automatically have restored the Lady Mary to the succession.

Charles Wriothesley states that the Archbishop declared Anne's marriage invalid on the supposition of a precontract with her former suitor, Henry Percy, Earl of Northumberland, and initially Cranmer did consider those grounds. Bishop Burnet asserts – without citing his source – that Anne would willingly have confessed to such a precontract in the hope of saving her life or, if the worst came to the worst, suffering the kinder death. But Percy himself thwarted her.

In the summer of 1523, according to the account of George Cavendish, Cardinal Wolsey's gentleman-usher Henry Percy and Anne Boleyn, headstrong young lovers, had secretly contracted to wed in the presence of witnesses, which was sufficient to create an impediment to any subsequent marriage with other partners. But by law, such a precontract *per verba de praesenti* would have been invalid because Percy had been betrothed since 1516 to Lady Mary Talbot, whom he married in September 1523 after being forced by Cardinal Wolsey, on the King's orders, to part from Anne. In the summer of 1532, the Countess of Northumberland had applied to Parliament for a divorce on the grounds that her husband had been precontracted to Anne at the time of their marriage, but the Earl had that July sworn on oath that he had not been (see his letter below), whereupon Parliament had turned down his wife's petition.[3]

Undaunted, after Anne's arrest, Cranmer had again approached Northumberland on the subject of the precontract, and again Percy had denied its existence. A week later, Cranmer was forced to admit to Cromwell that he had as yet found no grounds for the desired annulment, at which Cromwell sent Sir Reynold Carnaby, one of the King's officers in the north and a man who would have known Percy well, to visit the Earl at Brook House, his residence in Newington Green, Hackney, north-east of London, and put pressure on him to confess that he had indeed been precontracted to Anne. But Northumberland would not allow himself to be bullied, and on 13 May, he sent an exasperated letter to Cromwell:

Mr Secretary,

This shall be to signify unto you that I perceive by Sir
Reynold Carnaby that there is a supposed precontract
between the Queen and me; whereupon I was not only
heretofore examined upon my oath before the Archbishops
of Canterbury and York, but also received the Blessed
Sacrament upon the same before the Duke of Norfolk and
other the King's Highness's Council learned in the spiritual
law; assuring you, Master Secretary, by the said oath and
Blessed Body which afore I received, and hereafter intend
to receive, that the same may be to my damnation if ever
there were any contract or promise of marriage between
her and me.[4]

Cromwell knew when he was beaten, and he directed Cranmer
to find other grounds for the annulment of the royal marriage.
In the end, according to Chapuys, the Archbishop found a solution that was somewhat embarrassing and damaging to the King's
honour, which may account for the proceedings being held *in
camera*. He cited the impediment raised by Henry's sexual liaison
with Mary Boleyn, which had placed him within the forbidden
degrees of affinity to her sister Anne.[5] In January 1528, the Pope,
anxious to do anything to please the King but grant him the
annulment he so desperately desired, had dealt with this impediment in a dispensation permitting Henry to marry anyone
within the forbidden degrees (so long as it were not his brother's
widow) as soon as he was free to do so; in 1533, after Henry had
broken with Rome, an Act of Parliament was passed permitting
marriage with the sister of a discarded mistress but that was
followed by the Dispensations Act of March 1534, which decreed
that existing papal dispensations would not be held as valid if they
were contrary to 'Holy Scripture and the laws of God'[6]. In the end
in declaring Anne's marriage null and void, Cranmer chose to
follow the old Canon Law.

The preamble to a new Act of Succession that would be passed by Parliament in July 1536 was to be suitably discreet: the union had been dissolved because of 'certain entirely just, true and lawful impediments hitherto not publicly known' and 'confessed by the Lady Anne before the most reverend father in God, Thomas, Archbishop of Canterbury',[7] presumably when he visited her on 16 May, and by the King, the other party, probably days before that, because at some stage the Archbishop had forwarded copies of articles of objection to the validity of the marriage to both Henry and Anne, 'that it might be for the salvation of their souls', and had summoned them to appear before his ecclesiastical court at Lambeth Palace to show why a sentence of nullity should not be passed.[8]

What exactly did Anne – and Henry – confess to Cranmer? It has been suggested that another possible ground for annulment was Anne's having used witchcraft to render Henry impotent, which had been recognised as an impediment since the twelfth century under canon law.[9] Yet while this construction may be placed on the evidence produced at George Boleyn's trial, it is clear that both Henry and Anne confessed to prior knowledge of a bar to their union, and that both their souls were in peril as a result, not just Anne's. Thus we should conclude that the true cause confessed to Cranmer was that Henry and Anne knew that their union was incestuous and invalid due to the existence of the impediment created by Henry's liaison with Mary Boleyn, and were aware that the Dispensations Act had rendered their marriage unlawful. What amounts effectively to confirmation of this can be found in the 1536 Act of Succession, which banned marriages between people who came within this particular degree of consanguinity.[10]

Certainly the impediment of consanguinity had been known of by both Anne and Henry when they entered into their illicit union. But they had married in good faith, because in 1533, the Pope's dispensation of 1528 could still have been cited. It was the Act of 1534 that rendered both the dispensation and the marriage invalid. Strictly speaking, the legitimacy of the Princess Elizabeth, who had been born before that date, of a marriage entered into in good faith, should never have been denied, but evidently Cranmer, Cromwell and the King were not interested in such legal niceties.

When Cranmer saw Anne at the Tower on 16 May, the purpose of his visit was not – as Kingston's letter makes clear – to provide spiritual consolation and administer the Holy Sacrament, but to obtain her admission of the impediment to her marriage, and her consent to the dissolution of that marriage and the disinheriting and bastardising of her child; and also to apprise her of the proctors whom the King had appointed to act for her, and to seek her approval of them.[11] It is more than likely, as will become apparent, that the Archbishop had instructions to offer her the kinder death by decapitation by the sword (as historians have long suspected), or even the hope of mercy, in return for her co-operation. He certainly discussed the possibility of her being spared the extreme penalty, probably as an inducement, and probably without committing himself, for after he had left, Anne was much more cheerful, and in his letter to Cromwell, Kingston reported that 'this day at dinner, the Queen said she should go to a nunnery, and is in hope of life';[12] her entering religion would render her marriage null and void.[13] It might be concluded, therefore, that she had agreed to the annulment without undue protest.

But it was a cruel deception. There would be no question of Anne being banished to a nunnery, which would have had to have been abroad anyway, since those in England were scheduled for dissolution. The only reward she would get for her co-operation was a mercifully quick end.

Weston's family were still making frantic efforts to save him, now offering the King 100,000 marks (over £11 million) in return for his life,[14] but Henry either was not told of this or remained impervious to bribery. Chapuys reported on 19 May that the French ambassadors Antoine de Castelnau, Bishop of Tarbes, and Jean, Sieur de Dinteville, had done their best to plead for Weston.[15] It is frustrating to discover that Jean de Dinteville's correspondence is missing for the two months covering Anne Boleyn's fall and its aftermath. Froude speculated that all his letters on that subject had been either set apart and lost, or destroyed. The latter is a distinct possibility, since Dinteville had found Henry VIII so terrifying that he begged to be recalled after his first audience in 1533, from which he had emerged visibly shaking.[16] He would not have wanted such sensitive letters falling into the wrong hands.

'Notwithstanding [the ambassadors'] intercession on Weston's behalf',[17] there was no hope of liberation for any of the condemned men. All were to be executed. It was after Kingston returned from seeing the King that he informed them they must prepare to die the next day, and that it would not be at Tyburn after all, or within the Tower, as John Husee had speculated, but on the public scaffold on Tower Hill; an anonymous contemporary account in the Vienna Archives confirms that they were executed 'on a scaffold in front of the Tower'.[18]

Kingston had been given very little notice to prepare for the coming executions. In his letter of the 16th (quoted above), he reminded Cromwell that

> the time is short, for the King supposeth the gentlemen to die tomorrow, and my lord of Rochford with the residue of gentlemen, and are yet without Dr Allryge, which I look for [Dr Allryge presumably being the chaplain who was to hear their final confessions and shrive them]; but I have told my lord of Rochford that he is to be in readiness tomorrow to suffer execution, and so he accepts it very well, and will do his best to be ready, notwithstanding he would have received his rights, which hath not been used, and in especial here.[19]

It was traditional – and indeed was perceived as a right and a privilege – for royal or noble persons condemned to death for treason to have the customary brutal sentence commuted by the King to beheading, which was seen as a more honourable way to die. But Kingston had as yet received no such instructions. He urged Cromwell: 'Sir, I shall desire you that we may know the King's pleasure here as shortly as may be, that we here may prepare for the same which is necessary, for the same we here have now may for to do execution. Sir, I pray you have good remembrance in all this for us to do, for we shall be ready always to our knowledge.'

Kingston's letter to Cromwell was dispatched after dinner on the 16th, probably in the afternoon, so the condemned men had several agonising hours to wait to hear how they would die. At length – and it may not have been until the next morning – word came that the King had been pleased graciously to commute the dread sentences to decapitation. Despite Bishop Burnet's later assertion that Smeaton was hanged, the contemporary *Lisle Letters* confirm that all five, including the low-born musician, 'suffered with the axe', as do Wriothesley (who says they 'were all beheaded'), Edward Hall, the anonymous Imperialist account,[20] the Grey Friars' Chronicle, the Histoire de la Royne Anne de Boullant and Cavendish, who refers to the great clemency extended by the King to Smeaton:

> And though by great favour I lose but my pate,
> Yet deserved have I cruelly to be martyred,
> As I am judged to be hanged, drawn and quartered.[21]

The musician was lucky. Such mercy on the part of the King whom the lowly Smeaton was said to have cuckolded was extraordinary. Pure logistics may have been a factor, for there was no gallows on Tower Hill; prisoners who were to suffer hanging were taken to Tyburn,[22] but it was more convenient to have the men all executed together, near the Tower. It is also possible that Henry commuted all the sentences because he knew the men personally.²³

Yet there could have been a deeply personal reason why Henry showed mercy. If he truly believed that these men had been Anne's lovers, he might not have wished to expose their bodies to the public gaze for castration and evisceration, perhaps feeling that that might only serve to underline their shameful crimes. He seems to have been concerned all along to minimise the scandal arising from the fall of the Queen, and to maintain discretion: witness his withdrawal into seclusion, his concern to observe all due ceremonial at every stage of the legal process, his granting to all the accused the most honourable form of execution, his concern that foreigners should not witness Anne's end (see p.321 below), his permitting her to be treated as a queen throughout, and his erasing of all reminders of her afterwards. Gruesome scenes on the public scaffold would only have given rise to more scandal, and had a more lasting impact; and they would have been at vari‑ance with the efforts the King and his ministers were making to deal with this scandal as discreetly as possible.

Young Weston spent his last evening writing out a list of his debts, 'as more plainly appeareth by a bill of the particulars written with his own hand'. They reveal insights into the glamorous and luxurious life he had so recently led, and into the members of his circle and those whose company he frequented. He owed money to many people: the King – two amounts of 40s. (£700) and 50 marks (£4,050); his father; his father's cook, Barnarde; his cousin Dingley; Thomas Boleyn, Earl of Wiltshire; Browne the draper; Jennings, a page of the Privy Chamber; and three 'broderers' (embroiderers), the King's own, Bradby and William, the latter being owed the substantial sum of £35 (£12,200), 'whereon he has a gown, a coat and a doublet of cloth of gold' – this alone shows how grand Weston had become through royal favour, since the sumptuary laws permitted only those of the rank of earl or above to wear embroidery, while only dukes and marquesses could wear cloth of gold. The fact that Weston owed money to Cornelius Heyss (or Hayes), the King's goldsmith, is further evidence of the status he had enjoyed. Other creditors included Peter the hosier; Bridges 'my tailor'; 'a poor woman that Hannesley of the tennis play had married, [in payment] for balls, I cannot tell how much'; Harde Derman 'at the gate'; Henry Seymour, a younger brother of Jane; Sir Francis Bryan; Sir Henry Parker, Lady Rochford's brother, then a page at court; Weston's saddler, shoemaker and barber; 'Jocelyne that was Mr Norris's servant'; John Norris; 'Secheper that playeth at the dice'; and Temple the fletcher. Altogether, the debts totalled a staggering £925.7s.2d (£323,150), enough to ruin Weston's family.

This list the condemned man enclosed with a farewell letter to his parents:

Father and Mother,
I shall humbly desire you, for the salvation of my soul, to discharge me of this bill, and to forgive me of all my offences that I have done to you, and in especial to my wife, which I desire for the love of God to forgive me and to pray for me, for I believe prayer will do me good. God's blessing have my children and mine.
By me, a great offender to God.[24]

It should be emphasised that such sentiments reflected the sixteenth-century view of the sinfulness of all human beings, and that in this context, Weston's words did not necessarily constitute an admission that he was guilty of the crimes for which he was to die. Brereton's wife Elizabeth certainly believed her husband to be innocent, and cherished a 'bracelet of gold, the which was the last token [he] sent me', bequeathing it to their son Thomas on her own death nine years later.[25]

It must have been later on the 16th that Kingston had another conversation with Anne's brother and again had occasion to write to Cromwell. Rochford was troubled in his conscience about a monk he had preferred, with Cromwell's help, to be Abbot of Valle Crucis Abbey; he was worried that, the abbey being suppressed, the Abbot would lose the pensions awarded him, and wanted the King, whose responsibility this now was, reminded of it. He had apparently asked Kingston to solicit Cromwell's help, and had also raised the matter with the tardy Dr Allryge, who had since arrived to offer spiritual consolation to the condemned men. That evening, Kingston went to see Rochford and

> showed him the clause of your letter. He answered that he had sent you word by Dr Allryge. Notwithstanding, he says that he made suit to you for the promotion of a white monk of the Tower Hill, and with your help he was promoted to the abbey of Valle Saint Crucis in Cheshire, and he had for his promotion £100, and at Whitsuntide next should receive £100 more, but for this the King has the obligations. He supposes the said abbey is suppressed and the Abbot undone, and his sureties also.

Kingston was hoping that Cromwell would put his prisoner's mind at rest, and added a postscript to his letter:

> You must help my lord of Rochford's conscience for the monk; and also he spake unto me for the Bishop of Dublin, for he must have of the said Bishop £250.

Kingston's letter was probably written late on 16 May, because he goes on to say that 'as yet, I have heard nothing of my lord of Canterbury, and the Queen much desires to be shriven'.[26] Cranmer had already visited her earlier that day and evidently had promised to return to hear her last confession, but he would not come again until early in the morning of 18 May. Aless states that Cranmer, 'to whom [Anne] was in the habit of confessing when she went to the Lord's table', was the one for 'whom she sent when she was in prison and knew that she should shortly die'.

Arrangements were by now in hand for the Queen's execution. Henry VIII had gone to the extraordinary trouble of sending for 'the hangman of Calais', Calais then being an English possession.[27] Decapitation by the sword was very rare in England but widely used in Europe;[28] it was a much cleaner, kinder and more precise method of execution than death by the axe. Evidently 'the sword of Calais'[29] was of some renown, being an expert executioner known for his swiftness and skill in cutting off heads.

Several authors, among them Winston Churchill, have asserted that, at the end of her trial, Anne had requested that, if the King would permit it, she wished to be beheaded with a sword, like the French nobility, and not, like the English nobility, with an axe. Friedmann says it is unknown why the King sent for a swordsman, but that, because of Anne's French education, she probably thought it more honourable to be beheaded by a sword. Yet there is no contemporary record of her requesting this method of execution.

Since burning was the penalty for women who committed treason, why did Henry VIII not only opt for the method of execution reserved for male traitors of gentle or noble birth, but also decide to spare Anne the axe? George Wyatt says that 'the King's conscience no doubt moved him to appointing the more honourable death'; not only was it the death reserved for the highborn, but it was less demeaning than being burned at the stake, for the flames, apart from inflicting sheer agony on the victim, could quickly burn away clothing and leave their nudity exposed to the public gaze, as had happened with Joan of Arc. It may be that Henry's conscience was troubling him – George Wyatt had spoken with people who had known him – but this was to be the first time ever that an English queen had been executed, so the official approach may have been that, condemned traitor though she now was, Anne was still the Queen of England, had been Henry's consort and was the mother of his daughter, and that therefore fitting treatment was called for, in line with her being royally lodged in the Tower, attended by ladies and servants, confessed by the Archbishop of Canterbury and richly garbed and bejewelled.[30] It may be that, considering Anne's rank – and the possibility of the tide of public sympathy turning in her favour – no one wanted a horrific scene on the scaffold, so steps were taken to minimise the risk of that happening.[31]

According to Charles V's sister, Mary of Hungary, who was Regent of the Netherlands, the King had sent for this headsman 'that the vengeance might be executed by [one of] the Emperor's subjects, as there were none in England skilful enough'.[32] This supports the claim in the 'Spanish Chronicle' that the headsman came from St Omer, which was then in Spanish-ruled Flanders. But perhaps Henry simply wanted Anne killed as humanely as possible; the warrant for her execution states that the King, moved by pity, was unwilling to send her to the stake,[33] which is substantiated by him securing the headsman's services at the handsome sum of £23.6s.8d (£7,800), which was for his 'rewards and apparel'.[34]

But there was probably another, more pragmatic reason for the King's decision. Given that Kingston was informed on 16 May, only the day after Anne's condemnation, that the headsman was on his way, and that Chapuys learned on the 17th that Anne was due to be executed the next morning, there can be no doubt that this executioner had been summoned before her trial. In the Tudor period, it took a fast rider four days to cover the two hundred miles from London to York, while in 1483, it had taken nearly two days for the news of Edward IV's death to be urgently conveyed from Westminster to Calais, probably using a relay system of messengers.[35] Thus, allowing for a quick Channel crossing – although that could take anything from a few hours to several days, depending on the wind and weather conditions – it would have taken a royal messenger, or relays of messengers, the best part of forty-eight hours to travel from London to Dover (a distance of seventy miles) and then make the twenty-mile boat trip to Calais; the journey would, of course, have been longer if, as the 'Spanish Chronicle' claimed (and its author would be a witness to Anne's execution), the headsman actually resided at St Omer, twenty-two miles further on. Then it would take another two or three days for him to make his slower way to England. Thus, if he was expected to arrive by the 18th (which he perhaps did, as there is no mention of him being delayed), he must have been sent for in advance of Anne's trial – even as early as the 12th, the day on which her co-accused were condemned, or the 13th, when her household was broken up, or – allowing for the fastest journey – on the 14th, at the latest. These calculations are supported by the account in the 'Spanish Chronicle', which states that the King 'sent a week before to St Omer for a headsman, and nine days after they sent, he arrived'. This suggests that, if he arrived on 18 May, or even early on the 19th, he had been summoned on the 9th or 10th. The dates may be incorrect, but these precise calculations show that people were aware that the executioner had been summoned well before the trial.

Thus the King had intended all along that Anne should be beheaded, and this not only pre-empted the verdict given at her trial, but also inflicted an added refinement of cruelty in keeping her in suspense for a whole day as to whether or not she would suffer the agony of burning. Since the executioner had already been sent for when Anne was sentenced to be burned or beheaded, there can be little doubt that the promise of a swifter death by the sword was used as a bargaining tool in securing her agreement to the annulment of her marriage.

Kingston had been gratified to hear about the headsman. 'I am

very glad of the executioner of Calais, for he can handle the matter,'
he wrote to Cromwell. Indeed, he was to handle it exceptionally
well, showing unexpected compassion and thoughtfulness towards
his victim.

'For the gentlemen, the sheriffs [of London] must make provision,' Kingston added, referring to an executioner; not for them
the sword of Calais, but the public hangman. 'As yet I hear of no
writ, but they are all ready and, I trust, clean to God. They shall
have warning in the morning.' As for his other prisoner, 'I shall
send at once for carpenters to make a scaffold of such a height
that all present may see it. If you wish more to be done, let me
know.'[36]

The 'Spanish Chronicle' states that Wyatt was told on 16 May
that no proceedings would be taken against him, and that it was
immediately after hearing this welcome news that he wrote to
the King to remind him that he had warned him not to marry
Anne Boleyn because she was a bad woman. That a prisoner in
the Tower should have written such a letter to Henry at this time
is utterly incredible; given the mood of the times, it would have
been taking an enormous risk. Wyatt, a diplomat and seasoned
courtier, would hardly have been so rash.

'Meanwhile, the [other] prisoners prepared to die, and took
the Sacrament.'[37]

Apprised only a short time beforehand of the time set for their
executions, the condemned men were 'led out of the Tower, all
closely guarded',[38] and beheaded early in the morning of
Wednesday, 17 May on a high scaffold 'at the Tower Hill'[39] before
large crowds, with a number of courtiers standing prominently
to the front.

Chapuys, who got his information from one of the ladies in
attendance on Anne, says that 'the Concubine saw them executed,
from the Tower, to aggravate her grief'.[40] It sounds as if she was
made to do so. Wyatt was also a witness. According to the 'Spanish

Chronicle', he was watching 'from a window in the Tower, and all the people thought that he also was to be brought out and executed'. The window was in the Bell Tower, as Wyatt makes clear in a poem about 'these bloody days' written probably later that summer:

> The Bell Tower showed me such sight
> That in my head sticks day and night;
> There did I lean out of a grate . . .[41]

It is unlikely that Anne was allowed to watch with Wyatt, so she may have been looking out from another room in the Bell Tower, or from high up in the Byward Tower, which also afforded a view of Tower Hill.

According to John Husee, the men all 'died very charitably'.[42] In the sixteenth century, great store was set by the way one met one's death. Redemption could be implicit in confession, repentance and resignation. There was also a code of etiquette to be observed on the scaffold, and it was customary for those about to die to make a pious farewell speech for the edification of those watching, in which they confessed their fault, acknowledged the justness of their fate and made their final peace with God before making a Christian end. Their words were meant to serve as a warning to others. This was not the place to deny one's guilt, or to criticise the King's justice; to do so might have led to a severer penalty being imposed, or could have rebounded on the often destitute relatives who were left behind, while those rash enough to plead innocence, such as the fourth Duke of Norfolk in 1572, would find the sheriff intervening to stop them.[43]

On this day, George Constantine was in the crowd, within earshot of the condemned men, and would tell Cromwell that he watched them die and 'heard them, and wrote every word they spake'. He added that 'in a manner' every one of them confessed, although clearly it was not necessarily to the crimes they were to suffer for. All admitted that they had deserved to die for having led sinful lives, but none alluded to the specific offences for which they had been condemned. They could have been acknowledging only the general sins of a lifetime.

Rochford, as the highest in rank, mounted the scaffold first and 'with a loud voice'[44] made a long and pious speech, of which several versions survive. Crispin de Milherve says that Rochford 'exhorted those who suffered with him to die without fear; and said to those that were about him that he came to die since it was the King's pleasure that it should be so. He exhorted all persons not to trust to courts, states and kings, but in God only' and prayed that he 'might be forgiven by all whom he had injured'. He admitted 'he deserved a heavier punishment for his other sins, but not-from the King, whom he had never offended. Yet he prayed God to give him a long and good life.' If these were truly his words, then this was as close to sniping at the King as a prisoner on a scaffold dared get, but Rochford would have realised that Henry could hardly take vengeance on his widow, since it was her evidence that had secured his death. In affirming that he had never offended the King, Rochford was, with his dying breath, proclaiming himself innocent of the charge of incest.

Another, similar version of this speech is in the *Chronicle of Calais*, which has Rochford stating:

Christian men, I am born under the law, and judged under the law, and die under the law, and the law has condemned me. Masters all, I am not come hither for to preach, but for to die, for I have deserved to die if I had twenty lives, more shamefully than can be devised, for I am a wretched sinner, and I have sinned shamefully. I have known no man so evil, and to rehearse my sins openly, it were no pleasure to you to hear them, nor yet for me to rehearse them, for God knoweth all. Therefore, masters all, I pray you take heed by me, and especially my lords and gentlemen of the court, the which I have been among, take heed by me and beware of such a fall, and I pray to God the Father, the Son and the Holy Ghost, three persons and one God, that my death may be an example unto you all. And beware, trust not in the vanity of the world, and especially in the flattering of the court. And I cry God mercy, and ask all the world forgiveness, as willingly as I would have forgiveness of God. And if I have offended any man that is not here now, either in thought, word or deed, and if ye here any such, I pray you heartily in my behalf, pray them to forgive me for God's sake. And yet, my masters all, I have one thing for to say to you: men do common and say that I have been a setter forth of the Word of God, and one that have favoured the Gospel of Christ; and because I would not that God's word should be slandered by me, I say unto you all, that if I had followed God's word in deed as I did read it and set it forth to my power, I had not come to this. I did read the Gospel of Christ, but I did not follow it. If I had, I had been a liv[ing] man among you. Therefore I pray you, masters all, for God's sake stick to the truth and follow it, for one good follower is worth three readers, as God knoweth.

Rochford's description of his sinfulness in this reliable account of his speech went way beyond what was normally required of a last confession, and goes a long way towards confirming the theory that he had indulged in what were then regarded as unnatural sexual practices.

There are many reported versions of Rochford's scaffold speech, and great similarities in all of them: he acknowledged his sinful life, regretted he had not followed the teachings of the Gospel he had preached, exhorted the people to beware the flatteries of the court, and submitted to the law that had condemned him. But there are a few significant discrepancies. Milherve and Chapuys both assert that Rochford denied that he had offended against the King, while the Portuguese account claims that he did acknowledge his crimes against God and his sovereign, and prayed Henry to pardon him. These discrepancies may have arisen from his words becoming garbled in the telling, or because different observers reported the passages that impressed them, while some either misheard what was said, or elaborated in order to make a political or moral point.[45]

Certainly Rochford spoke at some length before he submitted to the axe and died bravely as befitted a gentleman, and we cannot begin to imagine the thoughts of the men who were awaiting their turn to die. Even if the axe hit home cleanly, on the nape, it was a brutal death, for it did not so much as slice neatly through the neck as hew through flesh and bone. And because beheadings were rare in England, hanging being the customary form of judicial execution, executioners were often unpractised in the art. There was no guarantee of a swift end, and when Rochford 'lay upon the ground with his head on the block, the headsman gave three strokes'.[46]

According to Lancelot de Carles, when the other three gentlemen came to die, 'they said nothing, as if they had commissioned Rochford to speak for them' – or maybe they were too appalled at the butchery they had just witnessed to speak. The Imperialist account also claims that the four men who followed Rochford to the block 'said nothing except to pray for God's and the King's forgiveness, and to bid us pray for their souls'.[47] None spoke at length, yet obviously they did say more than Carles and the Imperialist – who may not have been able to hear everything – would have us believe, as the gist of their words was written down by other witnesses.

The Portuguese asserted that, after Rochford, 'Norris was beheaded, then Weston and Brereton, and Mark';[48] against this is the statement in the Histoire de la Royne Anne de Boullant, which also gives the order of the executions, that Weston was next to mount the scaffold. Yet it is more likely that Norris, who had been next in rank and importance after Rochford, came second. According to his man Constantine, 'the others confessed [he does not say to what], all but Mr Norris, who said almost nothing at all'. However, Burnet has him stating, 'I do not think that any gentleman of the court owes more to [the King] than I do, and hath been more ungrateful and regardless of it than I have.' The crowd might well have thought this to be an admission of guilt, but then he fearlessly spoke out in Anne's defence, and 'loyally averred that in his conscience, he thought the Queen innocent of these things laid to her charge; but whether she was or not, he would not accuse her of any thing, and he would die a thousand times rather than ruin an innocent person'. Constantine does not mention this brave and provocative declaration, but then his account of Rochford's speech is greatly truncated. The 'Spanish Chronicle' states that Norris 'made a great long prayer' and said he had been ungrateful to the King and had deserved death, but again, this source is unreliable.

Weston followed. 'I had thought to live in abomination yet this twenty or thirty years, and then to have made amends,' he said mournfully. 'I thought little I would come to this.' His mention of a life of 'abomination' might be understood to refer to illicit sexual acts, although there must have been those among his hearers who took it to mean his adultery with the Queen or just his general sinfulness. His last words were an exhortation to learn 'by example of him'.

Brereton was beheaded next. 'I have deserved to die if it were a thousand deaths,' he declared, possibly referring to his nefarious activities in Wales, 'but the cause whereof I die judge ye not. But if ye judge, judge the best.' Hearing him repeat this last sentence 'three or four times', and remembering that no witnesses had testified against Brereton at his trial, Constantine clearly *was* inclined to judge the best. 'If any of them was innocent, it was he,' he wrote, 'for if he were guilty, I say therefore that he died worst of them all.' He meant by the latter that Brereton, if guilty, should have made a less ambiguous speech, confessing his crimes and calling on God's forgiveness, for dying with a sin unconfessed would have been seen as inviting eternal damnation.[49] Brereton's admission that he deserved to die a thousand deaths seems a rather overstated confession of human frailty, and may suggest that he, like Rochford and Weston, was guilty of indulging in forbidden sexual practices.[50] The 'Spanish Chronicle' contradicts Constantine's evidence, and (probably falsely) asserts that Brereton said nothing but 'I have offended God and the King; pray for me.'

Finally it came to Smeaton's turn; being of low degree, he had been obliged to wait until last. By now, the block and the scaffold would have been awash with blood and piled with butchered bodies, so it is hardly surprising that he faltered when making his speech, which was brief and damning, and in which he declared 'he was justly punished for his misdeeds'.[51] 'Masters,' he cried, 'I pray you all pray for me, for I have deserved the death.'[52] Possibly he feared, even at this late stage, that he might be made to suffer the full horrors of a traitor's end if he protested his innocence, for the privilege of dying by the axe was not normally accorded to a 'varlet'[53] such as he. Milherve says that his confession of guilt gave rise to 'many reflections'. Maybe some wondered if he felt he deserved death for betraying Anne, rather than for having betrayed the King.[54]

The Imperialist commentator, who was certainly watching, reported that 'Brereton and Mark were afterwards quartered',[55] and on 2 June, Jean Hannaert of Lyons was to inform the Empress how 'the bodies were quartered'.[56] Yet it is possible that this eyewitness left immediately after the beheadings and merely assumed that the bodies were quartered, for no other witness makes any mention of quartering, and it was usually done so that the quarters could be displayed on spikes as a warning to would-be traitors. In this case, there is ample evidence that the 'bodies' and heads of all the men were buried that same day.

The executions sparked much comment. The conventional references to sinfulness in the scaffold speeches were clearly seen by some as confessions of guilt, thus further tarnishing Anne's reputation. George Constantine wrote that, to begin with, he himself and all true friends of the Gospel – that is, the reformists whom Anne had championed over the years – had found it impossible to credit what they had heard of the Queen. 'Now because she was a favourer of God's Word, at the leastwise so taken, I tell you few men would believe that she was so abominable. As I may be saved, before God, *I* could not believe it.' That was 'afore I heard them speak at their death. But on the scaffold, in a manner all confessed except Mr Norris', and Constantine found himself convinced that all were guilty as charged.

Milherve, more sympathetic, was of the opinion that all the men 'suffered a death which they had no way deserved'. Even the executioner 'shed tears, but the bloody corpses were allowed to lie on the scaffold for hours, half dressed',[57] after he and the Tower officials had stripped them of the clothing that was their perquisite. When Wyatt wrote, 'The axe is home, your heads be in the street' (in a poem he wrote during or soon after his captivity), he was not referring to the heads being displayed on pikes above London Bridge, as was customary after traitors had been beheaded, for both Chapuys and Wriothesley make it clear that the condemned men's 'bodies, with their heads, were buried in the Tower of London';[58] instead, Wyatt's words may be taken to mean that the heads had been lifted or rolled off the scaffold, and then left on the ground before being finally laden on to the cart that would trundle the remains of the five men back into the Tower.

Because he had been a nobleman, 'the lord of Rochford's body and head' were interred before the high altar[59] in the royal chapel of St Peter ad Vincula within the Tower, which had been founded in the twelfth century and largely rebuilt by Henry VIII in 1532, after a disastrous fire in 1512; the rest were laid to rest in the adjacent churchyard, with 'Mr Weston and Mr Norris in one grave' and 'Mr Brereton and Mark in another'.[60] Wriothesley states that 'the bodies with the heads' were placed in the graves, but Norris's family are said to have obtained permission to claim his head, which they later buried in the private chapel of Ockwells Manor, their house near Maidenhead, Berkshire.[61] That house still stands, but only parts of the chapel survive, with no clue as to where the head − if it was ever there at all − might rest.

The churchyard of St Peter ad Vincula surrounded the chapel and in those days extended into the area now covered by the Waterloo Block and the Jewel House. In 1841, when the foundations of the Waterloo Block were being dug, and during further excavation in 1964, many coffins and bones were found; these were buried in the crypt of the chapel.[62] We have no means of knowing if the remains of Anne Boleyn's alleged lovers were among them.

At court, people were still expecting 'many more' of the Queen's rumoured army of lovers to be arrested and beheaded,[63] while '*Trahitur et suspensus*' was written in the margin of the official record of the dead men's trials and convictions, to show that the sentence had been carried out.

'The Concubine will certainly be beheaded tomorrow, or on Friday at the latest,' Chapuys wrote on 17 May, 'and I think the King feels the time long that it is not done already.'[64] Whatever Chapuys had heard, it was not from Henry himself, but he would not have written this without some information on which to base it, and we might glean from his words some sense of Henry wanting everything all over and done with. It was customary for condemned prisoners to be executed with the minimum delay, but this was his queen and the mother of his child, whatever he believed she had done. Did he fear he might waver? Was this another reason for the frightening speed with which Anne had been arrested and condemned? It may be that Henry was 'persuaded to destroy her before he could change his mind'.[65]

Anne, meanwhile, had been escorted back to the Queen's lodgings, no doubt grievously shaken and distressed at witnessing the bloody deaths of her brother and her friends. It had been an all-too-brutal reminder of what she herself must face not many hours hence, for these executions would have left her in no doubt that she would imminently share the men's fate, and that hints about her being sent abroad to a convent had been merely a cruel ploy to gain her consent to the annulment. And she was right, for Kingston, having returned from discharging his grim duty on Tower Hill, now came to inform her that she was to die the following morning.

Kingston was surely relieved to be able to tell Anne that she was not to suffer the agony and horror of the flames but the kinder death by beheading, and that the King's mercy had extended to arranging for her to be dispatched by the sword. Whatever her sense of betrayal, Anne received the news calmly. When 'the day of her death was announced to her, she was more joyful than before'.[66] Her mind was apparently more exercised about what the men had said about her on the scaffold. She 'asked about the endurance of her brother and the others'[67] and wanted to know if any of them had protested her innocence, and when Kingston told 'how her brother and the other gentlemen had suffered and had sealed her innocence with their own blood, but that Mark had confessed he deserved to die, her face changed somewhat and she broke out into some passion, saying, "Has he not then cleared me of the public infamy he has brought me to? Alas, I fear his soul suffers for it, and that he is now punished for his false accusations! But for my brother and those others, I doubt not but they are now in the presence of that great King before whom I am to be tomorrow."' She was well aware that Smeaton's confession would give rise to 'many reflections'[68] as it still does today.

Between nine and eleven in the morning of 17 May,[69] 'having only God before his eyes', Archbishop Cranmer convened 'a solemn court' in 'a certain low chapel' (or crypt, perhaps the undercroft) at Lambeth Palace, where 'the doctors of the law' gathered for the purpose of annulling Anne's marriage.[70] Neither she nor Henry was present, despite both having received the summons to appear; they were represented by proctors. Strickland, followed by other writers, asserted that Anne was conveyed in privacy to Lambeth Palace, and that she attended the hearing, but there is no contemporary evidence for this.

The Queen was represented in court by her proctors, John Barbour and a rising diplomat, Dr Nicholas Wotton, both of whom had perhaps visited her at the Tower and obtained her formal consent to the dissolution of her marriage, although there is no evidence for their having done so; certainly they did not contest the annulment on her behalf.[71] Dr Richard Sampson, who would be rewarded with the bishopric of Chichester the following month, represented the King, alongside Thomas Bedyll, a royal chaplain and clerk to the Privy Council, and John Tregonwell, a lawyer, judge and Privy Councillor.

Also present were Cromwell, the Lord Chancellor, the Duke of Suffolk, the earls of Oxford and Sussex and other members of the King's Council,[72] while the formal witnesses were Richard Gwent, another royal chaplain who was Archdeacon of London; Edmund Bonner, Archdeacon of Leicester, who would in time become Bishop of London and gain notoriety as the 'Bloody Bonner' of the Marian persecutions of the 1550s; and Thomas Legh, a lawyer and diplomat. In the afternoon,[73] these persons heard Cranmer pronounce that, 'on the basis of some true, just and legitimate causes recently brought to our attention', the marriage that Henry VIII had schemed for six years to make was 'null and void, and had always been so', which made Anne's daughter – henceforth to be known as the Lady Elizabeth – a bastard. 'And so she was discharged, and was never lawful Queen of England, and there it was approved,' Wriothesley observed, not understanding Anne's true legal position with regard to her title.[74]

Cranmer's grounds for dissolving the marriage were not cited in his decree of nullity,[75] but it took Chapuys only two days to discover the grounds for the annulment: reliable informants told him that the Archbishop had pronounced Henry and Anne's marriage invalid 'on account of the King having had connection with her sister, and that, as both parties knew of this, the good faith of the parents cannot make the bastard [Elizabeth] legitimate [*sic*]'.[76] Such a judgement would only have been possible after Anne was safely condemned, because, given that she was aware of the impediment to her marriage, she could not technically have been guilty of adultery.[77]

On 19 May, Cranmer was to issue a dispensation for the King to marry Jane Seymour without prior publication of banns, even though both parties were within 'the third and third degrees of affinity'.[78] No such blood relationship existed between Henry and Jane Seymour, who were far more distant cousins, and Jane was not third cousin to either of his previous wives, so it is possible that Henry had at one time been involved in an unrecorded sexual affair with someone who was related within those degrees to Jane, or that Jane herself had been the mistress of a kinsman of the King; or Henry was perhaps a godparent to the child of one of Jane's close relatives, which would have created compaternity with the relevant parent and been as effective a barrier to marriage within the forbidden degrees of consanguinity as a blood relationship. Whatever the technicalities of the matter, the King was now a free man.

13

'For Now I Die'

On the night of 17–18 May, carpenters were set to work to build a 'new scaffold',[1] 'of such a height that all may see it'[2] 'having four or five steps'.[3] Wriothesley states that this was erected on 'the green within the Tower of London, by the White Tower', while the Lisle Letters and Anthony Anthony describe it as being put up 'before the House of Ordnance', a long, crumbling building (soon to be replaced) that stood on the north side of the Inner Ward, facing the White Tower; today, the Waterloo Barracks occupy part of the site of the House of Ordnance.[4]

In 2000, the Royal Armouries acquired a hitherto-unknown contemporary MS. account of the execution of Robert Devereux, Earl of Essex, in 1601, possibly written as an official report for the Privy Council and perhaps even for Elizabeth I herself. According to this document, Essex's scaffold was 'placed in the high court above Caesar's Tower'; in those days, people believed that Julius Caesar had built the White Tower. Thus it was almost certainly on the same site as Anne Boleyn's scaffold had stood, and probably all the other scaffolds erected for private executions in the Tudor period. This 'high court' was the largest open space in the Tower precincts, where tournaments had once been held, and it could accommodate large crowds of spectators.[5] The author of the 'Spanish Chronicle' corroborates this location, stating that 'they erected the scaffold in the great courtyard of the Tower'.

Dr Geoffrey Parnell, Keeper of Tower History at the Royal Armouries Museum, has established that the present Tower Green was adopted as the scaffold site in 1864 because Queen Victoria wished to mark the place where Anne Boleyn had been beheaded, and it was assumed that the green before St Peter ad Vincula was the correct location for executions, since three mutineers had been shot there in 1743.[6] This mistaken assumption was seemingly confirmed when Charles Wriothesley's chronicle was published in 1875, with its assertion that Anne met her end on 'the green' within the Tower. This was understood in the nineteenth century to refer only to the green before the chapel of St Peter ad Vincula. However, 'East Smithfield Green', as it was known in the sixteenth century, extended further east in Anne Boleyn's time.[7]

Thus Anne's scaffold was erected on the present parade ground north of the White Tower,[8] and the grim prophecy of the Abbot of Garadon was about to be fulfilled, at least in part, for even if the Queen was not to be burned, she was to meet her doom 'where the tower is white and another place green'.[9] Lancelot de Carles would observe of her end, 'Nothing notable has happened which has not been foretold.'

It is unlikely that Anne would have heard the builders hammering away from the Queen's apartments, as is traditionally supposed, although she was certainly up at two o'clock in the morning of 18 May, when her almoner, John Skip, arrived to offer spiritual support in her last hours. She spent the rest of the night in prayer with him until soon after dawn, when Cranmer came again, as he had promised, to hear her final confession and to celebrate Mass and give her Holy Communion. In these, her dying hours, she showed herself a devout Catholic with a pious devotion to the Eucharist, despite her reformist views.

'The Queen, in expectation of her last day, took the Sacrament.'[10] She insisted that Kingston be present. 'This morning,' he reported to Cromwell, 'she sent for me that I might be with her at such time as she received the good Lord, to the intent I should hear her speak as touching her innocency always to be clear.' Chapuys reported on the 19th: 'She confessed herself yesterday, and communicated, expecting to be executed. She requested it of those who had charge of it, and expressed the desire to be executed. No person ever showed greater willingness to die.'[11] Dr Ortiz, basing his account (written on 11 June) on information sent him by Chapuys, says, 'she complained that she had not been executed on Wednesday with her brother, saying that she hoped to have gone to Paradise with him'.[12]

But before Anne could go to her rest, she was determined to protest her innocence in the most effective way possible; to the sixteenth-century mind, the prospect of divine judgement was a chastening reality, and the fear of eternal perdition very real. Chapuys wrote: 'The lady who had charge of her' – either Lady Kingston or Lady Boleyn, who were both presumably present – 'has sent to tell me in great secrecy, that the Concubine, before and after receiving the Sacrament, affirmed to her, on the damnation of her soul, that she had never offended with her body against the King.'[13]

Anne's protestations of innocence, made when she believed that her execution was imminent, should surely be regarded as genuine. It is barely conceivable that she would have risked her immortal soul, on the brink of death and divine judgement as she believed herself to be, by lying, and hardly likely that she would have taken such a spiritual gamble in the interests of retrieving her earthly reputation. This was a time for confessing sins and making a final peace with God, not for bearing false witness.

Nonetheless, the wording of her confession is interesting. It may be that she merely wished to emphasise that she had been faithful to the King, but from her insistence that 'she had never offended *with her body*' against him, it might be inferred that she had offended in other ways, perhaps with her heart or her thoughts, and that she had perhaps secretly loved another, possibly Norris, but had never gone so far as to consummate that love.

On the morning of 18 May, a little before nine o'clock, the time appointed for the execution, Kingston received orders from Cromwell to 'have strangers [i.e. foreigners] conveyed out of the Tower'. There seems to have been official concern that foreign ambassadors would send home sympathetic reports of Anne's end that could reflect badly on the King. The Constable duly sent Richard Gresham, the Sheriff of London (and future Lord Mayor), and one William Cooke to see that this was done. This obliged him to delay the execution until midday, and he sent to inform Anne of this: the bringer of the difficult news was probably his wife.

It was not long before Anne summoned him, 'and at my coming, she said, "Master Kingston, I hear say I shall not die afore noon, and I am very sorry therefore, for I thought then to be dead and past my pain." I told her it should be no pain, it was so subtle; and then she said, "I have heard say the executioner was very good, and I have a little neck." And she put her hand about it, laughing heartily.' Kingston observed to Cromwell, 'I have seen many men and also women executed and all they have been in great sorrow, but to my knowledge, this lady has much joy and pleasure in death. Sir, her almoner is continually with her, and has been since two of the clock after midnight.'[14]

Both Chapuys and Kingston testified to Anne's readiness to die, and there can be little doubt that it was genuine. She had been accused, probably falsely, of the vilest of crimes, and she had lost nearly everything that mattered: her husband, her brother, her power, her married status, her friends, her possessions and her reputation. Her daughter had been branded a bastard and there was nothing she could do about it. Five men had died on her account. Her father had abandoned her. Her mother's grief was unimaginable. Barely recovered from a miscarriage, she herself had suffered three weeks of unthinkable anxiety and dread, and now she faced a violent death. The husband who had won her so dearly, but utterly abandoned her, had carried out his threat to lower her as much as he had raised her. There was little left to live for, so it is small wonder that she wanted her wretched existence to end. She had only her strong will and her faith to sustain her through these terrible final hours.

It had hardly seemed worth the effort to clear the Tower of foreigners, for 'the number of strangers passed not thirty', as Kingston informed Master Secretary, 'and not many of those armed; and the ambassador of the Emperor had a servant there, and [he was] honestly put out. Sir, if we have not an hour certain [i.e. for the execution], as it may be known in London, I think here will be but few, and I think a reasonable number were best, for I suppose she will declare herself to be a good woman for all but the King at the hour of her death.'[15] It is often claimed that Cromwell and Kingston kept postponing Anne's execution because they wished to pre-empt crowds gathering and the risk of demonstrations in her favour – both Chapuys and Constantine attest to the growing belief of the people that she had been unjustly condemned.[16] But it is clear from Kingston's letter that both he and Cromwell wanted a reasonable number of witnesses, so that justice could be seen to be properly done.[17] Chapuys was ill at this time, but could only deplore the fact that 'strangers were not to be admitted' to witness the execution,[18] since he would be obliged to rely on the testimony of Englishmen for his reports. He would have been vexed to learn that the author of the 'Spanish Chronicle', who had friends living within the Tower walls, managed to get into the fortress overnight, in defiance of the authorities, and 'took good note of all that passed'.

'Expecting her end', Anne had 'desired that no one would trouble her devotions that morning'. But when noon came, there was no dread summons, for sufficient time had to be allowed for spectators to gather. The fact that at least a thousand people found out when the execution was finally to take place, and would be present, indicates that news of its deferral spread quickly, and that there was never any determined attempt at a last-minute post-ponement to outfox would-be spectators. Had there been, it follows that only official visitors would have been admitted to the Tower.

But the delay was torture for Anne. 'When the appointed hour passed, she was disappointed.'[19] Kingston now had to inform her that her execution would be postponed until nine o'clock the following morning. Chapuys learned from his lady spy that, 'when the command came to put off the execution till today, she appeared very sorry, praying the Constable of the Tower that, for the honour of God, he would beg the King that, since she was in a good state and disposed for death, she might be dispatched immedi-ately'.[20] It was 'not that she desired death, but she had thought herself prepared to die, and feared that the delay might weaken her resolve'.[21] But Kingston was powerless to change the arrange-ments. It seems likely that word was now put about that the execution would take place early the next day.

In the hours that remained to her, Anne sought fortitude in prayer and in 'consoling her ladies several times, telling them that [death] was not a thing to be regretted by Christians, and she hoped to be quit of all unhappiness, with various other good counsels'.[22] She also reflected on the causes of her plight. 'The woman who has charge of her', who did 'not conceal anything' from Chapuys, sent to tell him 'that the said Messalina' could not imagine that anyone but Chapuys had got her in disgrace with the King, for 'from the moment of my arrival at this court [not, obviously, in 1529, the date of his original arrival at the English court, but on the previous 18 April[23]], the King no longer looked upon her with the same eyes as before'. This was surely misquoted, or an exaggeration, and there is plenty of eyewitness evidence to prove it. Chapuys was gratified that Anne held him accountable for her doom: 'I was flattered by the compliment, but it is well for me she did not escape, because, with her humanity, she would have cast me to the dogs!'[24]

Henry, meanwhile, was preparing for his wedding to Jane Seymour. On the evening of 18 May, he had himself rowed to Chelsea, where he visited Jane Seymour, who was carrying herself as if she were queen already, and her family.

Chapuys viewed Jane's discretion at this time as 'very commendable'.[25] Strickland, writing in Queen Victoria's reign, thought her conduct 'shameless', asserting that her willingness to entertain Henry VIII's courtship 'was the commencement of the severe calamities that befell her mistress. Scripture points out as an especial odium the circumstances of a handmaid taking the place of her mistress. A sickening sense of horror must pervade every right-feeling mind when the proceedings of the discreet Jane Seymour are considered. She received the addresses of her mistress's husband, she passively beheld the mortal anguish of Anne Boleyn, she saw a series of murderous accusations got up against the Queen, which finally brought her to the scaffold.' Strickland conveniently forgot that Anne, only a decade earlier, had begun scheming to supplant *her* royal mistress, and had later tried to compass that lady's death.

There is no record of Jane's feelings about the woman she had supplanted, who was awaiting death on the morrow a mile or so downriver, and whose crown she would shortly wear. In refusing the King's advances without removing herself from his presence, and accepting her role as his wife's replacement (which is just what Anne, in her day, had done), she behaved discreditably.[26] Probably she had had little choice in the matter, with the King ardently pursuing her and her family vigorously manoeuvring her into the most advantageous marriage a girl of her rank could ever make. Yet Jane was probably happy to comply: her championing of the cause of the Lady Mary shows her to have been Anne's enemy and implies that she did not accept Anne as Henry's true wife; she did not personally compass her end, although she was willing to exploit the situation to her own advantage, even when it became clear that her marriage to the King would be achieved literally over Anne's dead body. Her tacit – and chilling – complicity in Anne's destruction strongly suggests that she believed her former mistress deserving of the fate that lay in store for her.

Sleep eluded Anne on her last night. She spent the hours of darkness on her knees in prayer, or in conversation with her attendants. Chapuys was told that 'the night before she was beheaded, she talked and jested, saying, among other things, that those bragging, clever people who had invented an unheard-of name for the good Queen who would not be hard put to it to invent one for her, for they would call her *"la Royne Anne Sans Tête"* [Queen Anne Lackhead]. And then she laughed heartily, knowing she must die the next day.'[27] In a more sober moment, on 'the day before she was executed, she said she did not consider that she was condemned by Divine Judgement, except for having caused the ill-treatment of the princess, and for having conspired her death'.[28]

The cartographer and historian John Speed, who was born about sixteen years after these events, and whose book *The History of Great Britain* was published in 1611, recounts how, at the last, Anne tried to make her peace with the Lady Mary. He claimed that his story was 'a nobleman's relation', but omitted to name the nobleman concerned. Speed states that Anne

> took the Lady Kingston into her presence chamber, and there, locking the door upon them, willed her to sit down in the chair of estate. Lady Kingston answered that it was her duty to stand, and not to sit at all in her presence, much less upon the seat of state of her, the Queen.

'Ah, Madam,' replied Anne, 'that title is gone [*sic*]. I am a condemned person, and by law have no estate left me in this life, but for clearing of my conscience. I pray you sit down.'

'Well,' said Lady Kingston, 'I have often played the fool in my youth, and to fulfil your command I will do it once more in mine age.' And thereupon [she] sat down under the cloth of estate on the throne. Then the Queen most humbly fell on her knees before her and, holding up her hands, with tearful eyes beseeched her, as in the presence of God and His angels, and as she would answer to her before them when all should appear to judgement, that she would so fall down before the Lady Mary's Grace and in like manner ask her forgiveness for the wrongs she had done her; for, till that was accomplished, she said, her conscience could not be quiet.

Speed was highly respected as a historian in his day, and was elected a member of the Society of Antiquaries of London. By this means he became acquainted with the greatest scholars of the time, including William Camden, Elizabeth I's first biographer, Camden being one of several historians who contributed to Speed's great work. Speed had access to sources now lost to us; he himself says he consulted 'many manuscripts, notes and records' and that he had free access to the vast library of Sir Robert Cotton. His credentials are seemingly impeccable, and on the surface it sounds plausible that Anne, facing eternity, wished to make amends to the stepdaughter she had treated so unkindly, and perhaps hoped that Mary, in return, would look sympathetically on Anne's motherless daughter.

Apart from Anne's statement that her title was gone, the details sound authentic, and Lady Kingston is known to have visited Mary at Hunsdon on or before 26 May, a week after Anne's death; her visit is recorded in a letter of that date from Mary to Cromwell.

It is surprising, though, that Chapuys – who, on 20 May, reported Anne's observation that her execution was a divine judgement on her for her treatment of Mary – did not get to hear anything about Lady Kingston repeating Anne's words to Mary. We know he had an informant among Anne's ladies, although it may not have been Lady Kingston herself; yet if the latter had been charged by Anne with this mission, then surely she or Mary would have told Chapuys about it. For this reason, and the fact that it comes from such a vague source, most historians dismiss Speed's story as apocryphal. It appears that the chief purpose of Lady Kingston's visit was to advise Mary on how best to approach her father with a view to a reconciliation between them. She would also have been able to give Mary a first-hand account of Anne's last days and execution. But Chapuys states only that, in her final hours, Anne was adamant that her condemnation was a judgement of God. Full of remorse for her cruel treatment of Mary, and for plotting her death, she spoke often of her, her guilt clearly weighing heavily upon her conscience.[29]

Tradition once had it that Anne Boleyn composed two poems shortly before her execution.[30] Both express poignantly the kind of thoughts that must have been in her head at this time. Her authorship of them was attested to by Sir John Hawkins (1719–89): in his five-volume work *A History of Music*, a repository of valuable scholarly information, he states that these verses were communicated to him by 'a very judicious antiquary, lately deceased'. However, one of the poems, 'Queen Anne's Lament', was probably written by the composer Robert Johnson (c.1583–1633); it is a polemic protesting her innocence:

> Defiled is my name full sore,
> Through cruel spite and false report,
> That I may say for ever more,
> Farewell my joy, adieu comfort.

For wrongfully ye judge of me,
Unto my fame a mortal wound.
Seek what ye list, it will not be;
Ye seek for that can not be found.

The other poem, which is to be found in Additional MS. XV,
f.117 in the British Library, is earlier in date, and was set to music
by Robert Jordan, a former chaplain to Anne Boleyn. It is therefore possible that it was composed by Anne herself, for the lyrics
reveal how its author welcomes and embraces death, and the style
is in keeping with Anne's letters and mode of speech.

Oh Death, rock me asleep,
Bring on my quiet rest,
Let pass my very guiltless ghost
Out of my careful breast.
Toll on thou passing bell,
Ring out my doleful knell,
Let thy sound my death tell,
Death doth draw nigh,
There is no remedy.

My pains who can express?
Alas, they are so strong.
My dolour will not suffer strength
My life for to prolong.
Toll on thou passing bell,
Ring out my doleful knell,
Let thy sound my death tell,
Death doth draw nigh,
There is no remedy.

Alone in prison strange,
I wail my destiny:

Well worth this cruel hap that I
Should taste this misery.
Toll on thou passing bell,
Ring out my doleful knell,
Let thy sound my death tell,
Death doth draw nigh,
There is no remedy.

Farewell, my pleasures past,
Welcome, my present pain,
I feel my torments so increase
That life cannot remain.
Cease now, thou passing bell,
Rung is my doleful knell,
For its sound my death doth tell.
Death doth draw nigh;
Sound the knell dolefully, for now I die.

The Scotsman, Alexander Aless, had not had occasion to leave his London house for some days, so had heard nothing of the outcome of Anne's trial, but in the small hours of 19 May, he had a grim nightmare. He recounted it thus in a letter to Elizabeth I in 1559: 'I take to witness Christ, who shall judge the quick and the dead, that I am about to speak the truth. On the day on which the Queen was beheaded, at sunrise, between two and three o'clock, there was revealed to me (whether I was asleep or awake I know not) the Queen's neck, after her head had been cut off, and this so plainly that I could count the nerves, the veins and the arteries. Terrified by this dream, or vision, I immediately arose and, crossing the River Thames, I came to Lambeth, the Archbishop of Canterbury's palace, and I entered the garden in which he was walking.' Evidently Cranmer too had had trouble sleeping and was also disturbed in his mind.

'When the Archbishop saw me, he enquired why I had come

so early, for the clock had not yet struck four. I answered that I had been horrified in my sleep, and I told him the whole occurrence. He continued in silent wonder for a while.'

'Do you not know what is to happen today?' Cranmer asked. Aless 'answered that I had remained at home since the date of the Queen's imprisonment and knew nothing of what was going on. The Archbishop then raised his eyes to Heaven and said, "She who has been the Queen of England upon Earth will today become a queen in Heaven." So great was his grief that he could say nothing more, and then he burst into tears. Terrified at this announcement, I returned to London, sorrowing.' Cranmer, of course, had heard Anne's last confession only the morning before, and knew the truth about her innocence, so his observation is highly significant.[31] He also knew that the reformist cause was about to lose its greatest patroness.

'The execution of the Concubine took place at nine o'clock this morning in the Tower,' Chapuys reported to the Emperor on Friday, 19 May.[32] At seven o'clock, after hearing Mass after dawn and receiving the Sacrament from her almoner, Anne had eaten a little breakfast;[33] an hour later, 'at eight of the clock',[34] Kingston had appeared at the door.

'When the Constable came to tell her the hour approached and that she should make ready',[35] Anne was waiting for him. According to a letter dated 10 June 1536, which was written by a Portuguese observer who had managed to circumvent the ban on foreigners in order to witness the execution, she was 'wholly habited in a robe of black damask, made in such guise that the cape, which was white, did fall on the outer side thereof'. Elsewhere, he refers to the cape being 'a short mantle furred with ermines',[36] while Lancelot de Carles has it as a 'white collar'. An Imperialist observer states she was wearing a 'hood, which was in the English fashion'[37] – in other words, a gable hood. The 'Spanish Chronicle' describes the 'night robe of damask with a red damask skirt', but states that Anne wore 'a netted coif over her hair'. This was presumably under the gable hood, and was exposed when she later took it off.

The Histoire de la Royne Anne de Boullant describes this outfit slightly differently as 'a beautiful night-robe of heavy grey damask trimmed with fur, showing a crimson kirtle beneath, with a low neckline'. A night-robe at that time would have been a loose garment that either fell in folds from the shoulders or neckline, or was high-necked; sometimes worn open in the front, and lined or trimmed with fur, it was worn as a dressing gown would be worn today. Such garments were often made of rich materials such as velvet or damask, and examples may be seen in several contemporary portraits by Hans Holbein, notably the full-length of Christina of Denmark painted in 1538 (now in the National Gallery, London). In 1532, the year before their marriage, Henry VIII had ordered a sumptuous night-robe for Anne: it comprised thirteen yards of black satin, lined with eight yards of black taffeta, with a border of black velvet, the sleeves being lined with buckram to stiffen them.[38] Clearly, this was not the same nightgown as the one of damask lined with fur that Anne wore on the scaffold, but it would have been of a similar style, and because it had a low neckline, she would not need to take it off for her beheading.

The Histoire makes no mention of the cape. From medieval times through to the Elizabethan period, capes were usually garments such as the Portuguese described, deep collars of fur – ermine for royalty – worn over gowns or state robes. We might conjecture that Anne wore this garment to underline her royal status and bring home to spectators the enormity of her fate.

The red kirtle that Anne wore beneath the nightgown would also have had a low square neck. The word kirtle was then used to mean a fitted, sleeved jacket and wide-skirted petticoat (a full kirtle), or just a petticoat (a half kirtle). In this case, it may have been the former, given that the night-robe may have been open in the front. A noblewoman might wear several petticoats beneath her kirtle, depending on the weather, but the outer one would be of a rich fabric.

In choosing her attire for her last public appearance, Anne was probably making two statements: in the wearing of ermine, as has been noted, she was emphasising her queenly rank; and in vesting herself – like Mary, Queen of Scots, at the latter's execution fifty years later – in a kirtle of red, the liturgical colour of Catholic martyrdom, she was effectively proclaiming her innocence. The significance would not have been lost on any observers, or on Kingston.

'Acquit yourself of your charge,' Anne told him calmly, 'for I have been long prepared.'[39] In 1530, Chapuys had observed that Anne was 'braver than a lion', and it was never more true of her than on this last day of her life. And this when she must have been exhausted, having had very little sleep for two nights, as well as having endured the unimaginable stresses and fears of the past days.

Kingston gave her a purse containing £20 (£7,000) 'to give in alms before her death',[40] which would be her last queenly act. It was customary for a condemned person to pay the executioner his fee as well, but this was settled separately on this occasion. Chapuys says that 'when they came to lead her to the scaffold', Anne re-iterated what she had said the previous day, about her death being a divine judgement on her only on account of her ill-treatment of the Lady Mary.[41]

Sir Francis Bacon, in his *History of Henry the Eighth*, which was published in 1612, relates another of the probably apocryphal tales that have become part of the legend of Anne Boleyn's final days. He says that, before leaving her lodgings for that last short walk, she asked 'one of [her] privy chamber, faithful and generous, as she supposed', to take a message from her to the King, saying, 'Commend me to his Majesty, and tell him that he hath been ever constant in his career of advancing me. From a private gentle-woman, he made me a marchioness; from a marchioness to a queen; and now he hath left no higher degree of honour, he gives my innocency the crown of martyrdom as a saint in Heaven.' Unsurprisingly, the lady chosen as messenger 'durst not carry this to the King'; yet, says Bacon, who believed Anne to be innocent, 'tradition has truly transmitted it to posterity'.

Several eyewitness accounts of the execution refer to Anne being attended by 'four young ladies'.[42] Their identity is uncertain. Several historians have assumed that all four of the ladies who had waited – and spied – on Anne from her first day in the Tower were impressed to attend her to the scaffold,[43] but the Wriothesley and Harleian MSS accounts of her trial both make it clear that only two of those ladies – Lady Kingston and Lady Boleyn – waited on her after her condemnation. Neither could be described as a 'young' lady: Lady Kingston's first husband had died in 1515, and Lady Boleyn had probably been married by 1518. Lady Shelton was over fifty, and Mrs Coffin was probably in her mid-thirties; both had probably been dismissed four days earlier. Not by any stretch of the imagination could any of these matrons have been the 'maids' referred to both by Crispin de Milherve and the anonymous Portuguese witness in their accounts of Anne's execution.[44] Moreover, Lancelot de Carles makes it clear that, at her trial, Anne was attended by Lady Kingston, Lady Boleyn 'and her young ladies'. The young ladies remained in attendance thereafter.

There has long been a tradition that Margaret Wyatt, Lady Lee, sister of the poet Wyatt, attended Anne to the scaffold. In the eighteenth century, Thomas Gray copied a life of Sir Thomas Wyatt the Elder from one of the unpublished Harleian MSS;[45] in this, it was asserted that Margaret Wyatt[46] attended Anne at her execution. Margaret Wyatt perhaps knew Anne fairly well, for the Boleyns were neighbours in Kent, and Anne was certainly on familiar terms with Margaret's brother Thomas. Margaret was the wife of Sir Anthony Lee of Borston, Buckinghamshire. Her portrait by Holbein, depicting her at the age of thirty-four, is said to have been painted around 1540, and shows a middle-aged woman, too old to be referred to as a young lady or a maid.

It was Agnes Strickland who claimed in the nineteenth century that Anne was assigned two ladies who were sympathetic to her to serve her in her last hours. In fact, there were four of them, but there is no evidence in any contemporary source to support the claim that Margaret Wyatt was one of them and accompanied Anne to the scaffold. There was also a strong Wyatt family tradition that Anne gave Lady Lee a prayer book just before she was beheaded, but this dates only from the eighteenth century and is unlikely to have been based on fact (see note 89).

For more than a century, a tale has circulated that one of the 'young ladies' was Katherine Carey, the twelve-year-old daughter of Anne's sister Mary by her first husband, William Carey.[47] Katherine grew up to marry Sir Francis Knollys, and became a great favourite with Elizabeth I, Anne's daughter. There is, however, no contemporary evidence for Katherine Carey attending on Anne in the Tower – she would perhaps have been considered too young – and she is first recorded as a maid-of-honour in 1540, when she served Henry VIII's fourth wife, Anne of Cleves.

Anne Boleyn would thank the four young ladies who attended her to the scaffold for their diligent, faithful and true service;[48] at her end, they were 'weeping' and 'bewailing bitterly, shedding many tears', and appeared 'weak with anguish'[49] when they were performing the last offices for her. Yet none of the four ladies who had waited on her in the Tower had been kind to, or approving of, Anne, and not one seems to have been sympathetic, so it is therefore unlikely that they would have shown themselves so grieved at her passing. Although the Queen's household had been disbanded six days before, we can be almost certain that four of her former maids-of-honour had been summoned to attend her at her trial and in her last days, and that they had been a great support to her at this time. It seems that the King had been

moved by pity not only to grant Anne the more humane method
of execution, but also to extend to her this last kindness.

'The unhappy Queen, assisted by the Captain [Constable] of the
Tower, came forth',[50] with those 'four young ladies' following,[51]
down the stairs that led from the Queen's lodgings and out into
the courtyard that lay between the Jewel House and the King's
Hall. A grim procession was waiting there, ready to conduct the
prisoner to her execution. It set off immediately, led by a contin-
gent of two hundred Yeomen of the King's Guard. Later tales
erroneously had the executioner following next, traditionally
garbed in a tight-fitting black doublet and hose, with the upper
part of his face masked and a high, horn-shaped cap on his
head,[52] but he and his assistant were actually waiting on the scaffold, and were dressed in ordinary clothes. Behind the Yeomen
of the Guard came the officers of the Tower, and after them,
Anne, Kingston and possibly John Skip, Anne's almoner, bringing
up the rear, although the presence of a priest at the execution
is not recorded; it has been claimed – without any contemporary source being cited – that Anne was not allowed a priest on
the scaffold as she had not confessed her guilt,[53] but that may
not have been the case.

Anne was escorted across the palace courtyard and through the
massive twin towers of the Coldharbour Gate, which stood to
the west of the White Tower and led to the Inner Ward of the
fortress.[54] Ahead was the scaffold. The Queen 'went to her execution with an untroubled countenance',[55] although the hostile
author of the 'Spanish Chronicle' interpreted this as 'a devilish
spirit'.

Waiting for her was a vast crowd of 'a thousand people',[56] all
come to watch her die. Dr Ortiz, who again got his information
from Chapuys, wrote that 'La Ana was beheaded before many
people.'[57] There is no record of any stands being erected for the
onlookers at the execution, as has been claimed.[58] 'There were

present the Chancellor [Audley] and Master Cromwell [accompanied by his son Gregory] and many other of the King's Council, and quite a large number of other subjects.'[59] Also present was Henry VIII's bastard son, the Duke of Richmond,[60] who was doubtless there at his father's command,[61] as his representative, and may have wanted to watch because he believed that Anne had tried to poison him; he had come with his friend, the Earl of Surrey.[62] According to a later account, 'a malign smile seemed to pass over the features of the young Duke' at some point during the proceedings.[63]

Wiltshire was not present to see his daughter die, but the Dukes of Norfolk and Suffolk were there, along with 'earls, lords and nobles of this realm, the Mayor of London with the aldermen and sheriffs, and certain of the best crafts [guilds] of London'.[64] 'Some of the nobility and company of the City [were] admitted rather to be witnesses than spectators of [Anne's] death.'[65] It is unlikely that Wyatt was watching from a window, as he had done two days earlier. The poem he wrote mentions only the men who were executed, not the Queen, and he could not have seen their executions on Tower Hill, and Anne's on Tower Green, from the same window. Mercifully, the crowds around the scaffold probably obscured Anne's view of the newly dug graves in the burial ground of St Peter ad Vincula behind it.

The Imperialist observer[66] reveals that, despite Kingston's restrictions on foreigners, the gates of the Tower had been left open. Presumably there were guards posted to control admittance, but no one could say that the execution had been conducted in secrecy. Aless, a Scot, who would have been denied entry, seems to have been relieved: 'Although my lodging was not far distant from the place of execution, yet I could not become a witness of the butchery of such an illustrious lady.' Although interested, he evidently could not have borne to watch Anne's end, or those of 'the exalted personages' whom he mistakenly believed were to be 'beheaded along with her'. However, his landlord, 'who was a

Anne Boleyn in the Tower

'One hour she is determined to die, and the next much contrary to that.'

Anne Boleyn, Lady Shelton
The Queen thought it 'much unkindness in the King to put about me such as I never loved.'

Sir Thomas Wyatt
'These bloody days have broken my heart,' he mourned.

'To the King from the Lady in The Tower'

For centuries, controversy has raged over the authenticity of this letter.

Westminster Hall, where four of Anne Boleyn's co-accused were tried on 12 May 1536
'Suddenly the axe was turned towards them.'

Henry Percy, Earl of Northumberland

'May it be to my damnation if ever there were any contract or promise or marriage between her and me.'

Thomas Cranmer, Archbishop of Canterbury

'I think your Highness would not have gone so far if she had not been culpable.'

Sir Francis Weston and his wife, Anne Pickering
Weston referred to himself as 'a great offender to God.'

'Weston Esq. of Sutton Surrey'
This is almost certainly a portrait of
Sir Francis Weston.

Anne Boleyn driven mad:
a later, melodramatic image
'This lady has much joy and
pleasure in death.'

Carving from the Martin Tower

Anne Boleyn's falcon badge, without its crown and sceptre, in the Beauchamp Tower

The site of the Queen's Lodgings in The Tower of London, where Anne Boleyn was held prisoner in some splendour.

Gold and enamel pendant, made c.1520, and said to have been given by Anne Boleyn to Captain Gwyn on the day of her execution.

The site of the scaffold on which Anne Boleyn was executed.
It was built on the tournament ground before the old House of Ordnance, and faced the White Tower; it probably stood near the present doorway to the Waterloo Barracks.

The execution of Anne Boleyn
'The Queen suffered with sword this day, and died boldly.' This seventeenth-century woodcut incorrectly shows the headsman wielding an axe.

The Royal Chapel of St Peter ad Vincula, showing the so-called scaffold site
'The Queen's head and body were taken to a church in the Tower.'

Inside St Peter ad Vincula: Anne Boleyn is buried beneath the altar pavement
'God provided for her corpse sacred burial,
even in a place as it were consecrate to innocence.'

Memorial plaque said to mark the last resting place of Anne Boleyn
It is more likely, however, that her body lies beneath the slab commemorating Lady Rochford.

Carved initials of Henry VIII and Anne Boleyn in the vaulting above Anne Boleyn's Gateway, Hampton Court Palace. This carving was overlooked in the rush to replace Anne's initials with Jane Seymour's.

Queen Elizabeth I's ring of *c*.1575, with its portrait of Anne Boleyn.

It is possible that Elizabeth secretly commissioned a written defence of her mother.

servant of Cromwell's', was among the witnesses, and after he returned home at noon, he was able to impart to Aless information that the latter later imparted to Elizabeth I, much of which the landlord had picked up from other spectators.

A great murmur rose from the crowd as Anne appeared. 'Never had the Queen looked so beautiful,' reported the Portuguese witness.[67] 'Her face and complexion never were so beautiful,' echoed Lancelot de Carles. She walked slowly towards the scaffold, 'looking frequently behind her at her ladies',[68] or as if she perhaps expected at any moment to see a royal messenger come galloping into the Tower with a reprieve bearing the King's seal. As she walked past the crowd, Anne would have distributed the alms she had been given to the poorest-looking spectators. There is no record of her progress to the scaffold being accompanied by drum-rolls, as is so often portrayed in modern films.

In the nineteenth century, Agnes Strickland recorded a tradition handed down in the family of an officer of the guard who was supposedly on duty that day, escorting Anne to the scaffold. His name was Captain Gwyn, and she is said to have given him, in acknowledgement of his 'respectful conduct' to her, a small gold pendant in the form of a pistol chased with scrolls of foliage, the barrel being a miniature whistle and containing a set of toothpicks.[69] She told him it had been 'the first token the King gave her', and added 'that a serpent formed part of the device, and a serpent the giver had proved to her'. Strickland discovered that a Captain Gwyn did hold extensive property in Swansea in the reign of Henry VIII. The Gwyn family still had the trinket in their possession in the 1840s, but the tale does not ring true, for Anne's words are not in keeping with those she was shortly to utter on the scaffold, and it would have been sheer folly for a condemned traitor publicly to have denigrated the King in this way. The pendant is now in the Victoria and Albert Museum, and is thought to have been made around 1520.

The scaffold, 'no more than four or five feet high',[70] was draped

with black cloth and strewn with straw. On it, according to the
'Spanish Chronicle', waited 'many gentlemen, amongst them the
headsman, who was dressed like the rest, and not as executioner',
and his assistant. New clothes had been provided for the headsman,
paid for by the Constable, who would be reimbursed in due
course by the King. It seems that a conscious effort had been
made to spare the Queen the starker aspects of execution, with
the headsman unidentifiable and his sword concealed. There was
no block: prisoners being decapitated with a sword were required
to kneel upright.

Anne was composed when Kingston assisted her up the few
wooden steps, the four ladies following.[71] Although the anonymous Imperialist account states that she looked 'feeble and
stupefied',[72] as well she might have done after a sleepless night,
Lord Milherve says that 'when she was brought to the place of
execution, her looks were cheerful', a word used also by Hall,
while Wriothesley states that she showed to the people 'a goodly
smiling countenance'; the author of the 'Spanish Chronicle', whose
account of the execution is detailed and clearly that of an eyewitness, asserts that she was 'as gay as if she were not going to die'.

As soon as she had mounted the scaffold, Anne 'looked around
her on all sides to see the great number of people present', then
turned to Kingston and 'begged leave to speak to the people,
promising she would not speak a word that was not good'.[73] She
asked him 'not to hasten the signal for her death till she had
spoken that which she had a mind to say'. He 'gave her leave'
and indicated that she should proceed; whereupon, with a 'loving
countenance',[74] she faced the crowd and 'gracefully addressed the
people from the scaffold with a voice somewhat overcome by
weakness, but which gathered strength as she went on'.[75] There
are various versions of her speech, and most of them have her
acknowledging, as Dr Ortiz learned from Chapuys, that 'she died
by the laws of the kingdom'.[76]

In the Histoire de la Royne Anne de Boullant, Anne is recorded as saying that 'she was come to die, as she was judged by the law; she would accuse none, nor say anything of the ground upon which she was judged. She prayed heartily for the King, and called him a most merciful and gentle prince, and [said] that he had been always to her a good, gentle sovereign lord, and if any would meddle with her cause, she required them to judge the best. And so she took her leave of them, and of the world, and heartily desired they would pray for her.'

Hall gives a similar version of this speech, which suggests that it was substantially what Anne really said:

Good Christian people, I am come hither to die, according to law, for by the law I am judged to die, and therefore I will speak nothing against it. I come here only to die, and thus to yield myself humbly to the will of the King, my lord. And if, in my life, I did ever offend the King's Grace, surely with my death I do now atone. I come hither to accuse no man, nor to speak anything of that whereof I am accused, as I know full well that aught I say in my defence doth not appertain to you. I pray and beseech you all, good friends, to pray for the life of the King, my sovereign lord and yours, who is one of the best princes on the face of the earth, who has always treated me so well that better could not be, wherefore I submit to death with good will, humbly asking pardon of all the world. If any person will meddle with my cause, I require them to judge the best. Thus I take my leave of the world, and of you, and I heartily desire you all to pray for me. Oh Lord, have mercy on me! To God I commend my soul.

Wriothesley has Anne saying something similar: 'Masters, I here humbly submit me to the law as the law hath judged me, and as for mine offences, I here accuse no man; God knoweth them. I remit them to God, beseeching Him to have mercy on my soul, and I beseech Jesus save my sovereign and master the King, the most godly, noble and gentle Prince that is, and long to reign over you.'

Lancelot de Carles gives another version, in which Anne 'begged her hearers to forgive her if she had not used them all with becoming gentleness, and asked for their prayers. It was needless, she said, to relate why she was there, but she prayed the Judge of all the world to have compassion on those who had condemned her, and she begged them to pray for the King, in whom she had always found great kindness, fear of God and love of his subjects.' According to Milherve, Anne also said, 'Be not sorry to see me die thus, but pardon me from your hearts that I have not expressed to all about me that mildness that became me; and that I have not done that good that was in my power to do.' He adds that she prayed for those who were the procurers of her death.

The Imperialist source wrote that, 'raising her eyes to Heaven, she begged God and the King to forgive her offences, and she bade the people pray God to protect the King, for he was a good, kind, gracious and loving prince'.[77] Given that this was tantamount to an admission of guilt, he may have misheard her.

The Portuguese bystander had Anne blaming the cruelty of the law for her fate in a speech that echoes Hall's version:

Good friends, I am not come here to excuse or to justify myself, forasmuch as I know full well that aught that I could say in my defence doth not appertain to you, and that I could draw no hope of life from the same. But I come here only to die, and thus to yield myself humbly to the will of the King, my lord. And if in my life I did ever offend the King's Grace, surely with my death I do now atone for the same. And I blame not my judges, nor any other manner of person, nor anything save the cruel law of the land by which I die. But be this, and my faults, as they may, I beseech you all, good friends, to pray for the life of the King, my sovereign lord and yours, who is one of the best princes on the face of the Earth, and who hath always treated me so well that better could not be; wherefore I submit to death with a good will, humbly asking pardon of all the world.[78]

Anthony Anthony, another eyewitness, recorded Anne's speech as follows: 'You shall understand that I have submitted me unto the law, and so I am come hither to obey and fulfil the law. And so I can say no more, but I desire you all to be just and true unto the King, your sovereign, for he is a good, virtuous king and a goodly king, a victorious king, a bountiful king, for I have found his Grace always very good and loving unto me, and [he] has done much for me. Wherefore I pray God reward his Grace, praying you all to pray God for his life, that his Grace may reign long with you, and I pray you all for God's sake to pray for me.'

George Wyatt's version of Anne's words, probably taken from John Foxe's *Acts and Monuments of the Church*, echoes Hall's. This speech, Wyatt later observed, showed that Anne's love for the King was such that she chose 'to acquit and defend him by her words at her death'. Yet, as has been stated already, it was customary for condemned traitors to refrain from criticising the King's justice on the scaffold, and Anne would have been aware not only that her father's political survival and future at court depended on her, but also that her husband's anger might be visited upon their innocent child, whose future was now painfully uncertain.[79] Hence her refusal to say anything about her case, and her fulsome praise of the King – which, one would like to think, might have been delivered with just a touch of irony.

The author of the 'Spanish Chronicle', while initially fairly accurate in his version of Anne's speech, seems, as usual, to have embellished it, claiming that she said, 'Do not think, good people, that I am sorry to die, or that I have done anything to deserve this death. My fault has been my great pride, and the great crime I committed in getting the King to leave my mistress, Queen

Katherine for my sake, and I pray God to pardon me for it. I say to you all that everything they have accused me of is false, and the principal reason I am to die is Jane Seymour, as I was the cause of the ill that befell my mistress.' At this, supposedly, the gentlemen standing by 'would not let her say any more'.[80] Had this intervention really happened, more observers surely would have mentioned it.

John Husee aptly summed up Anne's dying speech, and those of the men who had been executed two days earlier, in a letter sent to Lady Lisle on 24 May: 'As to the confession of the Queen and others, they said little or nothing, but what was said was wondrously discreetly spoken.'[81] Anne's words were certainly moving, for 'the spectators could not refrain from tears'.[82] Her failure to admit her guilt would surely have been glaring – this was what Husee meant when he said that the Queen died 'boldly'[83] – and it certainly gave rise to much speculation.

Anne must have realised by now that there was no hope of a reprieve and that she had only minutes left to her. The 'Spanish Chronicle' states that she asked which gentleman was the headsman, and was told – by whom is not clear – 'that he would come presently, but that in the meanwhile it would be better for her to confess the truth and not be so obstinate, for she could not hope for pardon'. Anne replied, 'I know I shall have no pardon, but they shall know no more from me.'

'With the aid of her maids, she undressed her neck with great courage',[84] standing there as they 'stripped [her] of her short mantle furred with ermines. She herself took off her headdress', and 'a young lady presented her with a linen cap, into which she gathered her long hair',[85] so that the blow might not be impeded'.[86] According to the Portuguese account, which may have been embroidered somewhat, Anne was now heard to whisper, 'Alas, poor head. In a very brief space, thou wilt roll in the dust on the scaffold; and as in life you did not merit the crown of a queen, so in death you deserve not better doom than this.'[87]

However, these words have something of a ring of truth, since the hurriedly built scaffold may well have been dusted with sawdust.

As the Queen prepared for death, she was 'saying to her ladies that she asked them to pray for her'.[88] The Portuguese witness says she expressed her gratitude to them, declaring, 'And ye, my maids, who, whilst I lived, ever showed yourselves so diligent in my service, and who are now to be present at my last hour and mortal agony; as in good fortune ye were faithful to me, so even at this, my miserable death, ye do not forsake me. And as I cannot reward you for your true service to me, I pray you take comfort for my loss.' She told them not to be sorry to see her die, and begged their pardon for any harshness she had shown towards them. 'Howbeit, forget me not, and be always faithful to the King's Grace and to her whom with happier fortune ye may look to have as your queen and mistress. And esteem your honour far beyond your life, and in your prayers to the Lord Jesu, forget not to pray for my soul.'[89]

The end was very near. Seeing that Anne was not going to confess and that it was time to perform his office, the executioner came forward and knelt before her, saying, 'Madam, I crave your Majesty's pardon, for I am ordered to do this duty.' She gave it 'willingly'.

'I beg you to kneel and say your prayers,' he told her.[90]

This was the moment. She had perhaps been warned that she must remain very still if she wanted to avoid being horrifically injured by the sword.[91] Again, 'she appeared dazed' as she kneeled down, upright on both knees in the straw,[92] 'fastening her clothes about her feet',[93] a detail that was noted decades later by George Wyatt, who says she 'prepared to receive the stroke of death with resolution, so sedately as to cover her feet with her nether garments'. 'She asked that time for prayer should be granted her',[94] repeating, 'several times, "O Christ, receive my spirit"',[95] but her fear was evident. 'The poor lady kept looking about her. The headsman, being still in front of her, said in French, "Madam, do not fear. I will wait till you tell me."' Anne seemed fearful that her coif would be in the way of the blow, and told him, 'You will have to take this coif off,' pointing to it with her left hand.[96] Although he declined, presumably indicating that he did not need to, she kept her hand on the coif.

Eyewitness accounts of the execution differ; some spectators were closer than others, or had a less restricted view. The 'Spanish Chronicle' asserts that Anne refused to have her eyes bandaged and that her gaze disturbed the executioner, but three other witnesses state that one of her ladies, weeping, 'came forward to do the last office' and blindfolded her with 'a linen cloth'.[97] Aless, whose landlord related the details, says that Anne herself 'covered her eyes'. She was repeatedly saying 'with a fervent spirit',[98] over and over, 'Jesu, have pity on my soul! My God, have pity on my soul',[99] 'To Jesus Christ I commend my soul.'[100] 'The four ladies knelt in silent prayer';[101] the Portuguese says 'they withdrew themselves some little space, and knelt down over against the scaffold, bewailing bitterly and shedding many tears'. According to Aless, Anne now 'commanded the executioner to strike'.

As she knelt there and 'awaited the blow',[102] most of those present followed the example of the Lord Mayor, Sir John Aleyn, and sank to their knees, out of respect for the passing of a soul; only the dukes of Suffolk and Richmond remained resolutely standing.[103] Anne was still praying aloud, 'making no confession of her fault, but saying, "O Lord God, have pity on my soul! To Christ I commend my soul!"'[104] Strickland cites an unnamed source that gives her last words as 'In manuas tuas' – 'Into Thy hands.'

What happened next happened 'suddenly':[105] 'immediately, the executioner did his office'.[106] 'The Queen was beheaded according to the manner and custom of Paris, that is to say, with a sword',[107] which was probably of the finest Flemish steel,[108] and had been 'hidden under a heap of straw'.[109] It would have been blunt-tipped, around three or four feet in length, with a two-inch-wide double-edged blade and a leather-bound handle long enough to be gripped by both hands. A groove or 'fuller' was normally scored the whole length of the blade on either side of an execution sword, its purpose being to channel the blood away from the razor-sharp edge of the blade and so prevent it being blunted.[110]

The intention plainly was to distract Anne at the final moment. The executioner's English assistant had been 'told beforehand what to do', and as the headsman turned to the scaffold steps and called to the assistant, 'Bring me the sword,' Anne blindly moved her head 'towards the steps, still with her hand on her coif, and the headsman made a sign with his right hand for them to give him the sword'.[111] She was aware neither of him taking it, nor of his approach, for he had removed his shoes and come up stealthily behind her.[112] With his hand trembling,[113] for he was 'himself distressed',[114] he raised the sharp, heavy sword aloft, grasping it with both hands, and swung it in a circling motion around his head once or twice to gain the necessary momentum,[115] then 'without being noticed by the lady',[116] who was expecting the blow to descend from the other direction and 'not so much as shrinking at it',[117] he brought it down and swiftly 'divided her neck at a blow',[118] that 'fair neck' that the poet Wyatt had once praised in his admiring verse. Smitten 'off at a stroke',[119] the head was struck straight into the straw.[120]

'He did his office very well, before you could say a Paternoster,' reported Sir John Spelman, who was among the watching crowd. He added that as the Queen's head 'fell to the ground', he and other horrified onlookers witnessed 'her lips moving and her eyes moving', while Gregorio Leti, writing in the late seventeenth century, rather dramatically claims that those eyes seemed mournfully to look down on the broken body on the scaffold before glazing over in death, although his account presupposes that the executioner held up the head in the customary manner and cried, 'So perish all the King's enemies!' There is no record of that happening at Anne Boleyn's execution.

It may be that some sentient feeling briefly remained, although the movements Spelman witnessed could possibly have been a convulsive response of the body's reflexes to the shock of decapitation, rather than the last flickerings of consciousness, and they have been observed in various other victims of beheading down the centuries, particularly during the Terror in the French Revolution. Research undertaken in the late nineteenth century suggested that most die within two seconds, while a more modern estimate would be an average of thirteen seconds. Severing the spinal cord causes death, but not until the brain has been completely deprived, through massive haemorrhaging, of the oxygen in the blood that nourishes it. While that is happening, neurons are firing off in a vain attempt to counteract the blow that has precipitated the adrenalin rush and repair the damage done to the body, and the brain uses the oxygen that remains in the head.

In 1905, a French doctor observed that a decapitated criminal's eyelids and lips worked for five seconds before the face relaxed and the eyes rolled back, at which point he called out the man's name, only to see the eyes fixing themselves on him and the pupils focusing before the lids fell and the pupils glazed over. The whole process had taken twenty-five to thirty seconds. In 1989, the face of a man decapitated in a car accident registered shock, then terror, then grief, as the living eyes looked directly at the witness before dimming. In 1956, two French doctors concluded: 'Death is not instantaneous: every element survives decapitation. It is a savage vivisection.' In 1983, another medical study found that 'no matter how efficient the method of execution, at least two to three seconds of intense pain cannot be avoided'. However, once the spine is severed, the perception of pain recedes. Some victims have not responded at all to stimuli, so it must therefore be concluded that they were knocked unconscious by the impact of the blow, or fainted due to the dramatic loss in blood pressure, and felt virtually nothing, while others – including perhaps

Anne Boleyn – did experience a few dreadful moments of awareness of what was happening.

'When the head fell, a white handkerchief was thrown over it'
by one of the Queen's ladies.[121] The body lay slumped beside it.
At a given signal, the cannon along Tower Wharf were fired,
announcing Anne's death to the world.

The Queen was dead. Justice had to all intents and purposes been
done. 'It is said that, although the bodies and heads of those
executed the day before yesterday have been buried, her head
will be put upon the bridge [London Bridge], at least for some
time,' Chapuys wrote later that day,[122] but Anne was to be spared
that final indignity. Immediately, 'at the moment the poor lady
expired', her women made haste decently to dispose of her
remains,[123] refusing to allow any man to touch her.[124] An oft-
repeated popular tale has old women rushing forward from the
crowd to catch drops of Anne's blood for their charms and potions,
the blood of the condemned being regarded as especially potent,[125]
but again, there is no mention of this in contemporary sources.

As the spectators began to disperse, the Portuguese stayed and
watched as 'one of the four ladies' took up the severed head, still
covered with the white cloth, and carried it away. The other three
lifted the bleeding body of the dead woman, which had for so
long been the object of the King's ardent desire and, having reverently undressed it and 'wrapped [it] in a white covering',[126] placed
the remains 'in a chest which stood here ready, and carried them
to the chapel that is within the Tower';[127] Spelman says this was
an old elm chest that had been used for storing bow-staves, and
it would have been just long enough to take a headless corpse;
no provision had been made for a proper coffin, so this chest had
probably been fetched at the last minute from the Tower armouries,
and left lying ready beside the scaffold.[128]

'The head and body were taken up by the ladies, whom you
would have thought bereft of their souls, so languid and weak

were they with anguish, but, fearing that their mistress might be handled unworthily by inhuman men, they forced themselves to do this duty.'[129]

Jean Hannaert of Lyons also reported that 'the Queen's head and body were taken to a church in the Tower, accompanied by four ladies'.[130] That church was the royal chapel of St Peter ad Vincula, where Anne Boleyn was buried in the earth beneath the chancel pavement, 'the same day at afternoon',[131] in the presence of her ladies, who were 'sobbing woefully'; as it was gone noon, after which time Mass could not be celebrated, one of Anne's chaplains, Father Thirlwall, merely pronounced a blessing over the chest before it was interred.[132]

Since the execution was over soon after nine o'clock in the morning, and Anne's body was taken immediately into the chapel, we might wonder why there was at least a three-hour delay before it was buried. Perhaps Kingston had been expected to attend, but had then been busy all morning in the aftermath of the execution. What is most likely is that someone had to be found to lift the paving stones in the chancel and dig a shallow grave; Kingston, being very busy with his state prisoners and the arrangements for their executions, may have neglected to make provision for this earlier, just as he had neglected to provide Anne with a proper coffin.

What is certain is that Anne's attendants were made to strip the body of its expensive – and probably bloodstained – garments and jewellery, which were then distributed to the Tower officials as perquisites, as was customary after executions.[133] Later, these items would be redeemed by the King for a substantial sum. Possibly Henry did not want people cherishing mementoes of his dead wife. The sumptuary laws banned the lower orders from wearing such attire anyway – rich materials, furs and embroideries being reserved for those of high rank – so cash was probably very welcome in exchange.

Lancelot de Carles states that Anne was buried beside her

brother; his evidence may not be entirely accurate, as will be seen, and the authorities surely would not have thought it fitting for an incestuous brother and sister to lie together in death. Other evidence suggests that they were buried some distance apart, before the altar, where, as theirs were the first bodies to be buried in the chancel, there was plenty of space. 'God provided for her corpse sacred burial, even in [a] place as it were consecrate to innocence,' pronounced George Wyatt.

After the burial, observed Lancelot de Carles, Anne's ladies 'were as sheep without a shepherd', but they would not be left in that state for long because 'already the King has taken a fancy to a choice lady. Other great things are predicted of which the people are assured. If I see them take place, I will let you know, for never were such news. People say it is the year of marvels.'

'The Queen,' Husee reported only hours afterwards, 'suffered with sword this day . . . and died boldly.'[134] Referring to all who had died, he added, 'Jesu take them to His mercy.' Even Cromwell was impressed by Anne's bravery, and that of Rochford, and 'greatly praised the intelligence, wit and courage of the Concubine and her brother'.[135] 'She had reigned as queen three years lacking fourteen days, from her coronation to her death,' Wriothesley observed. The Imperialist witness believed that he had 'seen the prophecy of Merlin fulfilled'.[136]

Sometime after Anne's execution, in his prison in the Byward Tower, a distressed Thomas Wyatt again put pen to paper to write of the woman he had once passionately courted, his verses being an outpouring of woe at the unforeseen twists of fortune to which all human beings were subject, Anne more dramatically than most. It was a popular contemporary theme, and Wyatt – who had been so closely caught up in this tragedy – expressed it very movingly, and captured the horror of Anne's situation:

So freely wooed, so dearly bought,
So soon a queen, so soon low brought,
Hath not been seen, could not be thought.
            O! What is Fortune?

As slipper as ice, as fading as snow,
Like unto dice that a man doth throw,
Until it arises he shall not know
            What shall be his fortune!

They did her conduct to a tower of stone,
Wherein she would wail and lament her alone,
And condemned be, for help there was none.
            Lo! Such was her fortune.[137]

Writing on the day of her execution, Anne's chaplain, Matthew
Parker, was in no doubt that her soul was in 'blessed felicity with
God'. Her body, however, had been consigned to oblivion, for no
provision was made for any stone or memorial tablet to mark the
place where she lay.[138]

14

'When Death Hath Played His Part'

As Anne's head fell in the dust, with her body tumbling beside it, a signal was given and the guns on the Tower wharf were fired, announcing her end to the world. She had been one of the most powerful women ever to occupy the consort's throne, yet her rapid and cataclysmic overthrow illustrates just how fragile was the balance of power at the English court.

There had been no precedent for the trial and execution of an English queen, and Anne Boleyn's fall, with its attendant purge of the Privy Chamber, had been nothing less than sensational. At a stroke, Cromwell had eliminated or neutralised a whole faction, and many were touched by the tragedy.

Anne had never been popular; the common people had always disliked her. Just hours after her execution, Chapuys wrote from London, 'I cannot well describe the great joy the inhabitants of this city have lately experienced and manifested at the fall and ruin of the Concubine.' He added that many were elated at the prospect of the Lady Mary – whom they still regarded as the King's lawful heiress – being restored to favour,[1] for Anne's enmity towards her had been well known.

It is evident from Chapuys' dispatch that, at the time of Anne's beheading, people were ready to believe anything of her. The parson of Freshwater, Dorset, who was hostile to Henry VIII, was nevertheless in no doubt of her guilt: 'Lo, whilst the King and his Council were busy to put down abbeys and pull away the right of Holy Church, he was made a cuckold at home.'[2] Nicholas Shaxton, Bishop of Salisbury, spoke for many when he wrote to Cromwell on 23 May of 'the late Queen', declaring that she had 'sore slandered' the cause of reform, while 'that vice that she was found faulty of hath not the like in Christendom'. The Bishop did, in charity, pray that God would have mercy on her soul and pardon all her offences.[3]

It was a credulous and superstitious age. One of Cromwell's agents, John de Ponti, reported that the Master of Maison Dieu at Dover was telling people 'that the day before the Lady Anne Boleyn was beheaded, the tapers that stood about Queen Katherine's sepulchre kindled of themselves; and after Matins were done to *Deo gratias*, the said tapers quenched of themselves'. The King is said to have 'sent thirty men to [Peterborough] abbey', and they could see for themselves that 'it was true of this light continuing from day to day'.[4]

The ignorant folk who observed this phenomenon would have regarded it as a sign that the Deity approved of the King's punishment of the evil woman who had supplanted his true wife – Katherine of Aragon's cause had not been so soon forgotten.

In Catholic Europe, most people shared the view of the Emperor that, in destroying Anne, God had revealed His will. Antoine Perrenot de Granvelle, one of Charles V's chief advisers, wrote callously to Chapuys that the news was good music to his ears, and a subject for joyful mirth.[5] The Papal Nuncio in Lyons believed the Queen's fate to be the judgement of the Almighty. At the court of James V in Edinburgh, Lord William Howard, Anne's uncle, was shocked to see everyone so jubilant, and wrote urging Cromwell to tell him 'the truth' so that he should know how to deal with this.[6] A week after the execution, the merchant and diplomat, Edmund Harvel, wrote from Venice to Dr Thomas Starkey:

> The news of the Queen's case made a great tragedy, which was celebrated by all men's voices with admiration and great infamy to that woman to have betrayed that noble prince after such manner, who had exalted her so high and put himself to peril, not without perturbation of all the world, for her cause. God showed Himself a rightful judge to discover such high treason and iniquity. But all is for the best, and I reckon this the King's great fortune, that God would give him grace to see and touch with the hand what enemies and traitors he lived withal, of the which inconvenience his Grace is fair delivered, for with time there might have followed damage to his Grace inestimable.[7]

These were comparatively conservative reactions, for ever-wilder rumours were now proliferating. Even Chapuys, the arch-detractor of reform, did not swallow whole all he heard: 'Although the matter is not much to be relied on, many think that most of the new bishops *ont d'avoir leur Sainte Martin* [meaning, perhaps, that there was a globe of fire suspended above their heads, as appeared in popular representations of the saint], because, having persuaded the Concubine that she had no need to confess, she grew more audacious in vice; and moreover, they persuaded her that, according to the said [Lutheran] sect, it was lawful to seek aid elsewhere, even from her own relations, when her husband was not capable of satisfying her.' Reflecting on Anne's fate, the ambassador recalled how 'the Concubine, before her marriage with the King, said, to increase his love, that there was a prophecy that about this time, a queen of England would be burnt, but, to please the King, she [said she] did not care. After her marriage she boasted that the events mentioned in the prophecy had already been accomplished, and yet she was not condemned. But they might well have said to her, as was said to Caesar, "The ides have come, but not gone."[8] In the Privy Chamber, Sir Francis Bryan and his 'fellows' rejoiced at Anne's fall.[9]

Yet after her execution, increasingly, there emerged a strong sense that justice had been subverted, while reports of her dignity and courage on the scaffold gradually won her the latent admiration and sympathy of some who had previously reviled her. Even the unsympathetic George Constantine had 'never heard of queens that they should be thus handled, but I promise you there was much muttering of Queen Anne's death'. Alexander Aless, whose landlord had witnessed her execution, wrote that she had 'exhibited such constancy, patience and faith towards God that all the spectators, even her enemies and those persons who had previously rejoiced at her misfortune, testified and proclaimed her innocence and chastity'.

Aless's landlord invited some of those spectators to dinner a day or so later, and when these guests 'were thus talking at table in my hearing, without being questioned, they themselves answered the accusations brought against the Queen. It is no new thing, said they, that the King's chamberlains should dance with the ladies in the bedchamber. Nor can any proof of adultery be collected from the fact that the Queen's brother took her by the hand and led her into the dance among the other ladies, or handed her to another. It is a usual custom throughout the whole of Britain that ladies married and unmarried, even the most coy, kiss not only a brother, but any honourable person, even in public. It is also the custom with young women to write to their near relatives when they become pregnant, in order to receive their congratulations. The King also was most anxious for an heir, and longed for nothing more than to know that the

Queen was pregnant.' Some of these views must have been those of people associated with the court, who knew how things were conducted there.

'From such arguments as these, they affirmed that no probable suspicion of adultery could be collected, and that therefore there must have been some other reason which moved the King.' Aless thought it could have been 'the desire for an heir' and his being 'further strengthened in his desire for a new marriage by perceiving that all the male children to which the Queen gave birth came into this world dead. And further, the King was angry with the Queen because of the want of success which attended the embassy, which, at her instigation, he had despatched into Germany.' People were also speculating that Henry had got rid of Anne for fear that the Emperor, the Pope and the Catholic princes of Europe would band together against him, and because he was 'in danger from them on account of the change in religion'. There followed much speculation on what would happen to religion in England now that Anne was gone.

While Aless and his landlord's guests were talking, 'a servant of Cromwell's arrived from the court and, sitting down at the table, asked the landlord if he could let him have something to eat, for he was exceedingly hungry. While the food was being got ready, the other guests asked him what were his news? Where was the King? What was he doing? Was he sorry for the Queen? He answered by asking why should he be sorry for her? She had already betrayed him in secrecy, so now was he openly insulting her. For just as she, while the King was oppressed with the heavy cares of state, was enjoying herself with others, so he, while the Queen was being beheaded, was enjoying himself with another woman.'

His words provoked outrage. 'While we were all astonished and ordered him to hold his tongue, for he was saying what no one would believe, and he would bring himself into peril if others heard him talking thus, he answered, "You yourselves will speedily learn from other persons the truth of what I have been saying."' He was referring to the fact that the King was already betrothed to Jane Seymour. The landlord intervened, saying it was not fitting to discuss such things, and that he himself would 'go carefully into these matters' when he next went to court. Cromwell's servant retorted that 'he had the King's orders that none but that the councillors and secretaries should be admitted, and that the gate of the country house in which the King had secluded himself should be kept shut'. Undeterred, the landlord did go to court, and on his return, he was able to tell Aless that the King would shortly afterwards be married.

Aless, a Protestant recounting these events for Elizabeth I, was biased and probably exaggerating public opinion, yet his is not the only evidence for the small but growing swell of sympathy for Anne Boleyn. 'Although everybody rejoices at the execution of the Concubine,' Chapuys reported, 'there are some who murmur at the mode of procedure against her and the others, and people speak variously of the King, and it will not pacify the world when it is known what has passed, and is passing, between him and Mistress Jane Seymour. Already it sounds ill, in the ears of the people, that the King, having received such ignominy, has shown himself more glad than ever since the arrest of the Concubine.'[10] So soon, a legend was in the making.

As the murmuring spread, Anne began to be seen as a victim done away with on a flimsy pretext, particularly in the wake of Henry marrying Jane ten days after her beheading. That view was openly expressed in England just over a month after Anne Boleyn's execution, when an Oxfordshire man, John Hill of Eynsham, was brought before the local justices for saying that 'the King caused Mr Norris, Mr Weston and such as were put of late unto execution to be put to death only of pleasure', and that 'the King, for a fraud and a guile, caused Master Norris, Master Weston and the Queen to be put to death because he was made sure unto the Queen's Grace that now is half a year before'. Master Hill pleaded guilty and was thrown into prison. Another man, William Saunders, who had said much the same thing, was examined with him.[11]

It would surely have occurred to those who privately thought the same as John Hill that it could well have been the King, and not Cromwell, who had resolved to be rid not only of Anne but also of her powerful faction in the Privy Chamber, in order to clear the way for the rising stars, the Seymours.[12]

Although Chapuys famously referred to Anne in 1536 as 'the English Messalina or Agrippina', and Reginald Pole, Henry VIII's cousin and a stern Catholic, that same year called her 'a Jezebel and a sorceress', the reformer Philip Melanchthon was horrified at news of her death and its disastrous implications for any Protestant alliance with England: 'The reports from England are more than tragic. The Queen, accused rather than convicted of adultery, has suffered the penalty of death, and that catastrophe has wrought great changes in our plans. How dreadfully this calamity will dishonour the King. What a great change has suddenly been made.' As a Protestant, he was in no doubt that 'that blow came from Rome. In Rome, all these tricks and plots are contrived.'[13] In France, poems were written honouring Anne's memory,[14] while one French reformist, Etienne Dolet, raged that Anne had been condemned 'on a false charge of adultery'.[15]

Even the Emperor's sister, the politically acute Mary of Hungary, did not believe in Anne's guilt and was dismayed to hear of her fate: 'As none but the organist confessed, nor herself either, people think [the King] invented this device to get rid of her. Anyhow, no great wrong can be done to her, even in being suspected as wicked, for she is known to have been a worthless person. It is to be hoped, if hope be a right thing to entertain about such acts, that, when he is tired of this one, he will find some occasion of getting rid of her. I think wives will hardly be well contented if such customs become general,' she added drily. 'Although I have no desire to put myself in this danger, yet, being of the feminine gender, I will pray with the others that God may keep us from it.'[16] By 1538, the young Christina of Denmark, Duchess of Milan, a niece of Charles V – who, when Henry VIII later sued for her hand, was pertly to reply that if she had two heads, one would be at his Majesty's disposal – was voicing the kinder view that Anne Boleyn had been 'innocently put to death';[17] later still, in 1544, Jean de Luxembourg, Abbot of Ivry, asserted that Henry VIII had 'murdered' her.[18]

Although he had done so when Katherine of Aragon had died, Henry VIII did not mark Anne's death with celebrations and feasting. The royal household accounts for 19 May 1536 show the lowest expenditure for any day that year: £44.12s. (£15,600).[19] That was probably because, after hearing the guns signalling that he was a widower, Henry VIII left Whitehall in the morning to join Jane at Chelsea. 'The people will certainly be displeased at what has been told me, if it be true,' Chapuys wrote on the 20th, 'that yesterday, the King, immediately on receiving news of the decapitation of the Concubine, boarded his barge and went to [Mistress] Seymour, whom he has lodged a mile from him in a house by the river.'[20] By then, Sir Francis Bryan had already brought Jane the news that Anne was dead.

Henry did not, as legends have it, go hunting and wait in Richmond Park or Epping Forest for the Tower cannon to be fired,[21] and Chapuys' report belies the crude assertion made by Cromwell's servant to Aless that the King was 'enjoying himself with another woman' as Anne faced the executioner, although he might well have done so later on, as he spent the day quietly with Jane at Chelsea, and dined with her there in the evening.

Henry had still not appeared in public. John Husee, in his letter of 19 May that detailed the executions to Lord Lisle, stated apologetically that, despite having 'waited diligently and made all the friendship that I can make', he could 'find no ways to come to the King's presence. His Grace came not abroad these fourteen days, so that I have been, and yet am, at bay. I trust it be ere long, seeing that these matters of execution are past, to speak with his Grace, and then deliver your [gift of] spurs.' In the end, after all the frustrating delays, Lisle's request 'to have something of what came to his hands by these gentlemen's deaths' reached the King (as Henry was to explain a week later) 'too late, because all things were disposed long since, and there was nothing worth giving your Lordship'.[22]

By the time Anne died, preparations were already in train for the King's marriage to Jane Seymour. In the royal palaces, an army of carpenters, stonemasons, glaziers and seamstresses were busily removing Anne's initials, mottoes and falcon badge, and replacing them with Jane's initials and her emblem of a phoenix arising from a flaming castle;[23] that this was done in a hurry is evident from the fact that in some places, Anne's devices are still visible underneath; in others, they were clearly inaccessible or just over-looked. At Hampton Court, for example, her initials, entwined with Henry's, can still be seen adorning the vaulted ceiling of Anne Boleyn's Gateway, and her initials and badges are to be seen in the roof timbers of the great hall and in the Great Watching Chamber, while her falcon badge survives in the rood screen in King's College Chapel, Cambridge. On Henry's orders, a stained-glass window depicting St Anne, the fallen Queen's patron saint, was removed from the chapel royal at Hampton Court.[24] Portraits of Anne were probably taken down and hidden away, or destroyed, which would explain why no contemporary examples survive.

At Dover Castle, the King's master glazier, Galyon Hone, had just added 'the Queen's badge' to windows in the royal lodgings, for which he was paid £200 (£69,850); more money was wasted when the King had to pay him to replace the badges with those of Jane Seymour, in time for the summer's royal visit to Dover. Galyon Hone is also known to have replaced Anne's badges in the windows at Ampthill and Greenwich.[25] In the case of stone emblems, Anne's heraldic device of a leopard was more easily remodelled to look like Jane's panther 'by new making of the heads and tails'.[26] When news of Anne's fate reached Zurich, where Miles Coverdale's English Bible with its dedication to Henry and his 'dearest wife and most virtuous princess, Queen Anne' was being reprinted, Jane's name was hastily superimposed on the frontispiece.[27] Anne's name, and her image, were being thoroughly erased from view; it was as if she had never existed.

At Hever Castle, her family home, there is a posthumous reminder of her fate: on the stone newel of the spiral staircase leading to the Long Gallery, there is incised the cipher that appears in Henry VIII's love letters to her, and below it – at some unknown date – someone has carved an axe.

During the night after Anne's execution, Henry left Whitehall and was rowed upriver to Hampton Court; at six o'clock the following morning, 20 May, Jane Seymour was conveyed from Chelsea 'secretly by river to the King's lodgings' and they were betrothed there at nine o'clock. 'The King means it to be kept secret till Whitsuntide,' Chapuys added, 'but everybody begins already to murmur by suspicion, and several affirm that, long before the death of the other, there was some arrangement, which sounds ill in the ears of the people.'[28] Jane, Agnes Strickland sternly observed, had 'given her hand to the regal ruffian before his wife's corpse was cold. Yes, four-and-twenty hours had not elapsed since the sword was reddened with the blood of her mistress.'

News of the betrothal could not be kept secret for long. 'It is presumed that there shall be by midsummer a new coronation,' the perceptive Husee wrote on 24 May.[29] Six days earlier, Chapuys had expressed his doubts about Jane's virginity. 'Perhaps the King will be only too glad to be so far relieved of that difficulty,' he added mischievously. 'According to the account of the Concubine, he has neither vigour nor competence, and besides, he may marry her on condition that she is a maid, and when he wants a divorce, there will be plenty of witnesses ready to testify that she was not.'

Although Jane had proved useful to him and his friends, Chapuys was unimpressed by her: 'The said Seymour is not a woman of great wit, but she may have good understanding. It is said she inclines to be proud and haughty. She bears great love and reverence to the Princess. I know not if honours will make her change hereafter.'[30]

On the Sunday after Anne's execution, which was Ascension Day, 'the King wore white for mourning'.[31] That weekend, he ordered the settlement of an account submitted by Sir William Kingston in respect of expenses incurred in connection with the imprisonment of 'the late Queen': £100 (£34,900) 'for [the redeeming of] such jewels and apparel as [she] had in the Tower'; £25.4s.6d (£8,800) for her 'diet'; £23.6s.8d (£7,800) 'to the executioner of Calais for his reward and apparel'; and £20 (£7,000) for the alms Anne had distributed on the day of her death.[32] That came to the princely total of £168.11s.2d (£58,500), which would be paid in August. Some of Anne's outstanding debts were also settled by the King's comptroller – the rest would not be paid by Cromwell until February 1538 – and moneys owing to her totalling £1,073.6s.8d (£374,850) called in.[33] Meanwhile, Cromwell, on 20 May, had drawn up a list of 'Remembrances', and made a note to himself 'To remember . . . Sir William Kingston.'[34] He also remembered George Constantine, and how he had been a friend to Norris and sent details of the events in the Tower to John Barlow, once chaplain to the Boleyns. Constantine was briefly arrested, which suggests that Master Secretary was still anxious to control and censor information about Anne's fall.[35]

The news of Anne's execution had spread like wildfire through Europe. In Rome, the Pope, in the false hope that the English Reformation had been halted, suspended the excommunication process against Henry VIII. There was a virtual stampede to find a bride for the eligible royal widower. Charles V, on 18 May, before Anne Boleyn's death, had proposed, 'since the case [against Anne] is so manifest, as we suppose, by the divine will, and the King takes it to heart as he ought', a marriage for Henry with the Infanta of Portugal, 'as he is of amorous complexion and always desires to have a male child';[36] while on 24 May, the Bishop of Faenza reported that 'the Imperialists have offered the King of England the Queen of Hungary for a wife, but it is thought he will not take her as she is in bad health and not fit to bear children'.[37] The French were also keen to seize the advantage: Chapuys says that on the day after Anne Boleyn's execution, their ambassadors offered the King the hand of Madeleine of Valois, a daughter of Francis I. But Henry replied 'that she was too young for him, and he had too much experience of French upbringing in the case of the Concubine'.[38]

Of course, he was entertaining no thoughts of taking another foreign bride, and on 29 May, 'incontinent after the suffering of Queen Anne',[39] and before people in far-flung parts of the kingdom had even heard of Anne's death, he married Jane Seymour at Hampton Court.[40] It was thought strange by some that 'within one and the same month that saw Queen Anne flourishing, accused, condemned and executed', another was 'assumed into her place, both of bed and honour'.[41] A courier from England informed the Bishop of Faenza that Henry had 'showed the greatest preference for [Jane], even during the life of the other'.[42] It is easy to see why people were beginning to take a cynical view.

By 4 June, Henry VIII had emerged from seclusion and was again presiding over 'a great and triumphant court',[43] and on the 5th, the Queen's brother, Sir Edward Seymour, was created Viscount Beauchamp[44] and launched on the glittering path to power and, ultimately, tragedy.

On 7 June, the King brought Queen Jane by barge from Greenwich to Whitehall. London was *en fête*, and crowds lined the riverbanks. As the royal couple were rowed past the Tower, they saw it bedecked with fluttering pennants and streamers in honour of the occasion[45] – in stark contrast to the grim drama that had been played out within its walls not three weeks before. We might wonder if either Jane or Henry allowed their thoughts to dwell on the woman who had been its central player, and whose body was now decomposing beneath the pavement of the Tower chapel.

When Henry VIII reopened Parliament on 8 June 1536, Lord Chancellor Audley, in his speech to the King and both Houses, spoke of Anne Boleyn's crimes and the need to settle the succession on the issue of Queen Jane. 'Your Majesty, not knowing of any lawful impediments, entered into the bonds of the said unlawful marriage and advanced the Lady Anne to the sovereign state. Yet she, nevertheless, inflamed with pride and carnal desires of her body, confederated herself with her natural brother' and the other men accused with her, 'to the utter loss, disherison and desolation of this realm; and so, being confederate, she and they most traitorously committed and perpetrated divers detestable and abominable treasons, to the fearful peril and danger of your royal person, and to the fearful peril and danger of this realm, if God of His goodness had not in due time brought their said treasons to light. For the which, being plainly and manifestly proved, they were convict[ed] and attainted by due course and order of your common law of this realm, and have suffered according to the merits.'

Audley read out to both Houses the King's speech, in which Henry – possibly mounting a damage-limitation exercise to quell the rumours – publicly lamented that, having been so disappointed in his first two marriages, he had been obliged, for the welfare of his realm, to enter upon a third, 'a personal sacrifice not required of any ordinary man'.[46] Here the Lord Chancellor paused, then he asked, 'What man in middle life would not this deter from marrying a third time? Yet this, our most excellent Prince, not in any carnal concupiscence, but at the humble entreaty of his nobility, again condescended to contract matrimony, and hath, on the humble petition of the nobility, taken to himself a wife this time whose age and fine form give promise of issue.' There was resounding applause, and Audley, on behalf of the Lords and Commons, thanked the King for his selflessness and the care he had shown for his subjects. After that, the King left smiling benignly, confident that he had emerged from the whole tragic affair as the innocent party – as indeed those close to him made plain their conviction that he was. 'The King hath come out of hell into heaven for the gentleness in this [Queen] and the cursedness and unhappiness in the other,' Sir John Russell observed.[47]

The chief business of this Parliament was to ratify the condemnation of Anne Boleyn, as well as Cranmer's annulment of her marriage, which was sealed on 10 June and approved by the bishops in Convocation on the 21st and by both Houses of Parliament on the 28th.[48] Parliament's other priority – as Chapuys had predicted on 19 May – was to exclude 'the Concubine's little bastard' from ever succeeding to the throne,[49] and it now passed a new Act of Succession, declaring that the King's marriage to Anne was unlawful and that its issue, Elizabeth, was to be 'taken, reputed and accepted to be illegitimate, and utterly excluded and barred to claim, challenge or demand any inheritance as lawful heir to your Highness by lineal descent'. Instead, the crown was to pass to the heirs of Jane Seymour.[50]

A general pardon was thereupon issued to those persons who had been cast into prison for slandering Anne or calling her daughter a bastard.[51] Four years later, when French ambassadors showed themselves reluctant to consider Elizabeth as a bride for the French King's son, her great-uncle, the Duke of Norfolk, openly agreed with them that it would not be an 'honourable' match, and explained that 'the opinion of Queen Anne, her mother, was such that it was quite decided to consider her illegitimate'.[52]

No longer were the Boleyns a force to be reckoned with: their power and spirit had been crushed, their faction toppled and discredited in less than three weeks. Those who survived the purge, like the Howards and the late Queen's reformist protégés, had to keep their heads down in order to save themselves. Although Anne's parents had escaped being sent to the Tower, her father, Wiltshire – who had made no protest, nor expressed regret or grief at the fate of his son and daughter – was deprived of his lucrative office of Lord Privy Seal on 24 June, to be replaced by Cromwell on 2 July,[53] around the time when – had Anne's child gone to term – he would have become grandfather to the future king.

Nevertheless, Wiltshire retained his place at court and on the King's Council. He attended the christening of Prince Edward, the son whom Jane Seymour finally bore Henry VIII, in October 1537, helped to suppress the northern rebellion known as the Pilgrimage of Grace that year, and even, on one occasion, lent Cromwell his Garter insignia. In January 1538, we find him being 'well-entertained' at court.[54] After his wife, Elizabeth Howard, passed away in April that year,[55] there was talk of a marriage between him and the Lady Margaret Douglas, the King's niece.[56]

Clearly Wiltshire had not fallen far from favour, and when he died in March 1539, the King ordered masses to be said for his soul.[57] There is no evidence to support Sander's assertion that he 'died of grief', yet it would not be surprising if grief had been a factor in hastening his end. His fine tomb brass may be seen in St Peter's Church at Hever. Neither he nor his wife lived to see the triumphant accession of their granddaughter, Elizabeth I, in 1558. In 1540, Hever Castle, the family seat in Kent, was given to Anne of Cleves, Henry VIII's fourth wife, as part of her nullity settlement.

Mary Boleyn, Anne's sister, lived until 1543, dying in obscurity at Rochford Hall in Essex, a Boleyn property. Having incurred the wrath of Henry VIII and Anne Boleyn in 1534 for secretly marrying the impecunious William Stafford without their consent, she was banished from court and is not recorded there again.

Hence she probably had no further contact with her niece Elizabeth.

There has been speculation that George Boleyn perhaps left one son, his namesake, who became Dean of Lichfield under Elizabeth I and who described himself in his will as the kinsman of her cousin, Henry Carey, Lord Hunsdon, who was Mary Boleyn's grandson and Anne Boleyn's great-nephew. It is unlikely that the Dean could have been the son of George Boleyn and Jane Parker, since Thomas Boleyn's heir at his death was his daughter Mary. The name George – unusual in the Boleyn family – suggests he was Rochford's bastard. Barred from inheriting, and fatherless, with his Boleyn grandparents dead, it is entirely credible that, in November 1544, he should have entered Trinity Hall, Cambridge, as a sizar, a student of limited means who was charged reduced fees and given assistance with food and lodging whilst at university. A career in the Church was always the best option for gentlemen without independent means, and it was later claimed (by the antiquarian Browne Willis in his survey of Lichfield Cathedral, published in 1727 and based on original records and registers) that Elizabeth I wanted to appoint this kinsman Bishop of Worcester, but that he turned it down. But he was grateful for what she had done for him, and in his will, he stated, 'Her Majesty gave me all that ever I have.'[58]

Lady Rochford, 'a widow in black full woebegone',[59] retired from court after her husband's fall. After his execution, his confiscated assets, which had been inventoried, and now reverted to the Crown, were distributed among loyal courtiers such as the Earl of Sussex and Sir Thomas Cheyney; on 31 May 1536, no doubt to reward his willingness to condemn his son-in-law, Lady Rochford's father, Henry Parker, Lord Morley, was granted the lucrative office of chief steward of the manor of Hatfield Regis, which was part of the honour of Beaulieu in Essex, a royal palace that had been given to Lord Rochford and had also reverted to the Crown; in addition, he was appointed master of the deer in the forest there, and keeper of the park.[60]

Lady Rochford, however, was left in serious financial difficulties; even her rich court attire had been seized.[61] It was probably in late May that she was reduced to sending a begging letter to Cromwell, in whom, she declared, 'her special trust' reposed after God and the King, for he, Cromwell, was well known for his 'gentle manner to all them that be in such lamentable case'. She implored him 'to obtain from the King for her the stuff and plate of her husband', saying it was 'nothing to be regarded' by Henry, but would be to her 'a most high help and succour'. She reminded him that 'the King and her father paid 2,000 marks [£232,800] for her jointure to the Earl of Wiltshire, and she is only assured of 100 marks [£11,650] during the Earl's life', which, she wrote, 'is very hard for me to shift the world withal'. She prayed Master Secretary 'to inform the King of this' and make him think 'more tenderly' of her, assuring him of her 'prayers and service' for the rest of her life, and signing her letter as 'a poor desolate widow, without comfort, Jane Rochford'.[62] It seems that, despite the fact that she had furnished evidence that had helped their case, Jane had been overlooked by Henry and Cromwell in the hectic aftermath of Anne Boleyn's fall. Cromwell did see that she was well provided for:[63] he and the King acted immediately, Henry forcing her father-in-law, Wiltshire (who had control of her income), to increase her allowance to £100 (£34,900); understandably, the Earl did so reluctantly, bitterly insisting that Cromwell 'inform the King that I do this alonely for his pleasure'.[64] This was on 2 July 1536. However, Jane's jointure, the part of her marriage settlement allocated for her security in widowhood (which included Blickling Hall in Norfolk, where Anne Boleyn had probably been born), was not restored to her until after Wiltshire's death and that of his mother, Margaret Butler, in 1539.[65]

Lady Rochford perhaps sought refuge at her father's house, for it is unlikely that she was welcome at her father-in-law's castle at Hever; but she was back at court, as a lady-in-waiting to Jane Seymour, by the end of 1536. Her reappearance at court so soon after the fall of the Boleyns, and within months of her husband's death, suggests that she was being rewarded for her complicity, while other evidence implies that she was to go on being rewarded. In 1539, she obtained, probably through Cromwell's good offices, the passing of an Act of Parliament confirming her jointure and protecting her interest in certain Boleyn manors; this bill was passed after its three readings were rushed through on the same day, and it was signed by Henry VIII himself, who granted her two manors in Warwickshire at the same time.[66]

Jane continued to enjoy royal favour, and was to serve two of Henry's subsequent wives, Anne of Cleves and Katherine Howard, but in 1541, she rashly and 'traitorously' became a 'go-between' in Katherine's extramarital trysts with the courtier Thomas Culpeper; for which, these being discovered, she was arrested after the Queen, whom she betrayed under questioning. The theory that she abetted Katherine's adultery in order to wreak vengeance on Henry VIII for executing her husband is hardly convincing, given that it was her own evidence that had brought George Boleyn to the block. Lacey Baldwin Smith's description of Lady Rochford as 'a pathological meddler with the instincts of a procuress who achieves a vicarious pleasure from arranging assignations'[67] may not be far wide of the mark. Katherine Howard herself accused Jane of having a 'wicked imagination',[68] and of acting as *agent provocateur* for her own purposes; both behaved with 'unbelievable imbecility'.[69]

Taken to the Tower, 'that bawd the Lady Jane Rochford'[70] suffered a nervous collapse so severe that it was thought she had gone mad.[71] It did not save her. Parliament passed an Act of Attainder condemning her to death, and she followed Katherine Howard to the block on 13 February 1542. By the time Jane reached the scaffold, she was calm and resigned, although one bystander thought she spent too long a time dwelling on the 'several faults she had committed in her life'.[72] 'Good Christians,' she is reported to have said, 'God has permitted me to suffer this shameful doom as punishment for having contributed to my husband's death. I falsely accused him of loving, in an incestuous manner, his sister, Queen Anne Boleyn. For this I deserve to die. But I am guilty of no other crime.'[73] Her end, George Wyatt later observed, was 'a just punishment by law after her naughtiness'.

Less than twenty years later, George Cavendish observed that her 'slander for ever shall be rife' and that as a result of her deeds 'both early and late' in her life – which implies that her testimony against her husband was notorious – she would be called 'the woman of vice insatiate'. And so she has gone down in history, there having been just one not very convincing attempt, in 2007, to rehabilitate her memory.[74]

On the day of Anne's execution, Chapuys had reported that 'there are still two English gentlemen detained on her account, and it is suspected that there will be many more, because the King has said he believed that more than a hundred had had to do with her'.[75]

But there would be no more arrests. Corroborating Chapuys' account, John Husee informed Lord Lisle that 'Mr Page and Mr Wyatt remain still in the Tower. What shall become of them, God knoweth best.'[76] Cromwell secured their release on 14 June, Wyatt upon his father's surety for his good behaviour, and Page on condition that he never again came near the King or the court. The King soon made it clear that he was ready to receive Page back into favour, but Page decided that it was safer to stay away from court for the time being.[77] Later in 1536, however, he was appointed Sheriff of Surrey, and around this time resolved to become 'a daily courtier' again. The King was as good as his word and, in 1537, appointed Page chamberlain to the newborn Prince Edward. In September 1539, Henry personally granted him the dissolved priory of St Giles-in-the-Wood (later Beechwood Park) at Flamstead, Hertfordshire. After receiving various other grants and offices, including the property of the Knights of St John in

Kilburn, north of London, and being honoured by a visit by the young King Edward VI, Sir Richard died in prosperity in February 1548, leaving an only daughter and heiress, Elizabeth, the wife of Sir William Skipwith.

Henry was soon ready to welcome back Wyatt too. The 'Spanish Chronicle', referring to the letter that Wyatt had supposedly sent to him from the Tower, has the King saying, 'I am sorry I did not listen to thee when I was angry, but I was blinded by that bad woman.' This too is probably apocryphal. But Wyatt had been deeply affected, not only by his own plight, but also by that of the other accused, and during his imprisonment he had written another poem reflecting upon the fate of those who rose high at court only to experience the bitter reversal of fortune. Entitled *'Innocentia Veritas Viat Fides Circumdederunt me intimici me'* (the Latin title is based on Psalm 16, verse 9: 'My enemies surround my soul', and Wyatt's name – *Viat* – is surrounded by Innocence, Truth and Faith), it has each verse ending in a Latin phrase that aptly translates as 'Thunder rolls around the throne' (which is based on a line in Seneca's *Phaedra*, 'It thunders through the realms'), and reads:

> *V. Innocentia* [The 'V.' Stands for Wyatt; Innocence]
> *Verita Viat Fides* [Truth, Wyatt, faith]
> *Circumdederunt me inimici mei* [My enemies have
>   surrounded me]

> Who list his wealth and ease retain,
> Himself let him unknown contain.
> Press not too fast in at that gate
> Where the return stands by disdain,
> For sure, *circa Regna tonat.*

> The high mountains are blasted oft
> When the low valley is mild and soft.

Fortune with Health stands at debate;
The fall is grievous from aloft,
And sure, *circa Regna tonat.*

These bloody days have broken my heart,
My lust, my youth did then depart,
And blind desire of estate.
Who hastes to climb seeks to revert.
Of truth, *circa Regna tonat.*

The Bell Tower showed me such a sight
That in my head sticks day and night.
There did I lean out of a grate,
For all favour, glory or might,
That yet *circa Regna tonat.*

By proof, I say, there did I learn:
Wit helpeth not defence too yern [eager],
Of innocency to plead or prate.
Bear low, therefore, give God the stern,
For sure, *circa Regna tonat.*

Bitterly disillusioned with a courtier's existence, Wyatt seems to have spent only a brief time at court before returning to his father's castle at Allington for a time. It was probably then that he wrote (or completed) another, longer poem, in which he poured out the shock and deep sorrow he still felt at the brutal deaths of his friends; the immediacy of his misery suggests that it was begun soon afterwards, and completed later when he had had a chance to judge public opinion. The content of the poem shows that the executions were still very much the news of the moment, and speculation still rife, when it was written. Anne, the woman Wyatt had once loved, is not mentioned; no doubt – as with his other poems about her – he felt it was too dangerous to do so. And because of this, he made it clear in his verse that he dared not speak his feelings aloud, but that he knew they would be with him always:

> In mourning wise since daily I increase,
> Thus should I cloak the cause of all my grief;
> So pensive mind with tongue to hold his peace,
> My reason sayeth there can be no release;
> Wherefore, give ear, I humbly you require,
> The effects to know that this doth make me moan.
> The cause is great of all my doleful cheer,
> For those that were, and now be dead and gone.
>
> What thought to death dessert be now their call,
> As by their thoughts it doth appear right plain,
> Of force, I must lament that such a fall
> Should light on those so wealthy did reign;
> Though some perchance will say, of cruel heart,
> 'A traitor's death why should we thus bemoan?'
> But I, alas – set this offence apart –
> Must needs bewail the death of some begone.
>
> As for them all, I do not thus lament,
> But as of right, my reason doth me bind;
> But as the most doth all their deaths repent,
> Even so do I by force of moaning mind . . .

He went on to mention each of the condemned men in turn, saying of Rochford that 'many cry aloud, "It is great loss that thou art dead and gone."' It seems he thought that, of them all, Norris and Brereton at least were guilty:

Ah! Norris, Norris, my tears begin to run,
To think what hap did thee so lead or guide,
Whereby thou hast both these and thine undone,
That is bewailed in court on every side,
In place also where thou hast never been,
Both man and child doth piteously thee moan;
They say, 'Alas, thou art for ever seen
By their offences to be both dead and gone.'

As for Weston,

> . . . we that now in court doth lead our life
> Most part in mind dost thee lament and moan;
> But that thy faults we daily hear so rife,
> All we should weep that thou art dead and gone.
>
> Brereton, farewell, as one that least I knew.
> Great was thy love with divers, as I hear,
> But common voice doth not so sore thee rue
> As other twain that doth before appear.
> But yet no doubt but thy friends lament
> And other hear their piteous cry and moan,
> So doth each heart for the like wise relent,
> That thou givest cause thus to be dead and gone.

Smeaton, who had openly confessed and betrayed Anne, merited
only Wyatt's begrudging regret:

> Ah, Mark! What moan should I for thee make more,
> Since that thy death thou hast deserved best,
> Save only that mine eye is forced sore
> With piteous plaint to moan thee with the rest?
> A time thou hadst above thy poor degree,

> The fall whereof thy friends may well bemoan;
> A rotten twig upon so high a tree
> Hath slipped thy hold, and thou art dead and gone.

Wyatt concluded:

> And thus farewell, each one in hearty wise,
> The axe is home, your heads be in the street;
> The trickling tears doth fall so from mine eyes,
> I scarce may write, my paper is so wet.
> But what can hope, when death hath played his part,
> Though Nature's course will thus lament and moan?
> Leave sobs, therefore, and every Christian heart
> Pray for the souls of those be dead and gone.

Wyatt was to acquire the Lefèvre manuscript, which had been owned by Rochford and Smeaton. Among the proverbs he wrote on the flyleaves is one that reads: 'He that is an ass and thinks himself an hind, on leaping the ditch will realise the truth.' This was probably a comment on the fate of Mark Smeaton.[78]

By October 1536, Wyatt was serving with the royal forces that had been sent to suppress the Pilgrimage of Grace. He was back at court by 18 March 1537, when Henry VIII knighted him. For the rest of his life he would serve as ambassador to Charles V, before dying of pneumonia in the autumn of 1542. His poems were first published in 1557.

Despite his affinity with the Boleyns, Archbishop Cranmer survived the purge and continued to promote the cause of religious reform. He was burned at the stake for heresy, on the orders of Henry's daughter, Mary I, in 1556.

The Duke of Norfolk retained his post as Lord Treasurer, but deemed it politic, in the wake of the fall of his 'false, traitorous niece',[79] to retire from court for a time to his house at Kenninghall, and was not recalled until later in 1536, when he was needed to help put down the Pilgrimage of Grace. His absence from court enabled the Seymours to establish political ascendancy there, and thus was initiated the bitter rivalry between them and the Howards that was to endure for the rest of the reign.

After the arrest and disgrace of another allegedly adulterous niece, Queen Katherine Howard, in 1541, Norfolk again hastened to distance himself, writing to the King how he was in 'the greatest perplexity' because of 'the most abominable deeds done by two of my nieces'.[80] Late in 1546, Norfolk and his son Surrey were accused of treason and sent to the Tower. Surrey was executed, but the King, who died on 28 January 1547, held back from signing Norfolk's death warrant. The Duke spent the six years of Edward VI's reign in prison before being released by Mary I on her accession in 1553. He died in 1554.

The Lady Mary's supporters had good reason to believe that they had triumphed when Anne Boleyn was executed, but Mary's restoration to favour was not won so easily. Cromwell hastened to dissociate himself from the conservative faction after Anne's fall, and Mary and her friends found themselves isolated once more. Only after an acknowledgement that her mother's marriage had been incestuous and unlawful had been wrung out of Mary – a capitulation that was to haunt her for the rest of her days – would the King agree to be reconciled to her. Thereafter, however, she was welcomed back to court and given one half of 'the Boleyn's' jewels, some of which had once belonged to Katherine of Aragon; these were a gift from her father.[81] (Interestingly, along with twenty-seven diamond rings set with the letters HJ that were recorded among the King's effects late in 1537, after Jane Seymour's death, there were two rings with the initials HA, for Henry and Anne.[82]) In 1544, Mary and her half-sister Elizabeth were restored to the succession after Prince Edward and his heirs, but not legitimised.

Cromwell was raised to the peerage as Lord Cromwell of

Wimbledon on 9 July, and that same month was knighted and appointed Lord Privy Seal and 'Vicar General and Vice-Regent of the King in Spirituals'; he was also the recipient of several royal grants, no doubt by way of reward for his zeal in uncovering Anne Boleyn's alleged treason. In 1537, he secured as a bride for his son, Gregory, the great prize of Jane Seymour's sister Elizabeth.

Four years after the death of Anne, the woman he had brought to the scaffold, Cromwell himself fell victim to his enemies, who persuaded the King to have him arrested and attainted for treason and heresy. His desperate plea to Henry VIII – 'Most gracious Prince, I cry for mercy, mercy, mercy!' – went unheeded, and he met his end on 28 July 1540 on Tower Hill, where an inexperienced executioner took his head off with two strokes.

Cromwell's man, Sir Ralph Sadler – who was to serve as a diplomat under four Tudor monarchs – was granted Brereton's estate near Greenwich. An undated document of 1536 lists a considerable number of valuable grants made to Sir William FitzWilliam, who had been assiduous in bringing Anne down, and whose family connections were instrumental in her downfall. Sir Nicholas Carew, Sir Thomas Cheyney and Lord Chancellor Audley were all similarly rewarded for their support in ridding the King of his treacherous wife.[83]

The Duke of Richmond was appointed Warden of the Cinque Ports and Constable of Dover Castle in place of Rochford,[84] and Chancellor and Chamberlain of North Wales in place of Sir Henry Norris. Norris's house at Kew was given to Edward Seymour, Lord Beauchamp, while the office of park keeper at Windsor that he had held was bestowed on his brother John, a gentleman usher of the King's Chamber.[85] Weston's widow, Anne, remarried quickly; her second husband was Sir Henry Knyvett, that Gentleman of the Privy Chamber, who had helped her to fight for Francis's life. She bore him six children before his death in 1547, after which she married one John Vaughn, and died a very old lady in 1582. Her son by Weston was not restored in blood until 1549.

Seymour's brother Henry replaced Smeaton in the Privy Chamber.[86]

Those who had supported Mary also got some of the spoils of the Boleyn purge, and other rewards. Sir Francis Bryan, who had hoped to be made Groom of the Stool and Chief Gentleman of the Privy Chamber in place of Sir Henry Norris, had to be content merely with the latter office, since Cromwell secured the more important post of Groom of the Stool, the most influential position in the Privy Chamber, for his own man, Thomas Heneage,[87] a sure sign that the brief, uneasy coalition between Cromwell and the Imperialists was already breaking up. Both Bryan and Carew received a number of offices in June 1536. Carew remained in favour until 1538, when Cromwell engineered his arrest for involvement in the Duke of Exeter's supposed conspiracy against the King. Exeter and Lord Montagu, another alleged conspirator, were beheaded in 1538, Carew in 1539.

In June 1536, Urian Brereton, page of the Privy Chamber, was granted four properties and two hundred acres of land in Cheshire that had belonged to his late brother, William, while on 30 June, William Brereton's widow, Elizabeth Somerset, was generously granted 'all the goods, chattels, rents, fees and annuities belonging to the said William at the time of his attainder' with all debts and obligations then due to him.[88] The stampede for Brereton's many offices is ample evidence of the void his death had left in the Marches and his influence there.[89]

15

'The Concubine's
Little Bastard'

Anne's daughter Elizabeth was just two years and eight months old when her mother was put to death; she had been left at Greenwich during those dark days. Sarah Gristwood and Maria Perry have both raised the question of just how closely Elizabeth had bonded with her mother: nourished by a wet nurse from birth, she had been only three months old when she was removed from Anne's care and assigned her own household at Hatfield, away from the court, which the little girl was rarely to attend during her infancy. Thereafter she lived under the constant care of her Lady Mistress, the capable and aristocratic Margaret Bourchier, Lady Bryan, whom Henry VIII had made a baroness in her own right; and Anne had been merely an occasional visitor and a sender of costly gifts, never a constant presence in her child's life. So there could not have been a close relationship between them, and in later life Elizabeth, using the royal plural, was to write that she was 'more indebted to them that bringeth us up well than to our parents' – for her father had been a similarly distant figure.

Yet that was the norm for royal and aristocratic children in the sixteenth century, and the Queen's words should not be interpreted as a criticism. Thus it may well have been that Elizabeth's 'emotional life was unaffected by her mother's misfortunes'.[1] The loss of her mother – that remote being – may have had less impact on her than we imagine, its most vivid consequences perhaps being the change in her status and the cessation of pretty gifts. What counted most was that Lady Bryan, now a venerable sixty-eight, remained at the centre of the child's world, an ever-constant, stable and reassuring presence,[2] while Katherine Champernowne (later Astley), who was to replace her as the mother figure in Elizabeth's life, was already installed as one of her gentlewomen.[3]

During the weekend immediately following Anne's execution, when the King moved to Hampton Court, he gave orders for his daughter to be taken from Greenwich to the nursery palace at Hunsdon in the care of Lady Bryan. There is often an assumption that Elizabeth was spurned by her father in the weeks after her mother's death – indeed, it has been conjectured that he could not at that time bear to set eyes on her,[4] and even that he grossly neglected her,[5] for in August 1536, Lady Bryan had to beg Cromwell for new clothes to replace those that her charge had outgrown, revealing in the process that no one in Elizabeth's household had received instructions as to her changed status:

My Lady Elizabeth is put from that degree she was afore, and what degree she is of now I know not but by hearsay. Therefore I know not how to order her, nor myself, nor none of hers that I have the rule of, that is, her women and grooms; beseeching you that she may have some raiment. For she hath neither gown, nor kirtle, nor petticoat, nor no manner of linen, nor forsmocks [aprons?], nor kerchiefs, nor rails [nightgowns], nor body-stitchets [binding cloths or corsets], nor handkerchiefs, nor sleeves, nor mufflers, nor biggins [close caps in the style of Flemish beguines worn

by very young children for the purpose of aiding the closure
of the fontanelle].

Lady Bryan also mentioned disapprovingly that Elizabeth's
governor, Sir John Shelton, allowed the young child 'to dine and
sup every day at the board of estate', from which it is clear that
the little girl was still being treated as befitted the daughter of a
king. It is also clear that the recently widowed Lady Bryan feared
that her own authority was being undermined. 'A succourless and
redeless [i.e. without advice] creature', as she described herself,
she was obviously concerned that she might be dismissed in the
wake of her former mistress's fall and the radical change in her
charge's status, and begged Cromwell to 'be good to my little
lady and all hers'.[6]

Because it is evident that Elizabeth was still being treated as a
princess, this wardrobe crisis probably resulted from a mere administrative lapse, the King (to whom all decisions relating to Elizabeth
had been referred since her infancy) being away on his nuptial
progress in August, or followed an unexpected growth spurt. It
did not necessarily mean that Anne Boleyn's fall had undermined
Henry's affection for their daughter,[7] and there is no evidence
that she was out of favour. At the end of June, he gave orders for
her household to be reorganised, allocating her thirty-two servants.
Lady Bryan had told Cromwell she was sure the King would have
much cause for pride in his daughter, 'for she is as toward a child
and as gentle of conditions as ever I knew any in my life, Jesu
preserve her Grace'.[8] And on 21 July, the Lady Mary (now restored
to favour through the good offices of Cromwell and Jane Seymour)
had no compunction about writing to Henry from Hunsdon:
'My sister Elizabeth is in good health, and such a child toward
as I doubt not but your Highness shall have cause to rejoice of
in time coming.'[9]

When the King visited Mary at Hunsdon in August, he was
probably reunited with Elizabeth too, and she was soon to be

seen again at court, where the French Cardinal du Bellay observed that 'the King is very affectionate to her [and] loves her very much'.[10] Even so, that summer, she was the subject of much conjecture in a court that was still seething with gossip and speculation about Anne Boleyn's 'abominable and detestable' crimes.[11] Some of those tales undoubtedly concerned Elizabeth's paternity.

Chapuys himself reported – with more relish than truth – that 'the Archbishop of Canterbury declared by sentence that the Concubine's daughter was the bastard of Mr Norris, and not the King's daughter',[12] as the indictment had implied. This mistaken assumption reflects the gossip to which the secret proceedings at Lambeth undoubtedly gave rise, suggesting that the true grounds for Cranmer's annulment of Anne's marriage to the King were never openly divulged, and were the subject of much speculation. Dr Ortiz, the Emperor's ambassador in Rome, had already predicted, prematurely, as it turned out: 'It is intended to declare the child not to be the King's.'[13]

It was falsely claimed in the anonymous Portuguese letter written on 10 June 1536 that, after Anne's execution, 'the Council declared that the Queen's daughter was the child of her brother, and that she should be removed from her place [in the succession]',[14] while in the Low Countries rumour even had it that Elizabeth was the result of a casual encounter between her mother and a peasant: 'It is now said,' wrote Jean Hannaert of Lyons on 2 June, 'that her pretended daughter was taken from a poor man.'[15] In England, there was similar covert speculation.[16] If Elizabeth were not the King's daughter, then even the debased status of a royal bastard was not rightfully hers.[17] It was almost certainly because of the gossip that Lady Bryan was informed in August that 'it was the King's pleasure that my Lady Elizabeth shall keep her chamber and not come abroad'.[18]

There is evidence that the Lady Mary herself would take with her to the grave the belief that Mark Smeaton was Elizabeth's real father. When her half-sister was little, Mary played a mother's part to her and clearly cherished her dearly, but as Elizabeth grew more like Anne Boleyn, Mary's affections cooled, for every time she looked at her, she must have been reminded of the injuries, insults and ignominy she and her mother had suffered at Anne Boleyn's hands.[19]

As queen, when any sympathy for her half-sister had soured and there remained only suspicion and resentment, Mary was heard to remark several times on the resemblance between Elizabeth and Mark Smeaton,[20] and to say that Elizabeth's morals were no more admirable than her mother's had been. Shortly before her death, she confided to Bernardo de Fresneda, the confessor of her husband, King Philip II of Spain, that Elizabeth had 'the face and countenance of Mark Smeaton, who was a very handsome man', and thus 'was neither her sister nor the daughter of King Henry'.[21] Mary once sarcastically told Simon Renard, the Imperial ambassador, that Elizabeth was merely 'the offspring of one of whose good fame he might have heard, and who had received her punishment'.[22]

It would have been anathema to Mary 'to see the illegitimate child of a criminal who was punished as a public strumpet' inheriting the throne[23] – a child, moreover, who had 'a bewitching personality' and deplorable 'characteristics in which she resembled her mother'.[24] Thus Mary was perhaps deluding herself, since there is no evidence that Henry VIII ever doubted that Elizabeth was his daughter. As Alexander Aless told Elizabeth in 1559, citing it as proof of Anne Boleyn's innocence, 'Your father always acknowledged you as legitimate.' Doubtless she resembled him too greatly for there to be any doubt, something that several people would remark upon during the course of her life, among them those who observed that she looked more like him than Mary did; and one only has to look at the many portraits of Elizabeth I to see that she was her father's daughter, in colouring and in profile. Moreover, he was to restore her to the succession in 1544, something he would never have done had he any doubts about her paternity.

We might wonder if Mary was truly able to recall what Smeaton had looked like. Prior to 1529, he had been an obscure member of Cardinal Wolsey's household, and even after he was preferred to the Privy Chamber that year, he was apparently regarded as relatively lowly and insignificant. Mary herself had been sent away from court in 1531, and did not return until some months after Smeaton's execution, so even if she could remember him, she would not have laid eyes on him for five years. Possibly she was basing her assertions on the rumours that were circulating at that time, the speculation of others, or – which is most likely – malicious lies spread later by Elizabeth's enemies in the hope of impugning her claim to the throne. Or perhaps it was just wishful thinking on Mary's part, born of the vain hope of excluding Elizabeth from the succession.

There are some indications that Henry VIII was concerned lest Elizabeth showed signs of inheriting her mother's coquettish character and morals, which in itself is further evidence that he believed in Anne's guilt. He insisted that her household be staffed by 'ancient and sad [i.e. sober, serious] persons', and once turned down the application of a young gentlewoman in favour of that of one 'of elder years', grumbling that there were already too many young people around his daughter.[25] He was perhaps remembering the youthful crowd who had laughed and flirted with Anne Boleyn in her privy chamber, with disastrous consequences. He saw to it too that Elizabeth's rigorous education was framed so as to constrain her to the narrow paths of virtue, as well as to erudition, although this was by no means unusual at that time, women being universally regarded as morally weaker than men; yet this child, the daughter of so notorious a mother, would have been perceived as having more need of such instruction than most. It would be no exaggeration to say that, in this respect, Elizabeth would always bear the stigma of being Anne Boleyn's child.

Yet that stain, and the taint of bastardy, would have been far outweighed by her being the daughter of the King. And there was little shame, in that period, in having a mother who had perished on the scaffold. A Mantuan visitor to England was surprised to discover that 'many persons, members of whose families have been hanged and quartered, are accustomed to boast of it'. It was, he learned, the mark of a gentleman, to own such relations.[26]

We do not know when or how Elizabeth, a highly precocious little girl, discovered that her mother had 'suffered by sword',[27] but that she immediately noticed the change in her status is apparent in her sharp comment, made very soon after Anne's death, to Sir John Shelton, her governor and great-uncle: 'Why Governor, how hath it, yesterday my Lady Princess, and today but my Lady Elizabeth?' As Tracy Borman has pointed out, this proves that Elizabeth was not given any information to prepare her for her mother's death or even informed of it, but probably found out what had happened only gradually; for surely the grim truth was too harrowing to be disclosed in graphic detail to such a young child. She was at Hunsdon with Mary when Lady Kingston visited on 26 May 1536 and presumably gave a first-hand account of Anne's execution to the princess, but it is doubtful if Elizabeth was allowed to overhear it. What is most likely is that she learned of the death of her mother in careful stages from her kindly governesses, Lady Bryan and Katherine Champernowne.

But the subject seems to have remained a taboo one. The shocking details of Anne's crimes – adultery, incest, murder and the suspicion of witchcraft – were perhaps seen as too shameful to be openly discussed, let alone with her child. And given the dearth of surviving comments on her fate, it is possible that some people felt it was too dangerous or politically compromising to express an opinion. As has been demonstrated, the evidence we have suggests that most accepted the official line. So Elizabeth may have grown up to an awareness that there was a dark and dreadful mystery about her mother's fate that needed to be unravelled.

It would appear that Henry VIII himself, in giving orders that the child keep to her chamber when rumours about her paternity were rife, was determined to keep her in innocence as to what had happened to her mother for as long as possible, and spare her the gruesome details. Tellingly, when, in 1549, her stepfather, Admiral Thomas Seymour (who had tried to seduce her when she was a mere adolescent), informed one of Elizabeth's servants that he was going to Boulogne, which the English pronounced 'Boleyn', he added, 'No word of Boleyn!'[28] This is all at variance with the assertion that the child Elizabeth was probably subjected to a barrage of propaganda about her bastardy and the wickedness of her mother;[29] given the way in which Anne Boleyn's name, initials and images had been speedily and thoroughly obliterated, and that the King was rarely heard to refer to her again, the theory that, after 1536, she was a subject best avoided seems more credible.

For all the silence, however, Anne's terrible end, and the awareness that her father had ordered her mother's execution, however justified, must have overshadowed Elizabeth's childhood. Over the years, guarded revelations, gossip, rumour and innuendo, picked up from any number of sources, and the growing awareness of her bastard status, must have caused the maturing Elizabeth recurring distress and enduring insecurities, and certainly affected her emotional development. Her painful awareness of her mother's fate was probably one of the factors that prompted her decision never to marry. Another was almost certainly the execution of her father's fifth wife, Katherine Howard, in 1542, on charges of immorality that must have awakened painful thoughts of Anne Boleyn. Elizabeth was only eight then, but it was around this time that she announced to young Robert Dudley (who would recall this many years later, when he was Earl of Leicester and hoping to marry her himself), 'I will never marry.' Thomas Seymour's shocking, and ultimately fatal, attempts to seduce the adolescent Elizabeth would also have left their mark; he too may have seen her as easy game, her mother's daughter.

Elizabeth herself tried more than once to explain her aversion to marriage, and that she had such an aversion she made clear to Archbishop Parker in 1559, when 'she took occasion to speak in bitterness of the holy estate of matrimony'; indeed, she spoke so vehemently that Parker afterwards told her minister, William Cecil, he 'was in a horror to hear her'.[30] In 1561, she would tell a Scots envoy that the marital conflicts and disasters within her own family – she did not mention Anne Boleyn specifically – had led to her conviction that wedlock was an insecure state: 'Some say that this marriage was unlawful, some that one was a bastard, some other, to and fro, as they favoured or misliked. So many doubts of marriage was in all hands that I stand [in] awe myself to enter into marriage fearing the controversy.'[31] She was referring no doubt to her father's matrimonial career and to the disputed marriages of both his sisters. Four years later, in conversation with a French diplomat, Elizabeth expressed the fear that, were she to marry, her husband might 'carry out some evil wish, if he had one',[32] and later still, she once burst out that she 'hated the idea of marriage every day more, for reasons which she would not divulge to a twin soul, if she had one, much less to a living creature'.[33]

There were doubtless other repercussions too. Her tendency, in later life, to shy away from unpalatable facts and to fence around them – witness her prevarication over the death warrant of Mary, Queen of Scots – may also have had its roots in the traumas of her early childhood. She cannot have failed to draw comparisons between Anne Boleyn and the condemned Mary, and with others sentenced to beheading, including her cousin, Thomas Howard, 4th Duke of Norfolk; and her reluctance to send Mary and Norfolk to the block may have had a lot to do with her awareness of what had happened to her mother, as well as to her own near-brush with the headsman in 1554.

It cannot have been easy for the twenty-year-old Elizabeth, imprisoned in 1554 in the Tower by Mary I on suspicion of treason, and expecting daily to be summoned to the scaffold, to be incarcerated for three months in those same rooms in the Queen's lodgings that Anne Boleyn had occupied prior to her condemnation in 1536; in fact, we might conclude that Mary, who must have known where Anne had been held, had deliberately intended that Elizabeth should suffer this added refinement to her punishment. And Elizabeth's permitted perambulations took her along the wall walk, which overlooked the scaffold before the House of Ordnance, a scaffold built for the deposed nine-days Queen, Lady Jane Grey, on the exact place where Anne Boleyn had perished, and on which Anne's daughter might yet meet her end. Years later, when she was queen, Elizabeth revealed to a French nobleman that the prospect of the axe cleaving into her neck had been so terrible to her during those anxious days that she had resolved to ask that a French swordsman be sent for, to dispatch her as her mother had been dispatched.[34]

Elizabeth cannot but have thought of Anne when she came to the Tower in triumph, prior to her coronation in January 1559,[35] and again when she passed through a triumphal arch in Gracechurch Street during her state progress through the City of London to Westminster, for above her, as part of one of the pageants mounted in her honour, the 'Pageant of the Roses', the citizens had erected life-sized figures, seated together for the first time in twenty-three years, of 'King Henry the Eighth with a white and red rose in front of him, with the pomegranate [the symbol of their fortuitous fertility] between them, and Queen Anne Boleyn, mother of the present Queen, with a gold crown on the head and a gilt sceptre, and in front of her small branches of little roses [and] the coat of arms and device of the same Queen'.[36] Above them both was the figure of Elizabeth, 'seen in majesty'. The lightweight crown that Elizabeth wore after her coronation may have been the one made for Anne Boleyn in

1533.[37] There must have been many such reminders of her mother.

Elizabeth had been brought up to idolise Henry VIII, and clearly revered his memory, often referring to him with pride, and styling him 'her Majesty's dearest father' in official documents. She grew to maturity believing that he had always loved her, whatever he had thought of her mother, and that it was because of her close resemblance to him that he had ordered that she be reared as a king's daughter, rather than as the dubious offspring of a traitor, and left well provided for at his death.[38] 'She prides herself on her father and glories in him,' observed a Venetian envoy after she had ascended the throne in 1558.[39] When she rode in state through London before her coronation in 1559 and a man in the crowd cried, 'Remember old King Henry the Eighth!' she was seen to smile delightedly.[40] She seems to have borne Henry no grudge for his treatment of her mother, and to have regarded him as as much the victim of conspiracy as Anne; and in all her long life, she rarely referred to Anne Boleyn.[41]

This reticence is perhaps understandable, given the conspiracy of silence about Anne that had probably blighted Elizabeth's formative years. It has been said – incorrectly – that we do not know whether she believed her mother to have been wrongly convicted.[42] Unlike her half-sister Mary I, Elizabeth did not, when she came to the throne in 1558, have the annulment of her parents' marriage reversed by Parliament, and there was no official push to rehabilitate Anne Boleyn's reputation. There was much discussion about this at the time, and the decision not to repeal the 1536 Act of Succession was finally made on the advice of Sir Nicholas Bacon, then Lord Keeper of the Great Seal, who pointed out that, as Elizabeth was lawful heiress to the throne under the terms of the Act of Succession of 1544 and Henry VIII's will, there was no point in reviving the heated controversies about the validity of her parents' marriage, Anne's fall and her own legitimacy; this made sense, because Elizabeth's hold on the throne was still tenuous and there were many who already regarded her as a bastard, a heretic and a usurper. Instead, Parliament merely drew up a statute confirming her title – sparsely worded compared with that of Mary I – and passed another act confirming her as Anne Boleyn's sole heiress and enabling her to inherit her mother's property, forfeited on Anne's conviction for treason.[43]

Several writers have regarded as significant Elizabeth's failure to translate her mother's remains to a more honourable resting place, as James I was to do for his mother, the executed Mary, Queen of Scots, in 1612, when he had her body moved from Peterborough Cathedral to Westminster Abbey. Yet it is almost certain that, if the idea of moving Anne ever occurred to her, Elizabeth left well alone for the reasons Sir Nicholas Bacon had cited. It was just not advisable to revive old controversies and the dreadful events of 1536, and her presence at the re-interment of Anne Boleyn would have been the equivalent of making a provocative public statement that might impugn her father's memory and her own status. There was also the problem of the funeral rite, for Anne had died in the Catholic faith. Moreover, she was already buried in a royal chapel, so Elizabeth may have felt that, for many good reasons, she was better left there undisturbed.

In 1572, in the wake of her excommunication by the Pope, Elizabeth commanded Matthew Parker, now Archbishop of Canterbury, to search out the 1528 Papal bull of dispensation, authorising her parents' marriage. She chose not to publish it, but kept it at hand in case it became desirable to produce it as the basis for proclaiming herself legitimate in the eyes of the Roman as well as the English Church.

There can be little doubt as to Elizabeth's true opinion of the woman who had given birth to her. There are many clues. As early as 1544–5, she was painted, aged about ten or eleven, in a state portrait of Henry VIII and his family, wearing – astonishingly – one of Anne Boleyn's initial pendants, proclaiming to all posterity that she was her mother's daughter – and this, presumably, with the King's sanction. Thirty years later, around 1575, she commissioned a gold ring bearing the initial E in diamonds and R for Regina in blue enamel; it opened to reveal miniature enamelled reliefs of herself and Anne Boleyn. Thereafter, she wore this ring constantly, and it was only removed from her finger at her death, when it was taken to her successor, James VI of Scotland, as proof of her demise. The ring is now at Chequers, the Prime Minister's country retreat, primary evidence that Elizabeth kept her mother's image secretly with her for much of her adult life, and privately honoured her memory.[44]

In 1553, when her sister Mary ascended the throne, Elizabeth candidly intimated to Simon Renard, the Spanish ambassador, that the Queen was hostile towards her because of the injuries that she and her mother had been dealt by Anne Boleyn. Clearly Elizabeth was well informed. Foreign envoys also attributed Mary's increasing hostility to the fact that Elizabeth was Anne's daughter: 'She still resents the injuries inflicted on Queen Katherine, her lady mother, by the machinations of Anne Boleyn,' Renard observed. Later in Mary's reign, Elizabeth, in more bullish mood, openly – and rashly – voiced her opinion, to various people, that she was as legitimate as her sister, and of equal rank in blood as a daughter of Henry VIII. Her mother, she declared – ignoring the fact that she herself had been conceived out of wedlock – would never have cohabited with him 'unless by way of marriage with the authority of the Church and the intervention of the Primate of England'. She had acted in good faith according to her conscience, and lived and died in the church that had declared her marriage valid, all of which rendered her blameless and her daughter legitimate.[45] There was evidently no doubt in Elizabeth's mind that Anne had been a virtuous woman.

As queen, Elizabeth adopted Anne Boleyn's motto, '*Semper eadem*' ('Always the same'), and her badge of a crowned white falcon perched on a tree stump flowering with Tudor roses, which she had stamped on the bindings of her books. She may have felt that the tree stump, innocuous enough in her mother's day, had become symbolic of Anne being cut down before her time.[46] She owned a set of virginals bearing the Boleyn arms, which had probably once belonged to Anne; they are now in the Victoria and Albert Museum in London. Elizabeth openly prided herself on being 'the most English woman of the kingdom', and given that the Tudors came from Welsh stock, she must have been paying a discreet tribute to her mother's ancestry.[47]

She would do much – subject to their merits – for some of her relatives on her mother's side, notably the Careys: she created her cousin Henry Carey Lord Hunsdon and Captain of the Gentlemen Pensioners, the sovereign's personal guard; and she was grief-stricken when his sister Katherine, a gentlewoman of the Queen's Privy Chamber and wife to Sir Francis Knollys, died in 1569, for they had been very close. Both Henry and Katherine would have been able privately to tell Elizabeth many things about her mother, who had been their aunt and whom they had known in childhood. Katherine, as has been noted, may even have attended upon Anne in the Tower.

Then there were the Knollyses and the Sackvilles, the mysterious George Boleyn, and the unidentified 'Edmund Boleyn, her Grace's kinsman', who received a gift of £70 (£14,400);[48] and no doubt Elizabeth would have continued to show favour to her Howard cousins as well, had they not dabbled in treason or become too closely affiliated to the Catholic cause at a time when such a stance rendered one a political enemy. Elizabeth also made Anne's former chaplain, Matthew Parker, her first Archbishop of Canterbury. 'If I had not been so much bound to the mother,' a reluctant Parker confessed, 'I would not so soon have granted to serve the daughter in this place.'[49] He was, of course, referring to his promise to Anne to safeguard her daughter's welfare.

This is not the only testimony to Elizabeth's feelings about her mother. In 1561, she furiously demanded the immediate repression of a French tract in which Anne Boleyn was portrayed as a

'Jezebel' whose 'foul matrimony' was prompted by lust and whose brutal end was entirely justified.[50] Elizabeth was also greatly offended when, early in 1587, as she was agonising over signing the death warrant of Mary, Queen of Scots, Mary's son, James VI of Scotland, urging her to show mercy, tactlessly pointed out to her that 'King Henry VIII's reputation was never pre-judged but in the beheading of his bedfellow'. He was referring, of course, to Anne Boleyn.

When, in 1572, Elizabeth restored in blood a great favourite of hers, Henry, the son of Sir Henry Norris, and created him first Baron Norris of Rycote, she was tacitly acknowledging that Norris had 'died in a noble cause and in the justification of her mother's innocence'.[51] Yet her favour to Lord Rycote was not extended just on account of the fate of his father; it is more likely to have rested on his own merits and character.

A laudatory treatise on Anne Boleyn by her former chaplain, William Latymer, was almost certainly presented to Elizabeth I, to whom it was dedicated. Only a draft copy survives (in the Bodleian Library, Oxford), but that the Queen approved of its author's determination to rehabilitate her mother's memory is apparent in her lavishing many rewards on him.[52]

It is also possible that Queen Elizabeth commissioned by stealth George Wyatt's defence of her mother, written at the end of the sixteenth century. Wyatt himself claimed that he 'was entreated by *some who might command me* [author's italics] to further this endeavour', and that he had undertaken the writing of his life of Anne Boleyn at 'the request of him that hath been *by authority* set on work in this so important business, both for the singular gifts of God in him of learning, wisdom, integrity and virtue, and also the encouragement I have had of late from the right reverend my lord of Canterbury's Grace'. The Archbishop of Canterbury at that time was John Whitgift, who was a personal friend of Elizabeth and attended her on her deathbed in 1603.

Wyatt's memorial was never finished, so there is no dedication that might reveal the names of his patrons. Could it be that the Virgin Queen, nearing the end of her life, felt that the record should be set straight? Unlike Mary I, she had never had the annulment of her mother's marriage reversed, or the sentence on Anne, and she may have felt that by doing so, she would be reviving old scandals that might compromise her own legitimacy and even destabilise her crown. It would be in character, though, for her covertly to let it be known, through Whitgift and others, that she wanted Wyatt, whose extensive researches were evidently known of at court, to write a defence of Anne in answer to Nicholas Sander's calumnies, which had reflected so badly upon Anne Boleyn and herself.

But who was the unnamed man who had been 'by authority set on work in this so important business', and who had encouraged Wyatt to write his memorial? By whose authority had he done so? The fact that neither the authoriser nor the authorised are identified suggests that both wished to remain anonymous. The virtues enumerated by Wyatt were of the kind that were typically attributed to worthy persons at that time, so they do not help us. Yet the fact that Wyatt was asked to write his defence by a man who had been authorised to further this project, and was then encouraged in his labours by the Archbishop of Canterbury himself, who was close to Elizabeth and in a position to know the workings of her conscience and her mind, suggests that she herself was the prime mover.

The fact that the Archbishop had only begun encouraging Wyatt 'of late' implies perhaps that the unknown man who had commissioned the work had died. We might conjecture that he was Henry Carey, Lord Hunsdon, the chamberlain of Queen Elizabeth's household, who died in the spring of 1596. No one would have been better placed to ask Wyatt to write his defence, for Anne Boleyn was his aunt, he being the only son of her sister Mary, and he was close to the Queen.

Mary Boleyn, who had earned a reputation for promiscuity at

the courts of France and England,[53] had briefly been Henry VIII's mistress before he began pursuing her sister Anne, and it has been suggested that Henry Carey, who was born in March 1526, was in fact Henry VIII's bastard son. This was rumoured in the King's lifetime: in 1535, John Hale, the Vicar of Isleworth in Middlesex, reported how a nun of nearby Syon Abbey had pointed out 'young Master Carey' and told him that the boy was Henry's natural son. It should be remembered, however, that Hale, who was to be executed that year for denying the royal supremacy, also put about the unfounded rumour that 'the King's Grace had meddling with the Queen's mother',[54] which Henry himself denied.

It is highly unlikely that Henry VIII was Henry Carey's father. In 1519, when Elizabeth Blount had presented the King with a bastard son, Henry FitzRoy, he had immediately acknowledged him as his own, then brought him up in princely fashion. In 1525, with Katherine of Aragon having failed to bear the King a son, the crisis over the succession was acute. That year, Henry bestowed on FitzRoy two royal dukedoms. This was not just a swipe at Katherine, who was mortified at the bastard's public ennoblement, nor was it merely an affirmation that Henry was a virile man who could get sons on other women. Natural children were important, and a king could use them to extend his power base and affinity, make politically advantageous alliances with the nobility and enforce the royal authority in remote parts of the kingdom such as the north – where FitzRoy was to be sent as his father's deputy – and the Welsh Marches; and clearly Henry VIII understood this. He was in fact at this time, having no legitimate heir, grooming FitzRoy to succeed him on the throne.

Therefore it was in the King's interests, for many reasons, to acknowledge any bastards he might have, and consequently his failure to acknowledge Henry Carey is strong evidence that the boy was not his. Furthermore, there is no evidence that Mary Boleyn was the King's mistress at the time of her son's conception; the fact is, we do not know for certain when, or for how long, their affair took place, and its importance has probably been much over-stated.

It has been said that Henry would not have acknowledged the boy because his relationship with Mary Boleyn was an impediment to his marriage to her sister, yet it was not until 1527, more than a year after Henry Carey's birth, that Henry resolved upon marrying Anne. It has also been claimed that a series of royal grants made to William Carey in the 1520s[55] were to support young Henry Carey, yet William was the King's cousin (through his mother, Eleanor Beaufort) and an important and rising personage in the Privy Chamber who would doubtless have gone far had he not died young; these grants were an acknowledgement of his good service. Although he may have been a complacent husband, there is no evidence that he obligingly refrained from having sexual relations with an adulterous wife.

Henry's son or not, Henry Carey was certainly Elizabeth's cousin; she was to create him Lord Hunsdon on her accession in 1558, and he, a plain-spoken soldier, would serve her loyally all his life. He too, surely, with mortality encroaching, would have wanted the record set straight about his aunt. And if the Queen had authorised him to ask George Wyatt to write his memorial as a response to the calumnies of Sander, then we have in it Elizabeth's own views on her mother.

16

'A Work of God's Justice'

Anne Boleyn's contemporaries generally accepted the verdict of the ninety-five jurors who had sat on all the trials and commissions, and viewed her fall as 'an object lesson in morality'.[1] While her daughter Elizabeth's chances of becoming Queen seemed remote, there were virtually no attempts to rehabilitate Anne's reputation, and only a few dared to express any doubts as to the justness of the proceedings against her. People naturally – and prudently – took their cue from those in power, and one Edward Dudley was no doubt voicing the view of many when, in a letter to Cromwell dated 3 June 1536, he referred to her fall as 'the misfortune that has happened to England'.[2]

William Thomas, later Clerk of the Council to Edward VI, wrote a laudatory account of Henry VIII entitled *The Pilgrim* in 1546, which almost certainly reflects how the King's deeds were viewed by his subjects, and which was written in the form of a conversation with a disapproving Italian. Thomas says, in response to the charge that Henry 'chopped and changed [wives] at his pleasure', that 'with some of them, he hath had as ill luck as any poor man'. Anne Boleyn's 'liberal life were too shameful to rehearse'. Outwardly she appeared wise and imbued with good qualities and graces, but 'inwardly, she was all another dame than she seemed to be; for in satisfying of her carnal appetite, she fled not so much as the company of her own natural brother, besides the company of some three or four others, who were all so familiarly drawn to her train by her devilish devices'. It seemed, Thomas added drily, 'she was always well-occupied'. Henry, he wrote, 'was forced to proceed therein by way of open justice, where the matter was manifested unto the whole world'.

In 1553, Henry VIII's son and successor, Edward VI, when arguing with his justices over altering the succession in favour of Lady Jane Grey and passing over the rights of Mary and Elizabeth, told them: 'It was the fate of Elizabeth to have Anne Boleyn for a mother; this woman was indeed not only cast off by my father because she was more inclined to couple with a number of courtiers rather than reverencing her husband, so mighty a king, but also paid the penalty with her head – a greater proof of her guilt.'[3]

Writing in the Catholic Mary Tudor's reign, George Cavendish commented on how the memory of the woman who had 'reigned in joy' (something of an overstatement, this) was held in disdain by 'the world universal', that her name was slandered and that she was 'called of each man the most vicious Queen'. Jane Dormer, Duchess of Feria, the close confidante of Queen Mary, believed – like most Catholics – that Anne had sinned with all the men accused with her in a vain attempt to bear a son.[4] Cavendish, who also believed in Anne's guilt and that 'the sharped sword' had been her recompense, did little to dispel this view, having her remorseful shade lament her fall:

> I dread my faults shall thy paper pierce,
> That thus have loved and been to God unkind;
> Vices preferring, setting virtue behind,
> Hateful to God, to most men contrary,
> Spotted with pride, viciousness and cruelty.

Oh sorrowful woman, my body and my soul
Shall ever be burdened with slander detestable!
Fame in her register my defame will enrol,
And to erase out the same no man shall be able.
My life of late hath been so abominable:
Therefore my frailty I may both curse and ban,
Wishing to God I had never known man . . .
My epitaph shall be, The vicious Queen
Lyeth here, of late that justly lost her head,
Because that she did spot the King's bed.[5]

By and by, all those who had known Anne Boleyn passed away, and their memories of her were lost, and with them all sense of the real woman she had been.[6] Such was her infamy that her name had all but been erased from history, and it might have languished in obscurity had it not been for the fact that her daughter Elizabeth I became Queen of England in 1558. In the eyes of Catholic Europe, Elizabeth was a bastard, a heretic and a usurper, and the daughter of an infamous adulteress.[7] It was after that date that Anne's history became distorted by biased Protestant and Catholic writers to the point where it became just a series of myths.

Anne Boleyn was especially notorious in Catholic countries, where scandalous tales about her proliferated, as did the details of her supposed promiscuousness and witchcraft. Even today, in Spain and Portugal, an evil, scheming woman can be called an 'Ana-Bolena', and Anne was until recently portrayed as a demon in carnivals, while in Sicily, up to around 1850, there was a legend that she had been holed up under Mount Etna as punishment for her crimes.[8] It was in this climate that the slanders of Nicholas Sander and others – like Cardinal William Allen, who branded Anne 'an infamous courtesan' who had indulged in 'incestuous copulation' with Henry VIII, Elizabeth's 'supposed father' – were written, and this legacy that was to blight the European reputation of Elizabeth I.

But Anne's fame was not to be forever 'burdened with slander detestable'. As Cavendish's editor, Samuel Singer, put it in the early nineteenth century, 'Protestant writers have not been wanting in zeal to defend the Queen from all the unjust aspersions upon her character, and have almost considered her as a martyr to the cause of the reformed church'. This reversal took place after the accession of Anne's daughter, Elizabeth I, in 1558, when it suddenly became fashionable – and politic – to refer to the Queen's mother in laudatory terms, and Anne began to be once more hailed as the champion of religious reform.

'True religion in England had its commencement and its end with your mother,' Alexander Aless, the Scots reformist, told Elizabeth as early as 1559; elsewhere in his letter, he referred to Anne as 'that most holy Queen, your most pious mother'. He was convinced that she had died 'in consequence of her love for the doctrine of the Gospel when it was in its infancy', and because she had persuaded the King to befriend the Lutherans at Wittenberg. 'If other arguments of the truth of this were wanting, a single one would be sufficient, namely that before the embassy had returned, the Queen had been executed.' But since then, God had declared her innocence 'by the most indisputable miracles, proved by the testimonies of all godly men'. Of course, it was now permissible to talk up Anne's links to the Lutherans, and Aless was on a mission, seeing it as his sacred duty 'to write the history, or tragedy, of the death of your most holy mother, to afford consolation to the godly'. No one, as far as he knew, had yet published such a work, which indeed seems to have been the case, although it would not remain so for long.

At Elizabeth's coronation that year, the Gracechurch Street pageant showed that Anne Boleyn's image was no longer to remain hidden or forgotten. It was now permissible to speak her name, and to speak it with honour.

One of the first of Anne's early defenders was an anonymous author who had known her, and who was writing a defence of her between 1563 and 1570; his work – if it were ever finished – does not survive, and is only known through a reference to it by John Foxe in the 1570 edition of his *History of the Acts and Monuments of the Church* (popularly known as Foxe's *Book of Martyrs*, first published in 1563, and dedicated to Queen Elizabeth). Foxe wrote of Anne: 'Because more is also promised to be declared of her virtuous life (the Lord so permitting) by other who were then about her, I will cease in this matter further to proceed.' Foxe's wording suggests that there may have been more than one apologist.

John Foxe himself, who once enjoyed the patronage of Mary Howard, Duchess of Richmond, one of Anne's ladies, was one of the first to refer to Anne as a 'godly' woman, 'for sundry respects, whatsoever the cause was or quarrel objected against her'. Numbering her among the English martyrs, he wrote that an impenetrable mystery surrounded her fall, but because he expected that to be examined in the work to which he had referred, he did not elaborate himself upon it.[9]

First, her last words declared no less her faith in Christ than did her modesty utter forth the goodness of the cause, whatsoever it was. Besides that, this also may seem to give a great clearing unto her, that the King, [being] married in his whites [i.e. wedding clothes] unto another [so soon after her death] represented a great clearing of her. Certain this was, that for the singular gifts of her mind, so well instructed and given toward God, joined with like gentleness and pity towards men, there hath not been many such queens before her borne the crown of England. Principally, this commendation she left behind her, that during her life the religion of Christ had a right prosperous course. What a zealous defender she was of Christ's Gospel all the world doth know, and her acts do and will declare to the world's end. I marvel why Parliament, after the illegitimation of the marriage [was] enacted, should further proceed and charge her with such carnal desires as to misuse herself with her own natural brother, Lord Rochford, and others, being so contrary to all nature that no natural man will believe it.

Nor did the Elizabethans believe it. To them, Anne was a virtual saint. Although she had died in the orthodox Catholic faith, she had given impetus and encouragement to the cause of reform, and for this, succeeding generations brought up in the Anglican tradition were prepared to forgive her less endearing deeds. The Protestant scholar John Aylmer, famous as the tutor of Lady Jane Grey, was voicing the new received wisdom when he posed the question, 'Was not Queen Anne, the mother of the blessed woman, the chief, first and only cause of banishing the Beast of Rome with all his beggarly baggage?'

'She was a comforter and aider of all the professors of Christ's Gospels,' George Wyatt wrote. Her charities, benefactions, good works, alms and 'the heavenly flame burning in her' became 'the chief things that were remembered of her', and he concluded that 'this princely lady was elect of God'. It is not surprising, therefore, that Elizabethan chroniclers such as John Stow tended to omit the unpleasant details of Anne's fall. She and Henry VIII were portrayed rather as the righteous victims of Fortune or of unscrupulous, malicious schemers. These views would prevail in England right through the seventeenth century and into the eighteenth, a period during which Elizabeth I's accession day was celebrated as a national holiday.

William Shakespeare makes no mention of Anne's fall in his play *All is True*, or *Henry VIII* (now thought to have been a collaboration with John Fletcher), which was written around 1613, in the reign of James I, Elizabeth's successor, and focuses on Henry's love for 'Anne Bullen', her 'gentle mind and heavenly blessings', her coronation and the triumphant birth of the future Queen Elizabeth. However, when Francis Bacon did touch on the controversial aspects of Anne's life in *The Tragedy of Anne Boleyn*, a play that dates probably from the late 1580s, he thought it best to write in cipher. The first part of Bacon's play is very like Shakespeare's, but he goes boldly beyond the scope of *Henry VIII*, portraying Henry's disappointment in Elizabeth's sex, his fickle and changeable nature and how it prompted the false charges against Anne, the travesty of her trial, in which scene she is seen conducting herself nobly, and her cruel death.

Bacon wrote several other works in code, but there can be no doubt that this play – which was not deciphered until 1901 – was written in that manner because of its sensitive content, which might have offended Elizabeth I, and that it was never actually performed. Clearly, Bacon understood that the matters it dealt with were not to be spoken of. He wrote that such works would 'perchance remain in hiding until a future people furnish wits keener than those of our own times to open this heavily barred entrance-way and enter the house of treasure. Yet are we in hourly terror lest the Queen, our enemy at present, although likewise our mother, be cognisant of our invention.' All the same, Bacon's depiction of Anne is sympathetic and in keeping with the Elizabethan tradition. 'Every act and scene is a tender sacrifice,' he wrote, 'and an incense to her sweet memory.'

It was not until 1720 that modern historical research into the subject of Henry VIII's wives began. That was when the antiquarian John Strype embarked on the vast task of collecting, collating and preserving many important contemporary documents. This instituted a new tradition in historical study, which prompted independent analysis free – to a decreasing degree – of religious bias. From that time forward, public sympathy for Anne Boleyn began to burgeon, and one can detect in the works of eighteenth-century historians a certain antagonism towards Henry VIII, who was beginning to be regarded as an authoritarian bigot and a cruel lecher.

In the later eighteenth and early nineteenth centuries, the developing romantic movement in literature and the arts saw Anne Boleyn elevated to the status of tragic, wronged heroine, as she appears in Gaetano Donizetti's historically wildly inaccurate opera *Anna Bolena* (1830), in which she is portrayed as the tragic victim of treasonable intrigues at court and finally goes mad in the Tower. Jane Austen vilified Henry as a vile fornicator and sadist, and bitterly bewailed the fate of his unfortunate wives. Here again, a new, emotive and subjective tradition emerged, and it was in such a climate that Agnes Strickland wrote her celebrated *Lives of the Queens of England*, a landmark work in itself and the product of much original research, but heavily influenced by Victorian moral and social codes. She too wrote of Anne Boleyn in the romantic tradition, and clearly viewed Henry VIII as unspeakably wicked. Nevertheless, her work, much enjoyed by Queen Victoria (to whom it was dedicated), heralded a revival of interest in the Tudor queens.

From about 1850 onwards, we move into the great period of historical research, when a large number of documents were collated and published, many of them under the auspices of the Master of the Rolls. The monumental *Letters and Papers of the Reign of Henry VIII* was compiled, as were the foreign diplomatic calendars and the Tudor state papers, sources that are essential to our understanding of the period. This research prompted the publication of many history books with a fresh and analytical approach. The works of James Anthony Froude and Martin A.S. Hume achieved a more rational assessment of the history of Henry VIII's wives, while Paul Friedmann's *Anne Boleyn: A Chapter of English History* (1884) debunked many of the romantic legends about its subject and portrayed her as a scheming adventuress.

Froude felt that the unanimous verdict given by the peers and the grand juries proved that Anne must have committed at least some of the offences with which she was charged. Friedmann was of the opinion that Cromwell was speaking the truth when he referred to Anne's co-accused confessing to things 'so abominable that a great part of them were never given in evidence, but clearly kept secret',[10] and was 'by no means convinced that Anne did not commit offences quite as grave as those of which she was accused'. He thought it possible that she was guilty 'of crimes which it did not suit the convenience of the government to divulge'. He added that this was hinted at during her trial,[11] 'and although proof was not adduced, they were likely enough to have been true'. It is an interesting theory, and would explain why the evidence against Anne was destroyed, as Friedmann believed, and why the charges in the indictment seem so obviously contrived. It would also explain the odd remark Anne made when she was told by Kingston that she would not be held in a dungeon but in the Queen's lodgings – 'It is too good for me' – and her final confession, in which she declared she had never offended against the King with her body. Had she offended against him in some other way?

Yet what abominable offence could Anne have committed that had at all costs to be kept secret? Could it have been something that touched not only her honour but the King's too? Even if it had, Cromwell, that master of spin, could surely have turned it to Henry's advantage. If it was not a sexual offence, as Anne's last confession would appear to make clear, what other crime could her co-accused have disclosed? There is no evidence of any, and given that the charges against Anne were sensitive enough in their nature, and that Cromwell's reference to secret abominations was probably meant to convey nothing more than unmentionable sexual depravity, we can only conclude that Friedmann's theory does not bear close scrutiny.

The twentieth century witnessed an ever more impartial approach to research and historical interpretation, and the growth of post-Freudian analysis, with the historian evolving into a psychologist rather than a judge, which in itself led to some new conclusions being made, such as the theory that, because of the executions of her mother and Katherine Howard, Elizabeth I grew up equating marriage and sex with death, and consequently was too fearful to take a husband. Today, in the twenty-first century, a more rational and balanced approach prevails, yet it is rare to find a commentator who is devoid of all prejudice or preconception.

Because of the extreme polarity of Catholic and Protestant views of Anne Boleyn, the bias with which her contemporaries wrote of her, the romantic tradition, and the frustrating gaps in the source material for her life, she remains a controversial subject to this day. Rarely are historians entirely impartial about her. She is either a saint, a sinner, a wronged heroine, the feisty temptress beloved by film-makers, or – more recently – the prime cause and mover of the Reformation, a view that would have been unthinkable forty years ago, and which can sometimes be sweepingly overstated. Modern biographers increasingly tend to buy into the Protestant hagiographic view of Anne, a view that is supported only to a degree by contemporary evidence, and even now a religious bias is occasionally evident, as in the late Joanna Denny's anti-Catholic biography.

For centuries, Anne's partisans have seen her as a wronged woman whose wicked husband had her murdered in order to marry her handmaiden. Of course, this is only half the picture, but it underpins many perceptions of Anne even today. In 2005, a former Battle of Britain veteran, who had 'fallen in love' with the Queen during history lessons at school, tried unsuccessfully to persuade the Home Secretary either to pardon her or, preferably, declare her innocent.

Serious historians are now fairly united in believing Anne to have been guiltless of the crimes for which she died. John Scarisbrick found it 'difficult to believe that she was ever guilty of adultery or incest'. Professor Ives wrote stridently that, 'to substantiate nymphomania, incest and quadruple adultery, there is no evidence worth the name',[12] while Anne Somerset has called Anne the victim of 'a deadly combination of court intrigue and royal disfavour'.[13] Professor Loades is almost certainly correct in saying that she fell 'because of the dynamics of court politics, and the fact that her power over the King was based on nothing more durable than sexual chemistry'.[14]

There are few who have disagreed with this view. Back in 1902, A.F. Pollard felt that there must have been some 'colourable justification' for the charges, but Professor Bernard is now virtually alone in suggesting that Anne was quite possibly guilty, yet perhaps not of all the crimes of which she was accused, and not with all the men alleged to have been her lovers. Ives, however, concedes that the case against her must have been plausible enough to convince those ninety-five jurors of her guilt.

In assessing Anne's character and impact on history, we should ask ourselves how she would be viewed today if she had not perished on the scaffold. Her end was one of the most dramatic and shocking episodes in English history, her last days the best-documented period of her life, vividly described in the sources, while that powerful image of her on the scaffold, courageously facing a horrible death, has overlaid all previous conceptions of her.

Had Anne survived into old age – setting aside all other ramifications of that 'what if' – she might now be remembered merely as a ruthless 'other woman' who got her man and proved to be a none-too-popular queen. Had she borne the King no son, and lived to see her daughter succeed – which would probably have been in the late 1540s, when Anne herself would have been in her own late forties – something approaching the hagiographic Protestant view of her, as the lauded Elizabeth's mother, would certainly have prevailed, at least in England. But it is virtually certain that, dying in her bed, she would not have enjoyed the charismatic, romantic posthumous reputation that is hers today.

Conversely, Henry VIII's reputation has undoubtedly suffered as a result of his treatment of Anne Boleyn, and there is a popular misconception – even among some serious historians – that he had her 'murdered', even though she was executed in accordance with the law as it then stood. Sir Patrick Hastings, the former Attorney General, writing in 1950 about Anne Boleyn's 'appalling trial', called Henry 'one of the most unutterable blackguards who ever sat upon this or any other throne'. Jane Dunn sees him as a 'grotesque failure as a husband and father'; Linda Porter calls him 'a wife murderer', and refers to the 'obscene charade' of Anne's fall. Karen Lindsey, in her over-imaginative feminist perspective on Henry VIII's wives, asserts that Henry needed to kill Anne simply because he loathed her.

Eric Ives rightly draws attention to the oft-stated – and simplistic – view that, if Anne was innocent, then Henry VIII, Cromwell and many members of the Tudor establishment 'contrived or connived at cold-blooded murder'.[15] We have to remember that she was executed according to the due process of the law as it then stood. Virtually the whole of the establishment – the King, the Privy Council, the two grand juries, the twenty-six peers who sat in judgement at the trial, and the judges, not forgetting Parliament itself – all played their proper parts, and it may even be that the law was allowed to take its course without undue influence being brought to bear upon it. Certainly care was taken that the case be heard in public, and that some records of it were preserved for posterity to see. Because the depositions are missing, the Crown's case looks weak and contrived to modern eyes, but we can be certain that there was more to it than the surviving sources reveal. According to Cromwell, some of the evidence was so 'abominable' that it did not bear repetition in court, doubtless for the sake of the King's honour; he may have been exaggerating, but we just do not know. It is this lack of documentation that hampers our understanding of why Anne Boleyn was condemned. Above all, there is no evidence that Henry VIII did not believe in Anne's guilt, and it is barely credible that he sent six victims unnecessarily to the scaffold merely to satisfy 'a lust for superfluous butchery', as N. Brysson Morrison put it.

David Loades believes that Henry was able to deceive himself into believing the charges, and that, in the momentous events of 1536, he demonstrated for the first – and certainly not the last – time that his self-deception was 'capable of taking the form of a monstrous and amoral cruelty'.[16] Yet if one accepts the case for self-deception, one also has to accept the populist modern view of Henry as Starkey's 'great puppet' who was easily manipulated by clever advisers, a view that was effectively demolished more than thirty years ago by Lacey Baldwin Smith.[17] It is also worth remembering that Henry did not immediately accept at face value what his councillors told him about Anne's conduct, but insisted that they investigate further.

Yet Professor Loades makes a valid point in response to Henry's detractors who accuse him simplistically of sending Anne to the scaffold on trumped-up charges merely because she no longer pleased him: had this been the case, why hadn't he meted out the same punishment to Katherine of Aragon, who had defied him and been a constant thorn in his side for nine aggravating years?[18] His life would have been far less complicated with Katherine safely dead. Of course, she had powerful relations abroad, while Anne had no one to fight for her. Nevertheless, Katherine could legitimately have been accused of inciting the King's subjects to rebellion or her nephew, the Emperor, to make war on him, and charges of high treason could easily have been made to stick. No one could have complained about that, given that Katherine was betraying the man whom she staunchly insisted was her husband and her sovereign lord. This argues that Henry VIII did not lightly stoop to subverting the law to follow his own desires, and also that whatever evidence about Anne was laid before him, it must have been convincing.

Modern historians tend to view Cromwell's role in Anne's fall as 'hideously corrupt', as Hester Chapman has noted, yet she makes the point that he was operating in a period when justice yielded to expediency, and, as the principal Secretary of State, saw his duty as cutting away 'a malignant growth from the body politic'. Taking this line of argument to its logical conclusion, those co-operating in Anne's destruction acted as loyal subjects, putting the needs of the kingdom first.

Helen Miller has said that, if the King believed the charges against Anne, few others did. Yet, as has been demonstrated, the evidence shows that many at the time unquestioningly believed them. Had Elizabeth never succeeded to the throne, people might have continued to do so, and it might have been left to modern scholarship to rehabilitate Anne's reputation.

Notwithstanding all this, it is almost certain that there was a grievous miscarriage of justice. The circumstances of Anne's fall strongly suggest that she was framed; even her enemy Chapuys thought so. Nowadays, many historians would agree with David Loades that she was 'the victim of a political coup of great skill and ruthlessness', which also destroyed her faction.[19] Henry VIII virtually admitted as much when he told Jane Seymour that Anne had died 'in consequence of meddling too much in state affairs'.[20]

In assessing the surviving evidence for and against her guilt, the truth becomes staggeringly clear. Against Anne, we have merely her own account of compromising conversations and familiarity with Norris, Weston and Smeaton; reports of adverse testimony against her, with barely any details; and that odd remark − 'It is too good for me' − about being lodged in the Queen's apartments, rather than in a dungeon, which was made when she was in great distress.

In her favour, there are a multitude of compelling factors: the fact that she was involved in a life-or-death power struggle with Cromwell; his admission to Chapuys that he 'thought up and plotted' her fall; the incongruity of the charges, particularly that of plotting the King's death; the alteration of the dates in the Kent indictment; the discrepancies and illogicalities in both indictments; the striking absence of any evidence of Anne indulging in extra-marital affairs during the three years of her queenship, and of any real proofs of infidelity; the fact that no female attendants (without whose co-operation Anne could not have contrived any illicit meetings with her 'lovers') were arrested with her; the fact that four of her co-accused were convicted first, thus prejudicing her own trial; that crucial documents are missing from the case records in the *Baga de Secretis*; the superficial nature of the surviving evidence; the disbanding of Anne's household and the summoning of the executioner before her condemnation; the King telling Jane Seymour in advance that Anne would be condemned; Anne and others voicing the suspicion that there was some other reason for her fall than the crimes of which she was accused; her repeated denials of her guilt, and — above all — her last confession, in which, both before and after receiving the Holy Sacrament, she maintained her innocence.

In weighing up the evidence for and against her, the historian cannot but conclude that Anne Boleyn was the victim of a dreadful miscarriage of justice: and not only Anne and the men accused with her, but also the King himself, the Boleyn faction and — saddest of all — Elizabeth, who was to bear the scars of it all her life. In the absence of any real proof of Anne's guilt, and with her having been convicted only on suspicious evidence, there must be a very strong presumption that she went to her death an innocent woman.

Norfolk legend claimed that Anne Boleyn's body was removed from the Tower at some stage and reburied near her ancestors beneath a plain black marble tombstone in Salle Church near Blickling Hall, where she had been born.[21] That was debunked, however, when the stone was lifted a few years ago, and no remains were found beneath it. Early nineteenth-century tradition had it that a much smaller black slab in the ancient churchyard of the parish church at Horndon-on-the-Hill in Essex marked the place where her heart or her head had been buried, or that this was where her corpse had rested overnight on its way to Salle.[22] A similar legend is connected with an altar tomb in the churchyard of the disused Tudor church at East Horndon, Essex.[23]

There are other legends that Anne's heart was stolen and hidden in a church near Thetford, Norfolk,[24] or at Erwarton Church in Suffolk, where a heart-shaped tin casket was discovered in the chancel wall in 1836 or 1837, and reburied under the organ, beneath the Cornwallis memorial slab; even today, there is a notice in the church stating that it is on record that Anne's heart was buried in there by her uncle, Sir Philip Parker of Erwarton Hall. This is all highly unlikely, since heart burial had gone out of fashion in England by the end of the fourteenth century, while the uncle in question was in fact Sir Philip Calthorpe of Erwarton, who was married to Anne's aunt, Amata (or Amy) Boleyn, and died in 1549. Nevertheless, the legend is commemorated in the name of the local inn, the Queen's Head.

George Abbott, the Yeoman Warder who has written many books on the Tower of London, but does not in this instance quote his source, states that the vault in St Peter ad Vincula, in which Anne had indisputably been buried, was opened, and its contents viewed, in the reign of her daughter Elizabeth I. However, there was no vault, because the executed persons who were laid to rest before the altar were all buried in the earth beneath the chancel pavement, as later excavations would prove. Thus the anonymous Tudor observer could not have described what he saw, only what he was told, probably by Tower officials. But since the burials had all taken place within living memory, the information he recorded is likely to have been fairly accurate: 'The coffin of the Duke of Northumberland [executed for treason in 1554] rests besides that of the Duke of Somerset [executed 1552], between the coffins of the queens, Anne Boleyn and Katherine Howard, and next unto these last is the coffin of Lady Jane Grey [executed 1554]. Then comes the coffins of Thomas Seymour, Lord of Sudeley [executed 1549] and of the Lady Rochford; and lastly that of George Boleyn, that was brother to Queen Anne – all beheaded.'[25] This suggests that Anne and her brother were buried at opposite ends of the vault, and that Lady Rochford was interred beside her husband.

In the same period, the chronicler John Stow famously recorded, 'There lieth before the high altar in St Peter's Church, two dukes between two queens.'

In 1876, Queen Victoria approved the restoration of the dilapidated royal chapel of St Peter ad Vincula in the Tower, but only on condition that any disturbed remains be treated with the utmost reverence and that a careful record should be kept of any evidence that might aid identification. Before work began, it was noted that there was no memorial to mark the place where Anne Boleyn was buried.[26]

In November that year, excavations beneath the sunken altar pavement commenced, revealing the remains of most of the executed persons, some apparently still in the places they had occupied three centuries earlier. The excavation committee did not know for certain where the bodies of the Tudor victims had actually been interred. One of its six members, Doyne Bell, had drawn up a plan 'showing the relative positions in which it was believed that these persons had originally been buried'. He had done this 'after consulting various historical authorities', although he did not specify which ones. In fact, apart from Stow, there was no other reliable source he could have consulted, aside from the Elizabethan observer, and Bell's plan[27] shows that he had not seen that. Hence it was highly speculative, and inaccurate.

Worthy attempts were made to identify the remains. A heap of bones carefully arranged and assumed to be Anne Boleyn's, and found only two feet below the chancel floor 'in the place where [she] is said to have been buried', were thought to have been disturbed and disarrayed in 1750, when the lead coffin of one Hannah Beresford was buried two feet beneath them.[28] The skeleton assumed to be Anne Boleyn's was examined by a surgeon on the committee, Dr Frederic Mouat, and described by Bell, both of whom were present at the exhumation. It comprised the bones of 'a female of between twenty-five and thirty years of age, of a delicate frame of body, and who had been of slender and perfect proportions; the forehead and lower jaw were especially well-formed. The vertebrae were particularly small.' The committee thought that this bore witness to Anne Boleyn's 'little neck'.[29] This female had 'a well-formed round skull, intellectual forehead, straight orbital ridge, large eyes, oval face and rather square, full chin. The remains of the vertebrae and the bones of the lower limbs indicate a well-formed woman of middle height, with a short and slender neck. The hand and feet bones indicate deli- cate and well-shaped hands and feet, with tapering fingers and a narrow foot.' There was no evidence of a sixth fingernail, as described by George Wyatt. Judging from the vertebrae, Dr Mouat estimated the woman's height to have been 'five feet, or five feet three inches, not more'.

Dr Mouat confidently opined that the bones all belonged to the same person, and that they had lain in the earth for upwards of three hundred years, and voiced his opinion that these remains were 'all consistent with the published descriptions of Queen Anne Boleyn, and the bones of the skull might well belong to the person portrayed in the painting by Holbein in the collection of the Earl of Warwick'.[30]

Setting aside for a moment the question of age, Anne's authen- ticated portraits all show her as having a pointed chin, not a square one, while – as has been noted – no painting of her by Holbein is known to have survived. The portrait of Anne at Warwick Castle is an eighteenth-century copy in oils of Holbein's sketch of a lady who was not identified as Anne until 1649; this is discussed in the Appendix; other versions of the Warwick portrait are at Hever Castle and Hatfield House. Even today, these are still believed to portray Anne Boleyn.

We do not know how tall Anne Boleyn was. The hostile Nicholas Sander, writing fifty years after her death, called her 'rather tall of stature', but his account is in many ways suspect. Only one eyewitness description of the Queen survives, that of Francesco Sanuto, a Venetian diplomat, who described her as being 'of middling height',[31] which, in Tudor times as in the Victorian age, might have meant rather shorter than we would interpret 'middling height' today. But Sanuto also refers to her having a 'long neck', whereas the neck of the skeleton in the Tower was described as short.

More to the point, four other decapitated females had been buried in the chancel in Tudor times: Katherine Howard, Henry VIII's fifth wife, aged between sixteen and twenty-three, depending on which evidence for her age one accepts; Margaret Pole, Countess of Salisbury, aged sixty-eight; Lady Jane Grey, aged probably seventeen; and Lady Rochford, whose age at death is unknown, but who was of marriageable age (twelve or over) in 1524, and was thus born in 1512 at the latest. Forensic science was not exact in the Victorian age, and Dr Mouat's estimates of the ages of the deceased could have been inaccurate. It is just possible that the bones thought to be Anne Boleyn's – the diminutive slender female with a square jaw – actually belonged to Katherine Howard, miniatures of whom by Holbein show her with what could be a jutting square jaw.

It is interesting to note that, close by the remains of the Duke of Northumberland, in the place where Katherine Howard was thought to have been laid to rest, and whose remains were supposedly not found at all (and were thought either to have been dissolved in the quicklime that was found in the graves, or to have decomposed into dust), parts of the disarrayed skeletons of two woman were found. It was thought that they had been moved there in the eighteenth century to make room for other burials. One female, much advanced in years, was almost certainly Margaret Pole, Countess of Salisbury, who had been beheaded in 1541 at the age of 67.

The other skeleton was thought by Dr Mouat to have been that of a woman of 'rather delicate proportions', of 'about thirty to forty years of age, [but] probably forty years of age'. This female was 'of larger frame' than Katherine, who had been 'a very little girl', according to one French ambassador. Surely these bones belonged to Anne Boleyn, whose age at death has now been credibly established as about thirty-five, not twenty-nine, as the Victorians believed. It therefore follows that the two dukes, Somerset and Northumberland, were indeed buried between two queens, but that the queens were in opposite positions to the ones in which they were thought by the committee to have been laid to rest.

In April 1877, all the skeletons and bones – except the remains of Lord Rochford, Thomas Seymour and Lady Jane Grey, which had not been disturbed[32] – were reverently laid in individual leaden coffers, which were screwed down and placed inside oaken outer coffins one-inch thick, these being sealed with copper screws. A lead plaque bearing the name and arms of the person thought to be inside was affixed to the lid of each coffin, and all were decently reburied in the place where they were found, just four inches beneath the altar pavement, which was then concreted over and laid with decorative octagonal memorial slabs of green, red and white marble in a mosaic design, each having a border of yellow Sienna marble and the names and armorial crests of the deceased.[33]

The remains in the chancel were replaced in the order in which they were found, with the two dukes between the two queens, although these burials do not correspond to the memorial slabs. Presumably a space was left beneath the place where Katherine Howard's 'vanished' remains were supposed to lie. However, the partial skeleton of the woman that had been found there, and which – given the fact that other bones had been mistakenly identified as Anne Boleyn's in 1876 – no one thought to be of great significance, was buried as Lady Rochford.[34] Thus, we can be almost certain that Anne's memorial stone does not mark the last resting place of her actual remains, and that she lies beneath Lady Rochford's memorial.

The Victorian historian Thomas Babington Macaulay, referring to the chapel of St Peter ad Vincula, famously wrote:

There is no sadder spot on Earth. Death is there associated, not, as in Westminster and St Paul's, with genius and virtue, with public veneration and imperishable renown; not, as in our humblest churches and churchyards, with everything that is most endearing in social and domestic charities: but with whatever is darkest in human nature and in human destiny; with the savage triumph of implacable enemies, with the inconstancy, the ingratitude, the cowardice of friends, with all the miseries of fallen greatness and of blighted fame. Thither have been carried through successive ages, by the rude hands of gaolers, without one mourner following, the bleeding relics of the captains of armies, the leaders of parties and the ornaments of courts.

Each year, since at least the 1960s, on the anniversary of Anne Boleyn's execution, a bunch of red roses – such as appear on her coat of arms – has been delivered anonymously to the Tower, with a request that it be placed on her memorial. The flowers, sent by a shop in London on the instructions of an undisclosed firm of trustees, are always accompanied by a card bearing only the dedication *Queen Anne Boleyn 1536*. This request is complied with by the Yeoman Warders, who lay the flowers on Anne's grave and only remove them when they have withered.[35]

Anne Boleyn might have died in ignominy, but she left, all unwittingly, a rich heritage in her infant daughter, the child who grew up reluctant to speak her name, and who so nearly met the same fate as her mother.

Significantly, after complying with tradition and spending a week in the Tower palace prior to her coronation, Elizabeth I never stayed there again. The place held too many terrible memories of her imprisonment there in 1554, and of her mother's fate. She may well have been thinking of Anne as well as her own past experiences when, reining her horse to a standstill as she arrived at the Tower on that January day in 1559, she announced to the watching crowds, 'Some have fallen from being princes of this land to be prisoners in this place. I am raised from being a prisoner in this place to be a prince of this land. That dejection was a work of God's justice. This advancement is a work of His mercy.' One can sense the elation in her words, for she had overcome much, starting with the loss of her mother and her bastardy, to achieve her throne. This was Anne Boleyn's great legacy to England: her daughter, the unparalleled Virgin Queen, Elizabeth. How she would have gloried in and enjoyed Elizabeth's triumph.

Appendix: Legends

Legends about Anne abound. Her ghost has long been reported in at least a dozen places. At Blickling Hall in Norfolk, the house in which she had probably been born around 1501, the spectre of her father, Thomas Boleyn, seated in a coach drawn by headless horses and driven by a headless coachman, has been reportedly seen on many occasions, with the coach racing along country lanes to the door, followed by a blue light or screaming devils, or sometimes by a headless male corpse, said to be that of Lord Rochford, which is itself sometimes supposed to be dragged across hedges and ditches by four headless horses. This tale was probably well established by the eighteenth century.

According to some late Victorian versions, it is Anne herself who occupies the coach, dressed all in white and bathed in a red glow; she sits there headless, holding her bleeding head on her lap. Some have claimed that as soon as this spectral vision reaches the door of the hall, it vanishes; others assert that Anne alights and walks through every room of the house. A tradition grew up over the years that it made its appearance every year on 19 May, the anniversary of her execution.

By 1850, superstitious country folk were claiming that Thomas

Boleyn was condemned – as punishment for having connived at his daughter's fall – to drive his coach and horses once a year, for a thousand years from his death in 1539, over the twelve – or forty, according to later versions – bridges that lie between Wroxham and Blickling, including those at Belaugh, Coltishall, Hautbois, Aylsham and Burgh. He was said to be carrying his head, its tangled hair matted with blood, under his arm, and to have flames shooting from his mouth whilst performing this annual ritual, which is somewhat strange, as he died in his bed.[1] It was once said that anyone witnessing this coach would immediately be dragged down to hell. Despite this dire prediction, in 1940, Christina Hale, a member of the English Folklore Society, wrote that 'the occupants of the house are so used to this annual appearance that they take no notice if it',[2] although around that time the wife of the head gardener confessed she could never go to sleep on the night of 19 May until she had heard the crunch of coach wheels on gravel. In 1985, asked by the writer Richard Whittington-Egan if he believed in this apparition, an old local man replied that it was 'a load of old squit'.

Although Blickling was rebuilt in 1616–27, more than a century after Anne's birth, there are claims that her ghost has been seen in the drawing room, walking its corridors and, dressed in grey, reading a book in the long gallery. Around 1979, an apparition was seen there by a steward, but vanished almost immediately, leaving behind the book – on Hans Holbein's paintings – open at a portrait of herself. There is, in fact, no surviving portrait of Anne by Holbein, only two sketches by him that are unproven – and unlikely – to be her. One, formerly in the collection of the Earl of Bradford at Weston Park, is a portrait of a noblewoman who was identified as Anne only in 1649 and bears little resemblance to the standard portrait types, even though it has since been widely copied, as Anne, by several painters over the centuries (two notable examples are at Hever Castle and Warwick Castle). The other, in the Royal Collection at Windsor, of a blonde lady in a furred gown and nightcap, labelled 'Anna Bollein Queen', has been misidentified, as has been proved to be the case with sitters in other Holbein drawings labelled in the same hand; again, the lady in this picture bears little comparison to known paintings of Anne, and the coat of arms of the Wyatt family is sketched on the reverse, so it is possible that she was the promiscuous Elizabeth Brooke, and that this sketch was a companion portrait to that of her husband, Sir Thomas Wyatt.[3] So the ghost in this story – if there was indeed a ghost – may not have been Anne but someone else entirely.

As recently as 1985, Steve Ingram, a former administrator of Blickling Hall, was asleep one night in his flat there when he was awakened by the sound of light female footsteps advancing along the corridor and into his bedroom. He thought it was his wife, but then realised that she was asleep beside him, yet when he turned on the light, expecting to see a form standing at the end of the bed, there was no one there. One might be tempted to dismiss this as a dream, save for the fact that, the next morning, Mr Ingram's colleagues pointed out to him that the previous day had been 19 May.[4]

A former custodian of Blickling Hall, Dennis Mead, told the author Joan Forman that during the Second World War, a butler, one Hancock, had seen a woman wearing a long grey gown with a white lace collar and white mobcap walking across the lawn to the lake. He went up to her and asked her if she was looking for someone, to which she replied mysteriously, 'That for which I search has long since gone.' Hancock glanced up at the house at that moment, but when he turned back the woman had disappeared. Forman suggested to Mead that the costume she wore perhaps belonged to the seventeenth century, but he pointed out that Anne Boleyn had been wearing a grey gown, white coif and white cape on the day of her death.[5] However, the costume worn by the woman on the lawn would appear to be of a later date than the 1530s; lace was barely known in England then, and there is no record of Anne wearing a lace collar – or any collar at all – at her execution.

Norah Lofts reported a tale that a ghost called 'Old Bullen' haunted Blickling, and that a room called 'Old Bullen's Study' had such a bad atmosphere that the servants were too scared to enter it, so it was locked up, and its location is supposed to have long been forgotten.

Anne is also said to haunt Rochford Hall in Essex, which was formerly owned by her family and lived in by her sister Mary, with her second husband, William Stafford. In the 1920s, it was believed that Anne had been born there, and her ghost was said to appear in a large room called 'Anne Boleyn's Nursery', but the building dates from Henry VIII's reign, and since Mary Boleyn died there in 1543, we might wonder if it was her shade, not Anne's, that people claimed to have seen. At Wickford in Essex, at the turn of the year, Anne is said to travel in a phantom coach in the area where Runwell Hall, a house belonging to the Dean and Chapter of St Paul's Cathedral, once stood.

Surprisingly, there are few accounts of Anne Boleyn's ghost haunting Hampton Court, a royal residence where much supernatural activity has been reported. There is a late-nineteenth-century tale that she was seen drifting along a corridor wearing a sad face and a blue gown in which she is supposed to have been painted,[6] yet no such portrait exists. However, a female ghost in a blue velvet cloak has in recent years been reported in a grace-and-favour apartment that was once Katherine of Aragon's presence chamber. In 1945, Lady Baden-Powell, who had a grace-and-favour apartment just off the great hall, recorded in her diary that a visitor, a Mrs Hunt, sensed the presence of 'Queen Anne Boleyn!!' Anne, she went on, 'used my little turret room at the end of my bedroom as her secret praying room', and Mrs Hunt 'sees the Queen, who is beautiful, in the room'. Quite how Mrs Hunt made the identification is not recorded, and Anne Boleyn's apartments, the Queen's Lodgings that were built for her at Hampton

Court, were nowhere near this end of the hall. Adjacent to the hall, in the south-east corner of the Base Court, were the apartments refurbished by Henry VIII for Katherine Parr in 1543; prior to that date, they had been occupied by ladies-in-waiting of his previous wives.

Anne's ghost has also reportedly been seen on Christmas Eve, crossing a bridge over the River Eden on her way to Hever Castle, her family home in Kent, or as a wraith in white, gliding across the castle lawns; and she has apparently appeared at Windsor Castle, looking through a window in the Dean's Cloister or walking along the eastern parapet.[7] She is also said to walk every 19 May, on the anniversary of her execution, at Salle Church in Norfolk, where some of her Boleyn ancestors – including her grandparents – are buried, and where tradition once had it that her own remains were moved in secret. Norah Lofts related a tale told her by the sexton, who sat up to watch for this ghost; all he saw, however, was a hare, which ran around the church and then vanished. Lofts, a true East Anglian with an interest in the long tradition of witchcraft in that region, and a lively imagination, made the connection between witches and their familiars, hares having been so commonly associated with the latter that few Norfolk people would eat their meat.

Anne is also said to haunt thirteenth-century Bollin Hall, Cheshire (demolished in the 1840s), where local legend erroneously has it that she was born. Even though she had no connection with the place, she was at one time thought to be the White Lady seen in the grounds of a property owned by Jane Seymour's family, Marwell Hall, Hampshire, walking in the shade of the Yew Walk behind the hall. Local legend (falsely) claims that Henry VIII waited with Jane at Marwell for news of Anne Boleyn's death, having arranged for a chain of beacons to be lit to signal the event.

A ghostly vision of a barge, manned by shadowy grey oarsmen, taking Anne along the River Thames to the Tower, has been glimpsed passing the Water Tower of Lambeth Palace, despite the fact that in real life she was not conveyed so far upriver; and there are tales that her voice, moaning, crying and pleading for her life, echoes in the dark and ancient undercroft of the palace. These tales seem to be based on the untrue but oft-repeated assertion that she appeared before Archbishop Cranmer's ecclesiastical court in the undercroft on 17 May 1536, the day her marriage was dissolved, or even on the myth that she was tried there and, after being condemned, was taken down the steps of the Water Tower to the barge that would convey her back to the Tower.[8] Her ghost is also said to have appeared in Durham House Street off the Strand in London, in an ancient basement that is all that remains of Durham House, a former episcopal palace in which she once resided before her marriage. She is also said to be responsible for ghostly footsteps and lights in a shoe shop in Wisbech, on the premise of its proximity to Blickling, about forty miles away! The shade of a Tudor lady in green that manifests itself at the King's Manor in York cannot be Anne, despite claims to the contrary, for she never travelled so far north.

Predictably, there have been several tales of Anne's spirit appearing at the Tower of London. The figure of a headless woman in a Tudor gown has been seen several times near the Queen's House, formerly the Lieutenant's Lodging, the latter being where Anne was once thought to have been confined before her execution; since she was never held there, she cannot be the 'Grey Lady' in Tudor dress whose ghost haunts the building but can only be seen by females. The room next to the one in which Anne is supposed to have spent her last days is unaccountably colder than the other rooms in the house. In 1899, at a meeting of the Ghost Club, Lady Biddulph related how she had seen a lady with a red carnation over her right ear looking out of the window of Anne Boleyn's room in the Queen's House.[9] Even today, the room next door has an evil reputation because of its chill, forbidding atmosphere and strange perfumed odour, and because people have awoken there with a dreadful feeling of being suffocated, no child is permitted to sleep there.[10] However, these tales can have nothing to do with Anne Boleyn.

One night in 1864, a guardsman of the Sixtieth Rifles saw a white figure emerge from the dimness of a doorway of the Queen's House, where he was standing on duty. As it moved towards him, he challenged it, but as it came out of the shadows, he saw to his horror that it was headless and raised his bayonet, only to see the figure walk straight through it and himself. At that, he fainted with terror, and after being found by his angry commanding officer, was court-martialled for drunkenness and dereliction of his duty. Fortunately, two other people revealed that they too had seen the figure at that spot, and two other guardsmen swore that they had watched from a window of the Bloody Tower as it approached the sentry and had heard his scream of terror as he collapsed. In the face of this evidence, the court acquitted him.[11]

Later in the nineteenth century, a yeoman warder testified under oath to seeing a bluish form drifting across this area towards the Queen's House, while another soldier saw a woman in white coming out of that house soon after midnight; he could hear her heels tapping on the ground. He watched her walk towards Tower Green, but when she moved into a moonlit area, he was shocked to see that she had no head. He fled from his post, but when he explained what he had seen, he too escaped punishment. Similarly, in 1933, a soldier claimed to have seen the indistinct white form of a headless woman near the Bloody Tower; it seemed to rise out of the ground, then floated towards him; horrified, he thrust his bayonet at it, only to see it vanish.[12] Given that five different people saw this apparition at various times, there is perhaps some substance to these accounts, but the connection with the Queen's House again precludes any connection with Anne Boleyn.

In 1972, a nine-year-old girl from the North of England, visiting London for the first time with her parents, was standing by the scaffold site in the Tower, listening to a guide reciting the names of all the people who had been executed by the axe there. The child, who had no prior knowledge of Anne Boleyn, said to her mother that Anne had not been executed by the axe but by the sword, and afterwards described in detail the Queen's last moments, even asserting that the executioner had removed his shoes so as to come up behind her unawares and behead her.[13] The only thing she did not mention was that the scaffold site was in the wrong place!

In the late nineteenth century, an officer, peering through the windows of St Peter ad Vincula after seeing an unauthorised light inside at night, claimed to see the elegant figure of Anne Boleyn (whose face he said he recognised from portraits) at the head of a line of knights and ladies in period costume who were processing up the aisle towards the altar.[14] He watched astounded for a few moments until the procession and the light vanished.

There is a story that Anne's doleful ghost appears for a few moments at a time on autumn evenings in a dark corner of the upper room in the Martin Tower, but she was never held prisoner there (although her brother might have been), nor ever visited the Tower of London in the autumn.

One night in 1967, John Howden, a young soldier, patrolling near the White Tower, saw an eerie light in one of the upper windows, then a moving light illuminating a shape that passed from window to window. The next day, a warder told him he had probably seen the ghost of Anne Boleyn, who was supposed to haunt the White Tower and the Bloody Tower, and that many warders had seen her but did not normally discuss their experiences.[15] Again, the identification with Anne Boleyn must be incorrect, as she was not held in either building.

One might perhaps expect to glimpse the ghost of Anne at the Tower, but there are odder tales. In 1963, an Anglican clergyman, William Packenham Walsh, a canon of Peterborough Cathedral who had a life-long obsession with the executed Queen, published a book, *A Tudor Story: The Return of Anne Boleyn* –

which has been called 'a Christian morality tale' – about his many supposed exchanges with her discarnate soul, and even with that of a repentant Henry VIII, through mediums and automatic writing. His claim that one of her maids-of-honour was executed 'for her sake', for which there is no historical evidence, alone casts doubt on the reliability of his book, as do many other errors that have since been disproved by historians. In 2008, a woman claiming to be a witch advertised on eBay, the internet auction website, rings that allegedly have been infused with the spiritual essence of Anne Boleyn.

As a historian, I make no further comment on the veracity of these stories or the existence of ghosts. They are included here to illustrate how Anne Boleyn has become a figure of romantic mythology and a part of our national folk-lore.

Notes on Some of the Sources

Full details of the works mentioned are given in the Bibliography.

Anonymous accounts of Anne Boleyn's fall and execution:
1 Execution criminal hecha en Inglatierra el 16 [*sic*] de Mayo 1536, from the Vienna Archives. Anonymous Imperialist account of the executions of Anne Boleyn and her alleged lovers. This account is given in *LP* 911, firstly in an English translation, and then in French. The date is incorrect, and it is not known how soon after the executions this report was written, although the details were clearly very fresh in the author's mind. An English translation of the original Spanish MS., now in the Vienna Staatsarchiv, appears as notes in J.A. Froude's edition of William Thomas's *The Pilgrim* (a life of Henry VIII written in 1546); the French version is in Rymer's Foedera. Internal evidence suggests that the writer was not present at the executions on 17 May, but was an eyewitness to Anne Boleyn's death.

2 **Italian account by 'P.A.', perhaps a Venetian envoy, 2 June 1536**. A four-page Italian tract, which is identical in content and was published as *Il successo in la Morte della Regina de Inghilterra*

con il consenso del Consiglio di S.M., et la Morte di IIII gran Baroni del Regno (Bologna, 1536). It is reproduced in Alfred Hamy's *Entrevue de François Premier avec Henri VIII à Boulogne.*

3 **Anonymous letter written in London, 10 June 1536, translated from a Portuguese original in the convent of Alcobaca.** This is reproduced in *Excerpta Historica* (261) and given at LP 1107, which also mentions the Italian tract referred to above.

Pierre de Bourdeille, Seigneur de Brantôme (c.1540–1614) was a widely travelled soldier with close links to the French court, and knew many of the famous personages of his time. His rambling memoirs, which were not published until 1665–6, run into many volumes, and are witty, frank, sexually explicit and somewhat disjointed and unreliable, being a series of observations and random anecdotes, yet they provide a vivid picture of the licentious French court.

Lancelot de Carles: *Epistre contenant le proces criminel faict a l'encontre de la royne Anne Boullant d'Angleterre.* French poem describing the life of Anne Boleyn. *LP* 1036 is a translation from the French. Carles, later Bishop of Riez (d.1568/1570), was almoner to the Dauphin of France (the future Henri II), a renowned poet and man of letters, and the author of blazons and sacred poetry. In 1536, he was a diplomat attached to the French embassy in London, lodging in the house of Antoine de Castelnau, Bishop of Tarbes, the French ambassador. His letter describing Anne's fall was written in that city, in French verse, on 2 June 1536, within two weeks of her death, when Carles was still conscious of its impact. It was addressed to the Dauphin. Carles, who was present at Anne's trial, presents the charges against her as factual. His account was examined by Meteren, Burnet and his editor, Georges Ascoli, and has been re-examined by Professor Ives and Professor Bernard.

Ives suggests that Carles' poem be treated with caution, since it reflects the official government line. That has been questioned by Professor Bernard. It is true that in 1537, Henry VIII was presented with a 'French book written in the form of a tragedy [by] one Carle[s], being attendant and near about the ambassador'.[1] But was this the poem describing Anne Boleyn's fall? Certainly in that poem Henry VIII is generally portrayed in a sympathetic light, but would it have been politic of Carles to have asserted that on Anne's arrest, the Londoners rejoiced, hoping that the Lady Mary, the King's bastardised daughter, who was out of favour for defying her father, would be restored to the succession? Or that everyone was moved at the condemnation of the Queen's alleged lovers, and that even Anne's bitterest enemies pitied her? Would it have been tactful to have referred to Anne's 'fearful beauty', or to her giving voice to her suspicion that there was some other reason for her condemnation than the charges that had been preferred? Carles also has Lord Rochford complaining that he had been condemned on the evidence of only one woman, and Anne stating her conviction that she and her brother would be together in God's presence after their deaths. He states too that the people watching her execution were moved to tears. Taken together, much of this implied serious criticism of the King and his justice.

It may be, therefore, that the verse tragedy presented to Henry VIII by Lancelot de Carles in 1537 was not the poem he wrote on the fall of Anne Boleyn, but another work entirely, and that the former, based probably partly on sound intelligence and partly on official information leaked to the French embassy, was also a more objective work than has hitherto been suspected.

George Cavendish (c. 1500–61/2) was gentleman-usher to Henry VIII's chief minister, Cardinal Wolsey, from 1522 to 1530, and between 1554 and 1558 wrote the earliest biography of his late master. This is particularly useful for the early career of Anne Boleyn, as Cavendish was a well-placed eyewitness during this period to record events.

However, his admiration for Wolsey, his attachment to the old faith, to Katherine of Aragon and to Mary I, and his hatred for the Boleyn faction, all made him a biased observer, and his work has been challenged in parts by modern historians.

Cavendish is thought to have been the author of a series of tragic poems entitled *Metrical Visions* (Egerton MS. 2402), being the lamentations of fallen courtiers. Among the latter are Anne Boleyn's alleged lovers, whom Cavendish clearly believed guilty as charged. Given that he had retired from court in 1530, it is not known how he got his information, which is that of someone who was very well informed and knew his subjects personally.

George Constantine wrote a memorial to Thomas Cromwell in 1539, detailing the fall of Anne Boleyn and her alleged lovers in 1536. The original document does not survive, and is known only through the transcript sent in 1830 by the journalist, essayist and critic John Payne Collier to Thomas Amyot, Treasurer of the Society of Antiquaries. Branded as an outrageous forger in his lifetime, Collier's reputation has never recovered, despite the informed conclusions of Dewey Ganzel in *Fortune and Men's Eyes: The Career of John Payne Collier* (Oxford, 1982). According to this, Collier was largely innocent of those charges, and the defamation of his reputation was perhaps the most successful conspiracy in literary history. In fact, he was one of the foremost scholars of his age, and claims that he forged or embellished Constantine's memorial may be unfounded.

Jane Dormer (1538–1612) served as one of the future Elizabeth I's companions in childhood and adolescence, and later became one of Mary I's maids-of-honour and confidantes. When the Duke of Feria came to England in 1554 in the train of Mary's future husband, Philip of Spain, he fell in love with Jane and took her back to Spain as his wife. Many years later, she dictated her memoirs to her English secretary, Henry Clifford, who published them after her death, in 1643. They remain one of the best later

Catholic sources, although allowances must be made for a natural bias and an old lady's failing memory.

Edward Hall (c.1498–1547) was a Cambridge-educated lawyer. His chronicle has a strong patriotic bias in favour of Henry VIII, and a tendency to gloss over controversial issues. His true value is as an annalist, and his descriptions of state occasions and pageantry are informative and colourful.

Nicholas Harpsfield (1519?–75) was a Catholic propagandist who wrote two important works in the reign of Mary I: *A Treatise on the Pretended Divorce between King Henry VIII and Katherine of Aragon* (1556) and *The Life and Death of Sir Thomas More* (c.1557). Some of his material has been shown to be apocryphal.

Sir John Hayward (1560?–1627), a Cambridge-educated historian, wrote *The Life and Reign of King Edward the Sixt*, which was published in 1630 and is generally considered to be his masterpiece. He was conscientious and diligent in sourcing his information, researching from unpublished works, and a master of description who was impressively knowledgeable and impartial.

Sir William Kingston, Constable of the Tower: five letters to Thomas Cromwell concerning the imprisonment of Anne Boleyn, written in May 1536. The antiquary John Strype saw these letters before they were damaged in the disastrous Cottonian Library fire at Ashburnham House in 1731, and reproduced long extracts from them in his *Ecclesiastical Memorials of the Church of England under King Henry VIII* in 1721. The mutilated texts were printed in Singer's edition of Cavendish's life of Cardinal Wolsey in 1817, and they are also to be found in Ellis's *Original Letters Illustrative of English History* and in the *Letters and Papers of the Reign of Henry VIII*. The originals, with their charred margins, are now in the British Library:

Letter 1, undated, Cotton MS. Otho C. X. f.225 (f225)

Letter 2, undated, Cotton MS. Otho C. X. f.222 (f222)

Letter 3, undated, Cotton MS. Otho C. X. f.224b (f224b)

Letter 4, dated 16 May, Harleian MS. 283, f.134 (f134)

Letter 5, undated, Cotton MS. Otho C. X. f.223 (f223)

Singer also includes in this sequence Sir Edward Baynton's undated letter to Sir William FitzWilliam, sent while Anne Boleyn was in the Tower. This is Cotton MS. Otho C. X. f.209b.

Gregorio Leti (1630–1701) was an Italian historian whose life of Elizabeth I was written in 1682. Educated by Jesuits, he converted to the Protestant faith and for some years lived at the court of Louis XIV of France. He then came to Britain and wrote a history of England for Charles II, but fled to Amsterdam in 1683 after offending the King. Because his biography of Elizabeth was allegedly biased against Catholicism, it was suppressed by the Roman Catholic Church, and nearly all the original copies were destroyed. A French translation was published in 1692 in Amsterdam under the title *La Vie d'Elisabeth, Reine d'Angleterre*, but some of the original content is certainly missing. Leti researched his work in the libraries of the Earl of Anglesey (which boasted five thousand volumes) and Bishop Burnet, and perhaps used contemporary sources that are now lost, and although some passages are almost certainly apocryphal and contemporaries had no great opinion of Leti's veracity, there is something of interest in it for the historian.

Letters and Papers of the Reign of Henry VIII. This is a monumental archive of contemporary documents (some in abstract), now available online, and said to include at least one million separate facts about Henry VIII.

Clement Marot (1496–1544) and **Crispin, Lord of Milherve,** were two renowned French men of letters, whose writings are a valuable source of information on Anne Boleyn, whom Marot knew personally. Milherve, who was present at Anne's trial, wrote a separate metrical history, which was published in 1618.

Girolamo Pollini, an Italian Catholic historian, wrote his *Istoria dell' Ecclesiastica della Rivoluzion d'Inghilterra* in 1594. His work is biased in favour of Katherine of Aragon and Mary I, but while some passages appear to be apocryphal, much of what he wrote can be corroborated by other contemporary sources.

William Roper (1496–1578) wrote a highly regarded biography of his father-in-law, Sir Thomas More, around 1556. He was married to More's eldest daughter, Margaret, and his work, which has a strong Catholic bias, remains the primary source on Sir Thomas, to whom Roper was close.

Nicholas Sander (1530–81), one of Anne Boleyn's most virulent critics, was a Catholic who fled from England to Rome in the reign of Elizabeth I and became a Jesuit. His most famous work was his short and highly biased treatise on the Anglican Schism, *De Origine ac Progressu Schismatis Anglicani*, (*The Rise and Growth of the Anglican Schism*), which was published in 1585 in Rome and Cologne (and reprinted several times up to 1628) and reflected the damning Catholic view of Anne Boleyn. He was savagely critical of Henry VIII, but Anne, whom he regarded as the chief cause of the Reformation and vilified as 'the English Jezebel', was the chief object of his venom. He was responsible for several apocryphal but damaging slanders about her, such as the assertion that she was the bastard child of Henry VIII by her own mother, Elizabeth Howard, and the unsubstantiated tale that Anne herself was raped at the age of seven. Sander's work was received with outraged scorn in England, and it prompted George Wyatt's memoir of Anne, written in her defence. Wyatt called Sander 'the Romish fable-framer'. The reprinting of Sander's book in a French edition in 1673–4 spurred Bishop Burnet to write his history of the Reformation.

The Spanish Calendar (*Calendar of Letters, Despatches and State Papers relating to Negotiations between England and Spain, preserved in the Archives at Simancas and Elsewhere*). Informative and often biased, this vast array of documents incorporates Spanish and Imperial ambassadorial dispatches and correspondence (many of which are also reproduced in the *Letters and Papers of the Reign of Henry VIII*), and is by far the most useful diplomatic source.

The 'Spanish Chronicle': *The Chronicle of King Henry VIII of England* (*Cronico del Rey Enrico Ottavo de Inglaterra*). An often-controversial source, this was written before 1552 by a Spaniard living in London, who was perhaps an eyewitness (but not always a reliable one) to some of the events he describes. It has been attributed by some to Antonio de Guaras, who came to England in the train of Eustache Chapuys, the Imperial ambassador, in 1529. Much of the information it contains is based on hearsay and rumour, and its seemingly authentic detail is not always corroborated by other sources. As far back as 1905, M.A.S. Hume dismissed this source as being 'to a great extent hearsay' that 'truly represented the belief current at the time', while Ives has described it as 'garbled street gossip, strongly laced with the picaresque'.[2]

John Stow (1525–1605), author of *The Annals of England* (1592) and *A Survey of London* (1598), was an antiquarian writing in the reign of Elizabeth I.

Agnes Strickland's monumental *Lives of the Queens of England*, dedicated to Queen Victoria, in whose reign it was published, is now much outdated, but in its day it was a milestone of historical research, for Strickland was indefatigable in seeking out original source material, travelling around the country to look at documents in private collections. She also made use of secondary works that were respected at the time, but her work reflects the values of the Victorian age and is highly subjective. Its chief value lies in the scattered original sources that it cites.

Charles Wriothesley, Windsor Herald (1508–62), was the first cousin of Thomas Wriothesley, Earl of Southampton and Lord Chancellor of England (from 1544), and wrote the larger part of his chronicle over the years before 1552 (although it was not published until 1581). Well placed – he was in the service of Lord Chancellor Audley, and his cousin, the rising courtier Thomas Wriothesley, was Clerk of the Signet and Cromwell's man – and therefore well informed, he has been shown to be a highly reliable source.

George Wyatt's late-sixteenth-century eulogistic memoir of Anne Boleyn, written in answer to Sander's virulent attack on her, is one of the chief primary sources for her life. Wyatt (1554–1624), of Boxley, Kent, was the grandson of the poet, Sir Thomas Wyatt, Anne's Kentish neighbour and sometime admirer, and he had been fascinated by tales of Anne from his youth, when he had 'gathered many notes touching this lady'.

Wyatt himself wrote that he had had 'the peculiar means, more than others, to come to some more particular knowledge' of his subject. Much of his information came from anecdotes handed down in his family, from George Cavendish's *Life of Cardinal Wolsey*, a copy of which he owned, and from the reminiscences of three ladies: his mother, Jane Haute, who had married his father Thomas, the poet's son, the year after Anne Boleyn's death; Anne Gainsford (later the wife of George Zouche of Codnor), who had been Queen Anne's maid-of-honour 'that first attended on her both before and after she was queen', and afterwards served Jane Seymour in the same capacity; and an unidentified 'lady of noble birth, living in those times, and well-acquainted with the persons' about whom Wyatt wrote. Much of this source material survives in the Wyatt MSS in the British Library (Loan MS. 15) in the form of drafts, notes and extracts from various works. Wyatt's work, which was left unfinished, is so strongly biased in Anne's favour as to be virtually hagiographic, and virulently anti-Catholic.

Select Bibliography

Primary Sources

Additional MSS, British Library

Aless, Alexander: 'Letter to Elizabeth I, 1 September 1559' (see
  Calendar of State Papers, Foreign Series, of the Reign of Elizabeth,
  below, entry 1303)

Allen, Cardinal William: *An Admonition to the Nobility and People of
  England and Ireland Concerning the Present Wars* (Antwerp, 1588)

Anthony, Anthony: Chronicle (known only from notes made by
  Thomas Tourneur in his copy of Lord Herbert of Cherbury's *Life
  and Raigne of King Henry the Eighth*, Bodleian Folio Delta 624)

Ashmole MSS, Bodleian Library, Oxford

Bacon, Sir Francis: *The Tragedy of Anne Boleyn: A Drama In Cipher* (ed.
  Elizabeth Wells Gallup, London and Detroit, 1901)

Baga de Secretis (The Bag of Secrets), 1499–1537; Court of King's
  Bench (Crown Side) Indictments, and documents of state trials
  (National Archives, KB/2; reproduced in Wriothesley)

Bourbon, Nicolas: *Nicolae Borbonii Vandoperani Lingonensis, Nugarum
  libri octo* (Basel, 1540)

Brantôme, Pierre de Bourdeille, Seigneur de: *Lives of Gallant Ladies*
(trans. R. Gibbings, London, 1924)

Burnet, Gilbert, Bishop of Salisbury: *History of the Reformation of the
Church of England* (1679, 1682 and 1714; 7 vols., ed. N. Pocock,
Oxford, 1865)

*Calendar of Letters, Despatches and State Papers relating to Negotiations
between England and Spain, preserved in the Archives at Simancas and
Elsewhere* (17 vols., ed. G.A. Bergenroth, P. de Goyangos, Garrett
Mattingley, R. Tyler et al., H.M.S.O., London, 1862–1965)

*Calendar of Letters and Papers, Foreign and Domestic, of the Reign of
Henry VIII* (21 vols. in 33 parts, ed. J.S. Brewer, James Gairdner and
R. Brodie, H.M.S.O., London, 1862–1932)

*Calendar of State Papers, Foreign Series, of the Reign of Elizabeth, Vol. I,
1558–9* (23 vols., ed. Joseph Stevenson and A.J. Crosby et al.,
London, 1863–1950)

*Calendar of State Papers and Manuscripts relating to English Affairs
preserved in the Archives of Venice and in the other Libraries of Northern
Italy* (7 vols., ed. L. Rawdon-Brown, Cavendish Bentinck et al.,
H.M.S.O., London, 1864–1947)

Camden, William: *Annales rerum Anglicarum et Hibernicarum regnante
Elizabetha* (London, 1615)

Carles, Lancelot de: *Letter containing the criminal trial brought against the
Queen Anne Boleyn of England* (MSS Fr. 1742 and 2370,
Bibliothèque Nationale, Paris, written 1536, published Lyons, 1545,
of which a copy is in the British Library; published as 'Epistre
contenant le proces criminel faict à l'encontre de la royne Anne
Boullant d'Angleterre' (in *La Grande Bretagne devant l'Opinion
Française* by Georges Ascoli, Paris, 1927)

Cavendish, George: *The Life and Death of Cardinal Wolsey* (London,
1557; ed. R. Sylvester, Early English Texts Society, 1959; ed. Roger
Lockyer, The Folio Society, 1962)

Cavendish, George: *Metrical Visions* (published in Vol. 2 of S.W.
Singer's edition of George Cavendish's *The Life of Cardinal Wolsey*,
London, 1825)

The Chronicle of Calais in the Reigns of Henry VII and Henry VIII, to the year 1540 (attributed to Richard Turpin; ed. J.G. Nichols, Camden Society, XXV, 1846)

The Chronicle of King Henry VIII of England (*Cronico del Rey Enrico Ottavo de Inglaterra*, sometimes attributed to Antonio de Guaras; also known as 'The Spanish Chronicle'; ed. M.A.S. Hume, 1889)

Clifford, Henry: *Life of Jane Dormer, Duchess of Feria* (1643; ed. E.E. Estcourt and J. Stevenson, 1887)

Collected Poems of Sir Thomas Wyatt (ed. J. Daalder, Oxford, 1975)

Concilia Magnae Britanniae et Hiberniae (4 vols., ed. David Wilkins, London, 1737)

Constantine, George: 'Memorial from George Constantine to Thomas, Lord Cromwell' (ed. Thomas Amyot, *Archaeologia*, XXIII, 1831)

Corpus Reformatorum (ed. C.G. Bretschneider and H.E. Bindseil, Halle and Brunswick, 1834–1900)

Cotton MSS, British Library

Dolet, Etienne: *Epigram* (Lyons, 1538)

Excerpta Historica (ed. S. Bentley and H. Nicolas, 1831)

Foxe, John: *History of the Acts and Monuments of the Church* (*Foxe's Book of Martyrs*) (1563; ed. G. Townshend and S.R. Cattley, 8 vols., London, 1837–1841)

Fuller, Thomas: *History of the Worthies of England* (1662)

Gascoigne, George: *A Hundred Sundry Flowers Bound up in One Small Poesie* (ed. Richard Smith, London, 1573)

Gascoigne, George: *The Posies of George Gascoigne Esquire* (ed. Richard Smith, London, 1575)

Gruffydd, Ellis: A History of Wales, written by Ellis Griffith, a soldier of Calais, in Welsh (1550) (National Library of Wales MS. 5276D)

Guicciardini, Lodovico: *Comentarii di Lodovico Guicciardini Delle cose piu memorabilia seguite in Europa: specialmente in questi paesi bassi: dalla pace di Cambrai, del M.D. XXIX, insino a tutto l'Anno M.D.LX* (Venice, 1565)

Hall, Edward: *The Triumphant Reign of King Henry the Eighth* (London, 1547; 2 vols., ed. C. Whibley and T.C. and E.C. Jack, 1904)

Hargrave MSS, British Library

Harleian MSS, British Library

Harpsfield, Nicholas: *The Life and Death of Thomas More, Knight* (London, c.1557; ed. E.V. Hitchcock and R.W. Chambers, Early English Texts Society, London, 1935)

Hayward, Sir John: *Life of King Edward the Sixt* (London, 1630)

Herbert, Edward, 1st Baron Herbert of Cherbury: *The Life and Raigne of King Henry the Eighth* (London, 1649)

Heylin, Peter: *Ecclesia Restaurata, or the History of the Reformation of the Church of England* (London, 1661)

Histoire de la Royne Anne de Boullant (MS., before 1550, in the Bibliothèque Nationale, Paris)

'Household Expenses of the Princess Elizabeth during her Residence at Hatfield October 1, 1551 to September 30, 1552' (ed. Viscount Strangford, *Camden Miscellany*, II, Old Series LV, London, 1853)

Il successo in la Morte della Regina de Inghilterra con il consenso del Consiglio di S.M., et la Morte di IIII gran Baroni del Regno (Bologna, 1536)

Journals of the House of Lords, Vol. I, 1509–1577 (London, 1802)

Lancashire and Cheshire Cases in the Court of Star Chamber (ed. R. Stewart-Brown, Record Society of Lancashire and Cheshire, LXXI, 1916)

Latymer, William: Treatise on Anne Boleyn (Bodleian Library, Oxford, MS. Don. C.42)

Letters and Accounts of William Brereton (ed. E.W. Ives, Lancashire and Cheshire Record Society, Vol. CXVI, 1976)

The Letters of King Henry VIII (ed. Muriel St Clair Byrne, London, 1936)

Letters and Papers, Foreign and Domestic, of the Reign of Henry VIII (21 vols. In 33 parts, ed. J.S. Brewer, James Gairdner, R. Brodie et. al., 1862–1932)

The Lisle Letters (6 vols., ed. Muriel St Clair Byrne, London and
  Chicago, 1981)
The Love Letters of Henry VIII (ed. Henry Savage, London, 1949)
The Love Letters of Henry VIII (ed. Jasper Ridley, 1988)

Meteren, E. van: *Historie der Nederlandscher . . . oorlogen ende
  geschiedenissen* (Delft, 1599, 1609)
Milherve, Crispin, Lord de: *Metrical History* (1618)
*Miscellaneous Antiquities, or a Collection of Curious Papers, either republished
  from scarce tracts, or now first printed from original MSS* (from the collections
  of Horace Walpole and Thomas Gray, including a Life of Sir Thomas
  Wyatt the Elder, copied from an unpublished Harleian MS.; 2 vols.,
  ed. Horace Walpole, privately printed at Strawberry Hill, 1772)
Miscellaneous Writings and Letters of Thomas Cranmer (ed. J.E. Fox,
  Parker Society, 1846)

National Archives (Public Record Office):
  E326: Ancient Deeds
  SP1: State Papers

Original Letters Illustrative of English History (11 vols. in 3 series, ed. Sir
  Henry Ellis, London, 1824, 1827 and 1846)

Parker, Matthew: *The Correspondence of Matthew Parker, 1535–1575* (ed.
  J. Bruce and T. Perowne, Parker Society, 1853)
Percy MSS, Alnwick Castle
Pocock, N.: *Records of the Reformation* (2 vols., Oxford, 1870)
Pollini, Girolamo: *Istoria dell' Ecclesiastica della Rivoluzion d'Inghilterra*
  (Rome, 1594)
*The Privy Purse Expenses of King Henry the Eighth from November
  MDXIX to December MDXXXII* (ed. Sir Nicholas Harris Nicolas,
  London, 1827)

Rawlinson MSS, Bodleian Library, Oxford
The Register of the Most Noble Order of the Garter (2 vols., ed. J. Anstis,
  London, 1724)

Relations Politiques de France avec l'Ecosse (5 vols., ed. A. Teulet, 1862)

The Reports of Sir John Spelman (ed. J.A. Baker, Selden Society, 93, 94, 1977, 1978)

Roper, William: *The Life of Sir Thomas More, Knight* (c1556; ed. E.V. Hitchcock, Early English Texts Society, CXCVII, 1935)

Rotuli Parliamentorum (7 vols., ed. J. Strachey et al., Records Commissioners, 1767–1832)

Royal MSS, British Library

Rymer, Thomas: *Foedera, Conventiones, et . . . Acta Publica inter Reges Angliae* (London, 1704–1717)

Sander, Nicholas: *Rise and Growth of the Anglican Schism* (*De Origine ac Progressu Schismatis Anglicani*, Rome, 1585) (ed. and trans. David Lewis, London, 1877)

Sanuto, Marino: *Diary* (59 vols., ed. R. Fullin, F. Stefani et. al., Venice, 1879–1903)

The 'Spanish Chronicle' (see *The Chronicle of King Henry VIII of England*)

Spelman, Sir John: *The Reports of Sir John Spelman* (B.L. Hargrave MS. 388, ff. 144v, 185–187v; 2 vols., ed. J.H. Baker, Seldon Society, London, 1976–1977)

State Papers of the Reign of Henry VIII (11 vols., Records Commissioners, 1831–1852)

State Trials, Vol. I: 1163–1600 (ed. D. Thomas, W. Cobbett and T.B. Rowell, London, 1972)

Statutes of the Realm (11 vols., Records Commissioners, London, 1810–1828)

Stow, John: *The Annals of England* (1592; ed. C.L. Kingsford, 2 vols., Oxford, 1908)

Strype, John: *Historical and Biographical Works* (59 vols., Oxford, 1812–1828)

Thomas, William, Clerk of the Council to Edward VI: *The Pilgrim: A Dialogue on the Life and Actions of King Henry the Eighth* (1546; ed. James Anthony Froude, London, 1861)

Vergil, Polydore: *Anglica Historia, A.D. 1485–1537* (trans. Denys Hay, Camden 3rd Series, LXXIV, Royal Historical Society, London, 1950)

'The Vitae Mariae Angliae Reginae of Robert Wingfield of Brantham' (ed. Diarmid McCulloch, *Camden Miscellany* XXVIII, Camden Society, 4th Series, XXIX, London, 1984)

Wilkins, D.: *Concilia Magnae Britanniae et Hiberniae* (London, 1737)

Wriothesley, Charles, Windsor Herald: *A Chronicle of England in the Reigns of the Tudors from 1485 to 1559* (2 vols., ed. William Douglas Hamilton, Camden Society, 2nd Series, X and XX, 1875, 1877)

Wyatt, George: *Extracts from the Life of the Virtuous, Christian and Renowned Queen Anne Boleigne* (published privately, 1817, and publicly as an appendix to Vol. 2 of S.W. Singer's edition of George Cavendish's *The Life of Cardinal Wolsey*, London, 1825)

Wyatt, George: *The Papers of George Wyatt Esquire* (ed. D.M. Loades, Royal Historical Society, London, 1968)

Wyatt, Sir Thomas: *The Complete Poems* (ed. R.A. Rebholz, London, 1978)

Secondary Sources

Abbott, Geoffrey: *Ghosts of the Tower of London* (London, 1980)

Abbott, Geoffrey: *Mysteries of the Tower of London* (Nelson, Lancs., 1998)

Abbott, Geoffrey: *Severed Heads: British Beheadings Through the Ages* (London, 2000)

Ackroyd, Peter: *The Life of Thomas More* (London, 1998)

Albert, Marvin H.: *The Divorce* (London, 1966)

Anonymous: 'Henry VIII and Anne Boleyn' (*Royal Romances*, XXXI, London, 1991)

Armstrong, C.A.J.: 'Some Examples of the Distribution and Speed of News in England at the Time of the Wars of the Roses' (*Headstart History*, Vol. I, no. 2, 1991)

Arnold, Janet: 'The Coronation Portrait of Queen Elizabeth I' (*Burlington Magazine*, CXX, November 1978)

Ascoli, G.: *La Grande Bretagne devant l'opinion francaise* (Paris, 1927)

Baden-Powell, Olave, Lady: *Window on My Heart* (London, 1962)

Bagley, J.J.: *Henry VIII and His Times* (London, 1962)

Batey, Mavis: 'Basing House Garden History' (*Garden History*, XV, 2, Autumn 1987)

Bayley, John Whitcombe: *The History and Antiquities of the Tower of London, with Biographical Anecdotes of Royal and Distinguished Persons, deduced from Records, State Papers and Manuscripts, and from other original and authentic sources* (London, 1821)

Beckingsale, B.W.: *Thomas Cromwell, Tudor Minister* (London, 1978)

Bell, Doyne C.: *Notices of the Historic Persons Buried in the Chapel of St Peter ad Vincula in the Tower of London, with an Account of the Discovery of the Supposed Remains of Queen Anne Boleyn* (London, 1877)

Benger, Elizabeth Ogilvy: *Memoirs of the Life of Anne Boleyn, Queen of Henry VIII* (London, 1821)

Bernard, G.W.: 'Anne Boleyn's Religion' (*Historical Journal*, XXXIV, 1991)

Bernard, G.W.: 'The Fall of Anne Boleyn' (*English Historical Review*, CVI, 1991)

Bernard, G.W.: 'The Fall of Anne Boleyn: A Rejoinder' (*English Historical Review*, CVII, 424, July 1992)

Bernard, G.W.: *The King's Reformation: Henry VIII and the Making of the English Church* (Yale, 2005)

Bindoff, S.T.: *Tudor England* (1950)

Borman, Tracy: *Elizabeth's Women* (London, 2009)

Bowle, John: *Henry VIII: A Biography* (London, 1965)

Brayley, Edward Wedlake; Brewer, James Norris; and Nightingale, Joseph: *London and Middlesex*, Vol. 4 (London, 1816)

Brewer's British Royalty (ed. David Williamson, London, 1996)

Brigden, Susan: *New Worlds, Lost Worlds: The Rule of the Tudors, 1485–1603* (London, 2000)

Brook, V.J.: *A Life of Archbishop Parker* (1962)

Brooke, Xanthe, and Crombie, David: *Henry VIII Revealed: Holbein's Portrait and its Legacy* (London, 2003)

Bruce, Marie Louise: *Anne Boleyn* (London, 1972)

Brysson Morrison, N.: *The Private Life of Henry VIII* (London, 1964)

Bush, M.L.: 'The Lisle-Seymour Land Disputes: A Study of Power and Influence in the 1530s' (*Historical Journal*, IX, 1966)

Carley, J.P.: *The Books of King Henry VIII and his Wives* (London, 2004)

Chapman, Hester W.: *Anne Boleyn* (London, 1974)

Chapman, Hester W.: *Two Tudor Portraits* (London, 1960)

Childs, Jessie: *Henry VIII's Last Victim: The Life and Times of Henry Howard, Earl of Surrey* (London, 2006)

Churchill, Winston: *A History of the English-Speaking Peoples* (4 vols., London, 1956–1958)

Clark, Andrew: *The Life and Times of Anthony Wood, Antiquary of Oxford, 1632–1695, described by himself* (5 vols., Oxford Historical Society, 1891–1900)

The Complete Peerage (ed. G.H. White et al., St Catherine's Press, 1910–1959)

Cutts, H.: 'On an Incised Sepulchral Slab in East Horndon Church' (*Transactions of the Essex Archaeological Society*, V, 1873)

Deans, R. Storry: *The Trials of Five Queens* (London, 1909)

Denny, Joanna: *Anne Boleyn* (London, 2004)

Denny, Joanna: *Katherine Howard: A Tudor Conspiracy* (London, 2005)

Dickens, A.G.: *Thomas Cromwell and the English Reformation* (1959)

Dictionary of National Biography (22 vols., ed. Sir Leslie Stephen and Sir Sidney Lee, 1885–1901; Oxford, 1998 edition)

Dodson, Aidan: *The Royal Tombs of Great Britain: An Illustrated History* (London, 2004)

Doran, Susan: *The Tudor Chronicles 1485–1603* (London, 2008)

Dowling, Maria: 'The Fall of Anne Boleyn Revisited' (*English Historical Review*, July 1993)

Du Cann, C.G.L.: *English Treason Trials* (London, 1964)

Dunn, Jane: *Elizabeth and Mary: Cousins, Rivals, Queens* (London, 2003)

Elizabeth: The Exhibition at the National Maritime Museum (catalogue, ed. Susan Doran, guest curator David Starkey, London, 2003)

Elton, G.R.: *England under the Tudors* (London, 1955)

Elton, G.R.: 'The Good Duke' (*Historical Journal*, XII, 1969)

Elton, G.R.: *Policy and Police: The Enforcement of the Reformation in the Age of Thomas Cromwell* (Cambridge, 1972)

Elton, G.R.: *The Tudor Revolution in Government* (Cambridge, 1953)

Erickson, Carolly: *Anne Boleyn* (London, 1984)

Erickson, Carolly: *Bloody Mary* (London, 1978)

Erickson, Carolly: *The First Elizabeth* (London, 1999)

Erickson, Carolly: *Great Harry* (London, 1980)

Foister, Susan: *Holbein in England* (London, 2006)

Forman, Joan: *Haunted Royal Homes* (Norwich, 1987)

Forty-Six Lives (ed. Hubert G. Wright, London, 1943)

Fox, Julia: *Jane Boleyn, The Infamous Lady Rochford* (London, 2007)

Fraser, Antonia: *The Six Wives of Henry VIII* (London, 1992)

Friedmann, Paul: *Anne Boleyn: A Chapter of English History, 1527–1536* (2 vols., London, 1884)

Froude, James Anthony: *The Divorce of Catherine of Aragon* (London, 1891)

Froude, James Anthony: *History of England* (London, 1856–1870)

Fuller, T. Anna: *The Spear and the Spindle: Ancestors of Sir Francis Bryan (d.1550), Kt.* (Bowie, Maryland, 1993)

Gristwood, Sarah: *Elizabeth and Leicester* (London, 2007)

Gross, Pamela: *Jane the Quene, Third Consort of Henry VIII (Studies in British History)* (New York, 1999)

Gwyn, Peter: *The King's Cardinal: The Rise and Fall of Thomas Wolsey* (London, 1990)

Hackett, Francis: *Henry the Eighth* (London, 1929)

Hamer, Colin: *Anne Boleyn: One short life that changed the English-speaking world* (Leominster, 2007)

Hammond, Peter: *The Tower of London* (Historic Royal Palaces, 1987)

Hamy, Alfred: *Entrevue de Francois Premier avec Henri VIII a Boulogne-sur-Mer en 1532* (Paris, 1898)

Handbook of British Chronology (ed. F.M. Powicke and E.B. Fryde, Royal Historical Society, 1961)

Hare, Augustus J. C.: *Walks in London* (vol. 2, London, 1878)

Harrison, David: *Tudor England* (2 vols., 1953)

Hastings, Patrick: *Famous and Infamous Cases* (London, 1950)

Hayward, Maria: *Dress at the Court of King Henry VIII* (Leeds, 2007)

Hearsey, John E.N.: *The Tower* (London, 1960)

Henry VIII: A European Court in England (ed. David Starkey, London, 1991)

The History of the King's Works, Vols. 3 and 4 (ed. H. Colvin, 1975, 1982)

Hume, Martin A.S.: *The Wives of Henry the Eighth* (London, 1905)

Hutchinson, Robert: *The Last Days of Henry VIII* (London, 2005)

Impey, Edward, and Parnell, Geoffrey: *The Tower of London: The Official Illustrated History* (London, 2000)

Ives, Eric W.: 'Court and County Palatine: The Career of William Brereton' (*Transactions of the Historic Society of Lancashire and Cheshire*, CXXIII, 1972)

Ives, Eric W.: 'Faction at the Court of Henry VIII: The Fall of Anne Boleyn' (*The Journal of the Historical Association*, LVII, 190, June 1972)

Ives, Eric W.: 'The Fall of Anne Boleyn Reconsidered' (*English Historical Review*, CVII, 424, July 1992)

Ives, Eric W.: 'A Frenchman at the Court of Anne Boleyn' (*History Today*, August 1998)

Ives, Eric: *The Life and Death of Anne Boleyn, 'The Most Happy'* (Oxford, 2004)

Ives, Eric W.: 'Stress, Faction and Ideology in Early Tudor England' (*Historical Journal*, XXXIV, 1991)

Jaffe, Deborah: *What's Left of Henry VIII* (Shepperton, Surrey, 1995)

James, Susan: *Catherine Parr: Henry VIII's Last Love* (Stroud, 2008)

Jankofsky, Klaus P.: 'Public Executions in England in the Late Middle Ages: The Indignity and Dignity of Death' (*Omega: The Journal of Death and Dying*, X, 1979)

Jenkins, Elizabeth: *Elizabeth the Great* (London, 1958)

Jenner, Heather: *Royal Wives* (London, 1967)

Johnson, Paul: *Elizabeth I: A Study in Power and Intellect* (London, 1974)

Jones, Richard: *Haunted Houses of Britain and Ireland* (London, 2005)

Jones, Richard: *Haunted London* (London, 2004)

Jones, Richard: *Walking Haunted London* (London, 1999)

Kelly, Henry Ansgar: *The Matrimonial Trials of Henry VIII* (Stanford, California, 1976)

Kittredge, G.L.: *Witchcraft in Old and New England* (Cambridge, Mass., 1929)

Lacey, Robert: *The Life and Times of Henry VIII* (London, 1972)

Levine, Mortimer: 'Henry VIII's Use of His Spiritual and Temporal Jurisdictions in His Great Causes of Matrimony, Legitimacy and Succession' (*Historical Journal*, X, 1967)

Levine, Mortimer: *Tudor Dynastic Problems, 1460–1571* (London, 1973)

Lewis, Lesley: *The Thomas More Family Group Portraits After Holbein* (Leominster, 1998)

Lindsay, Philip: *The Secret of Henry VIII* (London, 1953)

Lindsey, Karen: *Divorced, Beheaded, Survived: A Feminist Reinterpretation of the Wives of Henry VIII* (Reading, Mass., 1995)

Lloyd, Christopher, and Thurley, Simon: *Henry VIII: Images of a Tudor King* (Oxford, 1990)

Loach, Jennifer: *Edward VI* (New Haven and London, 1999)

Loades, David: *Chronicles of the Tudor Kings* (London 1990)

Loades, David: *Elizabeth I: The Golden Reign of Gloriana* (The National Archives, 2003)

Loades, David: *Henry VIII: Court, Church and Conflict* (The National Archives, 2007)

Loades, David: *Henry VIII and His Queens* (Stroud, 1994)

Loades, David: *Mary Tudor: A Life* (Oxford, 1989)

Loades, David: *Mary Tudor: The Tragical History of the First Queen of England* (The National Archives, 2006)

Lofts, Norah: *Anne Boleyn* (London, 1979)

Lowinsky, Edward E.: *A Music Book for Anne Boleyn* (Toronto, 1970)

Luke, Mary M.: *Catherine the Queen* (London, 1967)

Mackie, J.D.: *The Earlier Tudors, 1485–1558* (Oxford, 1952)

Manning, James Alexander: *The Lives of the Speakers of the House of Commons* (London, 1851)

Martienssen, Anthony: *Queen Katherine Parr* (London, 1973)

Mathew, David: *The Courtiers of Henry VIII* (London, 1970)

Matthews, Rupert: *Haunted London* (Andover, 1993)

Mattingly, Garrett: *Catherine of Aragon* (London, 1942)

Merriam, Tom: *The Identity of Shakespeare in 'Henry VIII'* (Tokyo, 2005)

Michell, R.: *The Carews of Beddington* (London Borough of Sutton Libraries and Arts Services, 1981)

Miller, Helen: *Henry VIII and the English Nobility* (Oxford, 1986)

Minney, R.J.: *The Tower of London* (London, 1970)

Morris, Christopher: *The Tudors* (London, 1955)

Muir, Kenneth: *Life and Letters of Sir Thomas Wyatt* (Liverpool, 1963)

Murphy, Beverley A.: *Bastard Prince: Henry VIII's Lost Son* (Stroud, 2001)

Neale, J.E.: *Elizabeth I and Her Parliaments, 1559–1581* (London, 1953)

Neale, J.E.: *Queen Elizabeth I* (London, 1934)

Nichols, J.: *The History and Antiquities of the Parish of Lambeth* (London, 1786)

Norris, Herbert: *Tudor Costume and Fashion* (London, 1938)

Norton, Elizabeth: *Anne Boleyn, Henry VIII's Obsession* (Stroud, 2008)

On a Manuscript Book of Prayers in a Binding of Gold Enamelled, said to have been given by Queen Anne Boleyn to a lady of the Wyatt Family: together with a Transcript of its Contents (ed. Robert Marsham, publisher not stated, 7 March 1872)

Parnell, Geoffrey: 'Diary of a Death at Daybreak' (*BBC History Magazine*, II, 2, February 2001)

Paul, John E.: *Catherine of Aragon and her Friends* (London, 1966)

Perry, Maria: *The Word of A Prince: A Life of Elizabeth I* (Woodbridge, 1990)

Plowden, Alison: *The House of Tudor* (London, 1976)

Plowden, Alison: *Tudor Women: Queens and Commoners* (London, 1979)

Pollard, A.F.: *Henry VIII* (London, 1902)

Pollard, A.F.: *Thomas Cranmer and the English Reformation, 1489–1556* (London, 1965)

Porter, Linda: *Mary Tudor: The First Queen* (London, 2007)

Prescott, H.F.M.: *Mary Tudor: The Spanish Tudor* (London, 1940, revised 1952)

Pugh, T.B.: 'The Marcher Lordships' (*Welsh History Review*, XIV, 1988–1989)

The Renaissance at Sutton Place (The Sutton Place Heritage Trust, 1983)

Rex, Richard: *The Tudors* (Stroud, 2002)

Richardson, Ruth Elizabeth: *Mistress Blanche, Queen Elizabeth I's Confidante* (Little Logaston, 2007)

Ridley, Jasper: *Elizabeth I* (London, 1987)

Ridley, Jasper: *Henry VIII* (London, 1984)

Rival, Paul: *The Six Wives of Henry VIII* (London, 1937)

Rivals in Power: Lives and Letters of the Great Tudor Dynasties (ed. David Starkey, London, 1990)

Routh, C.R.N.: *Who's Who in Tudor England* (London, 1990)

Rowse, A.L.: *The Tower of London in the History of the Nation* (London, 1974)

Saunders, Beatrice: *Henry the Eighth* (London, 1963)

Scarisbrick, J.J.: *Henry VIII* (London, 1968)

Sergeant, Philip W.: *The Life of Anne Boleyn* (London, 1924)

Seymour, William: *Ordeal by Ambition: An English Family in the Shadow of the Tudors* (London, 1972)

Sitwell, Edith: *The Queens and the Hive* (London, 1963)

Smith, Lacey Baldwin: *Henry VIII: The Mask of Royalty* (London, 1971)

Smith, Lacey Baldwin: *A Tudor Tragedy: The Life and Times of Catherine Howard* (London, 1961)

Snowden, Keith: *Katharine Parr, Our Northern Queen* (Pickering, 1994)

Somerset, Anne: *Elizabeth I* (London, 1991)

Starkey, David: *Elizabeth: Apprenticeship* (London, 2000)

Starkey, David: *The Reign of Henry VIII: Personalities and Politics* (London, 1991)

Starkey, David: *Six Wives: The Queens of Henry VIII* (London, 2003)

Strickland, Agnes: *Lives of the Queens of England* (8 vols., London, 1851; 6 vols., Bath, 1972)

Thomson, Patricia: *Sir Thomas Wyatt and his Background* (London, 1964)

The Tower of London: Its Buildings and Institutions (ed. John Charlton, H.M.S.O., London, 1978)

'Triumphs of English': Henry Parker, Lord Morley, Translator to the Tudor Court; New Essays in Interpretation* (ed. Marie Axton and James P. Carley, The British Library, 2000)

Tytler, Sarah: *Tudor Queens and Princesses* (London, 1896; reprinted New York, 2006)

Underwood, Peter: *Ghosts and How To See Them* (London, 1993)

Underwood, Peter: *Haunted London* (London, 1973)

Underwood, Peter: *This Haunted Isle* (London, 1984)

Van Duyn Southworth, John: *Monarch and Conspirators: The Wives and Woes of Henry VIII* (New York, 1973)

Wainewright, John B.: 'Thirlwall, 1536, Chaplain to Queen Anne Boleyn' (*Notes and Queries*, 1916)

Walder, John: *All Colour Book of Henry VIII* (London, 1973)

Waldman, Milton: *The Lady Mary* (London, 1972)

Warnicke, Retha: 'The Fall of Anne Boleyn: A Reassessment' (*History: The Journal of the Historical Association*, LXX, 228, February 1985)

Warnicke, Retha: *The Rise and Fall of Anne Boleyn: Family Politics at the Court of Henry VIII* (Cambridge, 1989)

Warnicke, Retha: 'Sexual Heresy at the Court of Henry VIII' (*Historical Journal*, XXX, 1987)

Watkins, Susan: *In Public and in Private: Elizabeth I and her World* (London, 1998)

Weir, Alison: *Britain's Royal Families: The Complete Genealogy* (London, 1989)

Weir, Alison: *Children of England: The Heirs of King Henry VIII* (London, 1996)

Weir, Alison: *Elizabeth the Queen* (London, 1998)

Weir, Alison: *Henry VIII: King and Court* (London, 2001)

Weir, Alison: *The Six Wives of Henry VIII* (London, 1991)

The Westminster Abbey Guide (London, 1953)

Westminster Abbey: Official Guide (London, 1966)

Westwood, Jennifer, and Simpson, Jacqueline: *The Penguin Book of Ghosts* (London, 2008)

Williams, Neville: *The Cardinal and the Secretary* (London, 1975)

Williams, Neville: *Elizabeth I, Queen of England* (London, 1967)

Williams, Neville: *Henry VIII and His Court* (London, 1971)

Williams, Neville: *The Life and Times of Elizabeth I* (London, 1972)

Wilson, Derek: *Hans Holbein: Portrait of an Unknown Man* (London, 1996)

Wilson, Derek: *In the Lion's Court: Power, Ambition and Sudden Death in the Reign of Henry VIII* (London, 2001)

Wilson, Derek: *The Tower of London: A Thousand Years* (London, 1978)

Wilson, Derek: *The Uncrowned Kings of England: The Black Legend of the Dudleys* (London, 2005)

Wormald, Jenny: 'The Usurped and Unjust Empire of Women' (*Journal of Ecclesiastical History*, XLII, 1991)

Younghusband, George: *The Tower From Within* (London, 1918)

Websites

www.british-history.ac.uk

Notes and References

Abbreviations used in this section:

Bernard   *The King's Reformation*
Ives   *The Life and Death of Anne Boleyn, 'The Most Happy'*
LP   *Letters and Papers, Foreign and Domestic, of the Reign of Henry VIII*
SC   Spanish Calendar: *Calendar of Letters, Despatches and State Papers relating to Negotiations between England and Spain*
VC   Venetian Calendar: *Calendar of State Papers and Manuscripts relating to English Affairs preserved in the Archives of Venice and in the other Libraries of Northern Italy*
Warnicke   *The Rise and Fall of Anne Boleyn*

Full titles of all works are listed in the Bibliography.

Prologue: 'The Solemn Joust'

1   Hall; VC; *LP*
2   Henry's skeleton, discovered in St George's Chapel in the early nineteenth century, measured 6' 2" in length. This should be compared with his armour in the Tower of London, which would fit a man of 6' 4". Strands of red hair adhered to the

King's skull. His armour measurements show that in 1534, his waist measured 37" and his chest 45".

3 VC
4 SC; *LP*; Brantôme; VC; Carles; George Wyatt; Sanuto
5 Carles; *LP*
6 Carles; Wriothesley; Constantine
7 Carles
8 Hall
9 Hall; Wriothesley

1: 'Occurrences that Presaged Evil'

1 Wriothesley. Although Hall dates Anne's miscarriage to early February, Wriothesley, who was better-informed, states that it occurred 'three days before Candlemas'. As Candlemas falls on 2 February, this suggests that the miscarriage happened on 30 January. However, Wriothesley cannot have been correct in this case, for the Imperial ambassador, Eustache Chapuys, who had been at court at the time, reported on 10 February that, 'on the day of the interment' of Katherine of Aragon, i.e. 29 January, 'the Concubine had an abortion'. Warnicke is therefore incorrect in dating the miscarriage to 19, then 30 January.
2 George Wyatt; *LP*
3 Wriothesley; Hall. For Anne Boleyn's miscarriage, see also George Wyatt and Clifford.
4 *LP*
5 Ibid.
6 Neale: *Queen Elizabeth I*
7 Pollini
8 Hall
9 For Katherine of Aragon, see Mattingly; Weir: *Six Wives*; Fraser; Starkey: *Six Wives*; Paul; Luke; Hume and Strickland.
10 Ives
11 SC
12 Ibid.
13 For Henry's pursuit of Anne Boleyn, see, for example, George

Wyatt; *LP*; SC and Cavendish: Wolsey. Henry VIII's seventeen surviving love letters to her are in the Vatican Library, and have been printed in several editions.

14 Cavendish: *Metrical Visions*

15 Smith: *Henry VIII*; Bernard

16 Bernard; National Archives: SPI/46; Pocock

17 Erickson: *First Elizabeth*

18 Loades: *Mary Tudor*

19 SC. It has been claimed recently that the Nidd Hall portrait of Anne Boleyn is based on Holbein's portrait of Jane Seymour, but there are significant differences, not least the AB brooch worn by the sitter, and the image is entirely compatible with Anne's verified portraits, and was engraved as Anne in 1618.

20 *LP*

21 SC

22 Cavendish: *Metrical Visions*

23 The evidence for Henry's growing disillusionment with Anne Boleyn is to be found in SC, GW and Roper.

24 *Rotuli Parliamentorum*

25 VC

26 Bibliothèque Nationale, Paris

27 SC

28 Ibid.

29 SC; *LP*; Fraser

30 *LP*

31 *LP*; Denny: *Anne Boleyn*

32 *LP*

33 Aless

34 *LP*

35 SC; Latymer. Latymer, Anne's chaplain, identifies her as Mary Shelton, who married Sir Anthony Heveningham in 1546, and who is the subject of a portrait sketch by Hans Holbein.

36 SC; *LP*

37 Roper

38 Wriothesley. For Henry VIII's courtship of Jane Seymour, see SC and Clifford.

39 *LP*

40 SC

41 For Jane Seymour's life, see Gross.

42 SC. Jane's portraits by Holbein and other artists bear this out.

43 Clifford

44 Warnicke: 'Fall'

45 *LP*

46 SC

47 *LP*

48 Ibid.

49 Ibid.

50 Foxe

51 *LP*

52 Ibid.

53 Hall

54 Vergil

55 SC

56 *LP*

57 Prescott; Williams: *Henry VIII and His Court*

58 Loades: *Mary Tudor*

59 Carles

60 *LP*

61 Ibid.

62 Ibid.

63 Ibid.

64 Ibid.

65 Ibid.

66 Wriothesley; cf. *Il Successo de la Morte della Regina*, an Italian
    poem of 2 June 1536, written in London, which also asserts that
    the shock 'caused her to give premature birth to a dead son'.
    Warnicke's theory that Anne miscarried on 19 January does not
    take account of the fact that the King's accident occurred on
    the 24th.

67 Wriothesley

68 Clifford. Sander also describes Anne Boleyn finding Jane
    Seymour sitting on Henry's knee.

69 George Wyatt
70 Clifford
71 SC
72 SC; Wriothesley
73 *LP*
74 Ibid.
75 George Wyatt
76 *LP*
77 *LP*; SC
78 *LP*
79 Fraser

2: 'The Scandal of Christendom'

1 Loades: *Tragical History*
2 Burnet
3 *LP*
4 Ives
5 *LP*
6 SC
7 George Wyatt
8 Lofts
9 Loades: *Mary Tudor*
10 *LP*
11 Loades: *Mary Tudor*
12 *LP*
13 Ibid.
14 SC
15 *LP*
16 Loades: *Mary Tudor*; Loades: *Henry VIII and His Queens*
17 Ives and Dowling, for example.
18 *LP*
19 Ibid.
20 For Mary Tudor, the future Mary I, see the biographies by Loades, Prescott and Erickson.
21 Warnicke: 'Fall'

22 Clifford
23 *LP*; Williams: *Henry VIII and His Court*; Warnicke: 'Fall'
24 *Lisle Letters*; *LP*; Ives
25 Fuller: *The Spear and the Spindle*
26 SC; Starkey: *Six Wives*
27 *Complete Peerage*
28 SC
29 Porter; Wilson: *Holbein*
30 *LP*
31 SC
32 Ibid.
33 Ibid.
34 Ibid.
35 Ibid.
36 *LP*
37 Ibid.
38 SC; Starkey: *Six Wives*
39 SC
40 Ibid.
41 Erickson: *Bloody Mary*
42 *LP*
43 Scarisbrick
44 SC; *LP*
45 SC
46 Porter
47 Ives
48 Friedmann; Loades: *Henry VIII and His Queens*
49 VC
50 SC
51 *Il successo de la Morte della Regina*
52 SC; *LP*. The dispatches of Chapuys and Jean de Dinteville, the French ambassador, attest to Anne Boleyn's unpopularity and her diminishing power.
53 Cited by Bernard
54 *LP*
55 Ibid.

56 *Chronicle of King Henry VIII*
57 *State Papers*
58 *LP*; Bernard
59 Carles
60 *LP*
61 VC; Vergil
62 SC
63 SC
64 *LP*; SC
65 Ibid.
66 *LP*
67 Bibliothèque Nationale, Paris
68 SC
69 *LP*
70 Loades: *Henry VIII and His Queens*
71 SC
72 Cited by Mathew
73 SC
74 Ibid.
75 Ibid.
76 Cavendish: *Metrical Visions*
77 Bernard
78 SC
79 Ibid.
80 Starkey: *Six Wives*
81 SC

3: 'The Frailty of Human Affairs'

1 *LP*
2 This report is dated 25 February, but must have been written earlier, as Anne was at York Place by the 24th.
3 Ives
4 *LP*
5 *Statutes of the Realm*
6 *LP*

7 Ibid.
8 Ibid.
9 Clifford
10 SC; Clifford
11 *LP*
12 Ibid.
13 Latymer
14 *LP*
15 *LP*; *Chronicle of King Henry VIII*
16 *LP*
17 SC; Loades: *Henry VIII and His Queens*
18 *LP*
19 Ibid.
20 Ibid.
21 *LP*; SC
22 *LP*
23 Wilson: *In the Lion's Court*
24 Warnicke: 'Fall'; Bush; Elton: 'The Good Duke'
25 Warnicke: 'Fall'; Seymour; Clifford; SC
26 Loades: *Henry VIII and His Queens*
27 *LP*
28 Prescott
29 Churchill
30 Ives; *LP*
31 SC; *LP*
32 Childs
33 SC; *LP*
34 Fraser
35 Warnicke
36 *LP*
37 Hamer
38 Ives; Gristwood; Porter
39 *LP*
40 Several historians give the date of this interview as 1 April, but
    in his report of it, dated that day, Chapuys wrote that he had
    seen Cromwell the evening before.

41 Warnicke: 'Fall'
42 *LP*
43 SC
44 Friedmann
45 *LP*
46 *Lisle Letters*; *LP*; Ives
47 Clifford
48 *LP*
49 *Henry VIII: A European Court in England*
50 *State Papers*
51 Wilson: *Uncrowned Kings*; Wilson: *In the Lion's Court*; Hamer;
     Bernard: 'Anne Boleyn's Religion'
52 *LP*
53 Ibid.
54 Hamer; Ives
55 Latymer
56 *LP*
57 Latymer; Ives
58 *LP*; Ives
59 *LP*
60 Ibid.
61 Froude: *Divorce*
62 *LP*
63 Ives
64 *LP*
65 Ibid.
66 *LP*; Friedmann
67 *LP*
68 SC
69 *LP*
70 Ibid.
71 Elton: *Tudor Revolution*
72 Ridley: *Henry VIII*
73 *LP*
74 Ibid.
75 SC

76　LP
77　Ibid.
78　Ridley: *Henry VIII*
79　Loades: *Henry VIII and His Queens*; Ives
80　LP
81　SC
82　LP
83　Friedmann
84　LP. Cromwell was to confide this to Chapuys on 6 June.
85　LP; SC
86　LP
87　SC

4: 'Plotting the Affair'

1　Loades: *Chronicles*
2　LP
3　Bagley
4　For the theory that Cromwell plotted Anne Boleyn's fall, see Ives.
5　Porter
6　Waldman
7　Froude: *Divorce*
8　Mathew
9　Loach
10　Wilson: *In the Lion's Court*
11　Friedmann
12　Wilson: *Tower*
13　Friedmann
14　*Rivals in Power*
15　Ives; Loades: *Mary Tudor*
16　Starkey: *Six Wives*
17　Ives
18　Loades: *Mary Tudor*
19　Ives; Gristwood
20　Sergeant

21 *LP*

22 Ibid.

23 Strype

24 Ives

25 Williams: *Henry VIII and His Court*

26 *LP*

27 Froude: *Divorce*

28 Friedmann; Froude: *Divorce*

29 Spelman

30 *LP*

31 The Beauforts were the descendants of John of Gaunt, Duke of Lancaster and fourth son of Edward III, by his mistress (later his third wife), Katherine Swynford. Gaunt's great-granddaughter, Margaret Beaufort, was Henry VIII's grandmother.

    Erickson (*Anne Boleyn*) suggests that it may not have been the wife of the 2nd Earl of Worcester who laid this evidence, but the widow of the 1st Earl, Eleanor Sutton. But she had remarried, to Lord Leonard Grey, Viscount Grane, so would then have been known as the Lady Grane or the Lady Grey, following the style adopted by her husband, who did not use his Irish title. She was, anyway, residing with him in Ireland at this time.

32 It was engraved by Francis Sandford, the seventeenth-century herald and genealogist, and restored by the 9th Duke of Beaufort in 1898.

33 *LP*

34 Starkey: *Six Wives*

35 *LP*

36 Ibid.

37 Ives: 'Fall Reconsidered'

38 Bernard: 'Fall'; Ives: 'Fall Reconsidered'. I can find no contemporary evidence to support claims on the internet that the Countess was Henry's mistress. If that were true, Elizabeth Browne's connection with Henry might explain her hostility towards the Queen, who might possibly have supplanted her in Henry's affections. It is more likely though that Elizabeth had bowed to pressure from her relatives to betray Anne, and that

she was worried about that hundred pounds she had borrowed without her husband's knowledge.

39 Warnicke: 'Sexual Heresy'

40 *LP*

41 *LP*; www.british-history.ac.uk

42 Warnicke

43 Ives

44 *LP*; Martienssen

45 *LP*

46 Milherve; Ives: 'Faction'

47 *LP*

48 Ives: 'Faction'

49 Warnicke

50 Spelman. *LP* has this incorrectly catalogued under 1531. Sir John Spelman's account is in Hargrave MS. 388, ff.187, 187v. Burnet, who had access to Spelman's Commonplace Book, and quoted him incorrectly, asserted that this page had been torn off and was incomplete, but that is not the case (see Ives: 'Faction', and Chapter 11 below).

51 Ives: 'Faction'

52 Sergeant; Ives; Warnicke

53 Cotton MS. Vespasian F.XIII, f.198; also in *LP*.

54 Ives

55 Fox

56 *Privy Purse Expenses*

57 *LP*; Ives

58 *LP*

59 Roper

60 Sir William Kingston's letters in *LP*

61 Thomas

62 Ives: 'Fall Reconsidered'

63 *Statutes of the Realm*

64 *LP*

65 Warnicke: 'Fall'; Bush

66 Loades: *Henry VIII and His Queens*

67 *LP*

68 SC
69 Loades: *Henry VIII and His Queens*
70 Ibid.
71 *LP*
72 Carles
73 Friedmann
74 Loades: *Henry VIII and His Queens*
75 Ives
76 Ridley: *Henry VIII*
77 Ibid.
78 Ives: 'Fall Reconsidered'
79 Ibid.
80 Warnicke
81 Neale: *Elizabeth*
82 *LP*
83 Murphy
84 *LP*
85 Ibid.
86 Ives: 'Fall Reconsidered'
87 Wriothesley. I am indebted to Glen Lucas for his translation of this and other documents in the *Baga de Secretis*.
88 Bernard
89 Ives
90 Fox
91 Friedmann
92 *Baga de Secretis*
93 Friedmann
94 *Baga de Secretis*
95 Miller; *Register of the Most Noble Order of the Garter*
96 Childs
97 *LP*
98 *Baga de Secretis*; Fox
99 Ives: 'Fall Reconsidered'
100 Ives
101 Ives: 'Fall Reconsidered'
102 Bernard

103　*LP*; Starkey: *Six Wives*

104　*State Papers*; SC; *LP*

105　I myself suggested that Anne might have been pregnant at this time, in my book *Henry VIII: King and Court* (2001), but after discussing the matter with John Guy, and reading the considered observations of David Starkey, I have been readily persuaded that I was probably wrong.

106　SC

107　*LP*

108　Denny: *Anne Boleyn*

109　Gristwood

110　Strype

111　*LP*

112　Wilson: *Uncrowned Kings*

113　*LP*

114　Ibid.

115　Denny: *Anne Boleyn*

116　*LP*; SC

117　*LP*

118　Ibid.

119　Ibid.

120　Ives: 'Faction'

121　*LP*

122　*LP*; Warnicke: 'Fall'

123　*LP*; *Lisle Letters*

5: 'Unlawful Lechery'

1　Aless

2　*LP*

3　SC

4　*LP*

5　Sergeant

6　Cavendish: *Wolsey*; Hall

7　Cavendish: *Metrical Visions*

8　Preface to Gascoigne, by Richard Smith

9 *LP*
10 Clark
11 Cavendish: *Metrical Visions*
12 Warnicke
13 Ibid.
14 *Chronicle of Calais*
15 Warnicke
16 Cited by Starkey: *Reign of Henry VIII*
17 Carles
18 Cavendish: *Metrical Visions*
19 Williams: *Henry VIII and His Court*; Friedmann
20 Spelman
21 *LP*
22 Cavendish: *Metrical Visions*
23 Ibid.
24 *Privy Purse Expenses*; Cavendish: *Metrical Visions*
25 Friedmann
26 Cavendish: *Metrical Visions*
27 *Privy Purse Expenses*; Carles
28 *LP*
29 Friedmann
30 Cavendish: *Metrical Visions*
31 Carles
32 National Archives, Exchequer: Augmentation Office records, Ancient Deeds Series B, E326
33 *LP*
34 *LP*; SC
35 *LP*
36 Ibid.
37 Cavendish: *Metrical Visions*
38 Murphy
39 Ives: 'Faction'; Childs
40 SC; *Letters and Accounts of William Brereton*
41 Cavendish: *Metrical Visions*
42 *LP*
43 *Letters and Accounts of William Brereton*; Murphy

44 Ives: 'Fall Reconsidered'
45 *LP*
46 Constantine; Murphy; Ives
47 Cavendish: *Metrical Visions*
48 Gwyn; *LP*; *Lancashire and Cheshire Cases in the Court of Star Chamber*
49 Murphy; Ives: 'Court and County Palatine'
50 Murphy
51 Ibid.
52 Warnicke
53 Clifford
54 *Chronicle of King Henry VIII*
55 *Privy Purse Expenses*; SC; Hall; Lowinsky. The 'Spanish Chronicle' incorrectly states that Mark was engaged by Anne Boleyn after Katherine of Aragon's death (*Chronicle of King Henry VIII*).
56 Ives
57 Cavendish: *Metrical Visions*
58 Guicciardini; Lowinsky
59 Lowinsky
60 Ibid.
61 *Chronicle of King Henry VIII*
62 Cavendish: *Metrical Visions*
63 Ibid.
64 *LP*; *Privy Purse Expenses*
65 Royal MS. 20, BXXI, fols. 2–3. This MS. later came into the possession of Sir Thomas Wyatt, the poet, whose name is also written on it. See Thomson; Lowinsky.
66 Ives: 'Stress, Faction and Ideology', and Wormald, for example.
67 Lowinsky
68 Ibid. The choir book is MS. 1070 of The Royal College of Music, London.
69 Wyatt: *Complete Poems*
70 Cavendish: *Metrical Visions*
71 Warnicke
72 *LP*
73 *Privy Purse Expenses*
74 Lowinsky

75 Cavendish: *Metrical Visions*
76 Warnicke
77 Pollard: *Henry VIII*
78 Ives: 'Faction'
79 Ives: 'Fall Reconsidered'
80 Warnicke: 'Fall'
81 *LP*
82 Ives: 'Fall Reconsidered'; Denny: *Anne Boleyn*
83 Bernard
84 Starkey: *Six Wives*
85 'Triumphs of English'
86 Cavendish: *Metrical Visions*
87 Fox
88 Hall
89 *LP*
90 Fox
91 Cavendish: *Metrical Visions*
92 *LP*; Froude, Note D, in Thomas (*LP* 911)
93 Friedmann
94 Fox
95 'Triumphs of English'; LP; Bernard: 'Fall'; Ives: 'Fall Reconsidered'
96 *Forty-Six Lives*
97 Warnicke: 'Fall'
98 Ibid.; *Forty-Six Lives*
99 For this theory, see Warnicke: 'Fall'
100 Ibid.; Additional MS. 12,060, ff20b, 23b; *Forty-Six Lives*
101 *Excerpta Historica* (*LP* 1107)
102 Fox, citing Carley
103 'Triumphs of English'
104 *Excerpta Historica* (*LP* 1107)
105 Warnicke

6: 'Turning Trust to Treason'

1 *LP*; *Lisle Letters*; *SC*; Ives
2 Milherve

3 Cavendish: *Metrical Visions*
4 Aless
5 Carles
6 *Chronicle of King Henry VIII*
7 *Lisle Letters*
8 Carles
9 Warnicke
10 *LP*. The letter is mutilated.
11 *LP*
12 Ives
13 Childs
14 Cited by Smith: *Henry VIII*
15 Aless
16 *LP*
17 Ibid.
18 Denny: *Anne Boleyn*
19 *Chronicle of King Henry VIII*
20 Wilson: *Holbein*; Constantine
21 Wriothesley
22 Constantine
23 Wilson: *Holbein*
24 Wriothesley
25 *LP*
26 Porter
27 *LP*
28 Ibid.
29 *Baga de Secretis*
30 Ives
31 Cavendish: *Metrical Visions*
32 *Lisle Letters*
33 Ives: 'Faction'; Smith: *Tudor Tragedy*
34 Carles
35 *Chronicle of King Henry VIII*
36 Carles
37 Ives: 'Faction'
38 Constantine

39 Cavendish: *Metrical Visions*
40 Carles
41 SC
42 Sergeant
43 *LP*
44 Ibid.
45 Ibid.
46 Wriothesley; *LP*; Carles; Ashmole MSS; Histoire de la Royne Anne de Boullant
47 Constantine
48 *LP*
49 Ibid.
50 SC
51 Wriothesley; *LP*
52 Ives

7: 'To The Tower'

 1 *LP*
 2 Deans
 3 Friedmann
 4 *LP*; Childs
 5 Denny: *Anne Boleyn*
 6 Lofts
 7 *LP*
 8 Sir John Hayward. Strickland confuses him with the playwright John Heywood.
 9 Ibid.
10 *LP*
11 Wriothesley
12 Sir John Hayward
13 *Lisle Letters*
14 Wriothesley
15 *LP*
16 Hall
17 Clark

18 Wriothesley

19 Ibid.

20 Its name appears thus in a plan of the Tower drawn in c.1597, which is only known from an engraving of the lost original done in 1742, which is now in the possession of the Society of Antiquaries of London.

21 Wriothesley

22 Warnicke asserts that Aless heard the cannon-fire on 30 April, but no one was committed to the Tower on that day — none of the accused were sent there until 2 May. She bases her assertion on Aless's statement, in his previous paragraph, that he was at Greenwich late at night on the 30th. However, he does not state when he returned to London. In the paragraph following the one in which he mentions hearing the cannon, he refers to news of the Queen's arrest spreading 'in the morning', i.e. the morning of 3 May. As she was imprisoned on the afternoon of the 2nd, he must have returned to Greenwich on that day. It is highly unlikely that the cannon was fired to mark the lowly Smeaton's committal to the Tower, as Warnicke suggests.

23 Fraser

24 Wriothesley; George Wyatt

25 George Wyatt

26 Wriothesley

27 Lofts

28 Warnicke is mistaken in suggesting that Anne was imprisoned in the Beauchamp Tower, also known as the Cobham Tower, which is some distance from the palace; that old tradition was disputed by Elizabeth Benger as far back as 1821.

29 *Tower of London*

30 Fraser

31 *LP*

32 *LP*. See Notes on Sources under Sir William Kingston.

33 Erickson: *Anne Boleyn*

34 'Triumphs of English'

35 *LP*

36 *LP*; Warnicke

37 *LP*
38 Ibid.
39 Cavendish: *Metrical Visions*
40 *LP*
41 Richardson
42 Hastings
43 Fraser
44 *LP*
45 Ibid.
46 Ibid.
47 Carles
48 *LP*; Friedmann
49 Cavendish: *Metrical Visions*
50 *Lisle Letters*
51 SC; *LP*
52 Friedmann
53 *LP*
54 Wriothesley

8: 'Stained in Her Reputation'

1   Du Cann
2   Erickson: *First Elizabeth*
3   Wriothesley (editorial notes)
4   *LP*
5   Ibid.
6   Ibid.
7   Ives
8   *LP*
9   Warnicke states incorrectly that this conversation with Weston had taken place a year earlier, but Kingston clearly stated that it occurred on 'Whitsun Monday last', i.e. 24 April 1536.
10 *LP*
11 Ibid.
12 Hume
13 *LP*; *Lisle Letters*; *Privy Purse Expenses*; Ives

14 *LP*

15 Friedmann

16 *LP*

17 Warnicke

18 Ibid.

19 Ives: 'Fall Reconsidered'

20 Warnicke: 'Fall'; Ives

21 Lindsey

22 *Lisle Letters*

23 *LP*

24 Ibid.

25 Erickson: *Great Harry*

26 SC; *LP*

27 Now a school known as Carew Manor.

28 *LP*

29 SC

30 *LP*

31 Constantine; Starkey: *Six Wives*

32 Hammond

33 Bell

34 Ives; Hamer; Strickland

35 Histoire de la Royne Anne de Boullant. Anthony Anthony says
    that Wyatt was taken to the Tower at 9.00 a.m. on 8 May, but
    he is not perhaps the most reliable observer, having almost
    certainly got the time of Smeaton's arrival there wrong. The
    Lisle Letters refer to Page being in the Tower on 8 May, not that
    he was taken there that day. Kingston's second report to
    Cromwell, probably written on the evening of 5 May, refers to
    the arrests of Wyatt and Page.

36 *LP*; *Lisle Letters*

37 Murphy

38 Friedmann

39 For Sir Thomas Wyatt, see Muir; Thomson and Wyatt: *Complete
    Poems*

40 *Rivals in Power*

41 Wyatt: *Complete Poems*; *LP*

42 George Wyatt
43 Ibid.
44 Ibid.
45 Ibid.
46 SC; *LP*
47 Ives: 'Faction'
48 Ibid.; Paul
49 Denny: *Anne Boleyn*
50 *LP*

9: 'The Most Mischievous and Abominable Treasons'

1 Fox
2 *LP*
3 Ives; Carles
4 *LP*
5 Ives
6 Starkey: *Six Wives*
7 Ives
8 *LP*
9 *Chronicle of King Henry VIII*
10 *LP*. The original is Cotton MS. Otho CX 228.
11 *LP*
12 *Love Letters of Henry VIII*, ed. Ridley
13 *Love Letters of Henry VIII*, ed. Savage
14 Strickland
15 Ibid.
16 *LP*
17 Ibid.
18 Ibid.
19 Ibid.
20 Ibid.
21 Ibid.
22 Ibid.
23 Murphy
24 *Lisle Letters*

25   Ibid.

26   *LP*

27   Ibid.

28   *Baga de Secretis*

29   Miller

30   *Baga de Secretis*. I am indebted to Glen Lucas for his translations of the indictments and summary of the offences cited in both.

31   Ibid.

32   Ives: 'Faction'

33   Warnicke: 'Fall'

34   Ives

35   Ibid.

36   George Wyatt

37   See Ives: 'Fall Reconsidered'

38   Bernard: 'Fall: Rejoinder'

39   *LP*

40   Ives

41   Bernard

42   Ibid.

43   *LP*

44   Ibid.

45   *Lisle Letters*

46   Lindsey

47   *State Papers*; Constantine; *LP*

48   Ives; Lindsey

49   Denny: *Anne Boleyn*

50   Williams: *Henry VIII and His Court*

51   *LP*; Fox

52   *Baga de Secretis*

53   *LP*

54   Ibid.

55   Friedmann

56   Ibid.

57   *LP*

58   Friedmann

59 SC
60 Carles

10: 'More Accused than Convicted'

1 Starkey: *Six Wives*
2 Cited by Strickland
3 Wriothesley; Starkey: *Six Wives*
4 Wriothesley
5 *Baga de Secretis*; Churchill
6 LP
7 Hamer; Denny: *Anne Boleyn*; Ives
8 Friedmann
9 Hastings
10 Wriothesley
11 Hastings
12 Spelman
13 Stow
14 *Baga de Secretis*
15 Spelman; SC
16 *Baga de Secretis*
17 Wriothesley (editorial notes)
18 Spelman
19 Wriothesley (editorial notes)
20 Constantine
21 Friedmann
22 Wriothesley; Spelman; *Baga de Secretis*
23 Carles
24 Ibid.
25 *Lisle Letters*
26 LP
27 Ibid.
28 *Lisle Letters*
29 Ives
30 *Complete Peerage*
31 *Lisle Letters*

32 Cf. *LP*.

33 *LP*

34 Ibid.

35 Ibid.

36 Ibid.

37 Ibid.

38 *Lisle Letters*

39 Carles

40 Ibid.

41 *Lisle Letters*

42 Ibid.

43 *LP*

44 Wriothesley

45 *Lisle Letters*

46 *Baga de Secretis*

47 *Baga de Secretis*; Friedmann. The latter lists only twenty-six
    peers.

48 *LP*

49 Ibid.

50 Ibid.

51 Ibid.

52 Ibid.

53 Ibid.

54 Ibid.

55 Ibid.

56 Ibid.

57 *LP*; Wriothesley; Starkey: *Six Wives*; Brayley, Brewer and
    Nightingale; Lewis; Batey

58 Roper

59 SC

60 Warnicke

61 SC; Warnicke: 'Fall'

62 Wriothesley

63 The original plan is lost, but a copy made in 1742 is now in the
    collection of the Society of Antiquaries of London.

64 Wriothesley; Harleian MSS
65 Benger
66 Wriothesley
67 Churchill; Miller
68 Wriothesley; Harleian MSS; *State Trials*
69 Constantine
70 *Complete Peerage*
71 *Baga de Secretis*
72 Miller; Friedmann
73 Wriothesley
74 Loades: *Henry VIII and His Queens*
75 Cavendish: *Wolsey*; *LP*; Percy MSS
76 *LP*
77 'Triumphs of English'
78 *Baga de Secretis*; Friedmann; *Complete Peerage*; *Dictionary of National Biography*
79 *Baga de Secretis*
80 Murphy
81 Friedmann
82 Snowden
83 *LP*
84 Ibid.
85 Ibid.
86 Wriothesley
87 SC
88 Churchill
89 SC
90 *LP*
91 Ives: 'Faction'
92 Froude, Note D in Thomas (*LP* 911)
93 Ives: 'Fall Reconsidered'
94 Starkey: *Six Wives*
95 *LP*
96 Burnet

11: 'Fighting Without a Weapon'

1 Wriothesley
2 Deans
3 Carles
4 Wriothesley
5 Carles
6 Younghusband
7 Carles
8 There is a fifteenth-century ceremonial axe in the Tower of London, but it is not known if this was the axe that was carried at Anne Boleyn's trial.
9 Carles
10 Aless
11 SC
12 Wriothesley; Carles
13 Wriothesley
14 Spelman
15 Carles
16 Childs; Fox
17 *LP*
18 This word is often mistranslated as 'medals' (*medailles*), but is more likely to be 'metals' (*metals*).
19 *LP*
20 Ibid.
21 Wriothesley; Ridley: *Henry VIII*
22 *LP*
23 Ibid.
24 Wriothesley
25 Burnet
26 *LP*
27 Cavendish: *Metrical Visions*
28 Dunn
29 Harleian MSS
30 *LP*
31 Milherve; Spelman

32 Fox
33 *Rivals in Power*
34 Hastings
35 Wriothesley
36 *Baga de Secretis*
37 *State Trials*
38 Loades: *Henry VIII and His Queens*
39 George Wyatt
40 Carles
41 Additional MSS
42 Carles; *LP*
43 *LP*
44 Levine
45 Ibid.
46 Kelly
47 Cited by Erickson: *First Elizabeth*
48 Harleian MSS
49 Warnicke
50 Wriothesley; Carles; Constantine; *Baga de Secretis*
51 Doran states that burning was the penalty for incest, but incest did not become a crime in England until 1908.
52 SC; *LP*; Ives
53 *LP*
54 Ibid.
55 Carles
56 *LP*
57 Spelman
58 Anthony
59 Harleian MSS
60 *LP*
61 SC
62 *LP*
63 Harleian MSS
64 Impey and Parnell; Fraser
65 *LP*
66 Wriothesley

67 Carles incorrectly states that Rochford was tried before Anne.
68 Wriothesley
69 SC; Carles; Thomas Fuller; *Excerpta Historica* (LP 1107); George Wyatt; Foxe
70 SC
71 *LP*
72 Ibid.
73 Carles
74 *Excerpta Historica* (LP 1107)
75 Loades: *Henry VIII and His Queens*
76 *LP*
77 Denny: *Anne Boleyn*
78 Norton
79 Dunn
80 Kittredge
81 Kelly
82 Cited by Denny: *Katherine Howard*
83 Fraser
84 SC
85 Warnicke
86 Erickson: *Bloody Mary*
87 *LP*
88 Carles
89 The site of the public gallows at Tyburn is by Marble Arch in London.
90 Wriothesley
91 Cited by Hamer
92 *LP*; Carles
93 *LP*
94 Wriothesley
95 *LP*
96 Ibid.
97 VC
98 *LP*
99 Ibid.

12: *'Just, True and Lawful Impediments'*

1 Chapman: *Anne Boleyn*
2 Loades: *Henry VIII and His Queens*
3 *LP*
4 *LP.* The original is Cotton Lib. Otho C.10.
5 Rymer; Wilkins; Ridley: *Henry VIII*
6 *Statutes of the Realm*
7 Ibid.
8 Wriothesley (editorial notes)
9 Warnicke
10 Loades: *Henry VIII and His Queens*
11 Wriothesley
12 *LP.* Ellis, the editor of *Original Letters*, misread Kingston's text, and mistook 'anonre' for Antwerp, when in fact it should read 'a nunnery'. In so doing, he perpetrated the myth that Anne believed she was to be sent abroad to a nunnery in Antwerp.
13 Kelly
14 *LP*
15 Ibid.
16 Ibid.
17 Ibid.
18 Froude, Note D in Thomas (*LP* 911)
19 *LP*
20 Froude, Note D in Thomas (*LP* 911)
21 Cavendish: *Metrical Visions*
22 Friedmann
23 Ridley: *Henry VIII*
24 *LP*
25 Her will is in the Cheshire Record Office: DCH/E 294.
26 *LP*
27 *Chronicle of Calais*
28 Abbott. In the eighteenth century, Horace Walpole recorded – with scant regard for accuracy – that 'the axe that beheaded Anne Boleyn' was on display at the Tower.
29 *Chronicle of Calais*

30 *LP*

31 Fraser

32 SC

33 National Archives C.193/3, f.80; Ives

34 *LP*

35 For examples of journey times in this period, see Armstrong.

36 *LP*

37 Carles

38 *Excerpta Historica* (*LP* 1107)

39 Wriothesley; *Lisle Letters*; SC; Froude, Note D in Thomas (*LP* 911); Starkey: *Six Wives*

40 *LP*

41 MS. in Trinity College, Dublin, discovered in 1959; Ives; Muir

42 *Lisle Letters*

43 *Rivals in Power*; Jankofsky; Warnicke

44 Wriothesley

45 According to the account in the reliable contemporary chronicle written by Charles Wriothesley, Rochford told the assembled people, 'Masters all, I am come hither not to preach and make a sermon, but to die as the law hath found me, and to the law I submit me, desiring you all, and specially you, my masters of the court, that you will trust on God specially, and not on the vanities of the world; for if I had so done, I think I had been alive as ye be now. Also I desire you to help to the setting forth of the true word of God, and whereas I am slandered by it, I have been diligent to read it and set it forth truly; but if I had been as diligent to observe it, and done and lived thereafter, as I was to read it and set it forth, I had not come hereto, wherefore I beseech you all to be workers and live thereafter, and not to read it and live not thereafter. As for mine offences, it can not prevail [benefit] you to hear them that I die here for, but I beseech God that I may be an example to you all, and that all you may beware [the text says 'be wayre', which could also mean 'be aware'] by me, and heartily I require you all to pray for me and to forgive me if I have offended you; and I forgive you all, and God save the King!'

In the contemporary Imperialist eyewitness account of the executions in the Vienna Archives (printed in Thomas), there is a very similar version of this speech, which was described by the writer as 'a very Catholic address to the people', in which Rochford said 'he had not come hither to preach but to serve as a mirror and example, acknowledging the crimes he had committed against God and against the King his sovereign; there was no occasion for him, he said, to repeat the cause for which he was condemned; they would have little pleasure in hearing him tell it. He prayed God, and he prayed the King, to pardon his offences; and all others whom he might have injured, he also prayed them to forgive him as heartily as he forgave everyone. He bade his hearers avoid the vanities of the world and the flatteries of the court, which had brought him to the shameful end that had overtaken him. Had he obeyed the lessons of that Gospel which he had so often read, he said he should not have fallen so far; it was worth more to be a good doer than a good reader. Finally, he forgave those who had adjudged him to die, and he desired them [the people] to pray for his soul.'

The Portuguese account, written on 10 June, has Rochford saying: 'From my mishap, ye may learn not to set your thoughts upon the vanities of this world, and least of all upon the flatteries of the court and the favours and treacheries of Fortune, which only raiseth men aloft that, with so much the greater force, she may dash them again upon the ground.' (*Excerpta Historica* (LP 1107)

In another version of his speech, Rochford declared: 'I was a great reader and a mighty debater of the Word of God, and one of those who most favoured the Gospel of Jesus Christ. Wherefore, lest the Word of God should be brought into reproach on my account, I now tell you all, Sirs, that if I had in very deed kept His holy word, even as I read and reasoned about it with all the strength of my wit, certain am I that I should not be in the piteous condition wherein I now stand. Truly and diligently did I read the Gospel of Jesus Christ, but I turned not to profit that which I did read; the which, had I done, of a surety I had not fallen into so great errors. Wherefore I do beseech you all, for the love of our Lord God, that ye do at all seasons hold by the truth, and speak it and embrace it; for beyond all peradventure, better profiteth he who readeth not and yet doeth well, than he who readeth much and yet liveth in sin.' (*LP*)

According to the author of the 'Spanish Chronicle', Rochford said, 'I beg you pray to God for me, for by the trial I have to pass through I am blameless, and never even knew that my sister was bad. Guiltless as I am, I pray God to have mercy on my soul.' This version was almost certainly fabricated.

George Constantine, far more concise, wrote that Rochford, after exhorting his companions to 'die courageously' and the crowd to 'live according to the Gospel, not in preaching, but in practise', said 'words to the effect that he had rather had a good liver according to the Gospel than ten babblers'. He added, 'I desire you that no man will be discouraged from the Gospel by my fall. For if I had lived according to the Gospel, as I loved it and spake of it, I had never come to this. As for mine offences, I cannot prevail you to hear them that I die here for, but I beseech God that I may be an example to you all.'

Chapuys, who, perhaps deliberately, misinterpreted Rochford's statements about religion, reported that he 'disclaimed all that he was charged with, confessing, however, that he had deserved death for having been so much contaminated, and having contaminated others, with these new sects, and he prayed everyone to abandon such heresies' (*LP*). Chapuys later informed Dr Ortiz that Rochford (whom Ortiz, in his report of 11 June, confused with Norris, 'the principal gentleman of the King's Chamber') 'said a great deal about the justice of his death, and that a favoured servant ought not to flatter his prince and consent to his desires, as he had done' (*LP*). It cannot have been Norris who uttered these words because according to the eyewitness accounts, he did not have 'a great deal' to say on the scaffold.

46 Abbott; *Chronicle of King Henry VIII*. While rejecting the speeches that the author of the 'Spanish Chronicle' put into the

mouths of the condemned, which he may not have been able to hear, we might yet accept his claim that three strokes were needed to behead Rochford, which any bystander could plainly have seen.

47 Froude, Note D in Thomas (*LP* 911)
48 Ibid.
49 Lofts
50 Warnicke
51 Carles
52 Constantine
53 SC
54 Brysson Morrison
55 Froude, Note D in Thomas (*LP* 911)
56 *LP*
57 Abbott
58 Wriothesley
59 Bayley
60 Wriothesley; Carles
61 Abbott. The Norris family had lived there until 1517, when Sir John Norris, Henry's father, had had to surrender the estate in return for a pardon for the murder of one John Enhold. Ockwells was then granted to John Norris's uncle, Sir Thomas Fettiplace, and it was the Fettiplaces who were supposed to have claimed Sir Henry Norris's head in 1536. A large part of the manor house was burned down in 1845.
62 Abbott
63 *LP*
64 Ibid.
65 Loades: *Henry VIII and His Queens*
66 Carles
67 Ibid.
68 Milherve
69 Wilkins
70 Wilkins; Wriothesley
71 Friedmann
72 *LP*; Wriothesley

73 Ives
74 Wriothesley
75 Kelly
76 *LP*
77 Ives: 'Fall Reconsidered'
78 *LP*; Rymer

13: 'For Now I Die'

1   *Lisle Letters*; The 'Spanish Chronicle' states that they brought Anne out to die 'the next morning' after the scaffold had been built.
2   *LP*
3   *Excerpta Historica* (*LP* 1107)
4   Ives; Parnell
5   Parnell
6   Ibid.
7   Ives; Parnell
8   Ives
9   *LP*
10 Carles
11 *LP*; SC
12 *LP*
13 Ibid.
14 Ibid.
15 Ibid.
16 As do George Wyatt and Camden.
17 Ives
18 *LP*
19 Carles
20 *LP*
21 Carles
22 Ibid.
23 Friedmann; Warnicke
24 *LP*
25 SC

26 Lindsey

27 *LP*

28 Ibid.

29 SC

30 See, for example, Strickland.

31 Ridley: *Henry VIII*

32 *LP*

33 Abbott

34 Wriothesley; *Chronicle of King Henry VIII*

35 Carles

36 *Excerpta Historica* (*LP* 1107)

37 Froude, Note D in Thomas (*LP* 911)

38 *LP*; Norris

39 Carles

40 *LP*

41 Ibid.

42 *Excerpta Historica* (*LP* 911); Histoire de la Royne Anne de Boullant; *LP*; Carles

43 Sergeant; Warnicke

44 Milherve; *Excerpta Historica* (*LP* 1107)

45 *Miscellaneous Antiquities*; Strickland

46 Some sources call her Mary, but there is no record of a Mary Wyatt, nor does a Mary Wyatt appear in the extensive pedigree drawn up by David Loades in his edition of George Wyatt's papers.

47 Hare; *Westminster Abbey* guidebooks

48 *Excerpta Historica* (*LP* 1107)

49 Froude, Note D in Thomas (*LP* 911); Carles

50 *Excerpta Historica* (*LP* 1107)

51 Froude, Note D in Thomas (*LP* 911); Histoire de la Royne Anne de Boullant; *LP*

52 Abbott; Younghusband

53 Chapman: *Anne Boleyn*

54 Ives; Impey and Parnell

55 Carles

56 *Lisle Letters*

57 *LP*
58 Foxe
59 *LP*; Wriothesley
60 Wriothesley
61 Murphy
62 Chapman: *Two Tudor Portraits*
63 Cited by Murphy
64 Wriothesley
65 Harleian MSS
66 Froude, Note D in Thomas (*LP* 911)
67 *Excerpta Historica* (*LP* 1107)
68 Histoire de la Royne Anne de Boullant; *LP*; Froude, Note D in Thomas (*LP* 911)
69 *Henry VIII: A European Court in England*
70 Histoire de la Royne Anne de Boullant
71 Froude, Note D in Thomas (*LP* 911)
72 Ibid.
73 *Chronicle of King Henry VIII*; Froude, Note D in Thomas (*LP* 911)
74 Wriothesley; Harleian MSS
75 Carles
76 *LP*
77 Froude, Note D in Thomas (*LP* 911)
78 *Excerpta Historica* (*LP* 1107)
79 Herbert; Strype
80 *Chronicle of King Henry VIII*
81 *LP*
82 Carles
83 Ives
84 Milherve
85 Froude, Note D in Thomas (*LP* 911); *Excerpta Historica* (*LP* 1107); Aless
86 Carles
87 *Excerpta Historica* (*LP* 1107)
88 Histoire de la Royne Anne de Boullant
89 *Excerpta Historica* (*LP* 1107). Wyatt family tradition had it that,

on the scaffold, Anne gave the prayer book she was carrying to Margaret Wyatt, who thereafter always wore it on a chain in her bosom (Strickland). It is sometimes claimed that this prayer book was the illuminated 'Hours of the Blessed Virgin Mary', which had been made for Anne in 1528 in France, and which she inscribed: *Remember me when you do pray, that hope doth lead from day to day.* This book is now on display at Anne's former family home, Hever Castle in Kent.

However, this cannot have been the prayer book that Anne is said to have given to Margaret Wyatt, which was preserved in the latter's family for generations, and was shown in 1721 to the engraver and antiquary George Vertue by its then owner, Mr George Wyatt of Charterhouse Square, London. It was also mentioned in Horace Walpole's *Miscellaneous Antiquities*, printed at Strawberry Hill in 1772. In 1817, George Wyatt's editor, Samuel Singer, claimed that the Wyatt prayer book was in the possession of the publisher Robert Triphook, who himself produced another edition of Wyatt's memoirs of Anne Boleyn, which was privately printed in that year. However, the description of Triphook's book differs from that of the Wyatt prayer book, which was then still in the family's possession.

The Wyatt prayer book is now Stowe MS. 956 in the British Library. It is bound in pure, richly chased gold enamelled in black, in an intricate pattern, and closely resembles one of Holbein's designs for jewellery and goldsmiths' work, having the same arabesque ornaments. It measures not quite two inches in length and just over an inch and a half in width, and has a ring for threading through a neck-chain or girdle. Small as it is, it contains 104 leaves of vellum, on which are inscribed metrical versions of twelve abridged Psalms by the Tudor lawyer and writer John Croke. Tiny prayer books like this one had been given by Anne Boleyn, in happier days, to all her ladies, as aids to devotion.

It is not inconceivable that Holbein himself designed this example for Anne Boleyn, although it is far more likely that it was commissioned for the Wyatts, as his original drawing shows the intials T.W.I., which are missing from the prayer book binding. These initials suggest that the prayer book was made to mark the marriage of the poet Wyatt's son, another Thomas Wyatt, to Jane Haute in 1537, a theory that is borne out by that indefatigable researcher George Wyatt's failure to mention it in his account of Anne Boleyn. Nor is it mentioned in the family memorials compiled by his descendant, Richard Wyatt, in 1727.

The tale of Anne giving the prayer book to Margaret Wyatt would appear to arise from a misreading of the first-recorded mention of the book in George Vertue's MSS; in his 'Notes on Fine Arts' (1745), he says he saw in the possession of Richard Wyatt 'a most curious little prayer book MS. on vellum, set in gold, ornaments graved gold, enamelled black – such as were given to Queen Anne Boleyn's maids of honour – and was thus given to one of the Wyatt family, and has been preserved for seven generations to this time'. This only states that Anne gave such books to her ladies – which is attested elsewhere – and that she gave one to a lady of the Wyatt family who served her. No mention is made of this gift being given on the scaffold, and that circumstance seems to have been inferred by later writers. There is also no record of any lady of the Wyatt family serving Anne Boleyn as a maid-of-honour. Jane Haute passed on what she knew of Anne Boleyn to her son George Wyatt, so if she knew anything about a prayer book, he would surely have recorded it. (See *On a Manuscript Book of Prayers*.)

90 *Chronicle of King Henry VIII*
91 Abbott
92 Wriothesley; *Excerpta Historica* (*LP* 1107)
93 Froude, Note D in Thomas (*LP* 911)
94 Aless
95 Carles
96 *Chronicle of King Henry VIII*
97 Carles; Froude, Note D in Thomas (*LP* 911); *Excerpta Historica* (*LP* 1107)
98 Harleian MSS

99 Histoire de la Royne Anne de Boullant; Froude: *Pilgrim* (*LP* 911)

100 Wriothesley

101 Histoire de la Royne Anne de Boullant

102 Ibid.

103 Younghusband

104 *Excerpta Historica* (*LP* 1107); George Wyatt

105 Wriothesley

106 Froude, Note D in Thomas (*LP* 911)

107 *Excerpta Historica* (*LP* 1107)

108 Ridley: *Henry VIII*

109 *Chronicle of King Henry VIII*

110 Abbott

111 *Chronicle of King Henry VIII*

112 Ibid.; Tytler; Strickland

113 George Wyatt

114 Carles

115 Abbott

116 *Chronicle of King Henry VIII*

117 George Wyatt

118 Carles

119 Wriothesley

120 *Chronicle of King Henry VIII*

121 Froude, Note D in Thomas (*LP* 911)

122 *LP*

123 Milherve; Histoire de la Royne Anne de Boullant

124 SC

125 Erickson: *First Elizabeth*

126 Carles

127 Froude, Note D in Thomas (*LP* 911)

128 Anthony; Abbott

129 Carles. Annabel Geddes, the former Director of the London Tourist Board who founded the London Dungeon, has suggested that Anne's head was sewn back onto her body by her women before burial, as Charles I's was in 1649, but no eyewitness account mentions this.

130 *LP*
131 Wriothesley
132 Wainewright; Wriothesley
133 Maria Hayward; Ives
134 *Lisle Letters*
135 *LP*
136 Froude, Note D in Thomas (*LP* 911)
137 Harleian MSS
138 Bell

14: 'When Death Hath Played His Part'

 1 *LP*
 2 Ibid.
 3 Ibid.
 4 *Corpus Reformatorum*
 5 SC
 6 *State Papers*
 7 *LP*
 8 Ibid.
 9 Ives: 'Faction'
10 *LP*
11 Ibid.
12 *LP*; Erickson: *First Elizabeth*
13 *LP*
14 Friedmann
15 Ives: 'Frenchman'
16 *LP*
17 Constantine
18 Friedmann
19 Williams: *Henry VIII and His Court*
20 *LP*
21 Jenkins
22 *Lisle Letters*
23 Rawlinson MSS
24 Gross

25 Additional MSS; Fraser

26 *History of the King's Works*; Fraser

27 Coverdale's Bible, with Anne Boleyn's initials embossed on the binding, is now in the British Library.

28 *LP*

29 *Lisle Letters*

30 *LP*

31 Hall

32 *LP*

33 Ibid.

34 Ibid.

35 *LP*; Warnicke

36 *LP*

37 Ibid.

38 *LP*

39 Foxe

40 *Lisle Letters*; *LP*

41 Harleian MSS

42 *LP*

43 *LP*; *Lisle Letters*

44 *LP*; *Lisle Letters*; *Complete Peerage*

45 Wriothesley

46 *Journals of the House of Lords*

47 *Lisle Letters*; *LP*

48 *LP*; Wriothesley (editorial notes); Kelly

49 *LP*

50 *Statutes of the Realm*

51 Elton: *Policy and Police*

52 *LP*

53 Ibid.

54 *Lisle Letters*; *LP*

55 She died at Reading Place, a tenement of the Abbot of Reading, in the Ward of Baynard's Castle in London, and was buried in the Howard aisle in St Mary's Church, Lambeth (*LP*; Nichols).

56 *LP*

57 Ibid.

58   *Dictionary of National Biography*; *Complete Peerage*

59   Cavendish: *Metrical Visions*

60   *LP*

61   Ibid.

62   *LP*. The original is Cotton MS. Vespasian, FXIII, f199.

63   Porter

64   *LP*

65   Ibid.

66   *LP*; Fox

67   Smith: *Tudor Tragedy*

68   Cited by Williams in *Henry VIII and His Court*.

69   Smith: *Tudor Tragedy*

70   *Statutes of the Realm*

71   SC

72   *LP*

73   Leti, Gregorio: *Vita di Elisabetta* (Amsterdam, 1692). Not always
     a reliable source, but given the other evidence about Lady
     Rochford, there may be some truth in this.

74   By Julia Fox in *Jane Boleyn*.

75   *LP*

76   *Lisle Letters*

77   *LP*; *Lisle Letters*

78   *Henry VIII: A European Court in England*

79   *LP*

80   Ibid.

81   Ibid.

82   Ibid.

83   Ibid. Later, in 1538, Audley was given Walden Abbey in Essex,
     which he converted into Audley End House; the present house
     was built on its site in the early seventeenth century.

84   Murphy

85   *LP*

86   *The Renaissance at Sutton Place*; *LP*; Royal MSS

87   *LP*

88   Ibid.

89   Murphy

15: 'The Concubine's Little Bastard'

 1 Neale: *Elizabeth*
 2 Williams: *Elizabeth*; *LP*
 3 *LP*
 4 Perry
 5 Waldman
 6 *LP*
 7 Neale
 8 *LP*
 9 Cotton MS. Otho
10 *LP*
11 Ibid.
12 Ibid.
13 Ibid.
14 *Excerpta Historica* (*LP* 1107)
15 *LP*
16 Ibid.
17 Erickson: *First Elizabeth*
18 *LP*
19 VC
20 Clifford; Prescott
21 VC
22 SC
23 VC
24 SC
25 *LP*
26 Cited by Neale in *Elizabeth*.
27 *Lisle Letters*
28 Cited by Somerset.
29 Ridley: *Elizabeth I*
30 Strype
31 Cited by Somerset.
32 *Relations Politiques de France avec l'Ecosse*
33 SC
34 Erickson: *First Elizabeth*

35 Gristwood
36 Foxe
37 Arnold
38 VC
39 Ibid.
40 Erickson: *First Elizabeth*
41 Jenkins. It is often stated that she made only two recorded references to Anne Boleyn, but that is not true.
42 Somerset
43 *Statutes of the Realm*; Ridley: *Elizabeth*; Neale: *Elizabeth I and Her Parliaments*; Johnson
44 Dunn
45 VC
46 Somerset
47 Ibid.
48 'Household Expenses'
49 Parker
50 *Calendar of State Papers, Foreign*; Borman. I am indebted to Dr Tracy Borman for drawing my attention to this reference.
51 Ives; Somerset; Ives: 'Fall Reconsidered'.
52 *Elizabeth*: Exhibition Catalogue
53 *LP*
54 Ibid.
55 Ibid.

16: 'A Work of God's Justice'

1 Ives: 'Faction'
2 *LP*
3 'Vitae Mariae'
4 Clifford
5 Cavendish: *Metrical Visions*
6 Friedmann
7 VC
8 Bruce; Loades: *Henry VIII and His Queens*
9 Warnicke: 'Fall'

10 *LP*
11 SC
12 Ives: 'Fall Reconsidered'
13 Somerset: *Ladies in Waiting*
14 Loades: *Henry VIII and His Queens*
15 Ives: 'Faction'
16 Loades: *Henry VIII and His Queens*
17 Smith: *Henry VIII*
18 Loades: *Henry VIII and His Queens*
19 Loades: *Mary Tudor*
20 *LP*
21 Strickland
22 Lofts; Strickland
23 Warnicke; Cutts
24 *Brewer's British Royalty*
25 Abbott
26 Bell
27 This plan is reproduced in Younghusband's *The Tower From Within*.
28 Dodson
29 *LP*
30 Bell
31 VC
32 Bell
33 Abbott
34 Bell
35 Abbott

Appendix: Legends

1 Forman; Jones; Underwood; Westwood and Simpson
2 Underwood
3 Foister
4 Forman
5 Forman; Underwood
6 Forman; Jones

7 Underwood
8 Ibid.
9 Ibid.
10 Abbott
11 Jones; Matthews; Underwood
12 Underwood
13 Ibid.
14 Forman; Abbott
15 Underwood

Notes on Some of the Sources

1 *LP*; Bernard: 'Fall'
2 Ives: 'Faction'

Genealogical Table 1: The Tudors

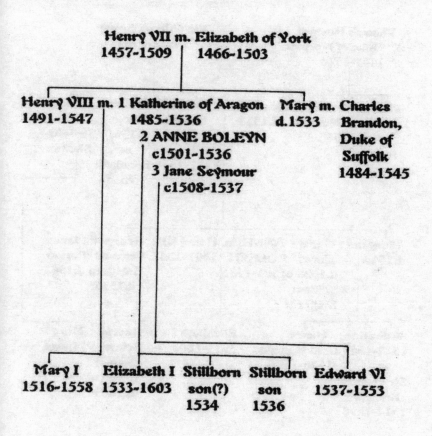

Henry VII m. Elizabeth of York
1457-1509   1466-1503

Henry VIII m. 1 Katherine of Aragon   Mary m. Charles
1491-1547   1485-1536   d.1533   Brandon,
                 2 ANNE BOLEYN   Duke of
                   c1501-1536   Suffolk
                 3 Jane Seymour   1484-1545
                   c1508-1537

Mary I   Elizabeth I   Stillborn   Stillborn   Edward VI
1516-1558   1533-1603   son(?)   son   1537-1553
                            1534   1536

Genealogical Table 2: The Boleyns

Thomas Howard,
2ⁿᵈ Duke of Norfolk
1443-1524

Sir William Boleyn
1451?-1505

Thomas Howard,
3ʳᵈ Duke of Norfolk
1473-1554

Elizabeth m. Thomas
d.1538   Boleyn
               Earl of
               Wiltshire
               1477-1539

Sir James
Boleyn
d.1561
m.
Elizabeth
Wood

Anne
m.
Sir John
Shelton

Mary m.1. William
d.1543   Carey
           d.1528
        2.William
          Stafford

ANNE m. Henry VIII
BOLEYN   1491-1547
c1501-1536

George m. Jane
Viscount Parker
Rochford d.1542
d.1536

?

Katherine   Henry
1524-1569 Lord Hunsdon
m.   1526-1596
Sir Francis
Knollys
1514-1596

Elizabeth I
1533-1603

George
Boleyn,
Dean of
Lichfield
d.1603

Mary
`Madge`

Genealogical Table 3: The FitzWilliam Connections

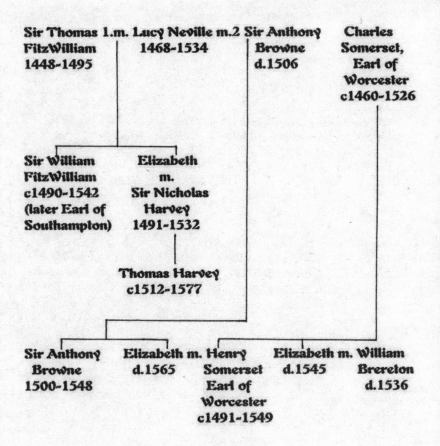

Sir Thomas FitzWilliam 1448-1495 1.m. Lucy Neville 1468-1534 m.2 Sir Anthony Browne d.1506

Charles Somerset, Earl of Worcester c1460-1526

Sir William FitzWilliam c1490-1542 (later Earl of Southampton)

Elizabeth m. Sir Nicholas Harvey 1491-1532

Thomas Harvey c1512-1577

Sir Anthony Browne 1500-1548

Elizabeth d.1565 m. Henry Somerset Earl of Worcester c1491-1549

Elizabeth d.1545 m. William Brereton d.1536

Index

Abbott, George 411

Act of Restraint of Appeals, 1533 115

Act of Succession, 1534 14, 41–2, 46, 74, 186, 234, 238, 276, 364, 388

Act of Succession, 1536 276, 296, 364, 388

Act of Succession, 1544 388

Act of Supremacy, 1534 44

Ainsworth, William Harrison 282

Aless, Alexander 20, 49, 51, 54, 66, 91–2, 106, 107, 111, 147–9, 153–4, 171, 185, 194, 264, 272, 278, 303, 329–30, 336–7, 344, 354–6, 358, 382, 399, 474

Aleyn, Sir John 265, 344

Alington, Sir Giles 115, 248

Allen, William, Cardinal 398

Allington Castle, Kent 223, 371

Allryge, Dr 298, 302

Ampthill, Beds. 359

Amsterdam, Holland 434

Amyot, Thomas 432

Anglesey, Earl of 434

Anne of Cleves, Queen of England 88–9, 108, 286, 334, 365, 368

Anthony, Anthony 140, 165, 265, 318, 341, 439, 476

Antwerp, Belgium 485

Ascoli, Georges 430

Ashburnham House, London 433

Askew, Anne 157, 216

Askew, William 248

Audley, Sir Thomas 79, 80, 112, 113, 168, 169, 188, 244, 250, 261, 263, 336, 363–4, 376, 437, 498

Austen, Jane 403

Aylmer, John 401

Aylsham, Norfolk 420

Bacon, Sir Francis 332–3, 401–2

Bacon, Sir Nicholas 388, 389

Baden-Powell, Lady 422

Baga de Secretis, National Archives
  113, 229, 263, 264, 265, 266–8,
  410

Baldwin, Sir John 113, 115, 227,
  232

Barbour, John 316

Barlow, John 361

Barnarde, Mr, the Westons' cook
  300

Barnes, Robert 253

Barton, Elizabeth 39

Baynard's Castle, London 56, 497

Baynton, Sir Edward 97, 102,
  152, 159, 192–4, 434

Beauchamp Tower, Tower of
  London 199, 270, 282, 293, 474

Beaufort, Eleanor 395

Beaufort, 9th Duke 465

Beaufort family 95, 140, 465

Beaufort, Margaret, Countess of
  Richmond and Derby 56, 143,
  465

Beaulieu Palace and Honour,
  Essex 125, 366

Beddington Park, Surrey 196, 198

Bedlam Hospital, London 253

Bedyll, Thomas 316

Beechwood Park, Herts 369

Belaugh, Norfolk 420

Bell, Doyne 412–13

Bell Tower, Tower of London
  281, 307, 371

Bellay, Jean, Cardinal du 11, 381

Benger, Elizabeth 282, 474

Beresford, Hannah 412

Bernard, George 406, 430–1

Bindoff, S.T. 160

Blickling Hall, Norfolk 1, 174,
  367, 410, 419, 420, 421, 422,
  424

Blount, Elizabeth, Lady Clinton
  263, 394

Blount, Gertrude, Marchioness of
  Exeter 28, 31, 39, 40, 62, 63,
  64, 67

Bodleian Library, Oxford 392

Boleyn, Amata/Amy 411

Boleyn, Anne, Lady Shelton
  41–3, 44, 174, 175–6, 283, 333

Boleyn, Anne, Queen of
  England:
  APPEARANCE 5–6, 13, 18, 30–1,
    200, 270–1, 276, 331–2, 337,
    342, 412–13
  ARGUMENTS FOR INNOCENCE OR
    GUILT 93–101, 103, 110–11,
    124, 137–9, 175, 178, 235–6,
    238–41, 404–10
  ARRANGEMENTS FOR EXECUTION
    303–6, 313, 321
  AT MAY DAY JOUSTS 5, 6, 7, 8,
    116, 159, 161
  ARREST 166–73, 177–8, 179,
    182, 183, 186, 189, 194, 197,
    215, 219
  BURIAL 348–9, 389
  CAREER 5, 431
  CHARACTER 6, 13–15, 17, 260,
    315, 319, 320, 321–2,

323–4, 332–3, 334–5, 337,
338–40, 386, 396–7, 406
EXECUTION 254, 260, 280, 292,
293, 300, 303–17, 318–60,
361–2, 369, 379, 381, 385,
410, 416, 419, 422, 423, 424,
426, 429, 431
EXECUTIONER 303–6, 310, 313,
321, 332, 335, 343, 344, 345,
361, 410
HOUSEHOLD INTERROGATED 7,
94, 106, 117, 123, 225
IMPRISONMENT IN THE TOWER
48, 136, 152–3, 169–73, 174,
176–9, 180, 182, 183, 185,
186, 189, 194, 199, 211–21,
243–4, 251, 269, 281–3, 297,
306, 315, 319, 320, 323,
325–6, 387, 403, 433
INDICTMENTS 31, 152, 160, 166,
213, 229–37, 239–41, 243,
245, 246, 249, 267, 271–2,
404, 409
LEGENDS ABOUT 22–3, 25,
332–3, 336, 356, 419–27
LETTER ALLEGEDLY WRITTEN IN
THE TOWER 216–21
MARRIAGE ANNULLED 29, 30,
60, 67, 74, 76, 87, 88, 90–1,
105, 107, 118–20, 179, 181,
186, 196, 224, 276, 280, 285,
293–7, 305, 315–17, 364,
381, 388, 393
MARRIAGE TO HENRY VIII 6,
9–37, 39, 41, 42, 46, 47, 49,
53–4, 56–7, 60–83, 85–111,

116–18, 143, 147, 152, 179,
181, 186, 189, 203, 270, 317
MISCARRIAGES 10, 12, 24–8,
32–4, 43, 53, 55, 61, 88,
109–10, 139, 178, 234, 287,
456, 458
PLOT AGAINST 22, 25, 38, 40,
44, 54, 65–70, 85–97, 104,
154, 219, 228, 409, 464
PROCEEDINGS AGAINST 107, 112,
121–2, 139, 159, 160, 186,
197, 220, 227–8
PROTESTS INNOCENCE 170,
176–9, 193, 220, 222–3, 255,
273, 315, 320, 410
RELATIONSHIP WITH DAUGHTER
ELIZABETH 9, 58, 117–18,
379–80, 378
RELATIONSHIP WITH LORD
ROCHFORD 87, 90, 125, 127,
129, 133, 141, 143, 145,
177, 213, 215, 231, 233,
234–5, 239, 242, 256, 257,
401
RELATIONSHIPS WITH SUPPOSED
LOVERS 6, 13–14, 91–101,
102, 103–4, 105, 107–8,
109, 110–11, 123–37,
144–6, 149–54, 178–9, 182,
190–1, 193–4, 199–210,
214–16, 230–4, 235–9, 241,
245, 251, 258, 262–3, 267,
381–2
REPUTATION 7, 13–15, 22–3,
48–9, 64, 93, 94, 101–4, 109,
137, 146, 185, 205–6, 259,

313, 320, 321–2, 388, 396, 406, 409

RELIGIOUS VIEWS 20–1, 31, 43, 45–6, 49, 52, 65, 66, 73, 90, 91, 153, 297, 365, 399

RIVALRY WITH CROMWELL 51–4, 64–71, 75, 77, 89–91

TRIAL 94, 112, 140, 153, 218, 227–9, 243–4, 245, 251, 256, 260–8, 269–81, 282, 283, 288–9, 303, 304, 305, 329, 333, 334, 351, 396, 402, 404, 407, 410, 430, 482, 488

UNKINDNESS TO KATHERINE OF ARAGON AND MARY TUDOR 21, 36, 40–5, 121, 180, 183–4, 196–7, 238, 325–7, 390

Boleyn, Edmund 391

Boleyn family 45, 51, 59, 112, 125, 333, 361, 366

Boleyn, George, Dean of Lichfield 144, 366

Boleyn, George, Viscount Rochford 6, 38, 39, 41, 45, 60, 76, 77, 79, 87, 90, 99, 111, 112, 125–7, 129, 130, 133, 135, 137–8, 139, 140, 141, 144, 145, 156, 160, 165, 175, 177, 180, 182, 184, 193, 198, 212, 213, 214, 215, 227, 231, 233, 234–5, 239, 242, 245, 247, 250, 251, 252, 253, 254, 256, 257, 260, 263, 266, 267, 272, 280, 283–9, 292–3, 298, 302, 308–10, 311, 312, 313, 349, 366, 368, 372,

374, 376, 391, 401, 411, 415, 419, 431

Boleyn, Sir James 174

Boleyn, Lady (see Wood, Elizabeth)

Boleyn, Mary 33–4, 56, 295, 296, 365–6, 393–5, 422

Boleyn, Thomas, Earl of Wiltshire 41, 60–1, 99, 111, 113, 114, 117, 125, 136, 156, 167, 178, 182, 247, 264–5, 300, 336, 345, 366, 367, 419

Bollin Hall, Cheshire 423

Bonner, Edmund, Archdeacon of Leicester, later Bishop of London 316

Bonvisi, Antonio 205

Borman, Tracy 384, 500

Bourbon, Nicholas 134

Bourchier, Elizabeth, Lady Page 199

Bourchier, Margaret, Lady Bryan 38, 40, 52, 378, 379–80, 381, 384

Bradby, Mr, borderer 300

Bradford, Earl of 420

Brandon, Charles, Duke of Suffolk 40, 100, 113, 114, 202–5, 206, 248, 261, 263, 275, 316, 336, 344

Brantôme, Seigneur de 13, 430

Braye, Anne, Lady Cobham 96

Brereton, Urian 31, 130, 377

Brereton, Sir William 6, 125, 130–3, 137–9, 156, 159–60, 162, 179, 182, 198, 204, 213,

216–17, 230–3, 236, 238, 242, 245, 247, 248, 249–50, 251, 253, 273, 274, 301, 310, 311–12, 314, 372–3, 376, 377

Bridges, Mr, tailor 301

British Library, London 96, 174, 216, 328

Brook House, Newington Green, Hackney 294

Brooke, Elizabeth, Lady Wyatt 200, 263, 421

Brooke, George, Lord Cobham 96–7, 263

Browne, Sir Anthony, the Elder 95

Browne, Sir Anthony, the Younger 95, 96, 99, 107, 121, 138, 158–9, 181

Browne, Elizabeth, Countess of Worcester 94, 95–6, 98, 103, 106, 107, 130, 133, 140, 150, 158–9, 178, 263, 274

Browne, George 60

Browne, Mr, draper 300

Bryan, Elizabeth, Lady Carew 40

Bryan family 38, 104

Bryan, Sir Francis 18, 37, 38–9, 40, 45, 70, 104, 121–2, 139, 141–2, 181–2, 191, 196, 206, 212, 253, 281, 289, 301, 354, 377

Bryan, Lady (*see* Bourchier, Margaret)

Brysson, Morrison N. 407

Buckingham, Duke of 114, 262

Buckley (or Bulkeley), Sir Richard 182–3

Buckley (or Bulkeley), Roland 182–3

Burgh, Norfolk 420

Burgh, Thomas, Lord 264

Burgos, Cardinal of 258

Burnet, Gilbert, Bishop of Salisbury 6–7, 145, 186, 216, 217, 219, 276, 283, 294, 299, 311, 430, 434, 436

Butler, Margaret, Lady Boleyn 311, 430, 434, 436

Byward Tower, Tower of London 170–1, 207, 307, 349

Calais, Executioner of 303–6, 361

Calais, France 94, 100, 116, 122, 136, 154, 201, 203, 264, 308

Calthorpe, Sir Philip 411

Cambridge, University of 57–8

Camden, William 281, 326

Carew, Sir Nicholas 37, 40, 45, 62, 104, 111, 112, 121, 139, 141–2, 181, 196, 211–12, 259, 376, 377

Carey, Henry, Lord Hunsdon 366, 391, 394–5

Carey, Katherine 334, 391

Carey, William 334

Carles, Lancelot de, later Bishop of Riez 14, 23, 34, 93, 94, 96, 98, 106, 107, 157, 158–60, 163, 165, 243–4, 249, 278, 283, 310, 319, 330, 333, 337, 348–9, 430–1

Carnaby, Sir Raynold 294

Casale, Gregory 258

Castelnau, Antoine de, Bishop of Tarbes 14, 18, 82–3, 141, 298, 430

Catesby Priory, Northants 73

Cavendish, George 51, 126, 128–9, 130, 131–2, 134, 136, 138–9, 140, 148, 158, 163, 167, 177, 294, 299, 369, 397, 399, 431–2, 433, 437

Cecil, William 118, 386

Champernowne, Katherine, later Mrs Astley 379, 384

Chapman, Hester 408–9

Chapuys, Eustache 9, 11, 13, 14–15, 17, 18, 19–20, 21–2, 23–4, 25–6, 28, 29, 30, 31–2, 33, 34, 35–8, 39–40, 42, 43–6, 47, 48, 50, 51, 52, 53, 54, 55, 56, 57, 59, 60, 61, 62, 63, 64–5, 66–70, 74, 75, 76–84, 85, 86, 89–90, 91, 93, 95, 104, 105, 108, 111–12, 118–21, 141, 144, 161–2, 163, 164, 165, 170, 179–82, 184, 189, 194, 196, 197–8, 202–3, 233, 245, 247–8, 249–50, 251, 259, 260, 261, 262–3, 264–5, 266, 267, 269, 271–2, 273, 278, 279, 280–1, 284, 287, 288, 289, 290, 295, 298, 304, 306, 309–10, 313, 314, 317, 320, 321, 322, 323–4, 325, 327, 330, 332, 335–6, 338, 347, 351–4, 356, 357, 358, 360, 361, 362, 364, 369, 381, 409, 436, 456, 460, 462, 488

Charles I, King of Great Britain 495

Charles II, King of Great Britain 434

Charles V, Holy Roman Emperor 15, 19–20, 21, 23, 36, 38, 45, 49, 53, 54, 56, 58–60, 65, 69–70, 74–84, 88, 89, 90, 105, 116, 117, 119, 120, 147, 179–80, 181, 189, 197, 239, 240, 245, 258, 260, 284–5, 290, 304, 322, 330, 352, 355, 357, 358, 361–2, 374, 381, 408

Charterhouse, London 250

Chelsea, London 259, 269, 281, 290, 324, 358, 360

Chequers, Bucks. 390

Cheyney, Sir Thomas 121, 181, 253, 366, 376

Christina of Denmark, Duchess of Milan 331, 358

Churchill, Sir Winston 303

Cirencester, Abbot of 241

Clement VII, Pope 10, 11, 58, 76, 82, 147, 197, 238, 295, 296–7

Clifford, Henry 432, 458

Cobham, Anne 96

Cobham, Eleanor, Duchess of Gloucester 29–30, 229

Cobham, 'Nan' 94, 96–7, 113, 263, 274

Coffin, Mrs (*see* Dymoke, Margaret)

Coffin, William 176, 226–7

Collier, John Payne 432

Collyweston, Northants. 56

Coltishall, Norfolk 420

Constantine, George 156–7, 162, 163, 164, 165, 198, 261–2, 277, 280, 287, 288–9, 307–8, 311–12, 313, 322, 354, 361, 432

Cooke, William 321

Corpus Christi College, Oxford 265

Cosyn (*see* Coffin)

Cotton, Sir Robert 326

Courtenay, Henry, Marquess of Exeter 28, 31, 32, 38, 39, 40, 62, 67, 104, 226, 263, 377

Coverdale, Miles 156, 360

Cranmer, Thomas, Archbishop of Canterbury 10, 20, 49, 73, 89, 91, 118, 119, 148, 185–9, 194, 224, 276, 293, 294, 295, 296, 297, 302–3, 304, 315–17, 319, 329–30, 364, 374, 381, 424

Croke, John 493

Cromwell, Gregory 336, 376

Cromwell, Richard 206, 207

Cromwell, Thomas, later Lord Cromwell of Wimbledon and Earl of Essex 20, 22, 38, 45, 48, 49–54, 56, 57, 58, 59–60, 64, 65, 66, 67, 68–74, 75, 76, 77, 79, 80, 81, 82, 83, 84, 85–6, 88–9, 90–3, 94–5, 96, 97–8, 100, 101, 104–6, 107, 108–9, 110, 111, 112, 113, 115, 116, 119, 120, 121, 122, 123–4, 127, 128, 131, 132, 133, 137, 138, 139–42, 145–6, 147–50, 151, 152, 155, 156, 157, 159, 160, 162, 163,

164, 167, 168, 169, 172, 173, 174, 175, 176, 177, 180, 181, 182, 183, 186, 189, 190–1, 192, 194, 195, 196, 199, 203, 204, 206, 207, 209, 211–12, 213, 214, 216, 217, 220, 222, 225–6, 227, 229, 236, 237, 238, 241, 242, 243, 244, 248, 252–3, 254, 256, 257, 263, 266–7, 270, 271, 274, 280, 282, 285, 287, 292–3, 294–5, 297, 298–9, 302, 306, 307–8, 316, 320, 321, 322, 326, 336, 337, 349, 351, 352, 355, 356, 357, 358, 361, 365, 367, 368, 369, 375–7, 379–80, 396, 403–4, 407, 408–9, 432, 433, 437

Croydon Palace, Surrey 209

Culpeper, Thomas 368

Cumberland, Earl of 264

Dacre, William, Lord of the North 264

Darrell, Elizabeth 201

Denny, Joanna 405

Deptford, Kent 232

Derman, Harde 301

Devereux, Robert, Earl of Essex 318

Dingley, cousin to Sir Francis Weston 300

Dinteville, Jean, Sieur de 46–7, 48, 298

Dispensations Act, 1534 295

Dolet, Etienne 357

Donizetti, Gaetano 403

Doran, Susan 483

Dormer, Jane, Duchess of Feria
24, 25, 235, 397, 432–3

Dormer, Robert 248

Douglas, Lady Margaret 365

Dover Castle, Kent 359, 376

Dover, Kent 116, 122, 305, 352

Dudley, Edward 396

Dudley, Sir John, later Duke of
Northumberland 242, 264,
411, 414, 415

Dudley, John, Lord 264

Dudley, Robert, Earl of Leicester
385–6

Dunn, Jane 407

Durham House, London 56, 424

Dymoke, Margaret, Mrs Coffin
(or Cosyn) 176, 189–90, 191,
214, 222, 226, 283, 314, 333

East Horndon Church, Essex 410

Edinburgh, Scotland 256, 353

Edward II, King of England 228

Edward III, King of England 465

Edward IV, King of England 11,
30, 39, 40, 304–5

Edward, son of Henry VIII by
Jane Seymour, later Edward VI
365, 369, 370, 375, 376, 396,
397

Eleanor of Aquitaine, Queen of
England 228

Elizabeth, daughter of Henry
VIII and Anne Boleyn, later
Elizabeth I, Queen of England
3, 9, 15, 16, 19, 21, 29, 38, 41,
42, 43, 45, 49, 53, 58, 70, 74,
75, 98, 101–2, 110, 114, 117,
118, 119, 121, 144, 148, 153,
154, 166, 186, 197–8, 234,
237, 238, 240, 260, 267, 281,
286, 317, 318, 326, 329, 334,
337, 356, 364, 365, 366, 375,
378–82, 383–95, 396, 397,
398, 399, 400, 402–3, 405, 406,
409, 410, 411, 416–17, 432, 435,
436

Ellis, Henry 216, 433

Eltham Palace, Kent 232–3, 240

Elyot, Sir Thomas 38, 63, 67

Englefield, Sir Thomas 113–14

English Folklore Society 420

Enhold, John 489

Epping Forest, Essex 358

Erasmus, Desiderius 35, 283

Erickson, Carolly 465

Erwarton Church, Suffolk 411

Erwarton Hall, Suffolk 411

Exchequer Palace, Calais 50

Exeter, Marchioness of (*see*
Blount, Gertrude)

Exeter, Marquess of (*see*
Courtenay, Henry)

Eyton, John ap Griffith 131

Faenza, Bishop of 23, 25, 33, 257,
264, 276, 279, 362

Felmingham, Ralph 256–7

Feria, Duke of 432

Fettiplace, Sir Thomas 489

Field of the Cloth of Gold, 1520
140

Fiennes de Clinton, Edward, Lord Clinton 263
Fiennes, Mary, Lady Norris 128
Fiennes, Richard, Lord Saye and Sele 264
Fiennes, Thomas, Lord Dacre of the South 128, 228, 248, 263
Fish, Simon 20
Fisher, John, Bishop of Rochester 47, 89, 115, 143, 145, 183–4, 238
FitzAlan, Henry, Lord Maltravers 263
FitzAlan, William, Earl of Arundel 263
FitzHerbert, Sir Anthony 113–14, 115
FitzJames, Sir John 113, 114–15
FitzRoy, Henry, Duke of Richmond 56, 111, 112, 114, 131, 132–3, 184, 199, 225, 239, 253, 260, 263–4, 336, 344, 376, 394
FitzWilliam, Elizabeth, Lady Harvey 98
FitzWilliam, Sir William, later Earl of Southampton 95, 96, 98–9, 100–1, 106, 107, 113–14, 152, 158, 159, 163–4, 167–8, 192, 216, 222, 243, 247–8, 250, 252, 256, 376, 434
Fletcher, John 401
Foliot, Margaret (or Anne), Mrs Stonor 174, 214
Forman, Joan 421
Forster, Giles 285

Fox, Julia 143–4
Foxe, John 102, 341, 400–1
Francis I, King of France 19, 47, 58, 59, 81, 112, 116, 147, 258, 362
Freshwater, Dorset 352
Fresneda, Bernardo de 382
Friedmann, Paul 87, 219, 262, 303, 403–4
Froude, James Anthony 86, 219, 266, 298, 403–4
Fulham Palace, London 209
Fuller, Thomas 57

Gainsford, Anne 145, 437–8
Gairdner, James 219
Gamage, Margaret, Lady William Howard 141
Grandon, Abbot of 22–3, 219
Ganzel, Dewey 432
Gardiner, Stephen, Bishop of Winchester 49, 91, 92, 116, 164, 191, 252–3, 257
Geddes, Annabel 495
Gracys, Norfolk 115
Grafton, Richard 158
Granfield, Diggory 154
Granfield, John 154
Granvelle, Antoine Perrenot de 352
Gray, Thomas 333
Great Hallingbury, Essex 122
Great Place, Stepney 84
Greenwich Palace, Kent 5, 9, 19–20, 23, 27, 55–7, 58, 63, 64, 76, 111, 116, 117, 118, 141,

149, 153, 154, 159–60, 166, 167, 168, 169, 170–1, 180, 181, 193, 222, 232, 233, 236, 237, 239, 240, 256

Gresham, Richard, Sheriff of London 249, 321

Greville, Honor, Lady Lisle 94, 97, 122, 198, 242, 254–5, 342

Grey, Edward, Lord of Powys 263

Grey, Elizabeth, Countess of Kildare 39–40, 67

Grey, Henry, Earl of Kent 264

Grey, Lady Jane 411, 414, 415

Grey, Lord Leonard, Viscount Grane 465

Gristwood, Sarah 3, 78

Gruffydd, Ellis 131

Guaras, Antonio 436

Guicciardini, Lodovico 134

Guildford, London 251

Guy, John 468

Gwent, Richard, Archdeacon of London 316

Gwyn, Captain 337

Haddon Hall, Derbyshire 176

Hale, Christina 420

Hale, John, Vicar of Isleworth 394

Hales, Sir Christopher 250, 265, 271

Hall, Edward 158, 299, 338, 339, 340, 341, 433

Hammulden, Joanna 47

Hampden, Sir John 248

Hampton Court Palace, Surrey 1, 3, 196, 211, 226, 227, 230, 233,

236, 239, 242, 243, 359–60, 362, 379, 422–3

Hancock, butler at Blickling Hall 421

Hannaert, Jean of Lyons 258, 312, 381

Hannesley, Mr 301

Harpsfield, Nicholas 204–5, 433

Harvel, Edmund 353

Harvey, Sir Nicholas 97, 98, 99

Harvey, Sir Thomas 98

Hastings, George, Earl of Huntingdon 263

Hastings, Sir Patrick 407

'Hasyllegh', Essex 56

Hatfield Place, Herts. 378, 413

Hatfield Regis, Essex 366

Hautbois, Norfolk 420

Haute, Jane, Lady Wyatt 437, 494

Hawkins, Sir John 327

Hayward, Sir John 433, 473

Heneage, Thomas 377

Henri II, King of France 430

Henry II, King of England 228

Henry IV, King of England 29, 229

Henry V, King of England 29

Henry VI, King of England 30

Henry VII, King of England 16

Henry VIII, King of England 1, 3, 5–7, 8, 9–98, 100–25, 127–31, 134–45, 147–56, 158–70, 173, 174, 175, 176–84, 186–9, 191, 192–5, 196–8, 199, 200–2, 203–6, 207, 208, 209, 211, 212, 213–14, 216–19,

220–1, 222–4, 225, 226, 227–8, 230–5, 238–40, 243–5, 256, 257, 259, 260, 261, 262, 263, 264, 265, 266, 269, 271–6, 277–81, 283–90, 292–308, 311–12, 313, 314, 315, 316, 317, 320, 321, 322, 323–5, 331, 332–5, 336, 337, 338, 339–41, 345, 347, 348, 349, 352, 353–70, 374, 375, 376, 377, 378, 379, 380–2, 384, 385, 387, 388, 389, 390, 391, 392, 394–5, 396, 397, 398, 399, 401–4, 410, 414, 422, 423, 427, 430–2, 433, 434, 435, 436

Herbert, Edward, Lord, of Cherbury 140, 216, 219, 265

Heron, Giles 115, 227

Heveningham, Sir Anthony 457

Hever Castle, Kent 1, 360, 365, 413, 420, 423, 493

Heylin, Peter 145

Heyss, Cornelius 301

Heywood, John 473

Hill, John, of Eynsham 386

Holbein, Hans 41, 46–8, 50–1, 72, 150, 331, 333–4, 413, 414, 420–1, 457, 458, 493–4

Hone, Galyon 359

Horenbout, Lucas 150

Horndon-on-the-Hill Church 410

Horsman, Margery 97, 156, 193, 216

Howard, Elizabeth, Countess of Wiltshire 13, 47, 178, 365, 391, 435

Howard, Henry, Earl of Surrey 240, 261, 275, 336, 375

Howard, Katherine, Queen of England 104, 139, 141, 161, 174, 209, 292, 368, 375, 385, 405, 411, 414, 415

Howard, Mary, Duchess of Richmond 114, 400

Howard, Thomas, 3rd Duke of Norfolk 13, 23–4, 25, 41, 47–8, 53, 80, 82–3, 111, 113–14, 115, 131, 141–2, 167–9, 170, 172, 174, 180, 240, 242, 243, 244–5, 247, 256–7, 261–2, 265, 269, 277, 280, 288, 295, 336, 364, 374–5, 386

Howard, Thomas, 4th Duke of Norfolk 275, 307, 386

Howard, Lord William 141, 256, 353

Howden, John 426

Hume, Martin A.S. 403, 436

Humphrey, Duke of Gloucester 29

Hungerford, Anthony 248

Hungerford, Walter 248

Hunsdon Palace, Herts. 142, 326, 379, 380–1, 384

Hunt, Mrs 422–3

Husee, John 94, 97, 98, 226, 251–6, 277–8, 298, 307, 342, 349, 358–9, 360, 369

Hussey, Anne, Lady 142

Ingram, Steve 421

Isabella of Angoulême, Queen of England 228

Isabella of France, Queen of England 228
Ives, Eric 2, 137–8, 233, 262, 405, 406, 407, 430–1, 436

Jacquetta of Luxembourg, Duchess of Bedford 30
James II, King of Great Britain 33
James V, King of Scots 256, 353
James VI and I, King of Scotland and England 261, 390, 392, 401
Jean de Luxembourg, Abbot of Ivry 358
Jennings, Mr, page 300
Joan of Navarre, Queen of England 29, 229
Jocelyne, servant to Henry Norris 301
John of Gaunt, Duke of Lancaster 33, 465
John, King of England 228
Johnson, Robert 327–8
Jordan, Robert 328
Joyce, Prioress of Catesby 57
Julius Caesar 318, 354

Katherine of Aragon, Queen of England 10–12, 15, 16, 18–19, 21–3, 26, 27, 28, 29, 31, 32, 35, 36, 37, 38, 39, 40, 42–3, 44–5, 46, 47, 48, 49–50, 52, 53, 58, 61, 63, 70, 76, 78, 87, 88, 115, 125, 135–6, 143, 170, 176, 179, 183, 184, 186, 197, 238, 239,

240, 244, 260, 276, 286, 293, 352, 358, 375, 390, 394, 408, 422, 432, 435
Kenninghall, Norfolk 374–5
Kent, Earl of (*see* Grey, Henry)
Kilburn, London 370
Kimbolton Castle, Hunts. 97
King's College and Chapel, Cambridge 72, 359
King's Lynn, Norfolk 61
King's Manor, York 424
Kingston, Sir William 167, 169, 170, 171, 172, 173, 174, 176–9, 189–91, 207, 211–16, 217, 220, 222, 223, 226, 241, 245, 248, 256, 267, 269–70, 276, 280, 282, 292–3, 297, 298–9, 302–3, 304, 305–6, 315, 320, 321–2, 323, 330, 332, 335, 336, 338, 348, 361, 384, 404, 433, 475, 476, 485
Kite, John, Bishop of Carlisle 289
Knights of St John 369–70
Knole, Kent 118, 186
Knollys family 391
Knollys, Sir Francis 334, 391
Knyvett, Sir Henry 252–3, 376

Lambeth Palace, London 186, 188, 296, 316, 329, 381, 424, 497
Lancaster, House of 16
Latimer, Lord (*see* Neville, John)
Latymer, William 73, 101–2, 224–5, 392, 457
Lee, Sir Anthony 333

Lee, Edward, Archbishop of York 295

Lee, Rowland, Bishop of Coventry and Lichfield 132, 223

Lefèvre, Jean 135, 144

Legh, Thomas 316

Leti, Gregorio 345, 434, 498

Lichfield Cathedral, Staffs. 366

Lieutenant's Lodging (The Queen's House), Tower of London 270, 281–3

Lindsey, Karen 407

Lisle, Lady (*see* Greville, Honor)

Lisle Letters 299, 318, 476, 490

Lisle, Lord (*see* Plantagenet, Arthur)

Lister, Sir Richard 113–14

Loades, David 406, 408

Lofts, Norah 422

London Bridge 313, 347

London, City of 16, 37, 52, 128, 156, 181, 288, 387

Longland, John, Bishop of Lincoln 225

Louis XIV, King of France 434

Lovell, Francis, Lord 127

Lovell, Frideswide, Lady Norris 127

Lucas, Glen 467, 478

Luke, Sir Walter 113–14, 115

Luther, Martin 20–1, 54

Macaulay, Thomas Babington 415–16

Machiavelli, Niccolo 51

Madeleine of Valois 362

Maison Dieu, Dover 352

Malory, Sir Thomas 168

Manners, Thomas, Earl of Rutland 263

'Margaret', called waiting woman to Anne Boleyn 155–6, 193

Marot, Clement 434–5

Martin Tower, Tower of London 198–9, 426

Marwell Hall, Hants' 423

Mary, daughter of Henry VIII and Katherine of Aragon, later Mary I, Queen of England 10, 12, 13, 15, 18, 19, 24, 29, 31, 32, 35, 36, 37, 38, 39, 40–5, 49, 52, 53, 59, 60, 61, 62, 63, 68, 69, 70, 74, 75, 79, 80, 82, 95, 100, 104, 120–1, 125, 141–3, 174, 175, 176, 180, 183, 184, 186, 197, 198, 203, 205, 228, 237, 238, 239, 240, 248, 260, 262–3, 286, 293, 325–7, 332, 351–2, 366, 374, 375, 377, 380–4, 386, 387, 388, 389, 390, 392, 393, 397, 422, 431, 432, 433, 435

Mary of Hungary, Regent of the Netherlands 304, 357, 362

Mary, Queen of Scots 332, 386, 389, 392

Matilda, Empress of Germany 15–16

Matilda of Flanders, Queen of England 228–9

Mead, Dennis 421

Melanchthon, Philip 21, 54, 70, 259, 357

Meteren, E. van 430

Milherve, Crispin de 270, 278–9, 308, 309–10, 312, 313, 333, 338, 340, 434–5

Miller, Helen 409

Montagu, Lord (*see* Pole, Henry)

Mordaunt, John, Lord 264

More, Sir Thomas 17–18, 30, 38, 47, 89, 102, 115, 143, 156, 171, 204, 205, 227, 228, 248, 259, 283, 433, 435

Mortimer, Roger 228

Mouat, Dr Frederic 412–13, 414–15

Musgrave, William 248

National Gallery, London 331

Neville, John, Lord Latimer 227, 264

Neville, Ralph, Earl of Westmoreland 113, 263

Neville, Richard, Earl of Warwick 30

New Hall Palace, Essex (*see* Beaulieu)

Nidd Hall, Yorkshire 13

Norfolk, Duke of (*see* Howard, Thomas)

Norris, Sir Edward 127

Norris, Sir Henry 6, 125, 127–30, 133, 137–8, 151–3, 154, 156, 158–60, 162–4, 165, 167, 175, 177, 178, 180, 182, 183, 190, 191, 192–4, 198, 204,

215–16, 221, 222–3, 225, 230, 231, 233, 234, 237, 241, 242, 245, 247, 249, 250–3, 266, 271, 272, 273, 274, 280, 301, 310–11, 313–14, 321, 356, 361, 372–3, 376, 377

Norris, Henry, Lord Norris of Rycote 392

Norris, Sir John 489

Norris, John 301

Northumberland, Duke of (*see* Dudley, Sir John)

Northumberland, Earl of (*see* Percy, Henry)

Nun Monkton Priory, Yorks. 73

Ockwells Manor, Maidenhead 314, 489

Orchard, Mary 174, 277

Ortiz, Dr Pedro 23, 25, 32, 34, 56, 164, 258, 264–5, 271–2, 276, 279, 320, 335, 338, 381, 488

Otterbourne, Sir Adam 256

Oxford, Earl of (*see* Vere, John de)

Oxford University 225

Page, Edmund 115

Page, Elizabeth, Lady Skipwith 370

Page, Sir Richard 199, 209, 211–12, 213, 242, 243, 251–2, 254, 369, 476

Paget, Sir William 36

Palmer, Thomas 248

Parham Park, Sussex 130
Paris, France 92, 257, 279, 344
Parker, Sir Henry 301
Parker, Henry, Lord Morley
121–2, 140, 142–3, 263, 366
Parker, Jane, Lady Rochford 96,
125, 140–6, 159, 160, 175–6,
212, 267, 283, 284, 286, 288–9,
301, 366–9, 411, 414
Parker, Margery 175
Parker, Matthew, later Archbishop
of Canterbury 118, 166, 350,
386, 389, 391
Parker, Sir Philip 411
Parnell, Dr Geoffrey 319
Parr, Katherine, Queen of
England 206, 264, 423
Pate, Richard 82, 116
Paul III, Pope 58–60, 258, 295
Paulet, Sir William, later
Marquess of Winchester
113–14, 167, 168, 243, 248,
256, 259
Percy, Henry, Earl of
Northumberland 48, 111, 120,
149, 181, 262, 277–8, 287,
294–5
Percy, Sir Thomas 149–50
Perry, Maria 378
Peter, hosier 301
Peterborough Abbey, later
Cathedral 10, 352, 382, 389,
426, 432
Philip II, King of Spain 382, 432
Pickering, Anne, Lady Weston
129–30, 376

Pickering, Sir Christopher 129
Pilgrimage of Grace 365, 374
Plantagenet, Arthur, Viscount
Lisle 94, 105, 107, 118, 154,
225–6, 251–2, 264, 277–8,
358–9
Pole family 38, 39
Pole, Geoffrey 38, 119
Pole, Henry, Lord Montague 38,
67, 119, 226, 263, 377
Pole, Margaret, Countess of
Salisbury 39, 43, 414
Pole, Reginald, Cardinal 39, 357
Pollard, A.F. 93, 406
Pollard, Sir Richard 272
Pollini, Girolamo 435
Ponti, John de 352
Port, Sir John 113–14
Porter, Linda 407
Portugal, Infanta of 362

Queen's Head Inn, Erwarton,
Suffolk 316, 366, 411

Radcliffe, Robert, Earl of Sussex
113, 114, 188, 263
Rayleigh, Essex 60
Reading, Abbot of 497
Reading Place, London 497
Reformation, English 20–1, 51,
52, 55, 65, 66, 74, 115, 238,
361, 405, 435, 436
Renard, Simon 382, 390
Richard II, King of England 249
Richard III, King of England 16,
30, 39, 127

Richmond, Countess of (*see* Beaufort, Margaret)

Richmond, Duke of (*see* FitzRoy, Henry)

Richmond Park, Surrey 358

Ridley, Jasper 219–21

Rochford Hall, Essex 365, 422

Rochford, Lady (*see* Parker, Jane)

Rochford, Lord (*see* Boleyn, George)

Rome, Italy 10, 23, 25, 51, 56, 60, 74, 75, 77, 105, 115, 116, 164, 201, 248, 258, 271, 279, 295, 357, 361, 381, 401, 435

Roper, Margaret 17

Roper, William 18, 435

Royal Armouries Museum, Tower of London 319

Royal Collection, Windsor 420–1

Royal College of Music, London 135, 470

Runwell Hall, Essex 422

Russell, Sir John 226, 251, 364

Sackville family 391

Sadler, Sir Ralph 376

Saffron Walden, Essex 130

St Botolph's Church, Aldgate 265

St Dunstan's Church, Stepney 84

St Giles in the Wood Priory, Flamstead, Herts. 369

St John, Alice, Lady Morley 140

St Mary's Church, Chepstow 95

St Mary's Church, Lambeth 497

St Omer, France 304–5

St Paul's Cathedral, London 416, 422

St Peter ad Vincula, Royal Chapel of, Tower of London 282, 313–14, 319, 336, 348, 411, 412, 415–16, 426

St Peter's Church, Hever 365, 412

Salisbury, Countess of (*see* Pole, Margaret)

Salisbury, Wilts. 46

Salle Church, Norfolk 410, 423

Sampson, Dr Richard, later Bishop of Chichester 119, 293, 316

Sander, Nicholas 6–7, 9, 13, 34, 38, 204, 205, 206, 265, 365, 393, 395, 398, 413, 435–6, 437, 458

Sandford, Francis 465

Sandwich, Kent 224

Sandys, Anne, Lady Weston 129

Sandys, William, Lord 113, 114, 168, 169, 188, 263

Sanuto, Francesco 413–14

Saunders, William 357

Savage, Henry 219

Saye and Sele, Lord (*see* Fiennes, Richard)

Scarisbrick, John 405

Scrope, Mary, Lady Kingston 174, 176, 177, 178–9, 215, 270, 280, 281, 283, 320, 325–7, 333, 384

Secheper, Mr 301

Seneca 370

Seymour, Sir Edward, later Lord
    Beauchamp, Earl of Hertford
    and Duke of Somerset 61–2,
    64, 78, 105, 252, 260, 357, 362,
    376
Seymour family 37–8, 45, 62, 65,
    80, 104, 183, 375, 423
Seymour, Henry 301, 377
Seymour, Jane, later Queen of
    England 18–19, 24–5, 26, 33,
    37–9, 45, 47, 55–7, 61, 63, 67,
    68, 69, 73, 86, 105, 109,
    111–12, 121, 142, 176, 183, 189,
    193, 195, 196, 197, 220, 240,
    244, 248, 256, 259, 264, 269,
    281, 287, 290–1, 301, 317, 324,
    342, 356, 357, 358, 359, 360,
    361, 362, 364, 365, 367–8, 375,
    376–7, 380, 409, 410, 423,
    437–8, 457
Seymour, Sir John 70, 259–60
Seymour, Lady (see Wentworth,
    Margaret)
Seymour, Sir Thomas, later Lord
    Seymour of Sudeley 61–2,
    206, 385, 411, 415
Shakespeare, William 401, 402
Shaxton, Nicholas, Bishop of
    Salisbury 352
Shelley, Edward 96
Shelley, Sir William 113–14, 115
Shelton, Sir John 41, 380, 384
Shelton, John 175
Shelton, Lady (see Boleyn, Anne)
Shelton, Mary (Madge) 17, 56,
    128, 141, 151, 175, 190–1, 457

Sidney, William 248
Singer, Samuel 399, 433, 493
Skip, John 66, 70–2, 152–3, 192,
    222, 319, 335
Smeaton, Mark 96, 125, 133–9,
    144, 148, 149–51, 155–6, 157–8,
    159, 160, 164, 165, 167, 179,
    193, 194, 198, 214–15, 216,
    221–3, 231–3, 235, 238–9, 242,
    244, 247–8, 249, 250, 266, 267,
    273, 299, 312, 315, 373–4, 377,
    381–2, 383, 409, 474, 476
Smith, Lacey Baldwin 368, 408
Smith, Richard 125
Smithfield, London 46
Society of Antiquaries of London
    432, 474, 480
Somerset, Anne 405–6
Somerset, Charles, 1st Earl of
    Worcester 95
Somerset, Duke of (see Seymour,
    Sir Edward)
Somerset, Elizabeth, Lady
    Brereton 130, 133, 179, 377
Somerset, Henry, 2nd Earl of
    Worcester 95, 130, 263, 465
Speed, John 325–6
Spelman, Sir John 7, 98, 113–14,
    115, 204, 265, 267, 274, 277,
    280, 283–4, 345, 346, 347,
    466
Staatsarchiv, Vienna 429, 487
Stafford, Henry, Lord 58, 112
Stafford, William 365, 422
Stanhope, Anne, Lady Seymour
    64, 252

Stanley, Thomas, Lord Monteagle
    263
Starkey, David 88, 267, 408, 468
Starkey, Dr Thomas 353
Statute of Treasons, 1351 104–5,
    151
Staverton, Richard 225
Stephen, King of England 16
Stokesley, John, Bishop of
    London 119–20
Stone Castle, Kent 97, 99
Stonor, Mrs (*see* Foliot, Margaret)
Stow, John 401, 412, 436
Strawberry Hill, Middlesex 493
Strickland, Agnes 58, 85, 86, 137,
    170, 219, 235, 273, 292, 316,
    324, 334, 337, 344, 360, 403,
    436–7, 493
Strype, John 174, 214–15, 221,
    402, 433
Stuart, Prince James Francis
    Edward 33
Suffolk, Duke of (*see* Brandon,
    Charles)
Surrey, Earl of (*see* Howard,
    Henry)
Sussex, Earl of (*see* Radcliffe,
    Robert)
Sutton, Eleanor, Countess of
    Worcester 465
Sutton Place, Guildford, Surrey 130
Swettenham, Master 132
Swynford, Katherine, Duchess of
    Lancaster 465
Syon Abbey, Middlesex 394

Tailboys, Lord 264
Talbot, Mary, Countess of
    Northumberland 294
Tarbes, Bishop of (Castelnau,
    Antoine de) (*see* Castelnau,
    Antoine de, Bishop of Tarbes)
Taylor, George 191
Tempest, Richard 248
Temple, Mr, fletcher 301
Thetford, Norfolk 411
Thirlwall, Father 348
Thomas, William 104, 396,
    429
Throckmorton, Sir Nicholas
    228
Tower Green (East Smithfield
    Green), Tower of London 270,
    281, 319, 336, 425
Tower Hill, London 207, 298, 299,
    302, 306, 307, 315, 336, 376
Tower of London 1, 2, 17, 31,
    128, 136, 165, 170–3, 174,
    176–9, 180, 182, 183, 185, 186,
    190, 194, 198–9, 207–8, 209,
    211, 212, 213, 215, 216, 217,
    219, 220, 221, 222, 224–5, 226,
    229, 242, 243–4, 248, 251–2,
    257, 258, 260–1, 265, 269–71,
    274, 277, 281–2, 288, 292–3,
    297, 298, 299–300, 302, 304,
    306–7, 313–14, 315, 316,
    318–19, 321, 322, 323, 330,
    333, 334, 335, 336, 337,
    347–50, 351, 358, 361, 362–3,
    365, 368, 370, 371, 372, 375,
    387, 391, 403, 410, 411, 412,

414, 416–17, 423–5, 426, 433, 474, 476, 482, 485
Tregonwell, John 316
Trinity Hall, Cambridge 366
Triphook, Robert 493
Troyes, Bailly of 141
Tuchet, John, Lord Audley 263
Tudor, Arthur, Prince of Wales 10, 16
Tudor, House of 16
Tudor, Mary, Queen of France, Duchess of Suffolk 203
Turner, Thomas 265
Tyburn, London 288, 298, 299
Tyndale, William 20
Tyrwhitt, Sir Robert 97, 100

Valle Crucis Abbey, Chesire 132, 302
Vaughn, John 376
Vere, John de, Earl of Oxford 113, 114, 168, 169, 188, 263, 265, 316, 493
Vertue, George 493
Victoria and Albert Museum, London 337, 391
Victoria, Queen of Great Britain 16, 319, 324, 403, 412, 436

Wallop, Sir John 49, 116, 253, 257
Walpole, Horace 485, 493
Walsh, William Packenham 426–7
Walsingham, Sir Edmund 171, 270

Warnicke, Retha 34–5, 52, 135, 138, 193, 234–5, 284, 456, 458, 474
Wars of the Roses 16
Warwick Castle 413, 420
Warwick, Earl of 413
Webb, Harry 191, 254
Wendon, Fr Ralph 46
Wentworth, Margaret, Lady Seymour 70, 264
Wentworth, Thomas, Lord 264
West, Thomas, Lord de la Warr 263
Westminster Abbey, London 389, 416
Westminster Hall, London 227, 247, 248–9, 251
Westminster, London 7, 112, 116, 162, 166, 188, 227, 228–33, 237, 242, 245, 247, 248–9, 251, 259, 304, 387, 389, 416
Westmoreland, Earl of (*see* Neville, Ralph)
Weston, Sir Francis 6, 125, 129–30, 133, 135, 137, 138, 156, 159–60, 175, 190, 191, 198, 204, 212, 213, 221, 225, 230, 231, 232–3, 238–9, 242, 245, 247, 250–4, 275, 297–8, 300–1, 310–11, 312, 314, 356, 373, 376, 409, 475
Weston, Henry 130
Weston, Margaret 225
Weston Park, Staffs 420
Weston, Sir Richard 129, 254

Whitehall Palace, London 11, 56, 57, 163–4, 165, 169, 177, 207, 209, 230, 243, 259, 292, 358, 360, 362

Whitgift, John, Archbishop of Canterbury 392–3

Whittington-Egan, Richard 420

Wickford, Essex 422

Wilder, Philip van 134

Wilkinson, Jane 102

William the Conqueror, King of England 228

William, Mr, broderer 300

Williams, John 255

Williams, Richard (*see* Cromwell, Richard)

Willis, Browne 366

Willoughby, Edward 248

Wiltshire, Bridget, Lady Wingfield 97–100, 156, 204, 267, 274

Wiltshire, Countess of (*see* Howard, Elizabeth)

Wiltshire, Earl of (*see* Boleyn, Thomas)

Wiltshire, Sir John 97

Windsor, Andrew, Lord 264

Windsor Castle, Berks. 240, 376, 420–1

Wingfield, Humphrey 204

Wingfield, Lady (*see* Wiltshire, Bridget)

Wingfield, Sir Richard 97

Wisbech, Cambs. 424

Wittenberg, Saxony 20–1, 54, 70, 91, 92, 399

Wolsey, Thomas, Cardinal 48, 50, 51, 67, 88, 95, 126, 132, 134, 170, 183, 199, 205, 209, 246–7, 253, 262, 294, 313

Wood, Elizabeth, Lady Boleyn 174, 175, 189, 214, 270, 280, 281, 283, 320, 333

Worcester, Countess of (*see* Browne, Elizabeth)

Worcester, Earls of (*see* Somerset)

Wotton, Dr Nicholas 316

Wriothesley, Charles, Windsor Herald 6, 108, 262, 276, 294, 313, 314, 318, 319, 338

Wriothesley, Thomas, later Earl of Southampton 66, 92, 107, 157, 253, 437

Wroxham, Norfolk 420

Wulfhall, Somerset 18

Wyatt family 200, 334, 421

Wyatt, George, of Boxley, Kent 10, 12, 19, 24, 25, 49, 102, 103, 144–5, 200, 202, 203, 206, 235–6, 241, 262, 266, 274, 284, 288, 303–4, 341, 343–4, 349, 369, 392, 395, 401, 413, 421, 435, 437–8, 456, 491, 493–4

Wyatt, George, of Charterhouse Square 493

Wyatt, Henry 223–4, 242, 371

Wyatt, Margaret, Lady Lee 333–4, 493, 494

Wyatt, Richard 494

Wyatt, Sir Thomas, the Elder 6, 102, 127, 129, 156, 199–209,

211, 213, 215, 216, 223–4, 236,
242, 243, 251–2, 254, 263, 289,
306–7, 313, 333, 334, 336,
339–40, 345, 349, 369, 370–4,
392–3, 421, 437, 470, 476, 493,
494
Wyatt, Sir Thomas, the Younger
437, 494
Wydeville, Elizabeth, Queen of
England 11, 30, 40

Wyke, Worcs. 227

York, Archbishop of (*see* Lee,
Edward)
York, City of 295
York, House of 16
York Place (*see* Whitehall Place)

Zouche, George, of Codnor 437
Zurich, Switzerland 360

www.vintage-books.co.uk